HERB BROOKS

HERB BROOKS

THE INSIDE STORY OF A
HOCKEY MASTERMIND

BY JOHN GILBERT

VOYAGEUR
PRESS

Brimming with creative inspiration, how-to projects, and useful information to enrich your everyday life, Quarto Knows is a favorite destination for those pursuing their interests and passions. Visit our site and dig deeper with our books into your area of interest: Quarto Creates, Quarto Cooks, Quarto Homes, Quarto Lives, Quarto Drives, Quarto Explores, Quarto Gifts, or Quarto Kids.

Inspiring | Educating | Creating | Entertaining

Paperback edition published in 2010 by MVP Books. First hardcover edition published in 2008 by Voyageur Press, an imprint of The Quarto Group, 401 Second Avenue North, Suite 310, Minneapolis, MN 55401 USA. T (612) 344-8100 F (612) 344-8692 www.QuartoKnows.com

MVP Books titles are also available at discount for retail, wholesale, promotional, and bulk purchase. For details, contact the Special Sales Manager by email at specialsales@quarto.com or by mail at The Quarto Group, Attn: Special Sales Manager, 401 Second Avenue North, Suite 310, Minneapolis, MN 55401 USA.

ISBN-13: 978-0-7603-3995-4

The Library of Congress has cataloged the hardcover edition as follows:

Gilbert, John, 1942-
  Herb Brooks : the inside story of a hockey mastermind / John Gilbert.
    p. cm.
  ISBN 978-0-7603-3241-2 (hb w/ jkt)
  1. Brooks, Herb, 1937-2003 2. Hockey coaches--Minnesota--Biography. I. Title.
  GV848.5.B76G55 2008
  796.962092--dc22
  [B]
                              2008023137

Editor: Dennis Pernu
Designer: Jennifer Bergstrom

Printed in USA

This one's for Herbie, and for a friendship I'll always cherish. He did it his way, and he did it well. Nobody can ever replace his dedication, honesty, and mystique, and I hope this helps keep him alive and forever young in our hearts and minds.

CONTENTS

INTRODUCTION

There are a lot of reasons I had to write this book. Mainly, though, I owe it to Herbie.

Watching, studying, and writing about hockey have been, and continue to be, an exciting and gratifying career. Trying to stay close to professional, college, and high school teams has been both challenging and rewarding, whether in the formative years of the 1960s, or in the highly sophisticated twenty-first century. Without question, the game will never be the same as it was in the late 1960s and through the 1970s. Among other teams I've covered, the University of Minnesota hockey program has been near and dear to my heart since I was a journalism student at "the U" in the 1960s and John Mariucci was the coach. When I started at the *Minneapolis Tribune* in 1967, I covered the Gophers and Minnesota's fabulous high school hockey, as both skyrocketed to prominence through the 1970s. It was no coincidence that both Minnesota high school hockey and the University of Minnesota hockey blossomed in parallel. The University of Minnesota teams comprised homegrown players throughout that era, arguably the most important and exciting two decades in the sport's history in Minnesota.

Having written about all the top high school players and teams, it was easy to be close to the Gophers, who were like a select team of the best prospects the high schools could produce. There was no Junior "A" United States Hockey League in the United States at the time, and no USA Hockey development program. Minnesota high school players were devoted to their communities, and equally devoted to go to "the U," even as walk-ons, for the chance to take on the constant horde of skilled Canadian players imported by other prominent American colleges. True, there also were top players from small pockets in New England and Michigan, and for a while an all–New England Boston College team joined Minnesota in comprising 100 percent U.S. players. But a lack of national championships eventually drove BC to add a few Canadian imports. No other college could have even imagined being made up of 100 percent home-state players, a feat the Gophers pulled off for most of three decades.

Herb Brooks was still playing when I first got to know him, and the first time I ever saw him coach, he was a young assistant to Glen Sonmor at Minnesota. It was definitely a career highlight of my thirty years at the *Tribune* (and later the *Star Tribune*) to cover those Gopher teams for the seven years Brooks coached them, from 1972 through 1979. It meant apportioning my time, because I was also covering the

National Hockey League's Minnesota North Stars, the World Hockey Association's colorful Minnesota Fighting Saints, regional small colleges, the national and Olympic programs, and the high schools. It was pure pleasure to try to capture and portray the color and passion of Gopher and high school games, because in those days, none of the players dreamed of playing beyond high school or college. And because there was little thought of careers with huge professional contracts, they played the game they loved with 100 percent intensity, for only their pride and their teammates. I treated college and high school games with the same passion as the Stanley Cup Finals, because they deserved it.

When Mariucci died, it was a stunning blow to all of us who knew and loved him. I was credited with being first to refer to Mariucci as the "Godfather of Minnesota Hockey," although that hit a nerve with Louie Nanne, who played for Maroosh at Minnesota and apparently had referred to John as his "Godfather," a nod to their common Italian heritage. That was before my time, but regardless, my christening of John as the whole state's godfather was because his impact on hockey went beyond nationality—he was most accurately the "Godfather of U.S. Hockey." Mariucci was never against Canadian players coming to U.S. colleges. In fact, he recruited Canadians such as Nanne and Murray Williamson, both of whom became All-Americans at Minnesota, and others, "Just to show I don't discriminate," he would grin. But he did fight to get the National Collegiate Athletic Association to restrict "over-age" Canadian recruits, who would play high-test Canadian major junior hockey through age twenty, then, if they didn't get an NHL offer, come to the States for a college scholarship. Mariucci saw that as exploiting U.S. hockey rather than helping it.

While fighting that fight, Mariucci cultivated the fertile but lightly seeded Minnesota youth and high school hockey fields, nurturing and finally generating a genuine movement. It was the same sort of craze that had afflicted his native Eveleth and first spread throughout Northern Minnesota, eventually reaching the Twin Cities and its fast-growing suburbs. That was about when I came onto the scene, in the mid-1960s, just in time to chronicle the rise of the Gophers and the upsurge in high school hockey. There were a lot of big-time sportswriters who knew every facet of the NHL—and there still are. Fewer in the media pay attention to college hockey, and fewer still to the high schools. My determination, and pleasure, was to try to encompass all of them and watch as that unique Minnesota perspective ultimately became intertwined.

The enthusiastic Glen Sonmor had been Mariucci's assistant and protégé, and he appreciated Mariucci's influence so much that when he succeeded Mariucci in

1966, he took Maroosh's dream and ran with it. A native of Hamilton, Ontario, Sonmor's colorful attitude spread to his teams, and the Gophers captured the interest of statewide hockey fans. Sonmor lifted the Gophers to a Western Collegiate Hockey Association title and an NCAA tournament championship game.

Then Herbie took over in 1972 and lifted the Minnesota program to unprecedented heights. That was shortly after the University of Minnesota-Duluth had gone Division I, and long before St. Cloud State, Mankato State, or Bemidji State even entertained such thoughts. To Mariucci's dismay, UMD chose to go mostly with Canadian imports, following the lead of other WCHA teams, and if it left the Gophers free to pick the best Minnesota high schoolers, not many thought Minnesotans were good enough on their own. Turns out they were, and it became a tradition that Mariucci had started, Sonmor expanded, and Brooks perfected.

From the time Brooks took the helm, I normally saw him, or at least talked to him, nearly every day. We also stayed in contact through the off-seasons. We exchanged tidbits of information from around the hockey world, talked about the numerous cars I reviewed for an automotive column I also wrote, and discussed other topics. It became common for Herbie to stop by my home in suburban Shoreview, or for me to drive to his place a few miles north to show him a particularly interesting car I was road-testing. We established a mutual respect that was everlasting.

Herbie demanded a high work ethic from himself and his players, and he appreciated that I worked beyond reasonable effort to study hockey and convey hockey news that went beyond the superficial. It didn't take long to realize he was something special as a coach who would try anything to extract the best from his players and teams. Sometimes he would invent psychological ploys, much the way Neal Broten might invent a move to get around a defender. Herbie had special confidantes, such as strength and conditioning coach Jack Blatherwick, but he seemed to appreciate an outside voice. He confided to me his innermost theories and ideas about the game, and I welcomed every opportunity to listen to his ideas. Occasionally, I challenged him with ideological questions based on observations I had made from watching NHL teams, or teams from the Soviet Union or Sweden. Even if my questions were simple, they were honest and they became more valid as I grew comfortable filtering such information through Herbie's uniquely creative mind. Herbie later told me those brainstorming sessions served as a source of checks and balances for him, helped reinforce some of his ideas, and pushed him to try his more inventive concepts. While putting his own teams together, he followed existing traditional guidelines at first, but remained alert for new ingredients for his teams' preparations.

When it came to studying the game, Herbie was a grad student moving swiftly toward becoming a professor, and I was an eager freshman, impatient to learn and discuss new hockey techniques wherever I could find them. It was always enjoyable to talk hockey with characters among the elite NHL coaches of that time, such as Fred Shero, Scotty Bowman, and Don Cherry, but while they were among the best in coaching NHL hockey, they had no knowledge of or experience with European variations of the game. Herbie, meanwhile, had played against and learned from the Europeans, and we frequently discussed their puck-control style. He ultimately started to practice such things as circling and regrouping with his Gopher teams, using each step to reinforce his cautious belief that there was a future for a "hybrid style." This was his term for his own idea of combining the creativity of the European collective style with the rock-solid Canadian defensive discipline, reinforced with the eager willingness to overachieve that was the greatly underrated asset of U.S. players, particularly Minnesota-bred high school players. That last factor was possibly the most important ingredient, so why wouldn't Brooks recruit only Minnesota kids, then push them to cover the skill and discipline ends?

One day in the spring of 1979, as Herbie was completing his third NCAA championship season with his most talented University of Minnesota team, I realized something was a little different when he called and asked me to meet him for lunch at Stub and Herb's, specifying a mid-afternoon time to ensure the place would be virtually empty. He was not the "Herb" in Stub and Herb's, but it was his favorite campus-area "saloon," as he called it—a corner restaurant and beer joint near the university campus, on Washington Avenue. He knew I didn't drink, but having a beer was not his objective. The place was only two blocks from Williams Arena, the long, huge barn of a building that housed the Gopher basketball team at one end and, at the time, the hockey team at the other.

"See you there," I said.

We often got together spontaneously for a quick lunch, but I couldn't help thinking how unusual it was for us to meet formally for lunch by appointment. When I arrived, Herb was sitting at a table just around the corner to the left of the entrance of the otherwise empty place. We ordered a couple of sandwiches, then Herb opened his briefcase and pulled out a large legal pad.

"This," he said, "is my organizational plan for the Olympic team."

Brooks laid his legal pad on the table. Always a stickler for details, he had the page filled with all sorts of notes surrounding a large circle he had drawn in the middle. Brooks had coached the U.S. National Team in the 1979 World Championships, but they didn't do well, finishing seventh as a thrown-together team of available players from the lowest echelon of the pros. It was, though, an invaluable learning experience for Brooks, who among other things learned he could go to battle with a young Boston University goaltender named Jim Craig.

Brooks explained that the circular chart was his flow chart, covering every imaginable position on the staff he would assemble for the 1980 U.S. Olympic hockey team. Spokes ran out from the center to names on the outer edges of the circle. He explained all the names he had put together, including Jack Blatherwick, his favorite physiological wizard, who studied and invented improved training techniques in the same manner Brooks concocted new breakout patterns and forechecks. Another spoke in the organizational wheel was Gary Smith, his Gopher trainer and a skilled medical man with a properly sarcastic sense of humor. Another was the colorful Doc Nagobads, a Latvian by birth who had served as team doctor for many U.S. teams, and who had become Herbie's long-time friend. Of course, Warren Strelow, Herbie's lifelong friend and neighbor in suburban Mahtomedi, would be asked along as goalie coach. Every detail was covered, from assistant coaches to specialists to equipment men.

I was both flattered and fascinated that he was showing me his secret plan, as he went around the circle, describing the roles he foresaw for each spoke. Being impressed with Herbie was not new to me, but being impressed to the point of being *silent* was definitely different. One of the reasons Herbie and I had developed an ever-closer bond was that we always knew we could count on each other for honest feedback. It might be supportive; it might be critical. It might stir up a huge argument between us, or it might lead to me heckling him about a game plan gone awry, or him heckling me for something in a story that might have been countered by a subsequent performance. Whatever, it invariably concluded with both of us laughing or imagining future scenarios that could be projected from there.

This time, I could only watch, until Herbie got around to the final spoke in his plan. "And this," he said, pointing toward the bottom of the page, "is you."

"*What?*" I asked.

"I want you to take a year's leave of absence from the *Tribune* and be the media contact guy for the Olympic team," Brooks said.

I was overwhelmed. I had never considered working in public relations—the "dark side" of journalism, if you're a reporter. I had spent a dozen years at the *Tribune*, where I was the only person with even the most remote interest in hockey on the sports staff of the largest publication, in the heart of the most intense hockey country in the United States. The sports editor who hired me, Larry Batson, was a brilliant man, and domineering. He once told me, "I don't know much about hockey, but I know just enough to know that I don't like it." There was no appropriate response to that, which was true of a lot of comments Batson tossed out. His directness was appreciated more in retrospect, when compared to his string of successors.

Batson noticed that I was eager to cover hockey at every level, so he decided to take advantage of my energy. I was already covering college and high school hockey, and also doing backup work on the North Stars. When the World Hockey Association started, I added the Minnesota Fighting Saints to my domain. Batson decided the only way to contain me was to make me control myself. He made me the paper's Hockey Department, as he called it, commanding me to cover the entire hockey spectrum but giving me the freedom to choose whichever game I decided would be biggest or make the most compelling story. When there were conflicts, other staff writers covered games I submitted as worthwhile. I frequently chose Gopher games over pro games when they were on the same weekend nights, because I could cover the pros during the rest of the week. I felt guilty when more veteran reporters were ordered to cover games I suggested, but I was totally consumed with the opportunity to take on the greatest possible assignment. I could expand my passion for the game at all levels and still steal enough time to coach the in-house bantam hockey team my older son, Jack, played on.

Every male sports journalist in the United States grows up with sufficient knowledge of baseball, football, and basketball to write competently about them. But when it comes to hockey, most reporters seem to write superficially about it, rather than risk exposing their lack of knowledge. I've always loved and played baseball, and as a kid I played quite a bit of basketball and enjoyed watching football. I read every word on the sports page and soon became aware that game reports from baseball, football, and basketball in the morning newspaper told me all I needed to know about those games. But I never read any stories that came close to adequately telling me what had happened in any hockey game. The score, who scored how many goals, and which goalie made a lot of saves, with a few quotes sprinkled in—usually only from the home team—was the superficial, formulaic norm. So, when I decided I wanted to become a sportswriter, I set out to learn all I could about hockey so that I could write about it with some degree of competence if the occasion ever arose.

There are millions of casual baseball, football, and basketball fans, but there are no casual hockey fans—you are either intensely into it, or you avoid it. Hockey is complex enough to repel those who aren't interested in its intricacies. To begin with, the ability to skate rivals any skill required of baseball, football, or basketball players. Remember when basketball followers insisted that Michael Jordan was the greatest *athlete* ever? Then he proved he wasn't by his inability to hit minor league curveballs. Hitting a baseball with a bat takes great skill, but try using a stick that has a 60-degree bend right where it seems it should be straight, to whack at a hard rubber object shaped like a tuna can, on a surface that is completely unnatural for both you and the object. Throw in the facts that your opponents are trying to knock you down and your teammates often move inconsistently with what the puck carrier seems to have in mind, and, out of hand, hockey is set apart from every other sport in difficulty, always spontaneous and improvisational, and never simple.

As hockey fans, we can be patient with those who don't understand hockey, or don't appreciate the athletic achievement of stickhandling around a defender to make a perfectly timed pass to a speeding teammate. But when it comes to writing about it, sportswriters should first be required to put on skates and try to play in any pickup game, just once, to appreciate its complexities.

Until the 1980 Winter Olympics loomed on the horizon, the *Minneapolis Tribune* had never shown more than passing interest in covering the Olympics. But the 1980 Games would be different. First, they would be held at Lake Placid. Second, along with the usual handful of Minnesota and Wisconsin skiers, skaters, and biathletes, the U.S. hockey team would be coached by St. Paul native Herb Brooks, who had just coached the University of Minnesota for seven years, winning its first three NCAA titles in the last six of those years. He would take a team of college and ex-college players of his own selection, including several Minnesotans, to fight the good fight against the evil hockey empire of the Soviet Union, the proud and often arrogant forces from Canada (who still consider hockey to be their own game), and the rising talents from Sweden, Finland, Czechoslovakia, West Germany, and the rest of the world. It was a David-and-Goliath thing, but these would be our own Davids against the rest of the world's Goliaths. The *Tribune* would send three reporters to cover the Games: Jon Roe to report on the main events in various sports, Joe Soucheray to do his trademark light and breezy early-career columns on whatever whims that moved him, and me specifically to cover the hockey team and the tournament.

Nobody, of course, could imagine that the 1980 Winter Olympics would end up with Brooks and his Team USA gang pulling off the Miracle on Ice. Everyone assumed that there would be a nice flow of homespun local-focus stories. Nobody guessed that what awaited them was an event that would galvanize the entire country and sporting world, and would be the springboard that made every reporter desperately eager to cover the next Olympics, certain that glory would be theirs as they chronicled the next gold medal. Overlooked in the rush was that a lot of those journalists started out at the 1980 Winter Games like a lot of fans in their indifference to the hockey team's hopeless cause. The horde of U.S. journalists could have been covering the hockey games, but chose instead to write about Eric Heiden's speed-skating glory, the futility of falling ski jumpers, and the faltering U.S. fortunes in various other events. Hockey wasn't big enough to them, and the fans reflected the media, as the first few U.S. hockey games didn't draw more than half-capacity crowds to the 8,000-seat arena or its press box.

For most journalists, covering the 1980 Winter Olympics meant grumbling about long days, late nights, deadlines, enormous crowds, impossible travel, and potential hypothermia. But to me, covering hockey at the Winter Olympics was an endless feast of the best things about the game. Herbie and the Minnesota-based U.S. team would be the primary focus, but I was excited about opportunities to watch the magically gifted Soviet Union and to marvel at the skill and creativity of the Swedes, Finns, and Czechs. It would be a labor of love. Journalists at such events have a tradition of complaining after three days about being overworked. Nine months beforehand, I knew it would be two weeks that would pass too fast. If there had been more space in the paper, I could have filled it all, every day, feeding off an adrenaline high that outlasted the Games.

With all of that building anticipation, here I was, sitting with Herb Brooks at Stub and Herb's while he offered me the chance of a lifetime—to be on the inside during the selection, formation, season-long world exhibition tour, and the Winter Olympics themselves, writing releases and promoting story ideas on a diverse group of players.

"So," Brooks said, "what do you say?"

"It's a great opportunity, Herbie," I said. "But I can't do it."

"What?" he asked, startled. This, as it turned out, would be the first of only a very few things in Brooks' carefully crafted blueprint that didn't go exactly as he had planned. I read the surprise on his face. Herb and I had grown to be close friends and had a high-test professional relationship. Cynics accused me of being Brooks' biggest booster, but I also was his biggest critic. I might have praised him more than others, but only because I covered his teams more extensively. I also zinged him, privately and in print, whenever I thought it was necessary.

"I'd love to be the PR man for your Olympic team," I told Brooks. "But I'd rather write about your team for the *Tribune*, and they've already told me I can go and cover the Olympics. Besides, if you screw up, who'll write about it, if I don't?"

"You bastard," he said, laughing. But he understood.

I knew I was forfeiting the chance to have the inside scoop on the U.S. team, but as it turned out, I was able to get the most comprehensive news on the team during the Games. Brooks exercised his stubbornness on the world stage, and his way of chastising the media was to announce that he would not attend his team's postgame press conferences. After making this announcement and storming out of the auditorium, he told me he would meet me privately in a small office near the dressing rooms back at the arena. Those sessions gave him a chance to vent and provided me with the incredible coup of exclusive interviews after every game.

After it was all over and the gold medal was in hand, back at the *Minneapolis Tribune*, the managing editor called me into his office and told me that Bantam Books had approached the paper. It had examined all the newspapers covering the hockey games and decided that the *Tribune*'s coverage was the most comprehensive. It wanted to reprint everything I had written in a paperback book, titled *Miracle on Ice*, which it could publish immediately. I was overwhelmed.

"That's great," I said.

"But we're not going to do it," he said.

"Why not?" I asked.

"We decided that if it's that good an idea, we'll do it ourselves."

That, too, would be fine with me. But somehow, the idea got pushed to the back burner, then taken completely off the stove—then forgotten. It never happened. Brooks told me about some fellows who were writing a book about the whole thing. "You're the only one who should write the book," he said. "You're the only reporter who was with this team from the time it was picked and throughout the whole season, and the only one who knows what really went on with this team."

I told him I would write the book, but I was going to wait. Books came out, movies and videos, too. Who can ever forget the first *Miracle on Ice* movie, where a rumpled Karl Malden pursed his lips and tried to convince us he was accurately depicting the smooth, slick Brooks? "Patti would rather have had Robert Redford play me, and then she would have played herself," Brooks said.

Several times, Brooks mentioned that he was waiting for me to write the book, in between coaching stops in Switzerland, New York, New Jersey, Minnesota, and then back to St. Cloud State University in Minnesota, when he took that program from Division III to Division I. He also coached the France team in the 1998 Olympics in Nagano, Japan, and returned to the NHL on an interim basis to coach the Pittsburgh Penguins for Craig Patrick, his old Olympic assistant, for part of a year. He agreed to coach the NHL pros representing the United States at the 2002 Winter Olympics in

Salt Lake City, where Canada played only one really good game in the tournament, but pulled the rug from under the United States in the gold-medal game to ruin Brooks' flawlessly choreographed undefeated masterpiece.

In the summer of 2003, I told Herb that, finally, I was going to write the book. I told him I had waited until he was through with coaching, so I could write a book that included the best stories and reminiscences from throughout his amazing coaching career. Certainly, the 1980 Olympic victory would be a big part of it, using the assembled facts, my published accounts, and tidbits pulled out of my yellowing notes, rather than impromptu recall. But Herbie was far more than a passionate coach who dropped out of the clouds for one magical Olympic year. After the 2002 Olympics, I had hopes he'd return to the NHL or to some college to work his unique coaching magic. But he insisted he wouldn't be doing any more coaching. It was time, I figured, to put it all together.

Tragically, Brooks was killed a couple of months later. On August 11, 2003, he apparently fell asleep at the wheel of his Toyota van, while driving home from a golf outing for a hockey fundraiser on the Iron Range. He died when the vehicle flipped over going off the freeway.

The news was crushing to our whole family. My wife, Joan, had treated Herb's aching back and shoulder with physical therapy, and he used to say she was the only person who could relieve his pain enough so that he could go golfing. My older son, Jack, was stick boy on Herb's first three Gopher teams, and years later Herb let my younger son, Jeff, into his Roseville hockey school a couple of years too young because Herb knew his feisty attitude would prevail. He knew all of us, we all knew him, and we all still feel the emptiness he left behind. I'm luckier than most, because every once in a while I can go back to my notes and relive so many of those treasured moments. That's why he was anxious for me to assemble all these notes into a book. He knew I could, and would, straighten out some of the discrepancies among the scattered reminiscences of him and his players.

My intention is not to write a biography, but rather to capture the best nuggets and stories that describe what made Herb Brooks the best hockey coach ever. One of the best goes back to when Brooks coached the New York Rangers. Many observers claim that he failed in that venture, even though he won a hundred games faster than any other coach in Ranger history. Most interesting, though, is that he turned a gang of mostly plodding, Canadian-stereotype, up-and-down players into a weaving, puck-controlling, quick-skating team that was a flat-out revolution in NHL hockey. It became a team that only a Wayne Gretzky could love for its creativity. The Rangers were the only NHL team that could throw a legitimate scare into the mighty New York Islanders, the Stanley Cup power of that time. I saw Herbie's Rangers early, and I saw them after he got the whole team convinced his concept would work. Witnessing the change in style, I wrote that he had transformed a herd of plow horses into Kentucky Derby thoroughbreds.

One of the key reasons for his success with the Rangers was Mark Pavelich—one of the true heroes of the 1980 Olympic team, and one who has remained unsung in every post-Olympic story and film. Pavelich joined Brooks and became the Rangers' master playmaker, the rink rat who blended perfectly with the flamboyance of Ron Duguay and the primitive presence of Nick Fotiu. It was as though Pav executed what was going on in Herbie's imagination. When Brooks left, or was dismissed from the Rangers, it was because he didn't like the politics of former stars who still influenced the club's hierarchy. Ted Sator was hired as the new coach. Sator was the exact opposite of Brooks and demanded that his players forget about the regrouping, circling stuff and change back to an up-and-down, dump-and-chase, traditional Canadian style. That is not a knock against Sator, who later, ironically, coached in Finland. At the time, he was just one among many coaches and general managers who believed the traditional style was the only style. Indeed, it may always remain the lifeblood of Canadian and NHL hockey, even while players from more innovative European systems prove their superiority on NHL and world stages.

Pavelich abruptly quit playing shortly after Sator took over. He left a six-figure salary in Manhattan and came home to Minnesota, to fish and live in the woods on the North Shore of Lake Superior. It was hard for many to understand why a highly skilled player would quit before he even approached his peak NHL potential. But Pav was an idealist. He played the game he loved in a way he could love. In a private interview at his home, Pavelich told me he left because the style Sator imposed was simply not fun. Pav always gave his utmost to the game, and it was always immensely fun to him. When it stopped being fun, he came home, with no regrets.

After the interview, I wrote a story about the whole situation in the *Minneapolis Tribune* and included the line: "Asking Mark Pavelich to play dump-and-chase hockey is like asking Picasso to paint your fence."

Brooks hadn't seen the story, so I told him about it, and he got a laugh out of the analogy. "That's a great line," Brooks said. "It's so good, I'm going to steal it. I'm telling you right now, I'm stealing it."

I laughed along with him.

Years later, and several months after Herbie died, a good friend of mine, Jess Myers, arranged to write a feature on Herb Brooks for the 2004 NCAA hockey tournament program. I knew Jess had never known Herbie or covered his teams, so I asked how he had gathered material for the feature. He said he had interviewed different people about Brooks, and that he got some good stuff from Herb's son, Danny.

"You'll love one story Danny told me about Herb," said Jess. "He said when Herb took over the Penguins for the second half of the [1999–2000] season, he said, 'Having a team with that much talent play the way they are is like having Picasso paint your fence.'"

Touché, Herbie.

CHAPTER 1

ONE OF A KIND

Herb Brooks was intelligent, intuitive, and stubborn—a powerful blend when it came to creating game plans and adjusting to game circumstances. The combination was never a problem when the intelligent and intuitive sides predominated, even though they defied conventional North American hockey thought.

Herbie was proud of his stubbornness. Always unwilling to compromise his principles, on many occasions he made stands that may have hindered his career advancement. This included his split from the New York Rangers and later from the New Jersey Devils, and his frequent battles with USA Hockey, particularly when it was known as the Amateur Hockey Association of the United States (AHAUS). He also ran into a few rough spots in his early years when his stubbornness prevailed over his intelligence and intuition, but he turned that part of his personality into a positive weapon as well. In fact, his stubborn determination was the catalyst for making the other two more cerebral qualities most effective.

Herb Brooks coached University of Minnesota hockey teams for seven seasons, from 1972 until 1979. His prime objective was to be loyal to the tradition he learned as a fan and player under John Mariucci. There couldn't have been a stronger foundation, and Brooks built upon it while raising the Gophers to the top competitive level in collegiate hockey. After only one year, his confidence bloomed and he raised the team's success, which brought even more confidence. Many coaches with good ideas never enjoy an upward spiral of success, but Herbie's beliefs led directly to the inexorable momentum of success and allowed him to live out the courage of his convictions.

The Gophers had always attracted a loyal following, although not as large as basketball in the 1960s, but the size of the crowds grew and grew until the Brooks teams started to win championships. Then the loyal fans outnumbered the 7,500 seats in the old Williams Arena, filling it to overflowing under the high, arched ceiling. The old Williams Arena is still in place, of course. A huge building resembling an aircraft hangar, it is still a fantastic location for the raised basketball floor surrounded by 15,000 seats and covering about two-thirds of the structure. At the west end, the remaining part of the structure is an oddly shaped facility where the hockey rink was once housed. The hockey end of Williams Arena was renamed Mariucci Arena in

1985. Later, when the university built a spectacular new hockey facility just across the street, the name Mariucci Arena went across the street, too. Brooks was correct in his assessment that "the new arena is beautiful, but it will never have the character of the old one." Character no, sightlines yes. The outdated hockey portion of the older facility was converted into a cozier venue for women's volleyball and basketball, and men's wrestling and gymnastics. But back in the final days with Herbie at the helm, crowds routinely topped 7,900, taxing the limits of the old barn, and the fire marshal.

In those days, Brooks had to conquer not only a league filled with powerful teams, but also a North American hockey mentality that is still a barrier in the twenty-first century. Hockey was Canada's game (and it still is, if you're Canadian). There was a time when Canada was the only country that played hockey at such a level, and because of that, the game established, and then nurtured, some deeply inbred traditions. Among them is the hard and fast rule to play "position" hockey. That means looking out from the goal, the left wing goes up and down the left boards, the right wing goes up and down the right boards, the center can wander some but pretty much stays between the wingers, and the defensemen stay back behind those three forwards. This positional style is not unlike soccer, where each position plays to support others; defenders advance the ball to midfielders, who, in turn, advance it to forwards. The Canadian game has always been played hard and passionately from Nova Scotia to Vancouver Island, and young teenagers leave home at sixteen for larger cities with better junior (under-twenty) developmental teams.

From 1942 to 1967, when the NHL had only six teams—in Montreal, Toronto, New York, Boston, Detroit, and Chicago—it was a tight clique of predominately Canadian players, Canadian coaches, and Canadian managers. If a U.S. player made a team, it was a novelty. In the 1930s and 1940s, among others there were John Mariucci and skilled goaltenders such as Frank Brimsek, Sam LoPresti, and Mike Karakas. All four came from tiny Eveleth, Minnesota, which is clearly the birthplace of U.S. hockey and is the rightful location of the U.S. Hockey Hall of Fame. Later, in the 1960s, the only U.S. player in the entire NHL for several years was Tommy Williams from Duluth, Minnesota.

Despite the fact that American cities paid the bills, NHL teams were Canadian-run and didn't give American players much of a chance to infiltrate "Canada's sport." American players and coaches simply followed along, playing the Canadian style at the youth, high school, college, and semipro levels.

It wasn't until the Soviet Union, Sweden, Czechoslovakia, and Finland started playing the game at a serious level that some startling alterations to the traditional style occurred. Soviet coach Anatoli Tarasov was the first to declare that the Soviet Union would develop its own style rather than copying the Canadians, because to copy Canada meant always to be second best. (Tarasov had some fascinating concepts, and any hockey fan who can find his book, *Road to Olympus*, will have a keepsake that is certain to make them rethink their theories of the game.) It was the Soviets who led the way in playing the game as a collective five-some, interchanging positions and crisscrossing wherever they chose, anywhere on the rink, rather than staying in predetermined lanes. The Soviets also broke new ground in physical training and the mental discipline of being tough enough to take a cheap shot and not throw down the gloves or retaliate in any way. Those traits were so foreign, so to speak, to North American hockey that NHL officials led the charge in ridiculing the Soviets, mistaking their unwillingness to fight as cowardice. To a lesser extent, the same was true of other European players, who were creative, brilliantly trained, and so totally disciplined that NHLers commonly referred to them as "Chicken Swedes."

About the same time when Europeans were developing their specific styles, Herb Brooks was finishing his playing career by skating on numerous U.S. National and Olympic teams. The story of how he was cut from the eventual gold-winning 1960 U.S. team is legendary, but he went on to play for the 1964 and 1968 Olympic teams and all the U.S. National Teams in that stretch. In those days, Canada generally sent the best of its many prolific senior teams, while the United States used mostly college players. The Europeans were not professionals, although they stretched the boundaries. Swedish players, for example, might hold day jobs, but they got jobs in cities where they also could play on teams in top amateur leagues. The Soviets focused on their Red Army team, although the Soviet Wings, representing the Soviet Air Force, and Spartak Moscow, also were significant powers in the Soviet Union's elite league. Players on those teams were, indeed, beneficiaries of the communist collective society. They might have served in the army or air force, but their only military duty was to their hockey team. They received financial support to play hockey, which made them pros to North Americans, even though they didn't command NHL-type salaries and still stood as amateurs to the International Olympic Committee.

Brooks, playing on those generally undermanned U.S. teams (they finished fifth with a 2-5 record in 1964, and sixth at 2-4-1 in 1968), soaked up the impressive but unconventional emerging styles and systems of the top European clubs. These bits of information resided, like the seeds of a prize-winning flowering plant, in the nether reaches of Herbie's fertile mind. He was smooth and slick as a player, but he admired all facets of the game. We can only guess when the germination process began, wherein he began pondering what would happen if you linked the best attributes of the varying European styles with the hardcore Canadian tradition, but it was clearly before 1972.

That year, Team Canada—a collection of NHL All-Stars—played the Soviets in an eight-game Summit Series. NHL observers, players, coaches, general managers, and owners were convinced to the point of arrogance that the NHL superstars would annihilate the red-clad players with unpronounceable names. Herb and I agreed that the Soviets would give the NHL stars more than they could cope with, and possibly shock the hockey world. And they did, even though Team Canada won in a dramatic comeback in the final two games to take the series 4-3-1.

Brooks paid close attention. He was heading into his first season as head coach of the Gophers. The traditional, stratified Canadian approach was still evident throughout college hockey in the United States. It wasn't just that the wide-open European game was a variation in style, such as a single-wing or T formation in football. At that time, the odd play of the Europeans was considered simply wrong.

When the Soviet Union proved the Canada-dominated NHL style had serious shortcomings, it inspired Brooks and advanced his beliefs. Still, Brooks moved cautiously at the University of Minnesota, gradually evolving toward more daring and adventurous ideas in practices long before he would turn his later Gopher teams loose, somewhat in desperation, in particularly tough games near the end of his college tenure.

Many critics insist that the sport's ruination lies in over-coaching young players with confusing and complex systems. It once reached the point where the very word "system" took on evil connotations. In Brooks' mind, his system simplified the game for his players. He didn't teach elaborate crisscrosses to be executed at the top of the left faceoff circle, much like a post-pattern in football or a pick in basketball. Instead, he refined his ideas to feature tough and disciplined North American defensive play, while setting his players free to be their most creative on offense.

Always the mind-game specialist, Brooks reached the point of making deals with his players: "You play the way I want you to play when we don't have the puck, and you can do whatever you want when we do have the puck." If the player got casual and slipped up on defensive coverage, his freedom was restricted until he covered all responsibilities. If he stuck with Brooks' defensive rules, the player was free to go out and make something happen, trusting his own skills to get it done. Brooks wanted to see players succeed by using their imagination and skills, rather than by fitting into a restrictive system that might negate such improvisation.

Throughout Herb's coaching career, cynics were plentiful. Some who knew him well claim he was mainly a master motivator. That includes those who think the game is too chaotic to be patterned by coaching, as well as those who worship at the altar of Canadian hockey and figure any success Brooks had was only because he motivated his players, even though they seemed to play "wrong."

Sometimes, even some of his own players seemed to rethink Brooks. Shortly after the 1980 Olympics, Steve Christoff, a quick and intuitive forward who had played three years for Brooks at Minnesota and on the 1980 team, confided that Brooks got a lot of credit for creative offensive ideas, "but really, he didn't coach us to do that much," Christoff said. "We were pretty much free to do whatever we wanted."

In 1973–74, Brooks' second year at Minnesota, the Gophers won their first NCAA title. Radio and television showed up to cover the team's games regularly, and newspapers grudgingly allotted more of their precious space for hockey stories and photos. Minnesota athletic director Paul Giel, who had to be talked into hiring Brooks in the first place by his old friend and football teammate Ken Yackel, marveled at Brooks' mercurial but unwavering dedication to success. As athletic director, Giel was a lot like Brooks was as a coach. He gave Brooks the necessary guidelines, then let him do his own thing. When Brooks pulled off a plan, perhaps challenging his boundaries, Giel would turn away, shaking his head and smiling, "Herbie, Herbie, Herbie . . ."

In the end, though, who can argue with Herbie's ability to set his team's goals idealistically—and sometimes unrealistically—high, and then drive his players to attain them? Who can say that he wasn't right when he stubbornly pushed to do things his way? Who can say that his powerful employers/adversaries weren't the ones who were wrong when their conservative traditions prevented them from appreciating his revolutionary ideas?

CHAPTER 2

EAST SIDER TO THE CORE

As a hockey player, Herb Brooks was a smooth, polished athlete, skating with a long, fluid stride that was always easily identifiable, whether he was winning a Minnesota State High School Hockey Tournament with St. Paul Johnson at the old St. Paul Auditorium, skating up and down the wing for John Mariucci's University of Minnesota Gophers, or moving up ice for several U.S. National Teams.

It's no surprise that Brooks became a coach who admired the same skating finesse he had, but he always sought to complement that finesse by selecting players who could supply other elements of the chemistry that he determined necessary to a winning potion. Scoring touch, of course, was one of the premier necessities, as was creativity—the ability to anticipate and either carry out or improvise productive playmaking with teammates. But skills weren't sufficient to impress Brooks on their own; they had to be complemented by toughness, a willingness to compete. No matter how skilled or full of finesse a player might be, Brooks learned early that every player had to be tough enough to take a beating, if necessary, to display whatever talent they had. A hustling overachiever with limited skills can often beat a more-skilled adversary whose intensity might waver. And no matter how big the star, even at the National Hockey League level, Brooks had no time for a player who wouldn't hustle and work hard to give his talent a chance to flourish.

Brooks never forgot his East Side teammates and high school buddies at Johnson, and he stayed in touch with some of them all his life. While, to many, he seemed consumed with hockey, he had numerous and varied interests, and some of the people he enjoyed hanging around with most had nothing to do with hockey. But Brooks' life and career were so interwoven with hockey that it's easy to overlook the fact that, for instance, he also was an outstanding baseball player. He spent several years playing first base for Whittaker Buick's prominent fast-pitch softball team in St. Paul.

"Herb was a good ballplayer, and I thought that was going to be his vocation," said Pauline Brooks, Herb's mom, during an interview in the spring of 2007. "He was always outside. We would have gone and watched him play more, but he never let us know where they were playing. He always kept to himself and he would never discuss anything he did. He might come home and say, 'We won,' but that would be about it."

That silent, pensive demeanor started early in his life. "As a baby, he was quiet," his mom recalled. "When he was little, he didn't have any problems in school. At least, if he did, he didn't tell us about them."

The Brooks family lived at 661 East Ivy in a duplex that his mom and brother best remembered as being "a half block from Hastings Pond." There were the parents, Herb (later known as Herb Sr.) and Pauline, and their sons Herbie and David, and daughter Gayle. Herb Sr. coached the Phalen Youth Club teams, from beginners to high school. Pauline skated long blades and taught her sons how to use the edges of their skate blades. Herb was four years older than David, and their personalities were farther apart than that.

"David talked about as much as Herb didn't," said their mom. "Herb took after me a little, I guess, as a cheap Swede. He watched his money like an old hawk. David was more like his dad. David would talk to anyone, but if you tried to draw Herb into conversation, it didn't work. You could strike up a conversation with David, but Herbie would cut you off."

Herb Brooks' quiet and aloof childhood left few memories of any disciplinary problems. That started at home, according to brother Dave, who said that at nap time, "you didn't move," and when their mom said it was suppertime at five o'clock, "you were there, with your feet off the chairs."

"I didn't ever have to discipline him," his mom said. "I only can remember one time. When he was little, he decided he wanted to dress up to be a pirate. He went through some things looking for just the right piece of material, and when he found a piece of white satin, he cut it up to make a costume. It was my wedding dress, and he had cut it right up the middle. I think I hollered at him a little bit that time. But never again. Of course, he never had another wedding dress to cut up, either."

Pauline also recalled that Herbie would go out in the garage and shoot pucks rather than visit with guests, including former Gopher coach Elwyn "Doc" Romnes, a close friend of Herb Sr. It was Herb Sr. who coached the neighborhood kids and was probably chiefly responsible for the creation of the Phalen Youth Club, but when it came to hockey, Pauline was a much more severe critic than Herb Sr.

"For all the shots he took in the garage, he never scored as many goals as he should have," said Pauline Brooks. "Rube Gustafson was his coach in high school, and I always thought they never gave Herbie the right break in high school. He played center and wing. He could have had a million goals, the way he tore down the ice, but then he'd stop and see who was coming. He'd rather set up his teammates than score himself."

Most of those youthful tendencies played out on his later coaching. That setup mentality explained why Brooks later appreciated playmakers. In his college recruiting, he sometimes carried his character and worker theory to an extreme, but his teams always were successful. It wasn't until his later Gopher teams when he infused more highly skilled players—and also won.

"In high school, he was very popular and well-liked," Dave recalled. "He was smart, and a good student. He had his own gang of friends, but he never brought any of the guys over to the house. He was always at the rink or the ball field. I can never remember him out late. Nine o'clock would be it. He liked his sleep, and he never was out carousing. He didn't have many dates, either, although he might go to dances."

Their mom said, "Herbie never brought a girl home, while David thought it was a parade. Herbie was so quiet, and David was a scalawag."

Dave Brooks, who followed Herbie through hockey stardom at Johnson and the University of Minnesota, was sitting right there in Pauline's room as she said that, and he had to grin.

"Herb and David shared the same room, but Herbie never discussed games with David, either," their mom said. Several months after my delightful interview with her, Pauline Brooks passed away at age ninety-seven.

"We had our stuff in the same closet," said Dave. "He'd never touch anything of mine out of respect, and I'd never touch anything of his out of fear. He had a lot of best friends, including Warren Strelow. And he never forgot where he came from. He came back to Falzone's Barber Shop every week for a haircut."

His mom and dad, obviously, were proud as their sons went on to fame at Johnson and then the University of Minnesota, where they played for John Mariucci, one of the most influential tutors Brooks had. Herbie later played some top-level amateur hockey and skated on seven national teams. But it was the one he didn't make that left Brooks with his favorite hockey story about himself as a player. He was playing for the U.S. team in 1960 as it prepared to go to Squaw Valley, California, for the Winter Olympics.

When it got down to the final cut for the 1960 team, Bill Cleary, a standout player who later became a close friend of Brooks and coach at Harvard, applied a little political pressure. He threatened to not play unless his brother, Bob Cleary, was added to the team. When the decision was made to cave in to Cleary's demands, somebody had to be cut. That person, cut the day before the Olympic Winter Games began, was Herb Brooks.

"I called home," Herb recalled, although he should have known better than to expect his dad to soothe his disappointment with any sympathy. "My dad said, 'Shake hands with the coach, turn in your jersey, wish your teammates good luck, and get your ass home.' So I did. After the U.S. won the gold medal, my dad said, 'Well, it looks like they cut the right guy.'"

There is every indication that Herb Brooks Sr. loved his sons. He had coached them all the way through youth hockey, and if he sometimes sounded a little gruff, that's the way it was. "I would say my dad didn't really make us a 'lovable' family," said Dave Brooks. "But you loved him, and you knew he loved you."

Growing up under the direction of Herb Sr. and Pauline, there always was the certainty that the boys would never lose that hardcore, East Side humility. For the rest of his life, Herb Brooks took considerable pride in telling that story about himself, climaxed by his dad's final, incisive proclamation. Then he'd laugh. When it came time to make tough, final decisions on players as a coach, Herb understood the issue from both sides.

CHAPTER 3

HERBIE THE PLAYER

While his most notable achievements in hockey came as a coach, Brooks always maintained that his greatest thrill was playing on the St. Paul Johnson team that won the Minnesota State High School Hockey Tournament in 1955. That championship came in the eleventh tournament, when the event was still in its formative years, before it evolved into the premier annual sports happening in Minnesota.

Of the first ten tournaments, Eveleth won five, Roseau, Hibbing, and Thief River Falls won one each, and Johnson won the other two. Johnson's third state title made the Governors the second most prolific winner, but more significantly helped the Twin Cities break through the dominant grip enjoyed by northern Minnesota teams in those early years.

Johnson won it for the fourth time in 1963, and it wasn't until 1969—the twenty-fifth tournament—when Edina became the second Twin Cities team to claim the championship. Edina's victory signaled major changes in the tournament, the start of the inevitable shift in power to the highly populated Twin Cities suburbs, and the first tournament played away from the dark, smoky, old St. Paul Auditorium. The event moved to Metropolitan Sports Center, home of the Minnesota North Stars in the National Hockey League. The reason for the move was that St. Paul was building the new Civic Center adjacent to the old auditorium, which the tournament had clearly outgrown.

For all historians and fans who look back to the tournament in its years at the auditorium, the St. Paul Johnson Governors, from the city's proud East Side, hold a special place as the only Twin Cities team that could win the title from the rink-savvy Northern Minnesota powers in the tournament's first twenty-five years.

On its way to winning the state title, Brooks' 1955 Johnson team played a peripheral role in a record-setting tournament event. Thief River Falls, the champion in 1954 and the heavy favorite in 1955, was engaged in a tie game with Minneapolis South in a first-round game, just before Johnson's first-round game. The game went into overtime, then another, and another. Finally, it was determined that Johnson's game with Roseau should start and that South and Thief River Falls could come back

Herb Brooks as a senior with the University of Minnesota Golden Gophers, 1958–59. *Courtesy University of Minnesota Athletics*

rested for another overtime. When the night was over, Johnson defeated Roseau 1-0, and Minneapolis South upset Thief River Falls in an incredible eleven-overtime battle.

Wendell Anderson, a Johnson defenseman who went on to play at the University of Minnesota and for U.S. National and Olympic teams, later became one of Minnesota's more popular governors. "Herbie's dad was my campaign manager," he told me. Anderson remembers Herbie well, but defers to his younger brother, Rod, who was a long-term coach at the Blake School in Hopkins. Always articulate and classy, Rod turned Blake into one of the perennial powers of private-school hockey in Minnesota. Rod not only was Herb's age and his teammate through youth and high school hockey, but the two played on the same line for the Johnson Governors, sharing the thrill of winning the 1955 state tournament as seniors.

"We grew up together," said Rod. "In eighth grade, they were living just off Payne Avenue, on Hyacinth, and I was on Wheelock Parkway. Herb, without question, was 'the good child.' Herbie was popular with the girls, but none of us dated much. Dating wasn't something we had time for, because we were always busy playing sports.

"I played for Herbie's dad, who coached us in peewees, which were what bantam age would be now [thirteen and fourteen]. Our peewee team was sponsored by Dutch Maid Cleaners. For all of us, 'Herb' was his dad, which is why Herbie was 'Herbie.'

"I was a wing, and Herbie was my center-ice man throughout high school. Herbie was a smoothie, a playmaker, and smart. But mostly he was a pretty skater, while I would go into the corners. He was a fine high school player, but remember, in those days there wasn't that much hitting in high school. Bodychecking was only allowed in the defensive zone. That was OK, because hitting was not Herbie's game anyway. Finesse was."

All the Johnson East Siders were close. Rod Anderson recalled how tight Herbie was with Warren Strelow, a goaltender for Johnson who graduated in 1951, four years earlier than Brooks and Anderson. "Warren was the goaltender when Johnson lost to Eveleth in the 1951 final. He had fifty saves against John Mayasich's last Eveleth team."

Naturally, the 1955 tournament remained a bigger highlight for Rod Anderson, just as it was for Brooks.

"When South and Thief River Falls played their eleven-overtime game, we started our game against Roseau between their overtimes," Rod said. "We beat Roseau 1-0. South finally beat Thief River Falls, and we beat South 3-1 in the semifinals. South had a very good team, with the Alms and Westbys playing. Then we beat a Minneapolis Southwest team 3-2 in the finals, and Herbie scored two of our three goals."

When Herbie went to play for Mariucci at Minnesota, he lived at home. Scholarship money wasn't being thrown around in those days. "Herbie lived at home when he went to college because it didn't cost him any money," David theorized.

In those days, freshmen were ineligible because colleges operated under the idea that it was important to get situated in college. So freshmen played on the freshman team. When Brooks became a senior, Lou Nanne was on the freshman team.

"I didn't play with Herbie at Minnesota, because I was on the freshman team," said Nanne. "But we practiced together. Later on, we played together at Rochester and on the Olympic team. He was a real good skater, and he was OK with the puck, pretty smart."

Dick Meredith preceded Brooks at the U and recalled "Herb used to tell me, 'My mom took me to games at Williams Arena, and I'd go down behind the goal to watch, and my mom would tell me that if I could ever skate as good as Dick Meredith, I could make it.' We played on the '60 Olympic team, and I would say he was such a good skater, you could almost say he was a fancy skater. He kicked his leg really high with each stride—he almost danced on his skates."

John Mayasich, still another former Gopher and 1960 Olympic star, played at Green Bay right up to the Olympics. Mayasich played in the era when there was no chance for any American to play in the NHL, and many who watched him set scoring records at Eveleth High School and at Minnesota claim he was the best player ever to come out of the state. Because he was such a lock for an Olympic spot in 1960, he was allowed to play for his Green Bay team right up until the Olympic Games and didn't spend any of the Olympic squad's exhibition schedule as Brooks' teammate.

"You'd have to say he was the most beautiful skater we ever saw, no question," said Mayasich. "And I know he played at Rochester . . . I think the best way to put it was that Herbie was a better coach than a player."

Brother Dave followed Herb to Minnesota and was one of Mariucci's all-time favorites. Maroosh loved to needle Dave, but he treated him like his own son. He centered Gary Schmalzbauer and Len Lilyholm on what was called the "Buzzsaw Line" for their hustling work ethic and effectiveness. But he came in just after Herb left the U.

"Dad and Herb were both hockey nuts," said Dave Brooks. "I had kind of a different approach to the game. Herbie worked out all the time, and I'd be on the couch, saying, 'Tell me what time the game is.' Herbie would be out running Lake Phalen with weights on his ankles when he was in college. I never did that. Drop the puck, I'd be ready. When I went to college, the first time John Mariucci saw me in the locker room he said, 'Brooks, you should have nylons on those legs.'

"Because I was four years behind him, I never had the chance to actually play with him until after college. We played on the 1964 Olympic team together."

Just as they had different approaches to conditioning, they also had different success—Herbie worked and skated and tended to not score, while Dave didn't work, but played smart and always seemed to find a way to score.

"We shared a desk in our room at home," said Dave, "and Herbie would leave a rule book sitting open, with underlines in red, yellow, and blue. I'd ask him, 'Why do you want to read that stuff over and over?' And Herbie would say, 'It's stuff I needed

Brooks was the last player cut from the 1960 U.S. Olympic team that went on to win the gold medal. Brooks would play for both the 1964 and 1968 Olympic teams, as well as several national teams, including the 1961 squad, for which this photo was taken.

to know that the ref didn't.' He'd know what was on page 33, paragraph 1, in the third sentence.

"When we were getting ready to try out for the '64 Olympic team, Herbie would be pumping iron and running Lake Phalen, and I'd be upstairs, watching TV. We had fifty guys from the East and fifty guys from the West, and we went to South St. Paul for a combined camp. We both made the team. He played defense, and I was a forward. I thought he was a great defenseman."

Because the United States had beaten the Soviet Union and won the gold medal in the 1960 games at Squaw Valley, the Soviets were loaded up for the 1964 games.

"In 1964, we were the defending champions," Dave recalled. "So we played the Russians in our first game at Innsbruck. They beat us 5-1 and I can't remember touching the puck more than once. Tom Yurkovich was our goaltender and he faced something like fifty-seven shots. It sounded like the bells of St. Mary's, they hit so many pipes. They had these crummy sticks and skates and uniforms, and it was 5-1. I remember thinking, 'We've been training four years for this?'"

It all worked out for both of them. Dave Brooks found a way to return to Austria and play for Kitzbühel. He said he scored "eighty or ninety points and had an enjoyable time." And Herbie came home, with more images of the wonders of collective hockey to file away in his mind for future usage.

While Herbie took on everything in his life with the same dedicated intensity, he was never able to set an example his younger brother would follow. And yet Herb always seemed to subtly envy the fact that while he worked hard for everything he got, Dave never seemed to work hard, always enjoyed life to the fullest, and seemed to succeed in everything he tried.

Herbie always got a wry smile on his face when Dave's name would come up. And after Herb started having great success as a coach, Dave willingly played the subservient role. He once began a talk at the University of Minnesota Blue Line Club by insisting from then on, he wanted to be known only as "HLB." "That's it," he'd say, "I'm HLB—Herbie's Little Brother." It was true: Dave was still enjoying life to the fullest, wheeling and dealing with real estate and turning everything he touched into a profit. But his big brother, Herbie, had finally proven that dedicated hard work and tireless attention to detail could work as well.

Years later, at Herb's funeral at the St. Paul Cathedral, I spotted David after the ceremony. We hugged and, amid his tears, Dave said, "I just want to be Herbie's Little Brother again."

CHAPTER 4

HERBIE CROSSES OVER

Herb Brooks continued to play hockey after his college days, focusing his attention on the U.S. National Teams for a decade. He played on national teams in 1961, 1962, 1965, and 1967—which prepared him for the U.S. Olympic teams in 1964 and 1968—as well as in 1970 and 1971. As a U.S. National player, the team he was best known for, of course, was the gold medal–winning 1960 Olympic team, from which Brooks was the last player cut.

Perhaps the most significant event in Brooks' life during those years, however, occurred when he was playing semipro hockey for the Rochester Mustangs and the South St. Paul Steers. While skating at Wakota Arena in South St. Paul, he was knocked into the boards by teammate Marv Jorde and suffered a broken arm. Jorde drove him to Divine Redeemer Hospital in South St. Paul, where he spent the night. While there, he met a young blonde nurse who ultimately became his wife. But it was hardly a love-at-first-sight, storybook romance.

"There were a lot of old people in the hospital," joked Patti Brooks. "He was the only unmarried young guy, and we ended up having a nice conversation. But it really was like two ships passing in the night.

"A while later, a friend and I went to a place in Somerset [Wisconsin]. My friend was talking to a guy and Herbie was standing there. I said, 'You look familiar.' Herbie said, 'I've heard lines in my life. . . .' I asked if he had been in the hospital, and it was him. We left the place and went to their apartment. We were all just sitting there talking, and Herbie got up and walked out of the room. I thought he went to the bathroom, but he never came back. He went to bed! So we left."

Ah, what a smooth operator. Later, though, Brooks sought Patti out.

"He called me at work," recalled Patti. "He had gotten my name from my friend. For our first date, he took me to a hockey game at the St. Paul Auditorium. It was the old minor league St. Paul Saints. It might as well have been cricket, because I didn't know a thing about hockey. I asked him a lot of dumb questions, but I never really got into the game. When he coached, I always went to the games, but for me, it was more of a social event.

"For him, after we got married, I think it was an escape to come home and not have to talk hockey. Sometimes I felt bad, when we'd be riding home from Gopher games. I know he wanted to talk hockey, but he never brought the game home with him."

While Herb kept playing on an amateur level, he also was a pragmatist and knew the limitations on American players hoping to play pro hockey in those days. While playing for the Rochester Mustangs in the old USHL amateur league (before that name became emblematic of junior hockey), he also brought his intensity and dedication to his job selling insurance for the St. Paul Companies.

During these years, Herb's friendships with Lou Nanne and Glen Sonmor altered his life and helped guide him from player to coach. Nanne and Brooks were teammates at Rochester and wound up being co-captains of the 1968 U.S. Olympic team after Nanne, a Canadian from Sault Ste. Marie, Ontario, had his citizenship hustled through so he could play on the U.S. team.

Heckling each other was part of the Brooks–Nanne relationship, and the heckling never ended. In later years, Brooks enjoyed joking about how when he and Nanne were roommates, he would get locked out of their room and have to sleep in the hallway when Nanne was entertaining a "friend." The story always brought howls of protest from Nanne, who insisted it was the smooth-talking Brooks who had the serious dates and left Louie locked out in the hall. Typical of Herbie, he enjoyed diverting attention for something he may have done by suggesting someone else had done it, knowing that listeners could never be sure who was telling the truth.

Sonmor, meanwhile, had been befriended by John Mariucci when, at the end of his career, Mariucci played with the young prospect on the Minneapolis Millers. "John was my teammate, and he had been with the Chicago Blackhawks," Sonmor recalled. "We were in the playoffs in Omaha and John said, 'Kid, all my teammates have always been Canadians, and you're the first one who ever finished high school. You're going to college.'

"So every summer, I'd come back from pro hockey and go to the University of Minnesota. I could come back for spring quarter after hockey and go to two summer sessions. During the 1954–55 season, the Rangers had sent me to Cleveland, and it was in February of 1955 in Pittsburgh that I got hit in the eye with a shot while I was in front of the goal. I was lying in the hospital in Pittsburgh. The doc was honest with me and said, 'You're not going to see out of that eye, so there'll be no games anymore, and you'll have a different life.' My daughter Kathy had been born four days earlier, and my wife, Marg, was still in the hospital in Cleveland, and I'm in the hospital in Pittsburgh, wondering what I was going to do.

"The phone rang, and it was John calling me. He was coaching the Gophers and calling from Minnesota. He said, 'Kid, don't worry about anything. I got you the freshman coaching job at Minnesota and you can finish up your degree while you're here.' You can imagine the difference that made to me."

In his first year as freshman coach, Sonmor finished his physical education degree. Herb Brooks was a freshman player at Minnesota that year. Freshmen weren't eligible to play varsity in those days, so making Minnesota's freshman team was an impressive transition for high school players. The freshman coach also served as an assistant varsity coach, which put Sonmor in a pivotal position when Mariucci went off to coach the U.S. Olympic team at Cortina d'Ampezzo, Italy, in 1956. Minnesota athletic director Marsh Ryman stepped in as interim coach. The hot-tempered Ryman always was close to hockey and intensely interested in it, but there was still an opportunity for Sonmor to do a lot of coaching.

"Everywhere we went, Marsh would get in a row with somebody, and he'd always threaten to never play them again," said Sonmor. "I'd have to calm him down. We had players like Ken Yackel and Jack McCartan on that Gopher team. After about five road games, the players started calling Marsh some kind of a nickname. It sounded like 'Rutra-cam,' and Marsh didn't know why, so he wanted me to find out."

As it turned out, the players thought Ryman was like a little general, but the opposite of General Douglas MacArthur. "Because MacArthur had said, 'I shall return,' and Ryman threatened that he and the Gophers would never return to every place we played," Sonmor explained, "the kids gave Marsh the nickname 'Ruhtracam,' which was MacArthur spelled backwards."

Mariucci returned to Minnesota and coached until the end of the 1965 season, when Ryman made the unpopular decision to dismiss him. Sonmor had gone on to study for his master's degree at Ohio State, where he also coached the fledgling program that became varsity. Mariucci advised Ryman that "Sonmor should be the guy," Sonmor recalled. Ultimately, Mariucci was hired by the Minnesota North Stars when the National Hockey League expanded in 1967.

Coincidentally, Herb and Patti Brooks were married in 1965, and while Brooks was flourishing as a young businessman, he was still playing hockey. Nanne was Sonmor's assistant. "After the [1968] Olympics were over, I was signed by the North Stars," Nanne said. "So I went to Marsh Ryman and got him to hire Herbie to replace me as assistant."

Sonmor welcomed Herbie with open arms for the 1968–69 season as a part-time varsity assistant coach. Brooks (whose son Danny was born in the spring of 1967) could keep playing on the side and remain dedicated to his insurance job. Although Sonmor had known Brooks for years, he recalled how instantly impressed he was with Brooks' dedicated focus to the game.

"I knew that Herbie was going to be an outstanding coach from the start," Sonmor said, "just watching him work with people, plus his knowledge of the game. He was so smart, a great student of the game. But in everything he had to do in his life, he was very thorough. I think people overlook that, for a coach, just pure intelligence is a great asset. Herbie was a brilliant guy with a brilliant mind. And he had a passion for hockey that few people have. He was innovative even then. He always had great ideas."

Sonmor was more of the Mariucci mold of coaching, emphasizing pure emotion and hard work more than systems. He was pragmatic in his pursuit of victory, but so impatient that he scoffed at such elementary tactics as designed breakouts or forechecking patterns. Brooks, on the other hand, had played for Mariucci, but had also played against and marveled at the Russians' systematized puck-control approach.

"Herbie had such a passion for the game that was so important to him," Sonmor added. "He was searching out stuff all the time, much more than I ever did, doing things like studying the Russians. I remember Anatoli Tarasov, the great Russian coach, came here and was speaking in the Twin Cities. I went over and listened to him. I was interested in hearing him, but Herbie would study what he said. It was obvious he would take coaching to a level beyond what others would do.

"I also had a chance to watch how he was around players, even as my assistant. For those of us who had a sense of the game, Herbie loved to talk hockey, and he was very, very special."

Brooks proved to be an effective recruiter and a bright and clever practice coach, while also complementing Sonmor's mercurial personality. One time, in a game in Duluth during the 1969–70 season, a bodycheck sent Mike Antonovich into the side boards adjacent to the visiting bench. There was no protective glass above the boards in those days, and when Antonovich hit the boards, his stick extended toward the seats. A fan, who had drawn Sonmor's notice for his relentless heckling of the Gophers, reached up, apparently to protect himself, and grabbed Antonovich's stick. Sonmor vaulted off the bench and into the stands. He and the fan engaged in a wild fistfight. Sonmor later joked that the fan held firmly onto his white shirt, ripping it to shreds, while Sonmor merely kept throwing punches.

Brooks, watching from the press box, raced downstairs, circled the arena, and hurried down to rinkside. It took authorities and security personnel about as long to restore order—clearing the section and breaking up the fight—as it did for Brooks to get to ice level. As he rounded the corner from the stairs to the scene of the incident, Brooks slipped and fell, sliding into some fans and observers, knocking over a couple of them, and briefly reigniting the whole melee.

The incident was retold with great humor afterward, particularly since the Gophers came back to win the game in overtime. After the game, in the cramped visitors' dressing room, Sonmor stood proudly atop a table and thrust his fist toward the ceiling, his sport coat still on and his tie still in place, but with his white shirt in tatters.

Sonmor's best team was that WCHA championship outfit of 1969–70, with Murray McLachlan in goal, Mike Antonovich as a freshman, and solid regulars and future pros in between. Unfortunately, they were knocked out before they could reach the NCAA tournament. A year later, the team started off struggling. Sonmor confided that he didn't think the 1970–71 team would be able to repeat as WCHA champs, but that he did think they might get it together later in the season and make a run at the NCAA. He turned out to be right on, and a spirited stretch drive led by Antonovich, Dean Blais, Bill Butters, Craig Sarner, Ron and Doug Peltier, Wally Olds, and John Matschke carried the Gophers to the NCAA Final Four in Syracuse, New York. (Before the basketball finals were given proprietary rights to the name, the NCAA ice hockey finals were also referred to as the Final Four; it was later that the hockey finals were renamed the Frozen Four.)

That season proved to be another turning point for Herb Brooks. "When we made it to the NCAA tournament in Syracuse, Marsh Ryman said he didn't have enough money to bring Herbie," said Sonmor.

Brooks quit as Gopher assistant over the matter and missed a rich weekend in Gopher hockey history, one which he had helped create and which Sonmor recalls as one of the highlights of his coaching career.

"We were down something like 5-2 against Harvard in the semifinals," said Sonmor. "We had made a lot of great comebacks that season, and we came back in that one. Antonovich came out of the corner and fed Johnny Matschke in front for a goal with eight seconds left, tying the game 5-5. We had Antonovich centering Matschke and Blais, then a second line with Ron and Doug Peltier and Sarner, and a third line with Jimmy Gambucci, who was only a freshman, centering John Harris and Bruce Carlson. We were going to play a short overtime, then they'd clear the ice for a longer second overtime. So I told the team we'd start out with Antonovich's line, then Peltier's line, then Antonovich's line again, and Peltier's line again, and then Gambucci's line.

"To remind them, I repeated it on the bench: 'Remember, Antonovich, Peltier, Antonovich, Peltier, and then we'll go to Gambucci.' Ronnie Peltier said, 'Don't worry, it'll be over by then.' Sure enough, he went out and scored the winner. But we lost 4-2 to Boston University in the final. I remember staying up all night afterward with [Harvard coach] Cooney Weiland, and he tried to convince me to convert Antonovich to defense."

Brooks missed all of that. But, as was typical of the Brooks magic, everything worked out in a strange and circuitous way.

Well, not everything.

The first game Brooks unofficially coached at the U was the annual intrasquad game featuring many talented walk-on prospects and varsity returnees. Sonmor watched from upstairs as Herbie coached one team and volunteer assistant Don Vaia coached the other. The game was fast and spirited, and with the score knotted 4-4 in the closing minutes, Herbie made his move. He pulled his goaltender. The other team blocked an attack, broke out of their zone, and scored into an empty net, costing Herbie's team the game.

"I was the goalie he pulled," said Ron Docken. "I never got to play because Murray McLachlan was so good, but at last here was my chance to beat him, or at least get a tie, then Herbie pulls me, they hit the open net, and I was the losing goalie after all."

Crazy? Maybe a little. But it was vintage Herbie. He would try anything to find a way to win, and he never considered that he might lose.

CHAPTER 5

A MATTER OF PRINCIPLE

L eaving Minnesota to coach junior hockey turned out to be a blessing in disguise for Herb Brooks, who found the value of players like Pat Phippen, and numerous others, for future dependability.

But skipping the 1971 NCAA tournament when he was told the university wouldn't pay his way to Syracuse was vintage Herbie. It proved how far his stubbornness would go in the name of principle, and it showed how far hockey still had to go, even in a state that embraced the game from mites to pros and a university whose team was attracting capacity crowds. Certainly all the assistants accompanied their teams when the Gopher football team went to the Rose Bowl in 1961 and 1962, but Sonmor went alone to coach the Gopher hockey team at the NCAAs, and Herbie bailed out.

When Sonmor got the news the university wouldn't pay for Brooks, he was unconcerned. He was certain he would find a way to get Brooks to Syracuse, thanks to an active Blue Line Club that operated under much more liberal rules than were later imposed by the NCAA. "I didn't worry about it, because we had a great group of boosters who had a fund that we could use for important things, so I knew we could get Herbie there," Sonmor said. "What I didn't take into account was that Herbie had heard about what happened, and he refused to go under any circumstances."

The stubborn stand could have forced Brooks out of hockey and into the business world forever. Instead, he was named coach of the fledgling Minnesota Junior Stars for the 1971–72 season. The junior concept made perfect sense in Minnesota. In those days, the University of Minnesota team was made up exclusively of Minnesota high school grads, but the Gophers were limited in scholarships. Sonmor, in fact, first had to divide up a four-year total of six full scholarships, parceling out partials to as many players as he could. Other players went to the university to fulfill their dream of playing on what amounted to a statewide all-star team, and were willing to earn roster spots as walk-ons with little hope of getting any financial help.

Other WCHA schools were less interested in developing younger Minnesota kids than in recruiting more experienced Canadian junior players. Using twenty or more full scholarship lures, most schools fought to attract top Canadian prospects who had played through age twenty in sixty-game Canadian junior seasons. The Canadian endgame, of course, was to play in the National Hockey League, whose teams couldn't draft amateurs until age twenty. When Canadian players finished junior hockey, those who didn't get pro offers would consider U.S. college scholarship offers.

Obviously, it was a tall order for the Minnesota high school kids at the University of Minnesota to challenge and beat Canadian-dominated teams, and the inequity provoked John Mariucci to try to persuade the NCAA to change its rules and level the playing surface. Naturally, more prominence for Minnesota and other U.S. players also aided the burgeoning Minnesota high school breeding ground. But while the elite high school players proved they could play, many others were overlooked or needed more development than the high school seasons could offer. High schools not only were limited to twenty-game seasons, but also their games consisted only of twelve-minute periods. It took serious lobbying by Mariucci disciples, such as Brooks, to prod the Minnesota State High School League to expand to fifteen-minute periods, and then seventeen-minute periods.

But back in 1970, a group of high school league critics and advocates of advancing Minnesota prospects got together to start a Midwestern junior operation. The Minnesota Junior Stars, named after the NHL North Stars, were first sponsored by the Win Stephens Buick dealership and then later owned and operated by KSTP radio and television owner Stanley Hubbard. The effort also led to junior teams in Rochester and Austin, Minnesota, and expanded into Iowa, Nebraska, and Wisconsin to form what became the USHL— the United States Hockey League—for junior-age (under-twenty) players.

The league evolved through the 1970s, '80s, and '90s to a level of sophistication in the twenty-first century where making money is an important business objective. Developing players for college was the USHL's initial objective, but that focus switched when teams learned that the NHL offered money to leagues and franchises that developed players. The NHL attempted to pay such seeding money to college programs, but was rejected by the NCAA. The money became, however, a great enticement for junior teams as years passed. Today, the high school programs' goal of social and hockey development is constantly threatened by junior teams that once depended on a broad base of talent from the high schools, but now annually try to lure the best Minnesota players to leave high school for the USHL. Taking a dozen elite high school players every season dilutes Minnesota high school hockey and threatens to tarnish its status as a development gold mine.

Furthermore, every high school player who leaves early for the USHL could instead finish high school and still be eligible for a season or two of juniors afterward.

Possibly the most short-sighted aspect of all of this, however, is that whenever a USHL team adds a high school player, it cuts an older player, essentially ending the career of a player who perhaps needed only another year to emerge—in other words, precisely the type of player the league was formed to develop.

In 1970, the USHL had more idealistic and less profitable plans, and Pat Phippen was a perfect example of what was best about the junior program. When Phippen graduated from Alexander Ramsey High School in Roseville, he was a skilled and shifty winger with great potential, but he wasn't offered a scholarship. He joined the Junior Stars, where he found a variety of good players who had been overlooked by colleges and universities for a variety of reasons.

"I joined the Junior Stars and we were the only Minnesota team playing junior hockey, and a lot of guys didn't qualify for college," said Phippen. "I had no idea what I'd have done without the Junior Stars. I wouldn't have had too many options."

Phippen was, at the time, aware of Herb Brooks and he remembered his first tryout with the Junior Stars.

"That was the craziest time," he said. "It wasn't really tryouts, because Herbie knew who was good enough. Our first game was against Thunder Bay, at Minnetonka [Minnesota] Arena. I remember Glen Sonmor was there, scouting."

Thunder Bay had Bill "Goldie" Goldthorpe, Willie Trognitz, Lee Fogolin, Danny Gruen, Rick Adduono—about a dozen guys who went on to play pro hockey. They were killers, and they intimidated everybody by simply coming at foes with an uncompromising, in-your-face style, literally as well as figuratively.

"Five minutes into our first game, there was a brawl," Phippen recalled. "There was blood everywhere, and a bunch of us looked at each other, wondering, 'What have we gotten into here?' We had two tough guys, Dave Hanson and [Jeff] Buzzy Parrish. A lot of us lost teeth and got beaten up pretty bad. I think we played them seventeen times that year, and we never beat 'em. It was a scary year, and there was blood on the ice at every game against them. Herbie hated every minute of it, and I think he kinda felt sorry for us. But it was kind of an experiment.

"I remember in one practice, I got hit and got a tooth knocked out," Phippen said. "I was going off the ice, and Herbie said, 'Where do you think you're going? Get back out there.' So I did."

The season—and especially the games against Thunder Bay—were not only basic combat training, but they were also overload training, for the players and the coach. Still, Brooks brought the Junior Stars home in second place in the league. His players attained more tangible rewards.

"We were gladiators when we played summer league at Bloomington after that season," Phippen said. "We weren't afraid of anybody."

Brooks ran the Junior Stars the same way he ran every team he coached—with a lot of skating and conditioning. He had Glenn Gostick, a memorable character who could recite famous quotations from Shakespeare to Shero with a scholarly articulation that befit his ever-present bowtie but seemed bizarre in any hockey training room. Goz ran off-ice conditioning drills for Brooks, who was always eager to find ways to ensure his teams were the best-conditioned.

When Brooks accepted the chance to take over the Gophers for the 1972–73 season, he lobbied for Doug Woog to take over the Junior Stars. Phippen remained and played a second year under Woog before joining Brooks for a fabulous stretch at Minnesota. Phippen laughed as he recalled the differences between the always-organized Brooks and Woog, who tended to be less organized and adjusted to game situations in a reactionary manner, which sometimes involved an in-your-face style on the bench.

"Herbie had everything planned out," Phippen said. "Woog was your buddy, or tried to be. Woog used to ask me what to do in certain situations. I always thought about that when he was coaching at the U, or later when he was a television analyst.

"I remember once we were playing against the Pembroke [Ontario] junior team, and Tim Young, who went on to the North Stars, was their third-line center," Phippen added. "David Lundeen, from Minneapolis Southwest, and who later played at Wisconsin, was on our team, and he got a bad penalty. Woog, our coach, was really mad, and as Lundeen headed for the penalty box, Woog gave Lundeen the finger. Lundeen gave him the finger right back.

"It was crazy, and a lot different than when Herbie coached."

CHAPTER 6

TRANSITION TO GOPHERS

Glen Sonmor was a big influence on Herb Brooks, and a specific bit of advice Sonmor received as a teenager in Hamilton, Ontario, may have been absorbed by Brooks at a vital juncture on his way toward becoming a premier coach.

"I had a fellow named George Farris as a coach in high school, and he threw me off the baseball team," Sonmor said. "I stomped away, and he let me go for a couple of weeks. Sure enough, I came back, and he made me apologize to my teammates and vow to stop being a disruption to the team. He also gave me some great advice.

"He said: 'Whatever you decide to do for a living, make sure it's something you enjoy.' I followed that advice."

Sonmor has not only lived his life to the fullest, and undoubtedly enjoyed every second of it, but he also went back years later, looked up Farris, and thanked him for that advice. Glen also put the same advice to further use.

"In November of 1971, we had gotten off to an awful start, and Mike Antonovich got hurt," Sonmor recalled of his final year at the University. "I had the chance to go to the Minnesota Fighting Saints, who were going to start play in the new World Hockey Association the next year, in October of 1972. They had to start putting the team together. At about the same time, Jack Kelley did the same thing with New England, leaving Boston University. That's when Jackie Parker took over at BU.

"Meanwhile," Sonmor continued, "Marsh Ryman got fired at the University of Minnesota, and Paul Giel came in as the new athletic director. Paul was not only a former star football and baseball player at the University, but also a great guy. John [Mariucci] had put me in school at the same time that Paul Giel was going to the U, and we were physical education majors at the same time. When Paul started as athletic director, about the first thing that happened was that I had to go in and tell him I was leaving as hockey coach.

"I didn't want to leave Paul Giel flat. Herbie was coaching the junior team and selling insurance, and I thought he should be the guy to take over the Gopher program. But he didn't want to leave his insurance company in the lurch. That's the kind of guy he was.

"I wouldn't have left the U if I didn't think Herbie would take the job. So I sat down with Herbie, and I was trying to talk him into staying in coaching and taking over when I left. He was working at the St. Paul Companies, and he said, 'I don't know, this insurance business is something that if you work at it, you can make a lot of money. My boss makes a lot of money and has this huge house . . .'

"So I asked him about what he actually did at work, and what it was like. 'Is it fun?' I asked him. 'Not really,' he said. But he was loyal. Then his boss suddenly dropped dead of a heart attack. Herbie was enamored by the way his mentor had made himself so successful, but that guy dropped dead. Part of my argument was that you can plan everything, but you never know what's going to happen. It made me realize once again that you'd better be doing something you love."

Without question, the challenge of the unknown and his love for hockey and coaching made for a far more tempting future for Brooks the Idealist, than the more conventional attraction of becoming a top-level business executive did for Brooks the Pragmatist.

Giel, a thoughtful, intelligent man, was considered by most to be an excellent fundraiser as athletic director. He also had tremendous insight and judgment of character. Still, he didn't know Brooks, but he did know Ken Yackel, his former All-American football teammate who was also a former pro hockey player. When Giel went to Yackel, he got the same referral: Yackel insisted Brooks should be the new coach. Yackel also agreed to finish the 1971–72 season as interim coach.

At Minnesota, the alumni welcomed each new season and group of players into their exclusive "club." Players at other colleges—even great players at prominent institutions—couldn't hope to enjoy an interconnected community of homegrown players like that fostered at the U. Boston University creates that filial atmosphere to some extent, and Boston College used to, before the Eagles branched out to continent-wide recruiting. But at the University of Minnesota, most of the alumni stayed in Minnesota and made their living in the state. Others who came from the outside to play at Minnesota —including Canadians such as Lou Nanne, Murray Williamson, and Murray McLachlan—were caught up in the spirit as well and remained in Minnesota after adopting the state's lifestyle.

A large and controversial nugget of inspiration for the passionate interaction among alumni developed when John Mariucci vehemently protested over-age Canadian recruits. He never protested the presence of Canadian imports, per se, but he was adamantly against the twenty-one-year-old freshmen who were brought in after completing their junior hockey apprenticeship for the pros to dominate younger American players. That, Mariucci argued, inhibited rather than encouraged the development of U.S. players. The rosters at the University of Denver, under Murray Armstrong, and Michigan Tech, under John MacInnes, were made up almost exclusively of Canadians.

When Minnesota made a stand and refused to play Denver, Mariucci got credit for the refusal. I learned the truth firsthand, however, when I got the chance to cover the Minnesota North Stars late in their first season and on into their first foray into the Stanley Cup Playoffs against the Los Angeles Kings. Mariucci told me many things in confidence whenever we found time to spend alone together, and in Los Angeles, during a long conversation on a sidewalk near the Ambassador Hotel, he told me that indeed, he would never refuse to play any team—including a powerhouse like Denver with its Canadian-loaded talent—because the chance to beat such a team was his way to prove his convictions.

Back inside the U's Cooke Hall offices, Ryman's tendencies toward bursts of temper and threats to refuse to play opponents he didn't like logically pointed to him as the person responsible for the University's refusal to play Denver. The two programs didn't play from the 1958–59 season until the 1971–72 season, which was long after Mariucci had been dismissed in 1966. In fact, the resumption of play came in the final year for both Sonmor and Ryman. During all those intervening years, standings had to be calculated by percentages because of the uneven game tallies. The controversy that arose from Minnesota's boycott may have pumped up its home-state pride in the Gopher program, but it also caused opponents to resent Minnesota. The Gophers became the focus of scorn for what was perceived as the school's pompous policy of all-Minnesota recruiting. And that was before any Minnesota team had ever won an NCAA hockey championship.

Not all ex-Gophers retained their intense love and loyalty to the program, of course, or at least remained free to show it. Bob Johnson was an excellent young coaching prospect at Colorado College who was hired by the University of Wisconsin to take its fledgling Division I program big-time. Mariucci, who had coached Johnson among his long legion of disciples, encouraged all of his ex-players to coach wherever the opportunity came, in hopes of broadening the base of U.S. talent.

Mariucci strongly encouraged Johnson to build the University of Wisconsin program from within the state, envisioning that Wisconsin could develop a high school network to rival Minnesota's, if Wisconsin youngsters grew up with the objective of playing for the Badgers. Instead, Johnson couldn't resist more instant success by following other U.S. college coaches to Western Canada's recruiting ground, where he could cultivate the same connections he had developed at Colorado College. Mariucci was sorely disappointed and, as usual, the ol' Godfather was right. Forty years later, Wisconsin's high school program is pretty good with a strong team or two, but not nearly as deep or broad as it could have been if it had adopted Mariucci's vision.

Under Johnson, Wisconsin moved from the ancient Hartmeyer Ice Arena to the shiny and bright new Dane County Coliseum. At the urging of Mariucci, and with Minnesota's eagerness to expand hockey to other Big Ten colleges, Sonmor took his Gopher teams down to play Wisconsin for a Wednesday game in Madison, even with important WCHA series before and after. It gave Sonmor a chance to rest All-America goaltender Murray McLachlan and to play Ron Docken, his outstanding backup.

Johnson, who always wore a red blazer, had a movie-star-like dressing room, with a star on the outside of the door and light bulbs surrounding the full-length mirrors inside. He was already being called "Badger Bob," a term usually spoken in derision because of Johnson's tendency to do things like manipulate the Wisconsin media to claim that the Gophers didn't play first-line players because they didn't respect the Badgers. That stirred up the Badgers, of course, and the passions of Wisconsin fans against Minnesota. It also stirred up Sonmor, his assistant Brooks, and the Gopher players. The rivalry intensity increased to a level that could accurately be described as hatred through the rest of the Sonmor–Johnson coaching matchups. It rose even higher through the Brooks regime.

That made it interesting in 1971, when Paul Giel was trying to buy time before deciding midseason whether to make Brooks the new coach to replace Sonmor. Inside the Gopher program, there was total consensus that Brooks would be the new coach. I reported it pretty much that way in the *Minneapolis Tribune*, which led to a humorous exchange with my "teammate," columnist Sid Hartman. An unflinching basketball advocate who either ignored hockey throughout his long career, or put it down as a minor sport with minimal interest outside a small cult of fans, Hartman liked Mariucci, and even got to know some players, including Nanne and Bob Johnson. But he was never close to Brooks, and certainly wasn't close to Sonmor, who hadn't played for the Gophers.

Hartman figured he could influence Giel, his "close personal friend" from Giel's football-hero days. After I had written that Brooks was the heir-apparent, Hartman strode up to my desk at the *Tribune* and said, "There's no way your boy Brooks will ever get the Gopher job. They're going to hire Bob Johnson." I laughed out loud, so stunned was I at the outrageous prediction. Johnson, universally disliked by

Minnesota hockey players, alumni, and fans, couldn't have gotten the job without causing mutiny within the program. Johnson continued to do an exceptional job as Badger Bob, and Hartman stayed away from Brooks and the Gopher hockey program for nearly all of the seven years Brooks coached there. When Team USA won the 1980 Olympics, Herbie was suddenly welcomed into Sid's vast legion of "close personal friends," ready or not.

When Sonmor left the U, Giel was pretty well convinced Brooks would be the next coach, but he persuaded Yackel to take over the team in December 1971 on an interim basis for the remainder of the season. Things didn't go well. Antonovich, who had missed the start of the season due to an injury, signed a contract to join Sonmor with the Fighting Saints, bypassing the rest of his junior year. Yackel tried to ram his entire playing system into the team in his first week on the job, but when the Gophers took their home ice that mid-December, they were slaughtered 15-3 by Minnesota-Duluth. Yackel tried to wipe the slate clean and told the players to go back to however they had been playing. Amazingly, the Gophers won 5-3 the next night. It was, however, a dismal season, and the team sputtered to an 8-24 league record, dead last in the WCHA. It was a program in need of total reconstruction.

In retrospect, it's impossible to know how much Sonmor's little tidbit of advice affected Herbie, but it may have been considerable. Brooks had always looked ahead to a graceful move to life after hockey. He had already started on the road to a successful business career that allowed him to assume the life of a suburban dad, with a beautiful wife and two young children. But his passion was hockey, and the attraction of doing something he so intensely loved needed only a spark to reach full fire. Sonmor's advice, to make sure he chose a path he loved, might have been that spark.

CHAPTER 7

RETURNING TO WILLIAMS ARENA

The old Williams Arena was a wonderful facility. Before the west end was converted to a compact gymnasium to host women and men's sports events too small for the large basketball arena on the eastern two-thirds of the building, it was a huge hockey arena, colorful and reeking with the character of years past. It could be called the greatest hockey arena where half the crowd had obstructed view, because the events that took place there on cold winter nights overcame the absurdly bad sightlines.

There were no seats at the ends. The press box was above the south-side stands, nearest University Avenue. The west wall was just that—a wall—with windows up high, and in the rare event of an afternoon game, strange shafts of light practically blinded players skating east to west. The eastern end was even stranger. Visiting teams insisted the rink was longer than the regulation two hundred feet and its corners were remarkably square compared to the more rounded shape of contemporary rinks. But the rink did measure the standard two hundred by eighty-five feet. The optical illusion was created by the adjoining basketball side of Williams, where stands surrounded the raised floor, which was (and still is) a highlight, if a bit dangerous. The first few rows of basketball fans sit at floor level and look up at the players. On the west end, the basketball stands rose upward from the court until they protruded into the east end of the hockey side. No problem. The architects simply created a peculiar facade that angled out over the goal at the eastern end before rising straight and flat to the ceiling. Skating toward the east gave the illusion of skating into a large cave under that overhang, and this design made the rink seem much longer than it was.

The hockey seats, wooden benches only, and only on the two sides of the rink, must have been designed by the same basketball people who designed the seating on the basketball half of the building. Trouble was that first-row fans had to peer over the boards to see halfway across the width of the rink. The next ten rows angled upward so gradually that few, while seated, could see over the heads of those in front of them. Anytime anything happened, first-row occupants jumped to their feet to see, which meant that everyone in the first ten or fifteen rows also had to stand in order to see anything. On the other hand, higher up, the rows of plank seats rose abruptly enough so most spectators in the top ten rows on both sides of the rink had great sightlines, except for a few seats obscured by the huge, arching girders. It was the only hockey arena where fans would moan if they got a seat in the first ten rows and be thrilled to get a seat in the upper reaches.

The press box hung from the ceiling on the south side of the building and had two levels, although nobody sat in the upper level. Across the rink, a balcony was affixed high above the north stands, providing by far the most spectacular view, almost like watching the game from an adjacent skyscraper. The balcony seats were so steeply stacked that you had to be careful climbing up and *really* careful coming back down. Those seats were for students and general admission, so when the arena doors opened more than an hour before game time, the whole building trembled from the knowledgeable fans who stampeded all the way around the arena and up the iron stairs to reach their favorite vantage points in the balcony.

Be it ever so strange, Williams Arena was home to the Gophers, and while I never heard a player complain about claustrophobia, going to the dressing rooms was a bit of a challenge. The Gophers' bench was on the north side, under the balcony; the visitors' bench was on the south side, and both were reached by a wide corridor. Just short of a pair of swinging doors that led to the outer concourse, a single door on the right opened on a steep staircase that seemed to plunge to nowhere. At the bottom of those many, steep, old, wooden steps, a ninety-degree turn to the right put you into a long, lower tunnel.

A small office on the immediate right was adjacent to a spacious dressing room for the visiting team during games and the junior varsity or freshman team on practice days. A fifty-yard walk down the long, tunnel-like hallway reached the home dressing room. Immediately beyond it was the trainers' room, and then the home basketball dressing room near a staircase that led up to the raised basketball floor. The athletic department tried not to schedule basketball and hockey games at the same time, so that both teams could use the training room.

The place was weird, but it was an imposing colossus for visitors when it was filled with cheering, chanting fans. There were a few games like that when I first watched Gopher hockey teams of John Mariucci as a student at the U, writing about them for the *Minnesota Daily* as assistant sports editor. I was apprehensive on my first trip there to watch practice, but I was overwhelmed by the warmth of Mariucci when I hesitantly introduced myself to his larger-than-legend self. I expected a hard-bitten Iron Ranger who would treat me like a young nuisance; instead, Maroosh immediately seemed to appreciate my eagerness to learn all I could about hockey, and to capture and relay the spontaneity and passion I found in every game. He took me under his wing, talked freely, and regaled me with colorful stories of his days with the Chicago Blackhawks, speaking both on and off the record. We became hard and fast friends for the rest of his life—a relationship I treasured then, and treasure even more in retrospect.

Sonmor was far different from Mariucci, but also similar in many ways, including his ability to always entertain. He replaced Mariucci while I was getting my early journalism experience back home, at the *Duluth News Tribune*. After migrating to the *Minneapolis Tribune* in the fall of 1967, I had the pleasure of covering most of Sonmor's teams firsthand. When Herb took the reins in 1972, I had been acquainted with him as a player and assistant coach, but didn't know much else about him, other than that he had some impressive and progressive ideas for the future. He was receptive to ideas from everywhere, if he thought they might raise the standards of the program, so I suggested a couple of things.

For one, Gopher hockey fans were free to pick up a mimeographed sheet with the numbered lineups of both teams as they entered the Williams Arena. That's the way it had always been. I recommended Herb should lobby for a different game program. First, it would be smaller, more like 5×8 inches rather than the full, letter-sized 8½×11, so hockey fans, who came dressed for the winter nights, could easily stuff it into a jacket pocket.

I also suggested listing the goaltenders separately regardless of number, then the defensemen separately, by number, and then the forwards by number, as well as including short background sketches of each player, Brooks, and his staff. There was no media guide for hockey in those days, so I volunteered to write much of the information as my own donation to the cause.

I gave Herbie full credit for a couple other clever ideas. One of the best was the proliferation of the Gopher logo: a horizontal Gopher, crouched low and skating hard, with an old leather helmet on his head and a bold, gold "M" on his maroon jersey. It was a wonderful symbol, one of those great sports icons that needed no words. It clearly said "Gopher Hockey."

While that logo adorned T-shirts, equipment bags, and many other items, a sudden array of large, maroon souvenir pins flooded the area, adorned with gold lettering that read, "Hockey Is for Tough Guys" and "Gopherhockey" (all one word).

Years later, I told Herbie what a great idea the pins were, and he said he had nothing to do with it, but that Tom Greenhoe, the hockey sports information director, or SID, had come up with the promotional gimmicks. All Herbie had done was offer his endorsement.

Greenhoe was a piece of work and seemed to fit in very well with the quirkiness of Williams Arena. A friendly fellow with a neat family, Greenhoe had been happy as the WCHA's most energetic SID when he was at Michigan Tech promoting all sports, but mostly the Division I hockey program. The University of Minnesota lured him away from Houghton, and he moved to the Twin Cities suburb of Coon Rapids to churn out tireless amounts of statistical information on the Gopher hockey team, much of it accurate.

Greenhoe was a friendly sort, and he enjoyed having the occasional celebratory drinks. He also smoked a nearly endless string of cigarettes. But he was pleasant to the point of greeting all, usually with a slap on the back, and he ran a pretty tight press box. On Fridays, Greenhoe stationed himself to glad-hand everyone at the Blue Line Club meetings held at noon at Jax Cafe, a neighborhood steakhouse in Northeast Minneapolis with an upstairs meeting room, above the bar. Greenhoe tended to stay at Jax after the meetings, not necessarily upstairs, and socialize until it was time to go to Williams Arena. On the off-chance a reporter needed something from Greenhoe on Friday afternoon, calling Jax was far more effective than calling the SID's office.

Because I was covering high school and NHL hockey as well as the Gophers, I was often writing feverishly before games and between periods, pecking at a small portable typewriter, as we did in those days, and Xeroxing our work to the newspaper office. I have dozens of notebooks, in which my notes are accented by a bold, diagonal line, sometimes ripping through the paper. I'd be writing notes when Greenhoe would spot me, walk up behind, and say, "Hiya, John," as he slapped me on the back with enough force to send my pen across and through the page.

Tom also did the media a great favor by ordering several large pizzas for reporters and photographers to eat between periods on the upper level of the two-tier press box. He didn't think we knew, but he'd always hide one or two in a cabinet to take home afterward. After we devoured what was on the table, any late-arriving media types who asked about the pizza were quietly informed that more was set aside for them inside the cabinet. They would be feasting heartily when the exasperated Greenhoe would catch them and try to remain calm.

Several years later, the fire marshal tightened up the rules restricting the number of standing-room tickets at Williams Arena and made the whole building no-smoking. That was long before no-smoking facilities were commonplace, but the fans seemed to appreciate the cleaner air, and it was a revelation to be able to see clearly across the arena to the balcony without the blue haze.

Greenhoe had a problem with the smoking ban and would sneak to the upper level every once in a while, open the cabinet door and crouch down, out of view, to hastily smoke a cigarette.

One night, uniformed university police came up the steps to the press box, caught Greenhoe in the act, and gave him a ticket. He was embarrassed and also dumbfounded. How did the police know he was stealing a smoke when he was crouched down out of sight on the otherwise uninhabited upper level of the press box? Turns out, a concerned fan sitting in the balcony on the other side of the building saw a column of blue smoke curling up toward the rafters, silhouetted against the dark wall, and notified a cop that the place might be on fire.

When Brooks took over the Gophers in the fall of 1972, his son Danny was five, and his daughter Kelly had just been born the previous December. Patti, who learned to enrich her marriage by establishing and nurturing parallel universes of work and family duties while her husband was lost amid X's and O's, attended every game. She still didn't have any idea what was happening on the ice, but the games became an important focal point of her social life.

"I had never heard of Paul Giel until he hired Herbie," said Patti, who was not only a non-sports fan, but was from Yankton, South Dakota, as well.

Of course, many elements of what Brooks wanted to build were already in place, including forwards Mike Polich, Dean Blais, Jimmy Gambucci, John Matschke, Cal Cossalter, John Harris, and Bruce Carlson, plus defensemen Bill Butters and John Perpich, and goaltender Brad Shelstad. All had suffered through that last-place finish the previous season and were appreciative to be included among Brooks' building blocks.

Brooks was so well organized that he was ready to go before he ever got on the ice. He enjoyed the "Hockey Is for Tough Guys" pins, and he started his practice of psych jobs. On the wall just outside the dressing room, where every player would see as they walked out to the dark hallway that led toward the rink, he affixed a sign. It said: "Passes come from the heart."

It was written by Anatoli Tarasov, the Father of Russian hockey, and while it perfectly stated the basis for the former Soviet Union's incredibly collective hockey mentality, it also perfectly described the unselfish attitude toward puck-control that Brooks would instill as a basic ingredient for his players.

CHAPTER 8

INHERITING THE
LAST-PLACE GOPHERS

In his two years as freshman coach at Minnesota, Brooks did a lot of recruiting, and he had gotten some prizes. Still there to play a pivotal role as captain four years later when Brooks returned as varsity coach was defenseman Bill Butters from the St. Paul suburb of White Bear Lake.

Butters, who performed a crucial duty for Brooks, went on to play in the World Hockey Association and later in the National Hockey League before becoming one of the most effective teaching coaches in Minnesota, and some say in the world. Butters became an assistant coach at Minnesota, and later a co-coach at Bethel College and a head coach at White Bear Lake Area High School. Everywhere he went, Butters displayed an unsurpassed ability to train young defensemen in the fundamentals of the position, which might be the most difficult chore in coaching hockey at any level. Butters gives credit to the same sort of instruction he received when he played for Herb Brooks, when he learned all the fundamentals as a freshman, and some new motivational concepts as a senior. He also learned important elements of recruiting and of simplifying the role a player is expected to play.

"When I was a senior at White Bear Lake, Herbie was selling insurance for St. Paul Fire and Marine, and also was freshman coach, and working as a referee who had a lot of our games," recalled Butters. "No question, he saw me play more than anybody, and he came out and talked to me about going to Minnesota.

"I came in on a half-scholarship, and it was the first year freshmen could play varsity," Butters added. "Dean Blais, Mike Antonovich, and Jimmy Gambucci played varsity right away, but I spent the season on the freshman team with Herbie as coach. A lot of coaches drop the puck and tell you to play, but Herbie would show you what to do. I learned the most I learned from any coach that year with Herbie on the freshman team.

"Glen was coaching the varsity, and he was great. He wanted you to work hard, and he could motivate you with all the rah-rah stuff, but Herbie could do everything, and he taught me things about skating, passing, improving my hands—I never played for another coach who was as good at teaching you everything you needed to improve your skill level."

In 1970–71, Butters played varsity on the team that went to the NCAA tournament. But Brooks had been perturbed enough about Minnesota not taking him to the 1971 NCAA tournament that he decided to leave. He quit on August 17, 1971, and went off to coach the Junior Stars.

Butters' sophomore high was followed by a junior low, when he and the Gophers suffered through the plunge to a miserable last-place season. The Gophers opened with eight consecutive WCHA games on the road in 1971. They were swept in the opening series at Duluth, 4-1 and 5-2, and lost 3-2 at Michigan State before winning 3-1. Minnesota lost 5-2 and 5-4 at Colorado College, and then lost 5-1 and 5-3 at Michigan Tech. After starting 1-7 in league play, the Gophers' first game at Williams Arena was a nonconference game against the 1972 U.S. Olympic team on December 7, 1971. The Murray Williamson–coached U.S. team that would go on to win the silver medal drilled the Gophers 8-0. The loss was bad enough, but Minnesota also lost Antonovich, who suffered torn knee ligaments and would never again play for the Gophers. Sonmor bailed, signing a contract to put together the Fighting Saints to start the following season. While Antonovich was recovering from the knee injury, Sonmor signed him as a charter member of the new WHA franchise.

Ken Yackel came in and set out to immediately change everything. A stickler for the sort of precision he had been teaching in his breakthrough hockey schools in suburban Edina, Minnesota, Yackel tried to systematize every step for what was essentially a freewheeling team with no particular breakout or forechecking system. Yackel may have crammed a year's worth of coaching into a week, and he had great hopes for his debut when the Gophers opened their home-ice WCHA play against Minnesota-Duluth. Nobody was prepared for the 15-3 clobbering by a very skilled UMD team up against a Gopher team that descended from hesitant, to very confused, to chaotic. The loss was the worst ever suffered by a Minnesota team, with the most goals ever allowed. Immediately after the game, Yackel asked, "Have they ever hanged a coach in effigy after the first game?" He was smart enough, though, to also immediately tell the players to forget his hastily installed system and go to back to "hitting the open man." Incredibly, twenty-four hours later, the Gophers relaxed and rebounded to upset UMD 5-3. Still, the team followed with a 1-7 slump and ended up 7-21 for last place in the WCHA, with an 8-24 overall record,

If 1971–72 was a season of harsh lessons for the Gophers, Brooks also was undergoing overload training as a coach with the Junior Stars, who were learning things beyond their inexperienced and wide-eyed years. For one thing, Brooks learned that no matter how much talent you gathered for a team, the players still had to be tough enough to let that talent shine through. The talent and newfound toughness did shine through enough for the Junior Stars to take second in the rugged USHL. But when Brooks took over as coach at Minnesota in the fall of 1972, he was ready for better things, the returning Gophers were certainly ready for better things, and Butters was the perfect young man in the right place at the right time for Herbie and his team.

"Herbie wanted to change the face of Gophers hockey," said Butters. "We didn't have a tough team, and it was obvious we didn't have a good team. He could make us a better team by recruiting better players, but he figured he could change our toughness in that first year.

"He called me in for a meeting. First, he said he was raising me from a half-scholarship to a full because he thought the Gopher captain should be on a full. Then he said he wanted me to start running guys over. I said that's how I always play, and he said, 'No, I mean now.' He wanted me to start running over some of our guys in practice.

"I said, 'But they're my teammates,' and he said, 'Do you want to be the captain? Do you want to keep your scholarship? Then do what I tell you.' He said he was setting the table, it was an honor to be captain, and that was the role where I could help the team the most. So I did it. Herbie didn't name names, so I assumed he meant everybody, and I ran over everybody I could."

That led to a few fights, and it probably didn't make Butters the most popular player on the team, but the team got better and more capable when things got ugly in game situations.

"I'll guarantee you, the guys hated practice more than games," Butters said. "First of all, whenever we scrimmaged, I'd be running guys over. Then he'd work us hard, too."

That whole first season was a test pattern for Brooks and the Gophers. They opened with a sweep of the University of Manitoba, but serious hockey prospects in Canada played junior hockey. Those who didn't get drafted by the NHL or receive a U.S. college scholarship might go to a Canadian college and play as a pastime while earning a degree. The tune-up was good, and it raised the level of optimism, but then things got serious in a hurry. Minnesota lost twice at Denver, then came home and lost 5-3 to Michigan State before gaining a 3-3 tie. The Gophers hit the road again and lost 3-2 at Notre Dame, before rebounding for Brooks' first WCHA victory—a rousing 7-1 romp over Notre Dame at South Bend.

Another trip to Ann Arbor brought another mixed weekend, beginning with a 7-6 loss to Michigan and ending with a resounding 7-3 victory. Back in Williams Arena, the Gophers tied Wisconsin 4-4, then beat the Badgers 4-2. A trip to St. Louis and a

6-5 victory over St. Louis University was followed by a 5-1 letdown loss to Wisconsin. Two more road trips saw the Gophers get swept at Michigan State and lose 6-3 to North Dakota before tying the Fighting Sioux 2-2. The Gophers were back home in mid-January with a 3-8-3 record in WCHA play, and 6-9-3 overall mark—not bad compared to last place, but nowhere near what Herb Brooks had in mind.

The opponent that January 19–20 weekend was Colorado College. During that memorable series, the Gophers, who had been run over by Bill Butters every practice, learned that when the chips were down, their captain would be making those runs on their behalf—and then some.

A scrap broke out behind the Gopher goal, with Butters typically in the middle of it. The officials waded in, separating the main combatants. They grabbed Butters and herded him toward the penalty box. As the escort reached the center faceoff circle, the refs noticed that the fight had erupted again. They told Butters to stay where he was and raced back to the end of the rink to restore order.

In the press box, I noticed that most of the players on the Colorado College bench right underneath us were standing and yelling at Butters. They were safe in the sanctity of their bench, presumably, and they had the strength of numbers. I looked down on Butters, standing in the center faceoff circle and he was glaring silently at the CC bench. The black-haired, stocky 5-foot-10 Butters could fool anyone with his expression, but his eyes betrayed his true emotion. As he stood there, I could see the rage building in Butters, as the whole CC team on the bench continued to taunt him.

Involuntarily, I stood up at my seat in the press box and said to nobody, "Don't do it, Butts!" From two hundred feet away, I could read his mind. Butters snapped into action. His feet churned, spinning like a dragster's rear wheels do before they bite traction, then he raced across the ice and hurtled over the boards, right onto the Colorado College bench. An amazing brawl ensued, but nobody would suggest Butters lost—at least not to his face. It was incredible.

I later wrote, "Butters glared at the bench and assessed the odds . . . 15 against 1. Pretty even." When order was restored, the Gophers completed a 3-2, 5-2 series sweep. Not everyone who was in Williams Arena that night remembers who won, but they all remember Butters and his infamous dive into the CC bench. Butters spent the rest of the game in the dressing room, having been tossed out for the granddaddy of all game disqualifications.

"It was pretty interesting, because in one year's time, we were coached by Glen Sonmor, Ken Yackel, and Herb Brooks," Butters said. "The real extremes were Glen, who had no tactical game plan but all the enthusiasm in the world, and

Yackel, who thought every move should be right out of his hockey-school book. Herbie turned out to be the best of both—he had the hockey-school tactical knowledge of Yackel, but he also had the motivational, challenging, and fun parts of Sonmor.

"The character stuff, to be tough enough, was every bit as important as tactics in Herbie's success. He had a lot of little tricks and catch-names, saying the first forechecker should go hard, the second should be alert to support him, and the third forward should stay back, as though playing centerfield. He could do it all—teach, coach, motivate, and you had to like and respect him."

Asked about the mind games, for which Brooks was later well-known, Butters said, "I never saw 'em. In my case, he called me in and told me my role. That's not a mind game—that's good coaching."

After the bench-hurtling routine, Brooks had to escort Butters into a meeting with Paul Giel. "He didn't want me to say a word," Butters said. "We got in there, and Herbie says, 'He's such an emotional player, and we don't want to lose that, but we've kept him in pretty good control. He just snapped in that one case and it won't happen again.'

"In reality, Herbie wanted our team to put a stake in the ground. And I was the stake."

The Gophers not only swept CC that weekend, but that series was the ignition for winning eight of their next ten games, including sweeps of North Dakota and Michigan in Williams Arena. The surge lifted the Gophers to 11-10-3—the first time Brooks and his charges reached the .500 mark. It didn't last, because two losses to UMD and a split at Wisconsin left them at 12-13-3 in the WCHA, still good enough to move up from tenth to sixth place. Being swept at Wisconsin in a league playoff series gave the Gophers a 15-16-3 overall record—one game under .500 in both the league and overall, which proved to be the perfect launching pad.

Butters created his own legend wherever the Gophers went that year. "We got thumped in Dane County Coliseum," Mike Polich recalled. "Their fans liked to pour it on by yelling all kinds of stuff, and their band would stand right in the first row. When they'd play, they'd aim their trombones over the top of the glass and blast away. Butters, by the time he got to his senior year, apparently had enough of that, and when we came out for the second-game warm-ups and their band was playing, Butters skated by and held his stick up. He knocked off all the trombones. Some of them ended up on the ice."

Patti Brooks recalled all seven of Herbie's Gopher teams, but holds special memories of that first one, which was filled with character—and characters.

"Herbie's first team was probably my favorite," she said. "I adored Bill Butters. He and his friend, Wacko, had once ridden bicycles naked around White Bear Lake. You've got to love that."

Butters laughed about that one. Wacko, he explained, is Doug Werlein, who now lives in Cambridge, Minnesota. "And it wasn't White Bear Lake, it was Bald Eagle Lake," Butters said, noting a smaller rural lake just west of White Bear Lake. "We didn't really go all the way around it, just a short segment of it. Wacko's buddy lived on Bald Eagle Lake. We had a bicycle built for two, so we thought it would be funny to ride up to his house naked. But the surprise was on us, because when we went up to the door, his buddy's girlfriend happened to be there, and she was the one who came to the door."

Butters tended to live for the shock value he could bring to normal life. And those days were long before his pro career with the Minnesota Fighting Saints and the North Stars, and his subsequent coaching years. It was also before Butters completely turned his life around with Hockey Ministries International. With this organization, he has gathered up friends such as Jack Carlson, Glen Sonmor, Wacko, and others, and travels the world to put on coaching clinics and advisory sessions to show players how to play hard and tough, but still be Christians.

For Gopher hockey fans, the pre-reformed Butters remains the standard of outrageous behavior, but to Patti Brooks he was also a sensitive, intelligent person.

"I remember the night at Williams Arena when he went into the Colorado College bench," said Patti. "I saw the look on his face. After that game, I remember Bill coming upstairs and asking if he could hold Kelly, my baby."

Butters remembers it, too. "That night was also my first date with Debbie," he said, as if, some thirty-five years after the fact, he was still pleasantly surprised she agreed to become his wife.

"Marry me? I was surprised she was still waiting for me," he said.

CHAPTER 9

RIGHTING THE GOOD SHIP GOPHER

"Herbie told me I was his first recruit," said Dick Spannbauer. "He may have told that to everybody, but he told me wherever I was thinking of going, I shouldn't pass up the chance to be a Gopher.

"Herbie came to our house because he wanted to visit each player at home," added Spannbauer, a huge and powerful defenseman for Hill-Murray School whose rugged capabilities were belied by his pleasant and engaging personality off the ice. "He wanted to make sure my mom and dad were home when he came. It was part of his personal study of players, just to see how a player treated his mom and dad."

The thoroughness with which Herb Brooks coached, and coaxed, his players was obvious, but what was less obvious was that he was every bit as thorough in his recruiting. After watching games and picking out prospects who showed the skill and tenacity Brooks sought, he wanted to meet and talk to the players and their families. He also wanted references, what might be called "third-person endorsements," to learn what kind of people, as well as players, he was recruiting.

Brooks knew all too well the influence that Canada always seemed to have on Minnesota hockey, and he also was a devotee of John Mariucci's philosophy of giving Minnesota players a chance to succeed in hockey's pecking order. At the same time, Brooks knew how advanced some players from Canada and outside the state were. While he didn't really have any intention of going outside the state in search of players, he was not above scouting what sort of parameters he might be facing. If he found out that he couldn't achieve success without recruiting out of state, he had no rules preventing the broadening of the University's boundaries. But he did feel the awesome pressure from the grassroots people in Minnesota hockey, particularly the high school coaches who worked so tirelessly to teach, train, and develop their players and teams.

Brooks paid no heed to the non-hockey members of the media who paid far more attention to the U football and basketball teams, both of which had always recruited their top stars from all over the country. Those media types always cynically questioned why the Gophers seemed so intent on staying in-state for their hockey players, and had no empathy for the integrity an athletic team could claim by being entirely from the home state.

Jack Blatherwick would become Brooks' training and conditioning guru after the coach left college hockey, but when Brooks started coaching at Minnesota, he barely knew who Blatherwick was.

"I was playing hockey in a men's league, for Midwest Federal, and Herbie was playing for Stephens Buick in the same league, and selling insurance," Blatherwick recalled. "I was coaching at Breck, when he got the Minnesota job. I knew who he was, but I didn't really know him at all."

Breck is an expensive private school, which in those days was located on the West Bank of the Mississippi River in South Minneapolis, just downstream from the university. Breck had its own arena, and it also had natural ice. Its walls were actually flaps that could be raised in case the ice surface needed some renewed chilling from outside.

Along with teaching and coaching, Blatherwick took care of the rink. You could say he was a progressive coach, as well. When the other seven teams in the private school state tournament stood grinning for their traditional team photos for the tournament program, Blatherwick parked a Zamboni and had his players sprawl in front of it, lean on it, or sit on it in all manner of casual array. It was obvious that although Breck was a pretty good team, the players had a good time. Any coach who would break from the rigid norm for a traditional team photo must be a cut above.

"I was flooding the hockey rink, and Herbie showed up," said Blatherwick. "He asked me if I thought high school coaches around Minnesota would resent it 'if I recruited a Canadian kid or two.'

"I said, 'Yes I do,'" Blatherwick recalled. "I always told him what I thought."

That was an integral part of their future relationship; they had a bond in their honesty, which was always more direct and candid than politically correct or even tactful. It was the honest opinions of high school hockey coaches that Brooks respected more than any unwritten recruiting rules.

Without a doubt, Blatherwick, and other high school coaches he respected, reinforced what Herbie already believed: the easy way to win in a hurry at Minnesota would be to follow the well-worn trails of all the other major college programs to Canada, from Nova Scotia to Vancouver Island. The harder way would be the right way: do it entirely with Minnesota high school kids, even if they were younger and less experienced. Brooks knew that some players might gain experience from going to junior hockey after high school, but he also knew from earlier recruiting and assisting at Minnesota that the spirit and determination of homegrown kids often compensated for lack of talent, and that there were more and more talented players coming out of the high schools every year.

While always a man of principle and character, Brooks had been through the warfare of junior hockey, so in his thoroughness he sought out special qualities.

In those days, Minnesota high school hockey was divided between public and private schools. They played each other and established some fantastic rivalries, such as Hill-Murray against St. Paul Johnson or White Bear Lake, and Duluth Cathedral against Duluth East. While they played each other during regular season, the private schools weren't allowed to play in the Minnesota State High School Tournament, which had grown to legendary proportions.

The private schools conducted their own tournament, on a smaller scale, with Duluth Cathedral and St. Paul's Hill High School emerging as the dominant private teams. Cathedral had colorful and exciting teams, very likely the best team in the state overall a couple of times, under Del Genereau, while future NHL coach Andre Beaulieu assembled a mighty team at the all-boys Catholic school called Hill, after the railroad baron James J. Hill.

Located in Maplewood, a suburb on the eastern boundary of St. Paul, Hill later merged with the nearby all-girls Archbishop Murray to become Hill-Murray. One of Hill-Murray's best teams had an imposing group of defensemen, particularly the large and dominant pair of Dave Langevin and Dick Spannbauer. Langevin, a tall, lanky, 6-foot-2, puck-rushing defenseman, went on to Minnesota-Duluth and then the New York Islanders, after which he took the assorted Stanley Cups on his resume and ended up in the U.S. Hockey Hall of Fame. Spannbauer was tall, too, but also *big*. At a time when hockey players were mostly 160 to 175 pounds, Spannbauer packed a rock-solid 215 pounds into his 6-foot-2 frame.

With the thought of rebuilding the Gopher program, and remembering the harsh realities of making the Junior Stars rugged enough to compete in the USHL, there was no question which Hill-Murray blueliner Brooks would pursue. "It's better to give than to receive" might be ideal for Christmastime, but "It's better to intimidate than be intimidated" was a much better motto for hockey success.

"Herbie always believed in muscle, and he wanted his teams to be a little more intimidating," Spannbauer said. "You knew that he had an idea of what to do, and that he was going to carry it out.

"My freshman year was Herbie's first year, and all six of the freshmen played. He cut some seniors, probably because of little disagreements, but after finishing last,

Herb Brooks patrols the Gopher bench in 1972–73, his first season as his alma mater's head coach. Number 24 is future 1980 Olympian Buzz Schneider. *Courtesy University of Minnesota Athletics*

we had no record of being successful. He probably used that line we heard a million times, 'Take two weeks off and then retire.'"

In preparation for his first year as head coach, Brooks recruited a solid crop of high schoolers, including Spannbauer, Warren Miller from South St. Paul, Bill "Buzz" Schneider from Babbitt, Pat Phippen from Ramsey, Tom O'Brien from Benilde, Brad Morrow from Anoka, and Tom Mohr, a goaltender from Hopkins Lindbergh. All went on to be impact players for the Gophers and, of course, Schneider—whose speed led me to nickname him the "Babbitt Rabbit" in the *Minneapolis Tribune*— went on to 1980 Olympic fame.

"Herbie was always into conditioning," said Spannbauer. "On Mondays, we got our butts kicked in practice. Tuesday, we'd do team concept things. We had Greg Hughes as assistant that first year, and then Tom Saterdalen. And sometimes we had Herbie by himself. But we always knew what was coming. We called 'em 'Herbies' from the start."

Every youth coach and high school coach has a drill that is usually called the "lightning drill." Players line up at the end boards and, on the whistle, skate hard to the center red line for a quick stop, dash back to the near blue line and stop. Then they go to the far blue line, back to the center red line, and finally to the far end boards. It's tough and grueling. And it's nothing compared to "Herbies."

In a Herbie, the players line up along the end boards and sprint to the near blue line, then all the way back to the end boards, then to the red line and all the way back, then the far blue and all the way back, then to the far end and all the way back.

There was no question it would take a couple of recruiting years to raise the caliber of the Gophers, but as he told captain Bill Butters, they could learn to get tougher immediately. Herbie and his "Herbies" would see to it that nobody else ever had a conditioning edge on the Gophers.

During his first season at the helm, Brooks intensified his recruiting, and after that 1972–73 season, he secured defenseman Russ Anderson from Minneapolis Washburn; forwards Joe Micheletti from Hibbing, Tim Rainey from Bloomington, John Sheridan from Minneapolis Patrick Henry, and Tom Vannelli from St. Paul Academy; and goaltender Bill Moen. Micheletti had been the star center on Hibbing's state championship team, but Brooks convinced him to switch back to defense, a favorite trick that he once performed himself—converting a good-skating, clever, stick-handling forward into a defenseman who could readily escape his zone and join the attack.

That second recruiting class plugged effectively into the style Brooks installed in his first season. Still, nobody who had watched Gopher hockey for all those years, without a single NCAA championship to show for it, was prepared for the season that 1973–74 was to become.

CHAPTER 10

BIGGEST GOAL—
INCREDIBLE SEASON

The long and rich history of University of Minnesota hockey is filled with highlights, but the 1973–74 season still stands out as its most pivotal year, lifting the Gophers to elite status among college hockey programs. It was the year Herb Brooks, in his second season, proved a lot of things to himself as well as to his players. Perhaps the biggest thing he learned was to shoot for the top and, once within reach of it, be prepared to snatch the big prize.

Also from that campaign, a shorthanded goal scored by Mike Polich in Boston Garden in March 1974 stands out as the most important single goal in Gopher hockey history. You could debate it, but why bother? The goal happened in the NCAA Final Four semifinals, after Boston University had roared back from a 3-0 deficit to gain a 4-4 tie with a dominant third period. The Terriers were suddenly faster, stronger, fresher, and full of fire, as if they were skating downhill, while the Gophers were hanging on, desperate to get to the end of regulation and perhaps catch their breath for overtime.

It appeared that BU, which had broken Minnesota's heart when Jack Kelley's Terriers claimed the 4-2 championship victory in 1971, was about to do it again, this time coached by a young Jackie Parker—before he demanded to be called by the more formal "Jack." Just when it appeared the slick Terrier power play would finish off Minnesota, Polich, a fiery little centerman from Hibbing, stole the puck and scored a spectacular goal in the closing seconds to give Minnesota a 5-4 triumph.

There was still a championship game to go, but pulling off that narrow escape against BU put the Gophers within reach of the title. At that moment, it appeared that whatever happened the next night would be frosting on the cake after what the Gophers accomplished in the semifinals.

After a last-place finish in 1971–72, and a .500 season in Brooks' first year, even reaching the Final Four seemed beyond comprehension to the Minnesota players and fans.

The Gophers played the first two weekends of the season at Williams Arena. Instead of launching them into their memorable season, those first four WCHA games made the final prize seem almost inconceivable at the time. They lost 3-2 and 8-2 to Wisconsin, then tied 4-4 and lost 4-3 against Michigan. The Gophers started 0-3-1, or 0-4-1 if you counted a 4-3 exhibition loss to UMD at the annual Hall of Fame game in Eveleth.

But Minnesota righted things and won six straight, putting together an 8-0-1 run—the Gophers' first real winning streak under Brooks. They never looked back, rising to second in a duel with powerful Denver and staying within reach of Tech at the top of the WCHA. Down the stretch, the Gophers went seven games unbeaten (4-0-3) to get within reach of second place before heading to Houghton, Michigan, to end the regular season.

That stretch run featured some stirring games. At Colorado College, for example, Minnesota won 2-1 and then survived a wild 6-6 tie. John Harris remembered that series among his recollections as a Gopher. He was one of seven seniors, along with goaltender Brad Shelstad, defensemen John Perpich and Doug Falls, and forwards Bruce Carlson, Cal Cossalter, and John Matschke. Shelstad was captain, while Matschke, Perpich, and Cossalter wore the "A" as alternate captains.

In Brooks' scheme, however, he wanted every player, and particularly every senior, to take accountability for the team's operation. Harris was often a spokesman in dealing with Brooks because he had a more outspoken personality—and fewer reservations about speaking out—than the captains.

"Most of the other seniors were pretty quiet, so Herb and I talked quite a bit," Harris said. "Everybody will talk about Herb's passion, but what sticks out to me is that he wasn't afraid to make a mistake, to try something that might not work."

In later years, Brooks encapsulated that adventurous attitude with one of his "Brooksisms": Make errors of commission, not omission.

"He treated each player individually, and he never had the philosophy that you had to treat everyone the same," Harris said. "The goal scorers had to score, but everybody had a role. He trusted certain guys to kill penalties, and he'd tell them, 'We can't win without you guys killing penalties.' It would get to the point when we'd get a penalty and he'd just look at them and they'd go over the boards and kill it. I remember Herb putting his arm around a backup goaltender, who probably wasn't going to play, and telling him he was the most important guy on the team for the coming week. 'Our forwards are scoring too many goals, so I want you to shut them down. Don't give 'em any goals in practice,' he told him. It was just his way of making everybody feel important in their role."

John Harris, who was on a golf scholarship, went on to win the 1993 U.S. Amateur Championship golf tournament. While he always was a superb golfer, he was totally focused on hockey under Brooks. "I'm not sure how much he actually wanted me," laughed Harris. "He wanted my brother Robby, who was a year behind me. When I was a junior, in Herb's first year, I didn't play much. I had to look at the line chart to see if I was dressing every week. But he had confidence in me, and when I was a senior, he made sure I'd take some ownership in the team, as captain. I walked in to see him once and said, 'Herb, a couple guys are unsure why they're not dressing, and I'm concerned you might lose these guys if you don't talk to them.' He said, 'You talk to them, and tell 'em to keep their chins up.'

"But sometimes he'd get on me, when he felt the need to jack up the team. When we went out to Colorado College on the next-to-last weekend of the season, CC played in the Broadmoor, which was right next to the Broadmoor Country Club. When we went out there, it was really nice weather, but I made sure I stayed away from the golf course. I never even looked at it, on purpose. But sure enough, we weren't getting anywhere on the power play, so halfway through it, he calls time out. He looks at me and says, 'Every time we get near a golf course, you go belly up.'

"I was mad. We went back out and scored right away. Then we scored again."

The Gophers were storming, even though they followed a 2-1 victory with a 6-6 tie, in which CC goaltender Eddie Mio made fifty-three saves.

Going "belly up" was another favorite cliché of Herbie's. He had to grope for new ones the following week, however, when Minnesota went to Houghton to end the regular season. Minnesota had a shot—albeit a long shot—at the WCHA title, but the Huskies whipped the Gophers 5-2 and 4-1, to finish first at 20-6-2.

Brooks put the clichés away, but not his psychology degree. Only Herbie could find a way to stash those two lopsided losses at Tech into his positive motivation storehouse.

When the playoffs began, the Gophers beat Michigan in a two-game, total-goal series. Brooks started in again, and while he always stored away favorite one-liners for future use, he told his players he knew they were "willing to pay the price," and he declared them as part of a "team of destiny." He used those phrases in public, too, and in interviews. He had the maroon buttons with "Hockey Is for Tough Guys" emblazoned in gold, and he manipulated to get "The Fastest Game in Town" established as the team's trademark catchphrase.

How dynamic was that, compared with the limp, lame "Pride on Ice" that became the team's lackluster motto a decade later? Brooks trumpeted the Fastest Game in Town theme wherever and whenever he could, knowing that in a state consumed with the Minnesota State High School Hockey Tournament, the North Stars in the NHL, and the Fighting Saints in the WHA, he had to get his team the notice it deserved. Who could argue? The Gophers threw themselves into battle with something approaching reckless abandon and lived up to the legacy of Mike Antonovich, flying through the air to score goals, and Bill Butters, flying through the air to start a brawl on the visiting bench.

After sweeping Michigan, the Gophers faced Denver, with a trip to Boston Garden on the line.

"I remember at Christmastime, when we were barely over .500, Herb said to Pat Phippen that this is where we're going to go with this team," said John Harris. "It turned out to be true, but a lot of things went our way. We had seven seniors and great chemistry. We had great goaltending, nobody got hurt, and we got huge breaks. Realistically, if we'd had to go to Denver, we probably would have lost, but we got them at home and won.

"In our first game against Denver, I went in two-on-one with Robby. I pulled the goalie over to me, then passed it across, and Robby had an open net, but he missed it. I got on Robby as we came off the ice, and I was still giving it to him on the bench, when Herb came over and yelled at me for yelling at Robby. I told him, 'This isn't player to player, it's brother to brother,' but he said, 'Don't ever talk to him like that!'

"Herb never yelled at Robby in his four years there. Robby was tough as nails on the ice, but he needed encouragement, not criticism. Herbie knew that, and he knew he could come at me a little differently, because I'd try to shove it up his ass, just to show him I could do it. A lot of times I went hard, and I was only trying to show Herb I could do it."

The mighty Pioneers, under coach Murray Armstrong, battled Minnesota to a 3-3 deadlock in the first game of the total-goal series, which put enormous pressure on the second game. Minnesota won it 2-1.

"I remember that second game against Denver," said Pat Phippen. "It was on a Sunday afternoon, the sun was coming through the windows, and both John and Robby Harris scored goals. They had Pete LoPresti in the nets, and they were loaded. I don't know how we beat them."

John Mariucci swelled with pride in assessing that 2-1 victory over Denver. "That may have been the biggest game in the history of the Minnesota program," Maroosh said.

Maybe, but a day after defeating Denver to advance to the NCAA Final Four, Brooks immediately relegated it to history.

"The day after we beat Denver to go to the NCAA, Glen Sonmor would have given us the day off," said John Harris. "But not Herbie. We started practice by standing at center ice for ten minutes while Herbie ripped us. 'You played Denver in your building, you *should* have won,' he said. 'You haven't done anything yet.' He'd been encouraging us for how well we played since losing at Tech, and now that we were going to the big show, he was like . . . back to training camp."

Upon arrival in Boston, the bus taking the Gophers to their hotel stopped by Boston Garden so the players could unload their equipment. Boston Garden! The place had magic in its name—until, that is, the Gophers started carrying their stuff down the darkened hallways to get to the dressing room. As they approached a corner, they heard a sound ahead and were startled to see a security cop coming toward them with leashes barely restraining two Dobermans. Later, they spotted a couple of rats of a size that made the presence of Dobermans seem logical.

Because he'd never been there before, Brooks couldn't have known he had the team poised just right as the West's No. 2 seed for the semifinal match with Boston University, the East's No. 1 seed. The Garden was rocking late in the third period, with the game tied 4-4. With each shift, a BU goal and a Gopher loss seemed more and more inevitable. In the final minute, there was hope the Gophers could make it to overtime and possibly regroup.

But with forty-four seconds remaining, Dick Spannbauer was whistled for a penalty. "A BU guy grabbed my stick," Spannbauer recalled. "I pulled on it, and he went flying, and they called me for hooking."

Brooks knew that just surviving to overtime might not be enough. He sent out Polich and Buzz Schneider for the kill. Polich had been so uptight all game he hadn't even gotten a shot on net, but he led the team in scoring with nineteen goals and fifty-two points, and in high-pressure moments, no one questioned Herbie's hunches.

Doug Falls, a vastly underrated defenseman from Minneapolis Southwest who had walked on at Minnesota was also on the penalty kill. He swatted the puck free, but the Terriers had a point man right there and kept it in the Gopher zone.

"When the puck went D-to-D, I anticipated it and went for the guy," said Polich. "I poked it by the guy, and got around him, and we had a two-on-one."

It unfolded in a flash. Polich raced up the left side, crossing the BU blue line. "I took a quick look at Buzzy," Polich said, "and then I thought, 'What the hell, I'll shoot.'"

Everything Polich did was sudden, with piano-wire tightness. With a quick backswing, he blasted a slapshot from outside the left faceoff circle. The forty-five-foot missile snared the net, far side.

The raucous crowd in Boston Garden fell silent as the Gophers erupted.

The way things work out in hockey, Polich had another season to play with the

Gophers before he signed a pro contract with Montreal, which had drafted him. He was sent to the Montreal Canadiens' Halifax, Nova Scotia, farm club, where he wound up roommates with Ed Walsh, the BU goaltender. They discussed the pivotal goal many, many times.

Everyone recalls the stunning goal. Some players thought that it was in the final minute, while some thought it was with ten seconds left. "Nope," said Polich. "It was thirteen. It's been lucky number thirteen for me ever since."

Interesting, considering Polich wore number seven.

Even in the euphoric aftermath of the stunning semifinal victory over BU, Brooks maintained his perspective. When he first spotted Spannbauer afterward, Brooks called him out. "Mike saved my ass, because I could have been the goat," said Spannbauer. "Herbie said, 'What happened?' and I said, 'Their guy was holding my stick.' And Herbie said, 'Next time, drop the stick.'"

John Harris recognized how Herb's coaching resembled a chess match.

"He got the most out of all his players by teaching them all sorts of neat little things to do on the ice, and he knew what buttons to push," Harris said. "But he never pushed a button unless he had an outcome in mind.

"I think Herbie really had a lot of fun that year," Harris added. "He very much wanted us to control the puck, and he'd always say they can't score if we've got the puck down in their end. He was innovative and creative, but still made the game fun. People think of him as being so young with the 1980 Olympic team, but think how young he was when he started coaching at the U. Those first couple of years, I think he wanted to see how far he could push us."

If Herbie's "team of destiny" routine had only a mild initial impact on his cynical players, the motto took hold at that point. If the Gophers weren't destined to win it all, they could have—indeed, should have—lost to BU in the semifinals. Boston University had the home rink, a powerhouse team, all the momentum in the world, and a power play. But what's momentum when it runs up against destiny?

"He wanted to win, but he also wanted to get the respect of other coaches," Harris said. "Glen Sonmor wanted to win by one goal. Herb wanted to win every game by as much as possible, and to win the game mentally, and to control the game. He wanted other coaches to realize when they lost that the win was planned."

Of course, the game's intrinsic spontaneity can easily disrupt the best-laid plans. But Herbie never overlooked any details, such as an ill-timed penalty.

"I think about Herb all the time and the stuff he did," Harris said. "He's gotten a lot smarter in my mind with every year since I stopped playing for him."

CHAPTER 11

AND NOW, THE FINAL

This was uncharted territory for Herb Brooks. On Saturday afternoon, March 15, 1974, in only his second season as head coach of the University of Minnesota, he had maneuvered his Gophers into the NCAA championship game. Brooks was always the picture of poise while coaching, but hours beforehand he was pacing nervously in the glass-encased corridor on the second floor of the Sonesta Hotel, overlooking the Charles River in Boston. Herbie was preparing the key phrases of his final pregame speech of the season, trying to determine the perfect time to walk into the large meeting room a few strides down the hall, where his players were eating their normal pregame meal.

It was the most nervous I think I ever saw Brooks. By comparison, John MacInnes, the wily old veteran coach of Michigan Tech, was far more relaxed. His Huskies had won the WCHA season championship, with Minnesota second, and had advanced to the championship game with a 6-5 overtime victory against Harvard. The Gophers went to Houghton, Michigan, for the final weekend of the regular season and the Huskies decisively punctuated their championship season by sweeping the series to finish nine points ahead of Minnesota.

The decisive series underscored the basic difference between the two teams: the veteran Tech squad, almost entirely populated with older Canadian imports, many with solid pro hockey futures, against the comparatively youthful and wide-eyed gang of homebred Minnesotans and their equally youthful coach, who was finding his way swiftly and already showing an intriguing mindset. Part of Brooks' psych job was to tell his players shortly after being swept at Houghton that Tech wasn't as strong as he'd thought, and that he was more and more convinced that Tech could be beaten. With that message repeated often enough leading up to the Final Four, it was now time for Brooks to deliver the final address.

There in the hallway, Herbie knew this could be the most important pregame talk of his neophyte career. He stood up straight, immediately regained his composure, and walked swiftly and assuredly into the meeting room.

"All right, gentlemen," Brooks began, "this is going to be the last time you'll have to put up with my clichés."

The players erupted, then built up to an ovation. Brooks was totally defused. It didn't matter what he said. The players had stopped him cold as if it was a comedian's setup line. Even so, Herbie played it perfectly. He laughed and then turned around and walked back out of the room. No magic phrases were required. Herbie knew his players were loose and ready, and that he had gotten his message across to them: Never mind how Tech won the league title by nine points, never mind how experienced and talented the Huskies were—it's all down to one game now, and we can win it all.

A key to that Gopher team was senior goaltender Brad Shelstad. He had never attained the glory he deserved, even back in high school. Shelstad played at Minneapolis Southwest for Dave Peterson and he was outstanding. But everyone who scouted him was unconvinced. Shelstad never seemed to move, and most scouts thought it was because he had no agility, not because he played his angles so well. But Peterson, formerly an outstanding goaltender himself, had turned Shelstad into the perfect protégé.

In college, he was a popular member of the team who entertained his teammates with some bizarre bits of twisted logic, as well as with moments of great goaltending. Once, when Shelstad was an underclassman, Glen Sonmor decided to take the team to Grand Forks, North Dakota, by train to build team unity. The most memorable event of the trip was Shelstad engaging senior Wally Olds in an unbelievable debate. Shelstad's stand was that when a bug is smashed by the windshield of a fast-moving train, at the precise moment of impact, both moving objects are frozen in time, meaning the bug actually stops the train for an instant. Olds was an A student, but Shelstad didn't do any worse than a tie in the debate.

Debate skills aside, Shelstad didn't dazzle anyone with his fancy footwork. He played the angles, stood firm, and stopped pucks. He posted a 3.30 goals-against average in Brooks' first season, which made him the top statistical returning goaltender for the 1973–74 season. He played well that senior year, and now here he was, carrying with him the hopes of the Gophers and their fans that maybe he, too, could stop an onrushing train.

Shelstad stood firm as the Gophers took a 1-0 lead against Tech in the first period on a goal by John Sheridan, then went up 2-0 in the second period, when John Perpich scored. Tech scored in the middle of the period to cut it to 2-1.

But the turning point of the game might have come just before the third period. Bill Steele, one of Michigan Tech's standouts, displaying arrogance that would have drawn stern reprimand from coach MacInnes if he had known about it, skated past Shelstad and said, "Now you're gonna sieve 'em." It was an old trick that would have shattered a lesser goaltender, but all it did was push Shelstad's tenacity over the top, and the Gophers went up 4-1 in the third.

The only response Tech could muster came when Mike Zuke, another standout, scored with forty-eight seconds remaining. But it was too little, far too late. The Gophers poured onto the Boston Garden ice with a 4-2 victory.

Shelstad was named to the NCAA all-tournament team, along with Mike Polich and defenseman Les Auge. Shelstad also had been voted to the *Denver Post*'s annual All-WCHA team after posting the league's best goals-against average, but he was not named All-America. "I'd rather be on the NCAA champs than be an All-American goalie from a seventh-place team," Shelstad remarked.

"Tech was the cream of the crop," said Polich. "Mike Zuke, Steve Jensen, Mike Usitalo, Bob D'Alvise, George Lyle, Bob Lorimer—they were loaded. We had no business beating them. . . . But none of that mattered. There was Herbie telling us every chance he got, 'These guys are ripe. It's out there for us, if we want it.' We didn't have any confidence at all against them, but there we were. Herbie got us to believe we could do it."

After Minnesota capped a 22-12-6 overall season with its first-ever NCAA championship, coach Herb Brooks never went into the dressing room. In what became his trademark maneuver, Brooks pushed his players hard, some to the brink, but he also knew this was their moment—one in a lifetime for some—and he didn't want to intrude.

Spannbauer later coached youth and high school teams in the Twin Cities, and said he appreciated what Brooks brought to the game at Minnesota. "I never put anybody on a pedestal," he said, "but I've got to hand it to Herbie. His second year, he was the same Herbie as the first year. My compliments to him. He recruited a bunch of guys that could definitely make it a better team—no prima donnas. Michigan Tech was number one, and they had a great team, but we beat 'em in a helluva game."

Brooks, after winning the championship, went out to add to his list of recruits already committed for the next season. "Winning the national championship will really open doors, but I'm leery of those jumping on the bandwagon," he said. "We've got to make sure people are dedicated to the U, win or lose, and those who just want to jump on a winner aren't what we're looking for. They'd go belly up when it mattered.

"I have a moral obligation to this year's players to find kids who'll fit right in. Also, I'm obligated to those who are leaving—they're not only good players, but good people. We have to recruit to fill immediate holes. We're not bringing in a goalie, because even though we're losing Brad Shelstad, the people coming back should fill up that hole. Someone like John Harris, though, will be awfully tough to replace. He had a great year, one that nobody foresaw, and we need someone to fill his shoes. That's the type of people I want—winners who are tough to replace."

The departing players also grew to appreciate Brooks' coaching.

"Herbie absolutely had some ideas about the game," said Spannbauer. "He wanted the first guy to go in hard and the third to stay high all the time, but the high winger allowed the defense to pinch all the time. Dean Blais was a senior when I was a freshman, and he always stayed high so I could pinch. Herbie also believed in puck movement. Don't just stand there, move and get open.

"When I coached, I put a lot of things I learned from Herbie to use. I told the players 'I cannot tell you how to use your imagination,' and I told them that 'it doesn't matter if you're a center or wing, get the puck.' I coached at Mahtomedi and with the Stillwater girls. When we'd do something, they'd ask, 'What's going to happen when the puck is dropped?' I'd tell them I didn't know either, but we were going to try to do it right."

Spannbauer may also have suggested to the girls to stay out of the penalty box—unless they had a Mike Polich type who could score a late shorthanded goal to save the team. "Believe me, I'll never forget how Polich's goal rescued me," said Spannbauer. "We get together and play golf every year, and if I didn't remember it, Polie would remind me."

CHAPTER 12

EXPECTATIONS, AND ONE ASSUMPTION

One of Herb Brooks' coaching legacies is to never take an opponent lightly. He convinced his players to always respect opponents and never get cocky. It was common for him to defuse the high of a victory by lighting into his players after a big triumph, to bring them back down to earth and start focusing on the next game.

That was almost always the case with Herbie, too. It may not have been evident during his first two seasons as University of Minnesota coach; his first year was dedicated to lifting the program out of the lower reaches of the WCHA, and the second year was that magical spiral that ended with the U's first NCAA title in 1974. On the way to that title, the Gophers were always reaching and climbing, then reaching out again, for the next rung in the ladder of upward mobility. There were no expectations, up to and including the final game.

Even Herbie had to learn a lesson of what happens if you expect victory or get a little bit overconfident, but he was a quick learner—as in instantaneous. That abrupt change can be traced directly to the final game of the 1974–75 season. That team, the one between the school's first two title years, 1974 and 1976, might have been the best of all the mid-1970s Gopher powerhouses, if you ask the Gopher players of that era. Pat Phippen, for example, played on all three of those teams.

"That 'middle' team between the two NCAA champions was better than the Olympic team," said Pat Phippen. "I don't know how we managed to beat Denver, then Boston University, and then Michigan Tech for the 1974 title, but I also have no idea how we lost to Tech in the 1975 final."

In analyzing Brooks' amazing tenure at Minnesota, a cursory glance at the 1974–75 season might figure as a typical drop-off, in which a national championship team lost enough firepower to need a year to reload for its next title. That wasn't true in Minnesota's case. A solid returning crop from the 1974 national championship team suffered a couple of early departures, but most of the top players returned and, coupled with what might stand as the best recruiting year in Minnesota history, that group made the 1974–75 Gopher team an imposing force.

Dick Spannbauer had done his job as a tough guy for the Gophers during his freshman and sophomore years, but Spannbauer and John Sheridan both left school to capitalize on big contracts being tossed around by the outlaw World Hockey Association. Sheridan signed with the Indianapolis Racers, Spannbauer with the Cincinnati Stingers. Their departures weren't devastating, only because Brooks recruited such an outstanding group.

The recruiting prizes for that 1974–75 season included Minneapolis Roosevelt's Reed Larson on defense and St. Paul Harding's Paul Holmgren at wing. Another nice addition was Tom Younghans, who had come out of St. Agnes High School and played so well at St. Mary's College that Don Joseph, his coach at the Division III college in Winona, Minnesota, urged him to transfer to Division I Minnesota. Larson, Holmgren, and Younghans all went on to National Hockey League careers, as did 1974–75 returnees Mike Polich, Warren Miller, Russ Anderson, and Joe Micheletti. Robin Larson (no relation to Reed) was accompanied on the blue line by Jim Boo, Joe Baker and Tony Dorn, three large defensemen. Forwards Mark Lambert, Bruce Lind, Dan Bonk, and Ken Yackel Jr. bolstered the offense.

Micheletti, who had been the star center of a state championship Hibbing High School team, later became a solid NHL defenseman for the St. Louis Blues. He was also one of Brooks' first successes at moving a clever centerman with great puck skills and playmaking ability to defense.

The Gophers opened with a 4-3 loss at UMD, then went to Eveleth to play UMD again in the U.S. Hockey Hall of Fame game. Clarence Campbell, the learned and colorful commissioner of the National Hockey League, had been invited to be the guest speaker. Campbell was well attuned to the scarcity of U.S. players in pro hockey, and he blamed U.S. colleges for failing to develop U.S. players.

"American sports of all kinds are associated with institutions, and they offer a great deal to be commended for, such as discipline, good facilities, and coaching," said Campbell. "Regrettably, from what I've seen, a high percentage of college players were not Americans. They were young men recruited from Canada, which means U.S. college hockey has limited the development of American hockey."

Mr. Campbell went on to say, "The Midwest Junior Hockey League and the University of Minnesota winning the NCAA championship with an all-American team were the biggest accomplishments for U.S. hockey."

As usual, Mr. Campbell—as he was always called, out of total respect, until the day he died—was correct in his assessment. His 1974 tribute to the University of Minnesota's NCAA title was fitting, particularly since many of those same

Gopher players were about to go into the Eveleth Hippodrome for the Hall's commemorative game.

The Eveleth Hippodrome is a classic old brick building, the cradle of Iron Range legends such as John Mariucci and John Mayasich, among many others. Its boards are sunk in concrete, with absolutely no give. The "Hipp" is only a block down the hill from what was Mitch's Bar, where fans, some of them ex-players with Hall of Fame credentials, could hustle between periods for a quick one and a hasty analysis of the game. The clock at the Hippodrome wouldn't start when it was supposed to that night, so after a few seconds of scrutiny, the scorekeeper delivered a quick, hard blow with his fist and it worked fine. It was a fitting prelude to a rugged game that the Gophers won 3-2 in overtime.

Minnesota then went off to Michigan State, where coach Amo Bessone had an explosive team, led by a spectacular line of Steve Colp, Tom Ross, and Daryl Rice. It took a Tom Vannelli goal in overtime of a rugged affair to claim a 4-3 victory.

The following night, with the Gophers up 1-0 in the second, Rice tied it for the Spartans. A few minutes earlier, Polich had earned an early respite. Penalized for tripping, he exited the penalty box, played for twenty seconds, and went right back in for offsetting roughing penalties. Brooks, fuming, benched Polich for the rest of the night and the Spartans went on to win 4-3 and gain a weekend split.

After the game, I asked Brooks about Polich. "We'll rise and fall with Michael Polich, but he's got to be a leader and lead by example," Brooks said. "I'll bet anything we would've won that game with Michael in the lineup in the third period, but maybe we'll win a lot more in the future this way, if he learns to control his temper."

Polich went on to have a fantastic season, leading the Gophers in scoring. After one outstanding late-season game, Brooks called me aside. "Remember when I benched Polich for all those penalties at Michigan State at the start of the season?" he asked me. "But look how that straightened him out and maybe led to how he played tonight."

"Right, Herbie," I said, sarcastically. "He's so disciplined that he only took three more misconducts as the year went along and set a personal record for penalties!"

Herbie laughed and abandoned the "rehabilitation" of Polich as the key to his top player's success. Polich not only led the Gophers in scoring, but he led all his teammates except Paul Holmgren in penalty minutes. Brooks realized the fire was a necessary part of Polich's performance, although he constantly tried various methods to harness it.

"Herbie didn't do much joking around with the players," said Polich. "He didn't become close to anyone. Right from the get-go, he taught us more tactics than I ever knew existed. If you won, Herbie never let you get too high. I remember one series I had something like seven points, so we're all out there the next Monday, skating around at practice. We weren't going too hard and Herbie skates up next to me and says, 'Michael, you had a great weekend, but now it looks like you're going to take a day off. Start thinking about that series coming up.'

"Herbie was the whole deal. He had all the X's and O's, and he also had the psychology to get you to play your best, even if it meant getting you to play great just because you wanted to show him. We had a routine of how we'd practice every week, when we'd go hard and when we'd ease off. With me, Herbie would put his line combinations up on a board every day. I was playing with Buzzy Schneider and Warren Miller on my wings, and I'd come in for Monday practice, look up and, 'Hmmm, I don't see my name anywhere on any line.' The trainer would come up to me and say, 'Herbie wants to see you.' I'd think, 'Oh-oh.' Herbie would say, 'Michael, you're taking misconducts and selfish penalties, and it's not good for the team.' He wouldn't be raving, or kicking, or screaming, or kicking the garbage can in the dressing room. He'd already done that. For two days, he'd let me think about it, and he might even say I shouldn't bother to come to practice.

"Before Thursday, he'd get me back in, maybe on the fourth line. The game would start, and before long, he'd work me back to my normal place. He wouldn't say a thing, but I'd be back on my line. After the second period, he'd walk alongside me coming back on the ice, and he'd say, 'Come on, Michael. Show these guys how to win the game.'

"Sure enough, for days you'd be thinking about how much you hated him, then he pats you on the rear end and you'd go out and play better than you ever did before. He was different with different guys. He didn't bark at Buzzy Schneider because he knew that Buzzy would see other guys getting yelled at and go even faster. He was always on Les Auge, because he knew he partied a lot. It didn't bother Les, which bothered Herbie."

One area where Brooks felt uneasy was with his goaltending. Shelstad was steady and consistent, and pleasantly daffy on occasion, but he graduated and eventually became a wise and thoughtful coach at Wadena-Deer Creek High School in central Minnesota. Jeff Tscherne was the heir-apparent—or maybe Bill Moen—and while Brooks said that he had no plans to bring in another goalie because those returnees could fill the role, both of them gave Brooks pause. Moen was quiet and retiring, and while skillful, he once asked to not come back to play too soon after a minor injury. Brooks, who always preferred guys who showed courage by playing hurt, lost some confidence in Moen's ability to handle the front-line job. In fact, Moen later transferred home to UMD. Tscherne, meanwhile, was daffy enough to forever erase that description from Shelstad's resume.

As the NCAA champion Gophers started off a lukewarm 5-5 in 1974–75, Brooks felt the need to take immediate action. Earlier in the year, he had spoken to an interesting non-prospect goaltender at a summer league game. Larry Thayer, who had played very well at Edina High School a couple of years prior, had attended a few colleges elsewhere but was now enrolled at the U. Brooks found him and coaxed him into joining the team after the season had already begun.

"I went to Normandale Junior College for one quarter in 1970," Thayer said. "Then I quit, and worked at Braemar [Arena in Edina] for a year. Then I went to Bemidji State in the winter of '72 for a couple of quarters. I was the third-leading scorer at right wing on an intramural team at Bemidji. After that spring, I stayed out of school in the fall, then I came to the U that winter because my girlfriend went there. In August, I talked to Herb during summer league at Braemar. I was driving the Zamboni and not playing."

Brooks pulled Thayer off the Zamboni to fit him for goalie pads.

"We were going along," said Mike Polich, "and all of a sudden, one day in practice we had this new goalie. I thought, 'Who is this guy?' I'd never heard of him, but he was really good."

For the 1974–75 season, Moen went 5-4, and Tscherne was 7-3 with a 3.30 goals-against average. Thayer, who was quiet but had a quick and wry wit, wasn't as quiet as Moen and certainly wasn't as wacky as Tscherne. More than that, he stepped in and played superbly, easing Brooks' goaltending anxiety with a 19-3-1 record, a 2.60 goals-against average and a .904 save percentage. The 5-5 Gophers went on a 22-2 surge that included an impressive sweep at Denver two weeks before the end of the regular season. Next up were showdowns with Michigan State in the final regular-season home series and Michigan Tech in Houghton.

Under Amo Bessone, the Spartans were always colorful, and in 1974–75 the coach had one of his best teams in his long tenure at MSU. His presence in Minneapolis assured that John Mariucci would show up for the Blue Line Club, where the two good friends would put much of the "good" in those good old days of Gopher hockey. (As close as they were, Mariucci always referred to Amo as if his name was pronounced "Emil.")

Speaking at the Blue Line Club before the series, Bessone remarked, "I always regretted that I didn't learn to speak Italian. Of course, I never knew I'd meet John Mariucci."

Mariucci took over the podium: "The only talking I used to do was to yell at Emil to shut up."

Later, Maroosh said, "I went to Denver last weekend because I wanted to witness two wins at Denver. I never thought I'd live long enough to have empathy for Murray Armstrong. But Herbie has done a fantastic job. He listened well. Some others who didn't listen as well are working for a living. But Herbie has to watch himself so he can be around as long as Emil. Coaches won't be around for twenty-eight years anymore—the athletic directors are a lot smarter these days."

Brooks didn't try to mix it up with those two. He turned analytical: "You have to live a scared life. Any time you stop and think you've got it made, you're in trouble. We'd like to win the WCHA because a team can get hot and win the NCAA, but you've got to be consistent for five months to win the WCHA. We're not going to blow it."

While Michigan State was at Minnesota, second-place Michigan Tech was at Wisconsin. With the scored tied 2-2 and the Gophers outshooting the Spartans in the second period, the public address announcer kept updating the score from Madison, where the hated Badgers were beating Tech. Minnesota took a 3-2 lead into the third, when the Gophers filled the net in a seven-minute span and cruised to an 8-3 victory.

With twenty-five seconds left, word came that with Wisconsin's victory, Minnesota had clinched the WCHA title. The game ended with a standing ovation. Thayer only needed seventeen saves, but it took thirty the next night en route to a 4-2 victory. "He's the calmest goalie I've seen," Mariucci said of Thayer. "Maybe he doesn't understand what's going on."

Next it was off to Houghton. The Gophers had swept Tech earlier at Williams Arena, and with the WCHA championship already in hand, there was no need to apply the whip. These two games were meaningless to Minnesota, and while it was the first time the team was in such a position under Brooks, it also was the first time he decided it was a good weekend to let the players coast a bit and recharge for the playoffs. But the 7-0 loss in the first game snapped a nine-game winning streak with rude emphasis. The Gophers played more seriously the next day but lost again, though by a more respectable 5-4 margin.

Herbie and the Gophers learned the hard way that they couldn't be tunnel-visioned about their objectives, because what the other team does can matter, too. Tech used the sweep as a springboard into the playoffs. The Gophers cruised through the first round, beating UMD twice, but settling the total-goal series with a 6-0 first game.

I suggested that despite the score and a flurry of goals, the Gophers didn't seem sharp. Brooks snapped, "We were tight, but you can't squeeze blood out of these guys every night. Our passes were off, it was not an artistic success, and we beat 'em 6-0. If we had a bad game, what about Duluth?"

After winning the second game 4-2, Brooks thought out loud as he looked ahead to Michigan and a series that would decide the return trip to the Final Four. "Our wingers were cheating up too high and UMD's point men could cover them," Brooks said. "We were loose at Tech, so I went to the other extreme, with two backcheckers, to tighten everything up. We'll loosen it up a little 'til we get where we want to be."

The Gophers had to rally from 1-0 and 3-2 deficits to tie Michigan 3-3 in the first game. In the second game, Tom Vannelli scored a hat trick and Minnesota prevailed 5-2. Athletic director Paul Giel presented the magnificent MacNaughton Cup to Brooks after the first period as the capacity crowd chanted "Her-bie! . . . Her-bie! . . ." When Michigan scored with 3:47 remaining, the crowd chanted in unison, "Who cares? . . . Who cares? . . ."

The triumph sent the Gophers to the NCAA Final Four in St. Louis. Tech, however, also was there. Perhaps still irked that Tech had trounced his Gophers on the final weekend of the regular season, Brooks continually put the Huskies down. He praised Michigan State, and repeatedly said the Michigan Wolverines were the toughest team the Gophers had seen: "In all due respect to the Techs and all, Michigan is the toughest team in the WCHA—the best team we've faced."

Tech had advanced to St. Louis by defeating Wisconsin. "Off the record," Brooks said, "Badger Bob couldn't get the Montreal Canadiens out of the International League."

In the semifinals, Minnesota beat Harvard 6-4. The hard way. A rebound goal to start the second period left the Gophers facing a 4-1 deficit.

In the third, Warren Miller took the game over, scoring a pure hat trick to turn a 4-2 deficit into a 5-4 Minnesota lead. An insurance goal made the final 6-4.

"That's the fastest team we've seen all year," said Brooks, afterward. "I told the players, 'I'm not trying to con you, but I've got a gut feeling we can get it done. I don't want any one-on-fives, but move the puck.'" Awakened at last, the Gophers kept the pressure on, though Harvard answered. When Thayer blocked a shot with twenty-five seconds remaining, a Harvard player slashed at Thayer's glove after the whistle. Holmgren moved in and a shoving match ensued. When Holmgren suggested possible punitive action, his adversary proved that even a Harvard education doesn't guarantee intelligence under fire. "I asked him if he'd like his nose rearranged," Holmgren said afterward, "and he said, 'Yeah.'"

Without dropping a glove, Holmgren threw a short left jab, right where a rearrangeable nose was positioned in those pre-facemask days. The Harvard player went down, and out—cold. It took several minutes to revive him, and while he was being tended to, Holmgren was assessed a rare five-minute roughing penalty. When they finally got the Harvard player to his feet and he had someone under each arm to help him through the nearby end door, he took a couple of steps off the ice and collapsed again. NCAA officials and Harvard fans went pale, while a couple dozen pro hockey scouts jumped out of their seats. This was a knockout—not a TKO, a real knockout—delivered with a short left-hand punch, glove and all.

In the second semifinal, Michigan Tech dismantled Boston University 6-3. "There is no comparison mentally to us this year and last," said John MacInnes. "Minnesota is faster than we are, but I think it'll be a physical final. We're not as physical as Minnesota. This year, the best team I saw was Minnesota, and the second best was Michigan."

It was an interesting contrast. MacInnes was full of praise for Minnesota, while Brooks had taken pains to declare that Michigan was the best team he and his Gophers had seen. Whether he really believed that, or it was an attempt to convince the Huskies they were not worthy of Minnesota's concern, it was intriguing. Either way, the coach and his players knew they'd have to play their best, every shift, to beat the Huskies.

Holmgren's punch was a major topic. Harvard coach Bill Cleary said Holmgren shouldn't be allowed to play in the final, pursuant to college hockey's fighting disqualification penalty. "The guy shouldn't be playing tomorrow, he's got no business being proud of that," said Cleary. But the officials hadn't DQ'd Holmgren and Brooks wasn't about to apologize, not with a rugged Tech team waiting.

"We're not going to run and hide, they're not going to run and hide," Brooks said. "After a while, you get tired of turning the other cheek, so we went out and got some guys so we could stand up and be counted."

About being ready for the final, Herbie added, "Your mind will do things that the body says cannot be done."

Vintage Herbie. One of his favorite motivational lines.

Brooks was sure of himself and of his team—a luxury he never had before. His first team had worked mightily to reach .500. His second traced a constant climb to claim the NCAA championship. And now, the WCHA title *and* a repeat trip to the NCAA final. Brooks also knew those two final regular-season setbacks would be added incentive to his team, which deserved far more respect than being tagged an underdog.

If Herbie was overconfident, it was the only time he allowed himself such a flighty luxury. If that also meant that the respect for opponents that he always demanded of himself and his players slipped just a bit, so be it. As it turned out, it was proof that, as sharp as Herbie was, there was always room for him to step back and absorb one more lesson.

Michigan Tech and the Gophers battled through a physical but even first period in the title game. The Gophers were on their heels, down 1-0, but they struggled to fight off Tech's momentum, and seemed to succeed. But then Tech took a 2-0 lead. The horn ending the first period was like the bell at the end of a boxing round, allowing a fighter to take a break after taking a couple of solid blows.

In the second period, Tech took a 3-0 lead. The Gophers came back hard. Midway through the second, Tom Vannelli's line came out on the power play, with Reed Larson and Mike Polich on the points. But Tech survived and before the second period ended, made it 4-0. Where was the magic? Where was the inspiration for a desperate rally? In the third, a Gopher power play fizzled and when Holmgren went off for a penalty, Tech scored.

It was 6-0. There would be no comeback. The colorful Tech fans sang "We love Canada" to taunt the all-Minnesota Gophers. Midway through the final period, Tom Younghans scored, but that was it. The Huskies had whipped the Gophers 6-1, sweet revenge for Tech and MacInnes. It also elevated Tech to an overall record of 32-10—one painful notch above the 31-10-1 Gophers.

Afterward, Brooks showed for the first time a changed demeanor. Instead of being feisty, angry, or defensive, he was analytical—philosophical, even. He had already absorbed the lesson. This was the first and only time he would be guilty of assuming his team would win.

"There are so many good, positive things to reflect on," Brooks said. "A good effort is the only way to achieve good peace of mind, and these people have done their thing. Because of a good attitude and extreme desire, sometimes they'd find themselves out of position. You have to contain it enough to stay in the context of positioning, and we didn't have good rhythm as a unit."

That loss was perhaps the biggest upset that Brooks, as a coach, would suffer at any level of hockey. As usual, he learned more from it than his players. Brooks now had convincing evidence of how difficult it was for a great team to avoid being overconfident and, indeed, blowing it.

Coming between the 1974 and 1976 titles, the 1975 final loss would also leave Minnesota one victory shy of three consecutive NCAA championships, a feat which only Michigan has accomplished, in NCAA hockey's formative years, 1951–53. Today, with more and more top underclassmen signing with the pros, three straight NCAA titles for any school seems unlikely, if not impossible.

The decisiveness of that 6-1 final loss left little room for equivocation. There wasn't a bad call, a misplay, or any single element that could have changed the outcome. It was a total thrashing. I knew Brooks had to be emotionally drained, so I was curious how long it would take him to unwind.

"When do you start over?" I asked him in the dressing room after the game.

Without hesitation, Brooks answered, "Monday."

CHAPTER 13

REBUILT FOR A TITLE RUN

In football, baseball, and basketball, the professional game sets the standard for the college level, but in North American hockey, where tradition long kept the professionals on a thin course of action, a few college teams—and even some Minnesota high school teams—were considerably more advanced in terms of coaching creativity and a willingness to try new and different concepts. One case in point was Herb Brooks. But even while he formulated styles and tactical ideas, Brooks was careful to uphold basic structural responsibilities. Somehow, he remained both an idealist and a pragmatist.

Brooks also continued to refine his motivational techniques, with gambits that ranged from brilliant to trite. The mind games were calculated to make an impact, even if by shock value.

A classic example was intended to ensure that his players would not let the overall success of the 1974–75 team—which some later called the best in Gopher history—erase the memory of that 6-1 loss to Michigan Tech in the NCAA title game.

The MacNaughton Cup the Gophers won that year as WCHA regular-season champs is a large and beautiful trophy, simple in style and ornate in detail, that was donated to the WCHA by Michigan Tech. After the Gophers lost the championship game to Tech, Brooks brought the team home and, in front of them all, carried the trophy across the Williams Arena dressing room, placed it in a urinal, and flushed it. The stunt didn't damage the cup, thankfully, but it made an indelible impression on Brooks' wide-eyed players.

A few things were missing for the 1975–76 season that followed. Mike Polich, the team's leading scorer and lone first-team All-WCHA player, had finished his four-year term, as had second-team defenseman Les Auge, Buzz Schneider, Rob Harris, and Tom Dahlheim. Larry Thayer, who led all goaltenders by a wide margin with a 2.50 goals-against average (no others were under 3.10), had used his only year of eligibility after all his transfers, and goalie Bill Moen had transferred to UMD. A large loss was Paul Holmgren, who, after a tremendous freshman season, took his intimidating form to pro hockey by signing with Glen Sonmor and the Minnesota Fighting Saints of the WHA. It wouldn't be long until he "graduated" to the Philadelphia Flyers, where he had an outstanding NHL career and years later coached the Flyers, before moving into the organization's front office.

If rebuilding was the order of the day, Brooks made some solid moves. His returnees included Jeff Tscherne in goal, as well as Tom Mohr from junior varsity. Returning defensemen were Reed Larson, Joe Micheletti, Russ Anderson, Joe Baker, Robin Larson, Brad Morrow, and Tony Dorn, with an eighth, Jim Boo, moving up from JV. Forward returnees were captain Pat Phippen, Warren Miller, Tom Vannelli, Mark Lambert, and Ken Yackel Jr., plus Bruce Lind, Dan Bonk, and Tim Rainey from JV.

Brooks brought in freshmen Steve Janaszak in goal, Bill Baker on defense, and a talented forward quartet of Don Madson, Phil Verchota, Tom Gorence, and Bob Fish. True, it was asking a lot from those freshmen to step in and play vital roles in a WCHA that was rich in depth and experience, but consider that Janaszak, Baker, and Verchota all went with Brooks to the 1980 Olympic team, and Gorence jumped to the NHL after two seasons. Madson, from Grand Rapids, Minnesota, was a clever and creative center who had a huge impact on the team. Fish, from Warroad, was studying medicine, and while he was a solid contributor, Brooks enjoyed sending him off to focus on his academics, using the old John Mariucci suggestion that he "take two weeks off and then retire."

Brooks recycled other one-liners—some of which survived to make it into the 1980 Olympic team's book of Brooksisms—the most notable being another one borrowed from Mariucci. John always had just the right twang of cynicism, and one of his masterpieces was delivered after somebody who had been playing poorly had an especially bad game, or shift. Maroosh would say: "Every day you're playing worse than the day before, and today you're playing like tomorrow."

Herbie loved that one—maybe John even used it on him a time or two. But in typical Herbie fashion, he couldn't resist embellishing it a little, saying, "Every day you're playing worse than the day before, and today you're playing like next week."

Across the border that season, Brooks' old rival Bob Johnson took a leave of absence from the University of Wisconsin to coach the 1976 U.S. Olympic hockey team. If Brooks was envious, he didn't let on, although he was perturbed that some of his players weren't selected for the team as the July 15 deadline for taking underclassmen came and went. It was part of the old Gopher–Badger feud and the battle of wills between two of the best coaches in the land.

The Olympic team scheduled games against WCHA teams throughout the 1975–76 season. On October 25, 1975, Brooks took Minnesota to Eveleth to play the U.S.

team in the Hall of Fame game. Badger Bob had chosen several of his own Wisconsin players for the U.S. team, including defenseman Bob Lundeen and forward Steve Alley, while turning the Badgers over to assistant Bill Rothwell for the season.

Among the other familiar rival faces on the U.S. team were goaltender Jim Warden and forward Steve Jensen from Michigan Tech. The Gophers—and Brooks—needed little more incentive than to face Badger Bob and some Tech guys. Minnesota cruised to a 5-2 victory.

Brooks couldn't have been prouder. "We dominated the thing from the opening whistle," he said, as if he was surprised himself. Then he tossed in a couple of zingers. "They've got twenty games under their belts, and this is our first, and we were the better team at the end. Yeah, there are some good young kids around the state of Minnesota."

The victory got the Gophers off to a good start, but they were headed for an extremely unusual season. After the Hall of Fame game, they went home to sweep St. Louis University. Brooks wasn't pleased with the first game: "We have seven new forwards, and we were too idealistic with the puck; it was like we were trying to fit a square plug in a round hole."

The second game was much better. "We used three different forechecking systems," Brooks said, then adding a little quip, "I looked through the rule book and nothing says we've got to use the same forecheck."

Next up was a big series with UMD at Williams Arena. The first game was great for the rivalry, with heavy hitting and alternating goals. Brooks' Gophers won the opener 5-4 in overtime and took the second game 4-2 to complete another sweep.

Captain Phippen and alternate captains Miller and Vannelli were not the most vocal guys in the Gopher dressing room, although Miller was the most likely of the three to remain silent. He grew up playing tough in South St. Paul, and later went on to play with the New York Rangers and Hartford Whalers. His teammates called him "Grumpy," because he always seemed to have a sullen, serious demeanor, but he was sharp and had a great wit for those close to him. Brooks never yelled at Miller and never used him as an example because he never had to. Miller played with an intensity that made him a prototype Brooks player.

Miller led by example, but proved to be a master of getting his point across without speaking. Tscherne, always a bit wacky, was also the polar opposite of the three captains. One day in the Williams Arena dressing room, as Tscherne was raving to anyone, everyone, and no one all at the same time, Miller calmly reached for a bucket of pucks, dumped them all out on the floor, and without saying a word picked up his stick and started shooting them at Tscherne until he got the message and shut up.

The best Michigan State team that coach Amo Bessone ever assembled became a huge rival for the Gophers, particularly that season. In late November, the Gophers earned a split in East Lansing against the Spartans and their explosive top line. Nobody in either program knew then of the epic battle that was yet to come, with an NCAA trip on the line.

After the Saturday night game, Herbie and I went out for a short time, then returned to our Kellogg Center hotel. Michigan State has a well-known hotel/restaurant management curriculum, and student-operated Kellogg Center was located right on campus. It was very efficient, but there was also an amazing number of exuberant coeds running around. Wisely, Herb always stayed on a different floor than his players, while my room was at the far end of the hallway on the players' floor. We were having a good discussion, so Herb was going to stop by my room. When we got to that floor, he detected some activity that he hadn't anticipated and decided to do a little room check. I left my door open, so I could hear what could have been a scene from *Animal House*.

Herbie knocked on a door down the hall, and assorted players, assuming it was a teammate, readily opened the door to find Herbie, who barged in and ordered some eager coeds to get their clothes and get out of there. Amid great squealing, shrieking, and hastily dressing young women running down the hallway, Herbie delivered a gruff message about being out of line. Then he came back to my room. "You should have seen the body on *that* one!" he'd say, laughing heartily. When he regained his composure, he reassumed the gruff demeanor and set out for two or three more rooms. He kept tagging up at my room, in his new self-appointed role as hall monitor, giving me progress reports between deep breaths. It was sort of like changing on the fly, so to speak.

The Gophers came home for their third straight split, this time against the Rothwell-led Badgers. Even after dropping the first game 4-2, Brooks couldn't pass up the chance to zing Bob Johnson. "They deserved the game," said Brooks, adding with a wink, "That was the best-coached Wisconsin team I've ever seen."

When rumors began to circulate that Johnson might want to add another couple college players to his Olympic roster, Brooks commented, "I don't think anybody should bail him out at the eleventh hour for bad selections. The WCHA had a July 15 deadline."

It wasn't until thirty years later—after the untimely deaths of Johnson and Brooks—that Vannelli learned he and Reed Larson were being sought by the Olympic team. Brooks never told them about Johnson's inquiry, or about his declining on their behalf. He knew Vannelli and Larson were pivotal to any Gopher success, but probably didn't believe even those two could help the U.S. cause.

The Gophers continued to be unbeatable some nights, while giving up too many goals on others. But there were some amazing high points and further indicators of the Brooks magic that was as yet uncontrolled. When the legendary Murray Armstrong brought Denver to Williams Arena in mid-January, the Pioneers rocked Tscherne and went up 4-0. Halfway through the second period, Brooks took the reins off the Gophers. "We started forechecking two men heavy halfway through the second period," said Brooks. "We got twenty-five shots in the second period. I can't remember ever getting more than that."

Forechecking is one thing, connecting on chances is something else. If the Pioneers were stunned, the Gophers were on fire. Vannelli scored twice early in the third as the Gophers went on to a 6-4 victory.

Two losses at the University of Michigan, however, followed. The Gophers were playing rough but ragged, giving up too many goals to get rolling on any major winning streaks. After that sweep at Ann Arbor, Brooks concocted another motivational ploy. Because Ann Arbor was a college town, and because there was a tight curfew on Thursday and Friday nights, the players always looked forward to a little freedom after Saturday night games. This time, Brooks ordered them all to meet in the captain's hotel room by midnight. There was considerable moaning and groaning, because that didn't leave enough time to shower, dress, and grab something to eat.

As midnight approached, the players started showing up at the captain's room. Inside, they were surprised to see that Brooks had stashed a dozen large pizzas, along with beverages. About one-third of the team didn't get there by midnight. As I walked down the hallway, I saw Herb standing in the corridor and stopped to talk, noting the players partying inside the room. The elevator would ding, and the players inside the room would go silent as Brooks put his hands on his hips and glared down the hallway. An arriving player would round the corner, see Brooks, and hear him bark, "You're late. Get your ass in here." They'd scurry along the wall as hastily as they could to reach the safe haven of the room. As they turned into the room, the players inside would erupt in laughter at how scared the new arrival was, and he would melt into a puddle of relief. That process was repeated three or four times, until all were inside. Then Brooks left.

Tom Younghans came out of the room and asked where Herbie had gone. I told him he'd simply left. "The guy is such a hard-ass," Younghans said. "You'd think he could at least come in and join us for a piece of pizza."

I explained that Herbie did his thing to get everybody back on the same page, but at the same time, he greatly valued player unity and felt he'd be intruding. "You think so?" Younghans asked. "I suppose he's really a hell of a guy, if you could ever get close enough to know him."

That short conversation always stayed with me. It showed how Brooks played with the minds of his players, how readily manipulated they were, and how he had his players fooled. It also was sad, though, because Herbie was a special human being, and even seniors, such as Younghans, didn't feel they knew Brooks at all.

However, Miller, a four-year Gopher regular, had Brooks figured out without talking to him. "No, Herbie would never let any player get close enough to really know him," said Miller. "But he did some unique things as coach. The one thing he did that stands out to me as maybe his best skill was to put the right personalities together. He got some good players, but no matter how much talent you've got, you're going nowhere unless you have the right personalities playing together—guys who really intermingle. He had a knack for putting the right guys together, and he'd get rid of guys who didn't fit in."

There is no gauge of how much Brooks' ploys worked for team unity, but the Gophers rebounded from the two losses at Ann Arbor to sweep at UMD.

The strange season took another turn in February, when Michigan State came to Williams Arena and swept the Gophers. Brooks was steamed. "To blow a two-goal lead at home in the third period," he said after the second game, "I don't know how the hell they lost six in a row, but we can't turn the game on and off."

At Wisconsin, the Gophers took a 1-0 lead, but the Badgers rallied to go up 2-1. The Gophers trailed 4-2 with six minutes left, but tied the game before Miller, who spent the day with a 102-degree fever, completed his hat trick in overtime. If that comeback was another hint of magic, reality struck the next night when the Badgers blitzed Minnesota 9-3. The regular season ended with the Gophers definitely not hitting on all cylinders, closing on a 4-6 slide that dropped them to third place.

In the playoffs, however, the Gophers started pulling in the same direction at home against Colorado College. Brooks went with Tom Mohr in goal, but the Gophers blew two leads and fell behind 4-3 early in the third. Then, the Gophers suddenly seemed to click, netting four unanswered goals for a 7-4 victory. "You've got to be either on the puck or on your check," said Brooks, "and we got caught between them. You can't have those extremes in performance in a game."

The two-game total-goal system made those last three goals imposing heading into the rematch, and the Gophers stormed to a 5-1 victory.

A scheduling oddity meant that the CC playoff series was on a Wednesday and Thursday, March 10 and 11. After winning the rare, midweek set, the third-place Gophers had to hurry to East Lansing to face Michigan State. A spot in the NCAA Final Four in Denver two weeks later would go to the winner. "Four games in five days, then two weeks off," muttered Brooks. Regardless, that Michigan State series remains a vivid memory for all who were in Munn Arena that weekend.

On the first night, the Gophers rallied from a 2-0 deficit in the third to earn a 2-2 tie, leaving the series up to the second game.

In case four games in five days wasn't grueling enough, the second game was an afternoon affair on Sunday, which would theoretically give the Gophers just enough time to catch a return flight home late Sunday from East Lansing.

Brooks switched from Mohr to Tscherne in goal, and came up with a good motivational line, "60 minutes to Denver," but he underestimated by almost half.

For two periods, the Spartans and Gophers matched offensive thrusts. Minnesota led 3-1 after a period. The intensity and the hard hitting led to a succession of power plays, and Minnesota went up 4-1 to open the second period. Daryl Rice countered on the MSU power play in the second, but Vannelli's backhander a minute later gave Minnesota a 6-2 lead. It was far from over, though, as the Spartans cut the lead to 6-4.

Michigan State came out flushed with momentum in the third and further trimmed Minnesota's lead to 6-5. The Spartans failed to click on another power play, but two seconds after the man-advantage expired, Rice completed his hat trick with the tying goal.

The Spartans figured that they might be able to jump the Gophers with a strong effort at the start of the overtime, and they swarmed into the Minnesota zone, firing twelve of the first thirteen shots in overtime. But the goofy Tscherne weathered it all and might have even inspired the Spartans to begin talking to themselves, because it was still 6-6 after the first overtime session.

They resurfaced the ice again and started a second twenty-minute overtime. This time the Gophers had an edge in shots, but were stymied. With both sides so exhausted they could hardly clear the puck from their end, it remained 6-6.

At 5:06 of the third overtime, referee Medo Martinello called a penalty on Michigan State for a flagrant trip. To his relief, he was able to penalize Younghans just thirteen seconds later. In the four-on-four situation, Bill Baker fed Don Madson on an all–Grand Rapids rush. Madson deked around one defender, then another, then a third, and closed on the goal. He fired a shot, got his own rebound, and wound up for another shot, but instead fed it to his left. Pat Phippen drilled it home from twenty-five feet for a 7-6 Gopher victory. The four games in five days endured by the Gophers actually included five games' worth of minutes. The crowd was drained too, as it rose to give both teams an ovation. The game went so long the Gophers missed their late flight home.

"I was going to be sedate after the game if we won, but everybody was flying over the boards, and I was with 'em," Brooks said. "A lot of things are expected of this team, and if we got beat, it wouldn't be because we died."

On the other side, Amo Bessone, wearing a green Spartan cap and with his ever-present cigar, said, "It was one of the best games I've ever seen. . . . I hope to hell he wins it all."

After going 4-6 to end the regular season, the Gophers' gutty performance—four straight playoff games in five days—began a winning streak to destiny. They had time to do a little laundry and rest before heading for Denver and the Final Four.

The 26-14-2 Gophers would take with them the baggage of an inconsistent season, as they joined WCHA champ Michigan Tech, Boston University, and Brown University in the Mile High City.

CHAPTER 14

THIRD FINAL, SECOND TITLE

Since the Gophers beat Tech in the 1974 final, then lost to Tech in the 1975 final, it seemed there was at least a chance the two teams would meet in the title game for the third straight season. But both 1976 semifinals seemed headed the other direction.

Tech might have taken Ivy League Brown lightly, and with four minutes remaining, the Huskies were looking at a 6-4 deficit. Tech tied it, but it wasn't until 2:13 of a second overtime that they eked out a 7-6 triumph.

To the Gophers, a two-overtime game might have seemed like child's play after their epic at Michigan State.

The crowd of 5,204 for Minnesota's semifinal against Boston University was genuinely into it. The BU band played the familiar five-note bit of the song "It Had to Be You" over and over again throughout the game, with the Terrier fans all chiming in—as in "It had to BU."

The Gopher crowd had established its own reputation for berating referees with a bit of light humor, particularly in games officiated by either of the familiar WCHA refs, Wilkie or Duffy. Whenever Don "Red" Wilkie made an unpopular call, a solid segment of Minnesota students would chant "A horse's tail is long and silky/Lift it up and you'll see Wilkie." Similarly, "A horse's tail is long and fluffy/Lift it up and you'll see Duffy." They hadn't yet found a way to heckle Medo Martinello, however. At Denver, Gopher backers settled for a large banner that read, "Spay the Terriers."

While the BU and Gopher fans engaged in some lighthearted rivalry in the stands, things were decidedly more intense on the ice.

It didn't take long for the rivalry between the teams' East-West cultures to surface. Big Russ Anderson was penalized at 0:33, and BU star forward Terry Meagher was called for slashing at 1:08. The Gophers were on the home Denver bench, directly under my station in the press box, with the penalty box adjacent. As Meagher headed toward the penalty box, there was an exchange between Meagher and players at the end of the Gopher bench, right where Gopher trainer Gary Smith was positioned. "He spit on me," Smith said later. Much later.

"When he spit on me," Smith added, "I said, 'Words are something, but spitting shows no class.' He reached around and hit me with his stick, so I grabbed his stick and took it away."

In an instant, there was chaos. The Gophers only had four skaters on the ice until Russ Anderson left the penalty box to even things up. The officials prevented a bench-clearing brawl and restored order. Then Mike Fidler came over from the BU side and told Smith not to touch any BU sticks. Again, it flared up.

The officials could have disqualified four or five from each side. Instead they assessed Meagher two minutes for the original slash, plus a game misconduct. Russ Anderson was given a game misconduct for leaving the penalty box, and Tim Rainey was sent to serve a Minnesota bench minor, presumably for the fiery trainer.

The incident set an ugly tone for the game. BU coach Parker later said, "Meagher got speared, so he slashed back. He was spat on first, so he spat back. We lost our top scoring forward, and they lost some thug of a defenseman."

Anderson, hardly a thug, went on to play fifteen years in the NHL. Then Parker was questioned about Minnesota's very effective penalty kill, which riled him even more. "I didn't think it was a good game," he said. "We had to play their style, to grab, hold, and interfere out front. The Minnesota penalty kill? It must have to be good."

Brooks chose to be a master of understatement. "There was a lot of emotion at the start," he said.

The first period was wide open but scoreless, and Tom Mohr was superb. The Gophers came out and outshot BU 16-7 in the second, but trailed 2-1.

In the third period, the Gophers erased the 2-1 deficit with goals from Tom Vannelli, Mark Lambert, and Tom Younghans to claim a 4-2 victory.

"Roses are red, violets are blue, we got four, they got two," said Lambert, a crafty centerman, who had exchanged enough on-ice banter with the Terriers to pretty much force himself to have a big game. "We had too much pride going for us. We heard so much about how good they were. I told their Canucks that if they were any good, they'd have gone right into pro hockey."

Parker was livid and convinced that the first-period scrap was contrived by Minnesota. Brooks was reserved, but he clearly loved the fact that the Gophers won the battle *and* the game. It put the Gophers back into their third straight final against Michigan Tech. Two years earlier, Minnesota had shocked Michigan Tech to win the title; one year earlier, the Gophers might have been a bit smug and were hammered by the Huskies. Now what? The only certainty was that Herb Brooks was not going to psych himself out, or allow his team to be cocky, this time around.

The puck dropped and the Huskies and Gophers sparred for position. A year earlier, Tech had taken a 2-0 lead in the first period. This time, though, the Huskies made it 3-0 in the first. The Gophers got one back at 17:05, but the first period ended 3-1. Brooks pulled Jeff Tscherne and sent in Tom Mohr, though more to shake up the troops than to pin any blame on Tscherne.

Whatever magic phrases Brooks uttered to his players during the first intermission break snapped the Gophers into a renewed sharpness. Don Madson darted in front of the Tech net and was grabbed for a holding penalty. With Reed Larson and Joe Micheletti manning the points, and Tom Vannelli feeding them, the power play clicked. Micheletti gunned a forty-five-footer into the net to cut the deficit to 3-2.

Midway through the period, and on the four-on-four, Vannelli stickhandled in on the right side and passed to Baker, who made a dazzling move and scored to tie the game 3-3.

Two minutes later, Reed Larson made a forceful rush in deep on the left side and left a perfect drop pass for Tom Gorence, who whistled a low shot past goalie Bruce Horsch's far side. Minnesota had turned a 3-0 deficit into a 4-3 lead, but Nels Goddard scored from the left point to tie it with thirty-six seconds left in the second period.

The third period was much more even, and it stayed 4-4 until 8:37, when Pat Phippen scored from the circle.

Mohr came up with key saves, clinging to that 5-4 edge. With thirty-nine seconds left, John MacInnes pulled Horsch for a sixth attacker, and nine seconds later, Warren Miller fired the puck into the empty net, clinching the game 6-4.

Brooks was both happy and relieved: "We were really on the ropes. I was relying on that inner fiber of this hockey club. We made a few adjustments to help us penetrate a little. This team might have had to overcome more than the '74 team, but one ingredient was the same: mental toughness and pride."

That's two ingredients, Herbie.

The afterglow of the 1976 championship will never fade, but the impact of the semifinal brawl between Minnesota and Boston University has lived on, too. Gary Smith, the Minnesota trainer, went on to a highly successful career as a physical trainer and was Herbie's trusted guy with the 1980 Olympic team.

"I've been able to watch a videotape of the fight," Smith said, years later. "You can see Terry Meagher spit on me, and then we have words, then he swings his stick at Mark Lambert, who was standing behind me. When he swung, he hit me, and I grabbed his stick. The penalty box was all one, with no barricade, so Meagher and Russ Anderson fought in the penalty box, and Meagher actually ended up on top of Russ.

"When the players were picking up all the dropped sticks, I was trying to help, and Fidler told me to keep my hands off the sticks," Smith added. "I said something back, and then Youngie [Tom Younghans] suckered him, and the whole thing started up again.

"Later, the NCAA investigated it. Herbie and I had to fly to Shawnee Mission, Kansas, and Paul Giel warned us to not complain no matter what they decided, because he knew a problem with basketball was coming. That was when [Gopher basketball coach] Bill Musselman had broken some rules. So when we got there, Jackie Parker was just leaving. When we testified, we got copies of the transcript of other testimony. I was pretty disappointed that Billy Cleary, the Harvard coach, said, 'The trainer was the perpetrator of the fight.'"

Cleary, always a stickler for gentlemanly protocol, was probably still steamed from the year before, when Paul Holmgren knocked out one of his players in the semifinals. It also was further evidence that the eastern teams assumed midwestern teams were crude and unrefined, while midwestern teams considered the eastern teams to be pretty boys. The NCAA, always trying to avoid any image of hooliganism, sided with the East.

"When they were through investigating, I was barred from the next year's NCAA tournament, and so was Mark Lambert," Smith said. "We didn't make it anyway, so it didn't matter."

BU players Jack O'Callahan and Mike Eruzione would be selected by Brooks for the 1980 U.S. Olympic team. But in 1976, Brooks saw the BU players, like everyone else "out East," as smug and spoiled, and he lumped public institutions such as Boston University with private ones, such as Boston College and Harvard.

"Herbie had everybody on our team fired up, saying, 'We're gonna beat these preppies and Canadians,'" said Smith. "Those [BU] guys were always cool to me during the Olympic year. And even since then, whenever there was any kind of reunion, Herbie always took care of guys like [goalie coach] Warren Strelow and me. Once Herbie died, Eruzione pretty much ran things, so I'm not included."

Cleary and Parker are both well-respected for their coaching, and became good friends of mine, and I later got to know Fidler, O'Callahan, and Eruzione very well. All are good guys, but presumably they'd never be in the market to buy an old maroon and gold "Hockey Is for Tough Guys" button.

CHAPTER 15

MAJOR TURNOVER

I t's easy to appreciate the Gopher championship seasons of 1974 and 1976, as well as the later one in 1979. All showed the stepping stones that Herb Brooks was both laying and following while establishing his coaching style.

He was installing more progressive systems, but he also was reluctant to try them in game conditions. He was progressive in his practices, but conservative in how he directed his players to play. Button-down jerseys and wingtip skates, if he could have found them.

That second NCAA championship may not have sunk in completely before Herb Brooks had to come to grips with the biggest turnover of core players in his tenure. Pat Phippen, Warren Miller, Tom Younghans, Bryan Fredrickson, Brad Morrow, and Tom Mohr—key fixtures in so many pressure situations—all had finished their eligibility. One reason why some of Brooks' friends privately thought he was better suited for the college game than the pros was the constantly revolving rosters.

Maybe he was lucky that he coached at Minnesota when high school hockey was booming, but then again, it was more likely booming partly because of the success Brooks was having with his all-Minnesota Gophers. The corresponding spike in high school hockey talent throughout the state was evident in the recruits Brooks brought in for the 1976–77 season: Rob McClanahan, Steve Christoff, Eric Strobel, Tim Harrer, Don Micheletti, Peter Hayek, and John Meredith.

When you add those names—and what they accomplished during their college years and beyond—with returnees that started with premier defensemen Reed Larson, Russ Anderson, Joe Micheletti, Bill Baker, Robin Larson, and Joe Baker, and also included forwards Tom Vannelli, Phil Verchota, Tom Gorence, Bruce Lind, Dan Bonk, Ken Yackel, Bob Fish, and Tim Rainey, it seemed there should have been no drop-off in Gopher fortunes. However, these freshmen all came in from their high school senior years.

"The league was really good back then," said Vannelli. "We had a JV with the Gophers, and most of the freshmen played on it. It was really hard for a kid coming right out of high school to be expected to do very well against the older players on other teams. The quality of Canadian players was much higher back then, because Major Junior players were still eligible."

Those older Canadian prospects from Junior A sometimes had two years and 150 games on the Gopher freshmen.

Although the teams the Gophers had outrun in 1975–76 were still bristling with returning talent, the 1976–77 Minnesota team could have been a contender if not for a string of unscheduled departures and injuries that seemed to plague them.

To start, Russ Anderson signed to turn pro. Still, Joe Micheletti, Reed Larson, and Bill Baker led the returning defensemen. All three would be at the top of any list of all-time best Gopher defensemen.

There also were some inconsistencies in goaltending. Brooks entrusted the 1976–77 team to the trio of senior Jeff Tscherne, little-used sophomore Steve Janaszak, and freshman Paul Joswiak. Warren Strelow—Herbie's close friend since childhood on St. Paul's East Side, and later his next-door neighbor in Mahtomedi, where Strelow coached the high school team—was brought in as goaltending coach and convinced Brooks to recruit Joswiak, his Mahtomedi netminder. Once Joswiak was at Minnesota, Strelow pushed Brooks to try a rotation of three netminders, which only fed Herbie's built-in anxiety about goaltenders and prevented what might have been a natural rotation of senior Tscherne and heir-apparent Janaszak from getting into any rhythm. Tscherne, who had led the WCHA the year before, was virtually pushed aside as a senior and faltered to a 6-7 record and a 5.10 goals-against average. Tscherne could not play up to his previous level, and Janaszak's rise to full potential was delayed.

A Hall of Fame victory over UMD in Eveleth, a nonconference split with St. Louis University, and a victory and tie against UMD opened the season. Then came a trip to the University of Michigan, where the Gophers dropped both games, 8-6 and 6-3.

Back home for Michigan State the next weekend, the Gophers were struggling without Joe Micheletti and Tom Vannelli, who had been struck in the face the previous weekend in Ann Arbor. In the third period of the Friday game, Bill Baker suffered a shoulder injury and would be out a month. The next night, Reed Larson went out with an injury. Then, before Thanksgiving, Tom Gorence suffered a sprained ankle.

In early December, as if to celebrate the restoration of their lineup, the Gophers beat Harvard 4-3 in overtime.

"We weren't particularly fond of overtime with four games in seven days, but we needed the win bad," said Brooks. "I said, 'If you want to play overtime, we will.' So we did. Enthusiasm and spirit were big factors for us. The fans help us play that way, but maybe the fact that we play that way is why there are 7,800 fans here."

Notre Dame brought a powerhouse team to the Twin Cities for the week between Christmas and New Year's, and played the Gophers at the St. Paul Civic Center in a memorable "neutral site" series. Charles "Lefty" Smith, Notre Dame's coach and a St. Paul native, wanted the games there for recruiting purposes, and the Fighting Irish won 6-5 in front of 9,704 fans. The next night, with 9,117 on hand, the Gophers came from behind in the third to win 3-2.

The Soviet Spartak team beat Minnesota 9-4 in an exhibition matchup on the day after New Year's. Getting an up-close look at the Soviet skaters, Brooks said, "We will bury you, and then they proceeded to do it. We were awed in the first period, and tried some things, against their defensive center breakout, and some other things."

A 7-1 drubbing at Madison followed in a chippy, penalty-filled game. Afterward, Gopher players showed off spear marks and grumbled about crosschecks. The next night, the youthful Gophers battled crosscheck for crosscheck, high-stick for high-stick, and beat the Badgers 5-4. "We were hurt, sick, undermanned, and we out-gutted them on their own ice," said Brooks, with fierce pride.

It was something less than proper sportsmanship, however, when Brooks decided to show his distaste for the Badgers, their coach, their arena, and their fans by refusing to shake hands with Bob Johnson after the game. "Why be phony about it?" he shrugged.

As January roared to its conclusion, the Gophers returned to East Lansing for the first time since the epic triple-overtime playoff victory the previous March. Brooks started Steve Janaszak in both games at East Lansing. In the first game, Minnesota managed four unanswered goals to win 4-3. In game two, Michigan State again jumped ahead 2-0. The Gophers forced overtime and Janaszak was simply spectacular. With thirty-two seconds showing, Tom Gorence drilled a shot home.

At 9-10-2 and finally healthy, the Gophers had twelve games left—enough for a surge. Right there next to Minnesota in the standings was Michigan Tech, and the two would resolve the rivalry of three straight NCAA title games in a fateful series at Houghton—their only two games of the season.

It was pretty ugly. The first period featured a lot of nasty stuff, and if there ever was a time when the Gophers were convinced they were being had by the officials, that game was it. Tech took an early lead, and after a half-dozen spirited charges went uncalled, Joe Micheletti was whistled for an inconsequential trip. After the whistle, a brawl broke loose in the corner. Referees Dennis Parrish and Don Wilkie tossed seven Gophers and five Tech skaters. While trying to break up the worst part of the fight, Wilkie took a stray punch and was knocked out.

Tech made it 4-0 before the second period ended. The Gophers cut into Tech's lead, but lost 6-3.

The rematch was stranger yet. With Tech up 4-2 and just three seconds remaining in the first period, Reed Larson skated the puck back along the boards to kill the clock. Warren Young, Tech's center, raced in after him, with no possible chance to make something of it. As he got within stick's reach of Larson, he swatted him lightly on the breezers, then slashed him as the horn sounded. Then he added one more slash. Larson whirled around and gave Young one slash across the shin pads. Referee John Ricci, a Houghton local called in because of Wilkie's injury the day before, skated directly to the scorer's table, obviously to call Larson for slashing.

Larson sped across the ice to confront Ricci. Tom Vannelli could tell Larson was angry and beat Larson to Ricci, where he tried to discuss it with the ref while positioning his own body strategically between the two. Like umpires in baseball, some hockey referees are able to ignore abuse so as not to be shown up by an angry player. Ricci's favorite trick was to gaze through or past a raging player, making it look like he was acknowledging the discussion. As Ricci gazed, Vannelli got no response, and Larson was incredulous that the ref would stare past them, as if in a trance.

With his hockey gloves still on, Larson reached over Vannelli's shoulder and lightly tapped Ricci on his chest, near his shoulder. Innocent as it was, Ricci appeared startled and stumbled back a step. He immediately turned to the scorer's table and gave Larson a game misconduct.

It would be the last moment in Reed Larson's spectacular college hockey career—January 30, 1977. Minnesota battled to the end, losing 7-5.

"We had three defensemen and eight forwards at the end," said Brooks. "The things we try to sell at Minnesota are the intangibles, and we were trying as hard at the end as at the beginning. The intangibles were never more apparent. If I was on the other team, I'd look at the Gophers and wonder what made them go."

The Gophers climbed aboard a coach bus after the game for the long ten-hour ride home through the night. "Before we left to come back, Herbie called me aside," Reed Larson remembered. "The guys were already on the bus, and Herb said he wanted to tell me that he thought they were going to suspend me."

Herbie's hunch was right on. The first report filed with the league from Michigan Tech referred to Larson's fingertip tap on Ricci as a punch. A faculty representative who was at the game filed a report that said he remembered seeing Larson "punch" the referee, then he added, "I just can't remember whether he had his stick in the hand he punched him with."

Somehow, the tap—albeit forbidden—had become a punch and possibly a stick assault. The word behind the scenes was that the league was considering suspending Larson for the rest of the season or even for a full calendar year. Brooks knew that before the season Larson had nearly signed with the Red Wings.

"If Detroit would've given me a decent offer, I wouldn't have been back for my junior year," Larson recalled. "They didn't, so we decided that if [Red Wings head coach] Alex Delvecchio was expecting me to sign for less, I'd go back to school for another year. We rode the bus Saturday night and got home Sunday morning. It turns out, Detroit was coming to town to play the North Stars, and later Sunday, I went down to [agent] Ron Simon's office, and Delvecchio was there. I signed, and I had to hurry home.

"I went to Met Center dressed like a campus hippie, and all I brought was my skates. They gave me all the equipment and uniform so I could play that night, and I figured I'd go home after the game and get packed. But when the game ended, they said no way, they were catching a charter right after the game and I had to dress like I was. Dennis Hextall was great, and he let me wear a couple of his leisure suits."

The loss of Reed Larson's toughness, character, and explosive shot from the point was too much for the Gophers. The next weekend they lost to, and then tied, Notre Dame. The following weekend in Duluth, the Gophers showed a glimmer of life against the Bulldogs, prompted by Bill Moen, their former goaltender who had transferred to UMD, and who was quoted saying one reason he left Minnesota was "I don't like the coach." The Gophers won 6-4 and 7-3.

But Minnesota limped to the finish, losing twice to Michigan and Colorado College at Williams Arena before winning twice at North Dakota. Against CC, Joswiak gave up a 3-0 first-period lead and was relieved by Tscherne. "I changed goalies more for the psychology than anything," Brooks said. "I didn't scream after the first, I screamed after the second when we almost gave 'em a breakaway goal. Then we gave up two stupid goals after we got ahead, off faceoff plays."

In the final regular-season weekend at North Dakota, Brooks decided to try a few new things to get ready for playoffs. He started Steve Janaszak in goal after pretty much leaving him out of the mix for over a month in favor of Mahtomedi freshman Joswiak, who had played well in several games, but really hadn't given Brooks the stopper he wanted. Minnesota beat the Sioux 7-4 and 8-6.

The ragged season was followed by a trip to South Bend to start the playoffs against Notre Dame, which was second to Wisconsin in the WCHA. The Irish had gone 2-1-1 against Minnesota, and coach Lefty Smith, the lovable former South St. Paul coach, could finally put away the Herbie demons that seemed to plague his team.

The Gophers were nearly run out of the building in the first game. They had no punch, no sustained offense, and Janaszak made fifty-eight stops in absorbing a 5-1 loss.

"It just wasn't our night," said Brooks. "We had no rhythm, no momentum, we didn't forecheck, and Notre Dame took it to us really good."

About the only good thing Brooks could pull from that game was the heroic play of Janaszak. Also, despite being whistled for nine penalties and a misconduct—compared to three minors for Notre Dame—the Gophers didn't allow a power-play goal.

There was absolutely no indication that, trailing by four goals halfway through a total-goal series, the Gophers had anything awaiting them except summer vacation.

It was Herbie time. He switched to Joswiak in goal. Since Rob Larson had a leg injury, he moved center Mark Lambert back to defense, and put Jimmy O'Neill at center between Rob McClanahan and Tom Gorence. Then he did his best to fire up the team for the task at hand.

Right away, Vannelli was called for tripping, and Irish star Brian Walsh connected for a power-play goal. The best way to start the second game of a total-goal series when trailing by four goals is *not* to give up the first goal. Notre Dame now led the series 6-1.

Vannelli came out of the box and promptly set up Phil Verchota to lift Minnesota into a 1-1 tie. Then O'Neill tallied for a 2-1 Minnesota lead. The atmosphere in South Bend was electrified. The Irish were playing well, but the Gophers were really jumping. O'Neill won a left-corner faceoff and fed Peter Hayek, who scored off the pass. Suddenly, Minnesota led the game 3-1 and had cut the total deficit to two. Notre Dame got one back, which should have snuffed the Gophers' hopes, but Vannelli ended the first period by taking a Joe Micheletti pass, darting around All-America blueliner Jack Brownschidle, and cutting in to jam a shot past Irish netminder John Peterson. In one period, the Gophers had stormed to a 4-2 lead, getting the total-goal deficit back down to a workable two goals.

Brooks saw more than just hope. "I told 'em, 'You're on the verge of the greatest comeback in the history of Minnesota hockey,'" Brooks later said.

As the second period began, it was as if the Gophers couldn't contain themselves. In the opening minute, O'Neill won another faceoff, and McClanahan rifled one past Peterson, boosting the lead to 5-2 and cutting the overall deficit to one.

The Irish fans may have been seized by the incredible game unfolding before them, but the Irish themselves were not—they came at the Gophers hard. Jim Boo blocked one shot, then Brian Walsh came in on the right side but shot off the left pipe. Another rush and Joswiak got another break when the puck hit a post and the net was dislodged.

In the final minute of the second period, Steve Christoff, the freshman from Richfield, charged in, but was hauled down. A delayed penalty was signaled, but Christoff didn't quit. He jammed a shot while down and Peterson blocked it, but Don Micheletti tried the rebound and Christoff steered it through at 19:20.

The Gophers were on fire, forechecking with abandon and overrunning the Irish. This was the wide-open, all-out attack Brooks had pushed his players to practice, a creative, high-tempo style in which the forwards rushed with the exuberance of neighborhood kids on an outdoor rink. This was his "sophisticated pond hockey," where everyone was free to try what they thought might work—or even invent something they had never tried before. There were no designs, no restraints. The Fighting Irish were left to play "normal" hockey—a traditional North American game—while the Gophers were freewheeling. With almost effortless ease, belied by their great intensity, the Gophers had stormed to a 7-2 lead in the second period and reversed a five-goal-total deficit to a one-goal advantage.

Lefty Smith changed goaltenders for the third period, but it didn't matter. Nothing seemed to get in the way of the Gopher flow. The Irish attacked, and Boo dived on a loose puck in the crease. A penalty shot was called. Don Fairholm beat Joswiak, but his shot rang off the left pipe and glanced away. Notre Dame attacked again and appeared to score a goal, but it was waved off for being kicked in.

At the other end, Jimmy O'Neill, emerging from obscurity, got free in front, and when his shot didn't go, Gorence slid the rebound across the goal mouth and McClanahan found an open net. The game score was 8-2, and the total-goal count was 9-7 for Minnesota.

The minutes ticked away, and the Gophers kept flying. Christoff completed the hat trick and the Gophers finished with six consecutive goals for a 9-2 rout and a 10-7 total-goal turnaround.

In the final seconds, the crowd, recovered from its shock, applauded—the Fighting Irish for a great season, and the Minnesota team for putting together the kind of game that presaged the miracle-work Brooks would be recognized for at Lake Placid.

"What can I say?" said Brooks afterward. "We beat one of the best hockey teams in the country tonight—in fact, one of the top two or three for sure."

With that, Herbie gave me a wink. He personally didn't believe Notre Dame was that good, but maybe that line had ignited his Gophers to overachieve.

Poor Lefty Smith. His great team, its great record, and its considerable potential were left shattered. Typically, though, Lefty demonstrated class. "Give Minnesota a pat on the back," he said, "from coach Brooks, right on down the line, including the goaltender."

How could any team follow that act? The next weekend, the Gophers headed for Madison to take on the mighty league-champion Badgers. Minnesota athletic director Paul Giel and Wisconsin athletic director Elroy Hirsch—a couple of ex-football stars—and league commissioner Burt Smith were all there to provide the proper decorum, although such pomp and ceremony was a stretch for Badger fans who held up banners such as "Kill Vannelli."

It was another two-game, total-goal series, and Brooks decided to go with Joswiak in goal against Julian Baretta, the league's top netminder. The Badgers went up 3-1 and made it 4-1 to start the second, but got one back at the midpoint of the middle period. But a strong Gopher attack in the third wasn't enough and Wisconsin pulled away, 9-5. Joswiak made fifty saves in an outstanding performance.

The score somehow seemed more daunting than the 5-1 deficit of the week before. Writing for the *Minneapolis Tribune*, I never passed up the chance for a smartass lead. "The Gophers have Wisconsin right where they want them," I wrote, spelling out the coincidental four-goal deficit of the previous weekend.

Herbie turned philosophical. Instead of fire and brimstone, his pregame comments included, "Rejoice in your suffering, because suffering will produce endurance, and endurance produces character, and character produces hope."

The Gophers started with something more resembling grim determination, forcing play, hitting, and putting all sorts of pressure on Badger netminder Mike Dibble. Tim Harrer scored the first goal, but Mike Eaves tied it 1-1, then Wisconsin blitzed Joswiak in the second and it was 5-1.

"I've been around the game all my life," said Bob Johnson. "Minnesota threw all they had at us in the first period, and the key goal was our first of the game, because it let us go into the dressing room even."

There was no stopping the Badgers, who pulled away to an 8-3 triumph.

Was it magic—a mini-miracle, even—when the Gophers overturned a four-goal deficit to beat Notre Dame in the total-goal series? Yes, indeed. Much like those doses of magic when they roared back from large deficits in other years to win shockers, or the sustained stretches that resulted in NCAA titles in 1974 and 1976. Was the magic missing at Madison, one week after the comeback against Notre Dame? Yes, pretty much. But all that really showed was that Brooks was like an eccentric sorcerer. He could summon up magic now and then, but even he couldn't completely control it.

CHAPTER 16

TYING IT ALL BACK TOGETHER AGAIN

The memorable comeback at Notre Dame in the 1977 playoff series may have been the highlight of the season, but even it couldn't obscure the disappointment of falling from 1976 NCAA champions to seventh-place in the WCHA. To make matters worse, the rival Badgers, who ended the Gopher playoff bid in the spring of 1977, went on to win the NCAA title.

I think Brooks enjoyed having his Gophers considered the WCHA's "Team of the '70s," and indeed, every player who played at least three years at Minnesota during Brooks' seven years there won at least one NCAA title, some two. Maybe Wisconsin's 1977 national title inspired Brooks to intensify his pursuit of a third title.

The Gophers moved on to the 1977–78 season without the graduated Tom Vannelli, who had been team scoring runner-up as a sophomore, and team scoring leader as both a junior and senior, not to mention the heart and soul of the 1976 NCAA championship team. Another key departure was Joe Micheletti, who had undergone a Brooks makeover from star centerman to standout defenseman, and was now ready for a lengthy tour of duty as an NHL defenseman. Tom Gorence, who signed a pro contract, and Bruce Lind also were gone, which meant the top four scorers had to be replaced. The early loss of Reed Larson the year before didn't help prospects for the new season, either.

The incoming freshman group was interesting. It was led by another player who would become a heart-and-soul Gopher: Steve Ulseth, a stocky sparkplug who actually walked on. He is always overlooked when alleged experts list their all-time Gophers, but his four years—in what might be considered the most competitive era in WCHA and college hockey history—stand tall.

Beginning with his freshman year, Ulseth's contributions helped rebuild Minnesota for a return to the pinnacle of college hockey. Other recruits for 1977–78 included Dave Terwilliger and Brad Doshan, both solid-working players; defensemen Bob Bergloff, who was solid and consistent; and rugged Mike Greeder, a force on the blue line for two seasons before going to the pros.

As a group, that freshman crop was far from the high-profile studs who arrived the previous year—Steve Christoff, Rob McClanahan, Eric Strobel, Don Micheletti, Tim Harrer, Bill Baker, Steve Janaszak, Peter Hayek, John Meredith—and who were arguably the top recruiting class in Minnesota history. Those players had aged a year and had inherited the responsibility of moving the Gophers up in the WCHA, which they did, rising from seventh to fourth in one of the strangest seasons in WCHA history. The top four teams were solidly above .500, while the remaining six were firmly entrenched below .500.

The Gophers seemed to take some heart from that fabulous playoff surge at Notre Dame the previous spring, starting the 1977–78 season at 5-1 in league play. But four straight losses at Michigan and Wisconsin set the scene for a season of ups and downs. Minnesota went 4-0 against UMD, and 3-1 against North Dakota and Michigan State, which was offset by going 1-3 against Wisconsin, and 0-2 against Michigan Tech.

As sophomores, the 1976–77 freshman class broke out in full bloom. Christoff, whose herky-jerky move made his quick shot more deceptive, led the team with sixty-six points in thirty-eight games.

The Gophers gave up too many goals, however, to make a run at the title. Janaszak had three shutouts and a 14-10-2 overall record, with a 3.85 goals-against and .890 save percentage. Backup Paul Joswiak was 8-4, with 3.91 and .885 stats.

The season's undulations might best be symbolized by the Gophers' February frustration against Colorado College. The Gophers swept a series from the Tigers in December, but later went to Colorado Springs and dropped both games. Even though the first round of playoffs looked good when the Gophers faced CC at Williams Arena, the teams tied 3-3 in the first game of the total-goal set, and the Tigers won 5-4 to end Minnesota's season. Losing at home, to a CC team that was below .500, did not sit well with Brooks, and it seemed as though the talented Gophers were still missing a couple of ingredients that could put them over the top.

Those missing links were still in high school in 1977–78, playing in the state high school tournament in March. Edina East defeated Grand Rapids for the state title in a 5-4 double-overtime thriller, which Grand Rapids and star goaltender Jim Jetland had dominated. In the first round, Roseau beat Rochester John Marshall 4-2, while Edina East nipped Minneapolis Roosevelt 3-2, despite a Roosevelt defenseman named Mike Ramsey setting up both goals. Hill-Murray, which had lost 1-0 to Grand Rapids in the first round, came back to crush coach Doug

Woog's South St. Paul team 5-0 as Steve Griffith notched two goals and one assist. Jeff Teal, a big centerman, had a goal and two assists in the first two games for John Marshall.

In the semifinals, Edina East beat Roseau 5-3, but Roseau's big line got two goals, one each by Neal Broten and Butsy Erickson, while Aaron Broten settled for two assists. Hill-Murray beat John Marshall 4-3 in overtime in the consolation final, as Griffith notched three assists, the third on the overtime winner against John Marshall goaltender Paul Butters. Then Roseau beat Mounds View 5-3 for third place in a classic show. Juniors Aaron Broten and Butsy Erickson scored twice each in the first period, and senior Neal Broten assisted on all four goals, breaking the record of Eveleth legend John Matchefts for most assists in a period. "I never heard of him," shrugged Neal afterward.

Herb Brooks was raking in prospects at the big show. He lured Neal Broten, Mike Ramsey, Jeff Teal, and Jim Jetland to Minnesota for the 1978–79 season, and pretty much secured Aaron Broten, Butsy Erickson, Steve Griffith, and Paul Butters for the following year.

One thing that never varied at Minnesota was the workload Brooks forced his players through. He believed that talent could win a lot of games, but he also believed that there was no excuse for being out-conditioned. His Gophers would never have to worry about that. It was heavy at times—heavier when the Gophers weren't contending for the title.

Some Gopher teammates from back then still contact each other frequently and discuss those college days. Bill Baker and Phil Verchota, for example, established impressive post-hockey careers in Minnesota, Verchota running a bank in Bemidji, and Baker a prominent dentist in Brainerd. Whenever one of them recalls an interesting tidbit from their playing days, they reach for the phone. One thing they always agree on is their disappointment that Brooks, even years afterward, could never really open up and let his old players know how much he appreciated their sacrifices back when they played for him.

Both still marvel at the totally dedicated practices Brooks ran, at his tactical wizardry, which at the time seemed only simple. Verchota and Baker also shared the uneasiness of being unsure where they stood in Brooks' constant manipulations.

"At Grand Rapids, I'd heard all about his coaching and his practices," said Baker. "I remember Bob Johnson and Rocket Rothwell recruiting me for Wisconsin and telling me how I'd be on the power play and everything. I really wanted to go to Minnesota, and every day I'd come home from school looking for an envelope with a big 'M' on it. When he came to sign me to a letter of intent, I think that was the last time I talked to him for four years.

"His practices were tough, and very new, with a lot of weaving and regrouping, and always with a defensive plan. He was ingenious. A student of the game."

Verchota, a big, smooth, and tough winger, played his high school hockey at Duluth East. Like Baker, he was sharp in the classroom, and while Brooks got on him frequently in the dressing room, Verchota often rolled his eyes and shook his head at some of the elementary psych jobs Brooks would pull.

"Nobody ever got comfortable on the team," said Verchota. "All the time he got on me, he knew that I'd try to fix whatever it was he thought was wrong. He knew our individual personalities and dealt with everybody differently. But every practice, you were trying to make the team for that next weekend. I never talked to anybody who thought they weren't liable to be cut."

In practice, Brooks used different colored jerseys to delineate who was playing together. One forward line would wear blue, one gold, one red, one black, and the defensemen might all wear green.

"You never knew which jersey you might be wearing," said Verchota. "I got so I'd come into the dressing room and the first thing I'd do would be to see what color jersey was hanging at my stall, and then see who else was wearing the same color.

"He had definite ideas of how disciplined we had to be on defense, and he had all kinds of little tips for how we should do it. Offensively, he had a system of keys that we all had to look for and react to. I never remember hearing him say anything about staying in a lane; we were free to think and react and we worked on it."

Baker and Verchota were teammates on the team that won the 1976 NCAA title, then on the team that plunged to seventh. They were also on the team that rose to fourth, and among the seniors who led the Gophers back to the top in the 1978–79 season. Finally, they both played for Brooks on the 1980 U.S. Olympic team. Baker went on to play several seasons of pro hockey with different NHL teams. Verchota, who always seemed the prototype NHL winger, never played pro in North America.

"Herbie allowed me to overachieve a little," said Verchota, "but I don't know that I was good enough for pro hockey. I just don't know if I had the physical staying power for the long pro season."

Verchota was right—and wrong. Brooks *did* allow him to overachieve, though "allowed" might not be the right word—"forced" to overachieve is more accurate. But Verchota was wrong about the pros. Not only was he good enough, but he also was strong enough and had the staying power. No pro team ever practiced as hard as

Brooks' Gopher teams did. For Verchota, college would have been good training for the NHL, where they play more games, but practice a lot less.

"Our practices were tougher than the games," Verchota acknowledged. "You got out of shape during the weekends."

Ah, but those weekends became more exciting, and more satisfying, during the 1978–79 season.

CHAPTER 17

BEST TEAM IN COLLEGE HOCKEY'S BEST YEAR

There are commonly held beliefs, usually true, that athletes keep getting better, stronger, faster, and more skilled with each advancing era. As the 1970s drew to a close, the National Hockey League was filled up and focusing on Canadian junior for new prospects. But the league also recognized that there was some exceptional talent in college hockey, especially the WCHA. At that point, the NHL wasn't moving in and swiping underclassmen from the colleges, so the improving level of U.S. players and Canadian players, whose families saw U.S. college scholarships as a more beneficial pathway to the future, made for tremendous improvements in college hockey.

Gopher fans in the twenty-first century are far more abundant and treated to expanded television coverage and the shiny palace of Mariucci Arena. They have been rewarded with some championships, but the college hockey rosters in the first decade of the twenty-first century can't compare to the skill level of the late 1970s.

For 1978–79, Minnesota's roster included the nucleus of Steve Christoff, Rob McClanahan, Eric Strobel, Don Micheletti, Tim Harrer, Phil Verchota, Steve Janaszak, and Steve Ulseth, and Brooks added two vital links among a very good recruiting crop. One was Neal Broten, the quick and creative center from Roseau with such electrifying improvisational sense that Brooks considered him the most-skilled player he ever coached with the Gophers.

How young was Broten? And how small was Roseau? One day, John Perpich, the former Gopher blueliner taking a turn as a grad assistant coach, asked Neal what he had done on one of his first freshman weekends.

"We got pizza," replied Broten.

"Oh, did you get anchovies?" asked Perpich.

"No," Broten answered. "We got Domino's."

The other key recruit was Mike Ramsey, the brilliant defenseman from Minneapolis Roosevelt who seemed instinctively skilled in defending, vacating the defensive zone, and providing intelligent thrusts to the offensive attack, even as a freshman. Broten and Ramsey were catalysts as freshmen, and together with fellow recruits Kevin Hartzell and Jeff Teal up front, Jim Jetland in goal, and Brian Zins on defense, they seemed to promise the Gophers a return to the pinnacle of college hockey.

Brooks, in fact, defied his own style and decided there was no use in creating his preferred underdog mentality. Instead he flat declared that this team would win the national championship. I was amazed—not that it couldn't happen, but that Brooks would quite eagerly climb out on such a limb.

Brooks also carried a bit of an extra mental load that year; he had been asked to coach the U.S. team both at the 1979 World Championships and in the 1980 Winter Olympics. Not that such cherished assignments pushed him to cockiness. If anyone congratulated him on the assignments, he was quick to point out, "Yeah, but I was their third choice." He knew that Billy Cleary of Harvard and John MacInnes of Michigan Tech had been offered the Olympic job, and both turned it down. They were outstanding coaches, so it seems inconceivable in retrospect that either would refuse the offer. But the historic achievements of 1980 tend to obscure what, at the time, seemed to be the futility of spending a year preparing a group of nonprofessional U.S. college players to face the super Soviet, Czechoslovakian, Swedish, and Finnish teams without any realistic hope of success.

It is incomprehensible to imagine what U.S. hockey would be like today had either Cleary or MacInnes coached the 1980 U.S. team, but it is virtually certain that there would have been no Miracle on Ice without the incredibly well-timed emergence of Herb Brooks as choreographer. That, however, was still a long way off, though it contributed to the backdrop as the most talented Gopher team ever embarked on the 1978–79 season to take on the strongest field ever in the WCHA, if not the nation.

A 5-3 Hall of Fame victory over North Dakota got things started, but the first hint of the special season to come emerged when Wisconsin brought a strong outfit to Williams Arena in the last weekend of October. The Badgers jumped ahead 2-0 early the first night, but the Gophers tied it and kept rolling to an 8-4 victory.

The next night, the Gophers jumped ahead after one, but the Badgers shut down the Gophers thereafter and won 9-5. "We didn't want to get in a shootout," said Badger Bob Johnson afterward. "We tried that last night, and it didn't work."

Bob's son Mark improved the already strong impression he had made on Brooks, centering two lines, because of an injured teammate, and recording three assists. Brooks, through nearly clenched teeth, said only, "It was a good hockey series."

The Gophers went to Michigan State and swept the Spartans with a pair of one-goal decisions. The second night, referees Dino Paniccia and Denny Parrish didn't win any points with Brooks for their penalty choices. "If you ask me about refs," Brooks said, "my only comment is 'no comment.'"

Minnesota-Duluth used to drive Brooks crazy. He always talked about how he didn't like Duluth and how he'd rather be in Des Moines. I was never sure whether he truly meant it, if it was a way to summon up a little extra edge against UMD, or if he was just zinging me a little because it was my hometown. He did the same with wife Patti's hometown of Yankton, South Dakota, which he always called "Shinbone," joking about it to the point where Patti not only tolerated it, but actually called it that herself.

In 1978–79, UMD had an outstanding team under coach Gus Hendrickson, an Eveleth native who had previously coached Grand Rapids to high school superiority. Bill Baker had played with Dan Lempe at Grand Rapids before coming to Minnesota. Lempe went to UMD, as did Mark Pavelich from Eveleth, and John Harrington and Gus' nephew Keith Hendrickson, both from Virginia, Minnesota. The Bulldogs also had a stocky Canadian defenseman named Curt Giles, who went on to become the best defenseman in Minnesota North Stars history.

It was an impressive show of college hockey talent when the two teams met in Duluth. The first game, Christoff strode into the UMD zone in overtime and rifled a thirty-five-footer past goalie Bill Perkl for a 5-4 Gopher victory.

The next night, Pavelich tipped one past Steve Janaszak, then set up Harrington for a 2-0 lead after one. Later, with UMD up 3-2, Pavelich lost a corner faceoff to McClanahan, who pulled the puck straight back to the end boards. No Gopher was there, however, so Pavelich darted in, scooped up the puck, went straight to the net, and jammed it in. Strobel tied it, but UMD scored again to earn a split.

"We could have moved into a tie for first, with Denver losing," said Brooks, "but it's a long season. Pav is their leader, but this game meant so much to Duluth, I can picture six thousand Duluth fans jumping off the Aerial Bridge if we'd won again."

It was only mid-November, but after sweeping at Colorado College, the Gophers went to 9-3 by also sweeping Michigan. The physically taxing sweep of Michigan at Williams Arena should have prepared the Gophers for anything, but next came a mid-December trip to North Dakota. The game started twenty minutes late because the Zamboni wouldn't start. The game was filled with fights that were, by tradition, called "roughing," and North Dakota smacked the Gophers 4-1. Afterward, Brooks chose to focus on Bob Iwabuchi, North Dakota's superb twenty-one-year-old freshman goaltender: "He has played more than our whole team, but he's a helluva goalkeeper."

The next night, the Gophers prevailed 6-3 despite being outshot 37-26.

The Michigan and North Dakota series were among the most intense Minnesota had played in years. The Michigan rematch in the second half of the season included a classic at Ann Arbor to open January. The game featured one of the most incredible periods in Gopher history. In the second, Michigan's big John Blum dropped Bill Baker with a high stick that saw him helped off the ice. Blum went for a major penalty, but Don Micheletti went for slashing a minute later. Ramsey blocked a point shot and fed McClanahan, who sailed in for a goal. Strobel went off for hooking, leaving the Gophers a man short while Blum still cooled his heels, but no matter. Ramsey threw another pass to McClanahan, who buzzed the defense and scored shorthanded for a 3-1 Gopher lead. Old Yost Ice Arena was pretty quiet. Thirty-eight seconds later, Harrer fed Bob Bergloff for a blast from the slot and Christoff converted the rebound for a 4-1 cushion.

It didn't stop. Micheletti scored, McClanahan completed a hat trick, Strobel scored, and Broten drilled in a slapshot for an 8-1 lead. Baker returned with seven stitches holding his nose together, and a minute later whistled in a goal from the point. Baker scored again in the third to finish a 10-1 romp.

Brooks behind the bench in 1978–79, his last season as Gopher head coach. *Courtesy University of Minnesota Athletics*

The eight goals in a single period was a Minnesota record. After the game, there was understandable jubilation in the Minnesota dressing room. Suddenly, though, an enormous crash stunned everyone to silence. Herbie had thrown a whole case of pop across the dressing room, and it crashed off the wall, narrowly missing a wide-eyed Strobel, who had just turned the corner coming out of the shower.

"Now you've done it!" Brooks yelled. The players looked at each other, then, quizzically, back to their coach.

"You've humiliated a very good hockey team, and they're going to really be out to get you guys tomorrow."

That was it. Phil Verchota had figured he'd heard it all, but was Brooks now trying that old "get ready for tomorrow" ploy after a record outburst and a 10-1 victory? He was indeed.

"We hurt ourselves tonight because it'll be just that much tougher tomorrow," Brooks added. "Eight goals in the second period? We've had teams that didn't get eight goals in a whole month."

Later, Brooks was quiet and collected. "McClanahan's stats are misleading," he said. "We go to him in checking situations, so he doesn't always get points. But he's so conscientious with his play without the puck, he isn't worried about scoring. But those two in a row he got in the second period were big ones."

The players, of course, didn't get to see the calm, rational side of Brooks. The next night, the Wolverines played better, but the Gophers were ready to turn it up a notch too, and left Ann Arbor with a huge sweep. The coach even had some nice words for the team.

"Goals-against is a team statistic," said Brooks. "But Janny was in charge tonight. He challenged the shooters. When you give up one goal for the weekend in a league noted for high scoring, you know you're doing something. . . .

"You never know when you'll get goals, but you *always* should check well."

In the other dressing room, Michigan coach Dan Farrell, who always seemed upbeat and friendly, was pleased with the way his team played, but having been outscored 31-8 in four games, he had seen enough of Minnesota. When asked if he thought Michigan might face the Gophers again in the playoffs, Farrell quickly said, "Christ, I hope not. I've had enough."

With the Gopher players and coach Brooks hitting on all cylinders, the team seemed destined to sail through the sixteen remaining WCHA games. But the league was too tough for any such assumptions. The Gophers were rolling, with a seven-game winning streak and an 11-1 stretch, but the rest of January was a disaster, starting the very next weekend in a 6-6 tie against UMD, followed by a shocking 6-1 loss to the Bulldogs at Williams Arena.

Again, the amazing skills of Mark Pavelich were almost mesmerizing and caused Brooks to fume about how he knew his friend, Gus Hendrickson, must have gone up to his hometown of Eveleth and gotten some grades changed to make Pavelich college-eligible. "Don't worry," I'd heckle Herbie, "you'll appreciate him a lot more next year."

Brooks fired back, "*Next* year? Why would I care about him next year?"

"Next year, when he's the star on your Olympic team," I casually answered.

Brooks said, "No way." But, obviously, the idea had already found a home in Brooks' mind.

The UMD series was followed by a split of one-goal games at Wisconsin and two losses at Denver. The 1-4-1 stretch cooled the Gophers, but they kept scoring and finding new ways to create offensive chances. The undulating season saw two victories over Michigan State by whopping 7-4 and 11-3 scores, two more high-scoring victories against Colorado College, and the two tough setbacks when Notre Dame swept them in South Bend. The Gophers whipped Michigan Tech, formerly their toughest foe, 6-2 and 7-3 at Williams Arena, setting up the season's final regular series.

North Dakota came to Williams Arena leading the WCHA with a 21-9 record, while the Gophers were three points behind with a 19-10-1 mark. The biggest crowd of the season—7,989—was in place early to see the clash of the two teams believed to be the best in the nation. The place was still dark when general admission fans stampeded in at 6:30 p.m. for the 8 p.m. game. Naturally, there was a huge roar when the Gophers came up the stairs for warm-ups, and later for the Minnesota rouser, the introductions, and the National Anthem.

And it worked. With the game not yet a minute old, Minnesota stormed to a 2-0 lead.

But the Fighting Sioux tied it later in the first. On the bench, Brooks watched Tim Harrer's stickhandling and said, "Timmy, I don't want you handling the puck— just shoot it." Less than two minutes later, with another power play, Harrer crossed the blue line and cut loose with a bullet that beat goalie Bob Iwabuchi to the upper right corner for a 3-2 Minnesota lead.

Still clinging to the 3-2 lead in the third after a rough and tumble middle stanza, the Gophers killed an early penalty, then Verchota galloped up the left side, caught a Bart Larson pass, and sent a forty-five-foot rocket into the upper right corner for a 4-2 lead. At 12:18, Broten yanked a right-corner faceoff back to Steve Christoff, who ripped a quick shot in off the far pipe. The goal was Christoff's thirty-fourth of the season, and the assist was Broten's fortieth of his freshman year.

The 5-2 victory left Minnesota (20-10-1) just one point behind the Sioux (21-10), with the regular-season title to be decided on the final day of the regular season.

The next night, 7,996 broke the season record of the previous night by seven. Before the game, word arrived that Amo Bessone had resigned at Michigan State, but the focus was on Williams Arena. The teams traded penalties, rushes, great chances, and brilliant saves. Sioux coach Gino Gasparini went with Bill Stankoven in goal against Janaszak, who had started all but four games. Every time the puck was whistled dead, there was a confrontation. The teams were scoreless through one period, the shots 10-10.

At 0:26 of the second period, Baker went off for hooking, and Bill Himmelright connected on the power play. Then Phil Sykes made it 2-0. The Gophers battled back, throwing seventeen shots at Stankoven in the middle period, but nothing would go in. In the midst of one of the Gopher swarms, North Dakota's Dave Christian broke up the left side and scored for a 3-0 lead. The Sioux came with more pressure, but Janaszak came up with several outstanding saves, earning an ovation in the closing minutes of the second. With forty-three seconds left, Broten twice stole the puck and ignited rushes. The first was foiled, but on the second, Broten came up the right side, turned Howard Walker inside out, carried into the circle, and passed to the slot. Christoff hammered a quick shot and Don Micheletti deflected it in at the crease.

Trailing 3-1, the Gophers still had a period to go, and the WCHA championship was still hanging there. Broten stickhandled in around Cary Eades, who grabbed him around the face for a takedown—and a couple of penalties. At 13:07, McClanahan won a left-corner faceoff back to the left point and Baker cranked up and scored with a slapshot to cut the deficit to 3-2.

Brooks pulled Janaszak with 1:08 remaining, but in the final seconds, Christian got the puck and skated in at the open net. He didn't just flip it in—he skated in alone at full speed, stopped at the crease, then blasted a slapshot into the empty goal, clinching a 4-2 victory and the MacNaughton Cup for the Fighting Sioux.

There was no time to feel bad about losing the league title, or to congratulate one another on a strong season. Michigan Tech was coming to town for playoffs. The Gophers seemed well-organized, until the game was ready to start and there was no linesman to complement referees Medo Martinello and Dino Paniccia. Incredibly, it was up to the coach to call the linesman, and Brooks had failed to do so. It seems he had a few other things on his mind.

Part of Brooks' strategy with his Gopher teams was to make everybody—including the fourth line—an important part of the team. In 1978–79, Brooks went with Dave "Twig" Terwilliger, John Meredith, and Brad Doshan—all veterans and character people who had their turns, however brief, on higher lines. Brooks told them that he'd play four lines regularly as much as possible, but warned them that they'd very likely be the ones to sit in tough third-period situations if he wanted to shorten the bench to three lines. However, he added, whenever there was a power play or a successful penalty kill, they would play the next shift, with the mission of a high-energy turn that would be sure to keep the Gopher momentum.

In that opening playoff game, the Gophers struck first, with Terwilliger taking a feed from Meredith and barging in to jam the puck through John Rockwell. Not only was it a 1-0 lead, it was also Terwilliger's first goal in two seasons of college hockey. Six minutes later, the fourth line struck again. Terwilliger passed from behind the net to Doshan, who pulled it between his legs to the right point, where Mike Ramsey fired a shot that Meredith deflected in. Not only was it a 2-0 lead, it was Meredith's first goal of his junior season.

Already being played without a linesman, the game almost lost Paniccia when he was clunked on the back of his head. None of that affected the Gophers, though, who went up 5-0, when Don Micheletti converted Ulseth's pass.

But the Gophers should have known Tech would not go down that easily. Sure enough, the Huskies outshot Minnesota 17-9 in the third and trimmed the final deficit to 5-3, giving Tech renewed hope for the second game of the total-goal series. It also gave Brooks the undivided attention of his players.

"I was irate," Brooks said. "I made a reference to the country song, 'Take This Job and Shove It,' and some guys took me literally. I was just mad because I don't want these guys to embarrass themselves by failing to reach their potential."

Brooks shook up the troops, putting Micheletti and Harrer on a line with McClanahan at center, Christoff and Verchota with Broten at center, and Ulseth and Strobel at wings with Teal. The Terwilliger-Doshan-Meredith line stayed intact—and started the game.

"Twig says, 'I guess we're starting,' just joking around," said Doshan. "Then Herb said who was starting, and Twig's jaw dropped."

Verchota and Strobel connected, followed by Micheletti, who scored twice in the second to make it 4-0. Micheletti completed his hat trick in the third and scored again on a Broten rebound. His four-goal outburst led a 6-1 Gophers romp and set up a second-round playoff matchup against UMD.

Only 1-2-1 that season against the Bulldogs, the Gophers had no reason to be overconfident. The first game drew a capacity 7,676 to Williams Arena, and the teams raged back and forth in a flurry of promising rushes—but no goals. It remained scoreless until Christoff scored his thirty-fifth of the season at 12:45 of the second. It stayed 1-0 until 5:53 of the third, when UMD's Mark Pavelich zigzagged into the left side and, with his back to the slot, whirled and scored on a power play. At 9:55, Tim Harrer scored from the slot and it ended 2-1. The Gophers outshot UMD 47-31, but Bill Perkl made forty-five saves.

In the second game, Minnesota took a 2-0 lead. UMD got one back and Broten answered, but the 3-1 lead vanished when John Harrington scored a power-play goal early in the second. The Bulldogs pulled even at 3-3, but Harrer scored to put Minnesota back up for the second intermission. Christoff and Micheletti scored in the third, and the Gophers escaped with a 6-3 victory.

"We got two egotistical penalties that gave them a good chance to get back in the game," said Brooks. "If we had stayed out of the box, they'd have had nothing going. But we beat a good hockey team, and we had to have a helluvan effort to do it."

Then he looked at me with that old gleam in his eye and smirked: "But I still don't want to go to Duluth. I'd rather go to Superior."

Supremacy in their half of the WCHA meant the Gophers advanced to face Bowling Green in a one-game playoff, with the winner going to the Final Four. Gopher fans knew all the intricacies of the playoffs—how North Dakota had beaten Wisconsin 4-2, but would have to finish off the Badgers in that total-goal series to reach the Final Four. As much as the Gopher fans loved to hate Wisconsin, they also knew that North Dakota was the more formidable challenge, so when the score from Grand Forks was announced at Williams Arena, with Wisconsin leading game two 7-6 at the second intermission, the Gopher fans started chanting "Let's Go Red! . . . Let's Go Red! . . ." it didn't help. North Dakota gained a 7-7 tie, winning the series and advancing.

The colorful Gopher fans poured into Williams Arena to see Minnesota face a comparatively unknown but strong Falcons team, which featured a trio of interesting players in defenseman Ken Morrow, center Mark Wells, and superstar George McPhee. Brooks had finally seemed to end his constant line-juggling—something that was fairly common, as he continued to evaluate and revise his most talented players in his efforts to extract their maximum potential. The juggling was a Montreal Canadiens–type of thing. Top teams either keep their lines together all year, or they interchange so frequently the players are comfortable playing with any combination.

The 1974 and 1976 NCAA title teams had interesting blends of hard-nosed and skilled players, reflecting Herbie's lunch-pail approach to success. Now that he had an immensely talented team, the ferocious competitiveness of the WCHA made winning streaks difficult to come by, and Herb juggled constantly.

Against Bowling Green, Brooks kept the lines together for the fourth straight game. The matchup was tense with a lot of stick work after the whistles. Referees Dewey Markus and Dino Paniccia gave each side an early penalty to settle things, but it stayed rugged throughout. The Gophers kept the tempo high and took charge midway through the opening period, going up 3-0 before the intermission.

But the momentum was difficult to maintain. Bowling Green scored a power-play goal, then got another on a deflection. Suddenly, it was 3-2. The Gophers got one back on a two-man advantage and scored again with three seconds remaining in the man-advantage. Harrer's power-play goal twenty-seven seconds into the third was enough insulation for a 6-3 victory.

The offense was impressive, but there was no mistake, the maroon and gold buttons that read "Hockey Is for Tough Guys" were still valid. The Gophers had logged ninety-six "takeouts" for the game, including a team record thirty-six in the first period. The body count was as important to setting the tempo as any of the goals.

"We knew we were going to have to keep them off the puck with an aggressive forecheck, and by finishing the checks," Brooks explained, noting that the victory would send the Gophers to the Final Four in Detroit's old Olympia Stadium. "Now it's easy. The hard part is over."

The Gophers would face New Hampshire, while North Dakota would face Dartmouth from the Ivy League in the other semifinal. The Gophers finally seemed to be rolling in high gear. In the four games since Brooks satisfied himself with his line combinations, everything seemed to click, particularly the unit of McClanahan centering Micheletti and Harrer. "I don't like to try to guess why he makes these changes," said McClanahan, of his all-junior line. "I always thought I could do it, and I especially wanted to try playing with Donny. I was with Timmy for a while, but the combination of all three of us worked. For a while, it might have been because of changing style, but I think I started cruising a little. Against Bowling Green, it's the first time I've really gone hard and felt like I could really fly. I can be satisfied if our line gets goals, even if I only get one once in a while."

At Detroit, the old Olympia had the aura of the old six-team NHL. It was about to go away in favor of Joe Louis Arena, and its last hurrah was the 1979 NCAA hockey Final Four. The big arena seemed even more cavernous when only 2,743 showed up to watch Minnesota—the lower seed wearing visiting maroon—face a potent New Hampshire team led by a big, strapping goal scorer named Ralph Cox. Brooks started Broten's line, and Christoff powered up the right side, turned the corner, and crossed the goal mouth, putting a backhander off goalie Greg Moffett and into the net at 0:35. It was Broten's forty-ninth assist, tying the school record set twenty-five years earlier by Johnny Mayasich.

The period ended 3-1, thanks to fifteen saves by Janaszak. At the end of the first period, Janaszak had gone behind the net to help kill the second straight penalty to Mike Greeder. While he was back there, the puck ricocheted off a seam in the boards and went right out front, where Cox whiffed on a bouncing puck with an open net facing him. It was a deserved break for Janaszak, who, as a senior, had simply stopped giving up bad goals and reflected a favorite line of former coach Glen Sonmor: "Luck is the residue of hard work."

The Wildcats outshot Minnesota again in the second period, 14-7, for a 29-17 edge, but Janaszak remained sharp. The only goal of the period came when Cox took a left-corner faceoff from Bob Francis and zinged his potent wrist shot into the upper right corner with 1:24 to go in the session. With the gap closed to 3-2 to begin the third, the Gophers gained a bit more breathing room after Strobel darted wide to beat a defenseman on the right side and scored into the short side at 1:53. Strobel's hat trick came at the best possible time. The third period was swift, up and down, and decidedly chippier as the game went on, but Janaszak held on to make thirty-seven saves.

"I felt beautiful," said Janaszak. "My heart was in my throat the whole time."

The rest of the Gophers were less enthusiastic. Ramsey wasn't exactly thrilled at playing in an NHL rink that had nowhere near the room of Williams Arena, with its deep, squarish corners and the nets that Brooks had talked his crew into moving out from the end boards a bit to leave extra playmaking room. "This rink is definitely a nightmare," said Ramsey. "There's nowhere to go behind the net."

That night, North Dakota spotted Dartmouth the first goal but came storming back, knocking "the Big Green" around and winning 4-2 to set up an all-WCHA final between the two storied rivals. In those days, there was no day off between the semifinals and final. Both teams, and their fans, were primed and ready. Gopher banners read, "The All-American Team," and "Golden Gophers—the homespun team—100% natural ingredients. Accept no substitutes." Fighting Sioux fans might have been more creative, but they probably couldn't find any place in Detroit to hunt the burrowing rodents they liked to use as post-goal litter back in Grand Forks.

Overall, North Dakota brought a 30-10-1 record into the final game, to Minnesota's 31-11-1. Any questions about the teams' intensity were answered in the first two minutes. North Dakota's Rob Mihulka knocked McClanahan to the ice and gave him a little extra shove after he was down. McClanahan got up and took a run at Mihulka and was called for high-sticking. Mihulka whirled and went after McClanahan again, but Micheletti knocked Mihulka down.

With Minnesota up 1-0 on Christoff's thirty-eighth goal of the season, the rough stuff continued. A lot of Gasparini's Sioux teams played an intimidating style and, of course, Brooks would never have his team intimidated. The Gophers, known for fast and forceful starts, grabbed a 3-1 lead by the first intermission, outshooting the Fighting Sioux 16-9 and matching them in a grueling, physical duel.

The second period, in which Bob Iwabuchi, who later said he had some fatigue and cramping from Friday night's game, replaced Bill Stankoven, was a case of irresistible force meets immovable object. With two minutes left, the tenacious Kevin Maxwell pulled the Sioux back to within one.

Then, at 2:48 of the third period, Broten created a play that is in every Gopher hockey highlight film ever made. Breaking up the left side, he slid the puck under the defenseman and tried to leap over him but tripped on his form. Iwabuchi reacted in a heartbeat and moved out toward the action, dropping to block the puck. Hurtling through the air, Broten stabbed at the puck, chipping it up and just over the startled Iwabuchi, who could only watch in dismay as the puck flew over him and settled into the net.

"I glanced up and could see he was coming out," said Broten afterward. "He came out kinda far and I was able to get it over him. I want to see it, too."

The Sioux kept coming. Marc Chorney shot from the left point into heavy traffic. In the tangle, the puck hit a Gopher defenseman and squirted in, and it was 4-3.

Christian put Erwin Martens in for a clean chance, but Janaszak snatched it with his glove. Moments later, he stopped Christian, too. Later, Mike Burggraf somehow got loose and the entire game teetered. But Janaszak stopped Burggraf—and then Micheletti leveled him.

And then it was over. The Gophers had won 4-3, with Broten's leaping, sprawling masterpiece standing up as the game-winner.

The team poured onto the ice in celebration, all except Brooks. I found him alone in the stick room. He was happy, and so was I, but I couldn't resist: "It must be more exciting to win the title when you know you've screwed the team up most of the season." We both laughed.

"I wish I could say we lost the last game of the regular season to set this one up," said Brooks, "but I can't."

Herbie looked back to the start of the season, when he predicted they'd win it all. "I put a lot of pressure on this team—more than ever," he said. "We had our ups and downs, and the most consistent thing about the club is its inconsistency. But we declared ourselves, and we backed it up.

"Sometimes, I didn't think this club wanted to win, or was capable of the effort needed to win. But I wouldn't let 'em admit that they couldn't do it. I reinforced it all year that too many people want to take the accolades after lying in the weeds."

For Ramsey, making the all-tournament team as a freshman from Roosevelt was mind-blowing. "At the start of the season, I played JV and just wanted to crack the lineup," he said. "Then to end up all-tournament . . . I learned a helluva lot about the game from Billy Baker, who took me through the ropes, how to handle myself, and he talked to me and encouraged me. If his ankle wasn't hurt, he probably would've been all-tournament."

As rough and pressure-filled as the game was, there were also some strategic gambits that Brooks had confronted. "In the second period, they came at us," said Brooks. "They brought two guys heavy on the strong side to pressure our defense. So we started throwing the puck around the weak side, and our forward in the slot would break for it."

Brilliant. Holding a forward in the slot for defensive purposes was typical, and that player, usually the center or weak-side wing, would curl for a breakout pass from the defenseman or posted winger on the strong-side boards. But with the Fighting Sioux crashing hard to take that away, Brooks pulled the string, and the Gophers started ringing the boards behind the net with the puck, seeming to throw it to nobody, except that the forward in the slot curled the other way, got to the puck unmolested, and was able to escape the pressure and get out of the zone.

That little tactical move was a jewel. It allowed the Gophers to win the last game Brooks ever coached at the University of Minnesota, but a year later, in the little town of Lake Placid, he would pull off a similar maneuver to help Team USA escape its zone against a high-pressure forecheck from the greatest hockey team in the world, wearing the CCCP of the Soviet Union.

For the moment, though, it was enough to have become the best team in the best year in college hockey history.

CHAPTER 18

LASTING LEGACY

It's possible that Herb Brooks learned as much from the banner 1978–79 season as his players did from him. He learned a lot about himself and refined how far he could push his players and how malleable they might be when juggled in all sorts of combinations. He also began trusting his uncanny knack for knowing when to try something that he knew would work.

It wasn't that the 1978–79 Gopher team won the NCAA title, or scored the most goals (later teams scored even more), but that team accomplished what it did in the most golden of golden eras of college hockey. Every team in the WCHA seemed loaded with skilled players, and the only casualties were the goaltenders. There were some great ones, but none could contain the league's incredible collection of scorers enough to post even a 3.00 goals-against average.

That team was not only the pinnacle of Brooks' college coaching career, but it also made a lasting impact on its players. Some of their stories are legendary in their descriptions of Brooks and the impact he had on his players.

Tom Vannelli, for example, wound up coaching at St. Thomas Academy thirty years after playing for Brooks at Minnesota. The 2008 team solidly beat Duluth Marshall, another private school, in the state's Class A final. Earlier in the season, however, Marshall had beaten St. Thomas Academy 9-2. When the players arrived at their arena for their first practice after that loss, they found their dressing room door locked. After much complaining, Vannelli let them know what the deal was.

"We were a little too high, and we forgot to appreciate what goes into being a good team," said Vannelli. "We had the luxury of our own arena, practicing there, and having our equipment in our own dressing room. . . . So I thought it might be good for all the players to come back down to earth a little, so maybe they'd appreciate what they had a little more."

Vannelli laughed when I suggested that was a Herbie-like trick. "He never did that," said Vannelli, "but he might have. It's definitely the kind of thing he would do to make a point, and I probably can trace the idea to having played for him."

Mike Polich, the catalyst center who preceded Vannelli, said, "Herbie had all the little ploys. He knew just how far to go with the refs, but more often than not, they'd end up penalizing the other team next. I remember when we'd be playing, and once in a while the other team might make a big play or get a goal, and they'd suddenly have the momentum for three or four shifts. We'd be taking a faceoff, and just as they were going to drop the puck, we'd hear, 'Hold it!' and Herbie would send out a late line change. Everybody waited, and the momentum stopped, and we'd take over again. I never saw anyone do it before, but it worked."

Brad Buetow, Herb's assistant in the later years, saw the trick too, which Herbie would pull with immaculate timing about once every two or three games. Brad knew it was a good idea, but didn't seem to realize that if he did it all the time, it would have no impact at all, except to make games last three hours and cause the officials to put in a rule making a late change illegal.

Another trick Polich remembered was when there was a sudden stoppage of play because a player lost a contact lens. The refs would help look, knowing how impossible it was to find a tiny, transparent lens on a 200×85-foot sheet of glistening white ice. No matter, the delay was an unofficial time-out, giving the Gopher power play or penalty kill a breather.

Later, the refs were prepared to give the Gophers a bench penalty for this trick, so Brooks embellished it. "Herbie would tell me to pop out a contact lens," said Phil Verchota. "So I'd pop it out and go look for it. Just about the time the refs were going to give us a penalty, Gary Smith would come out and look, and he'd find the missing lens. There was really nothing the refs could do then, and they never knew that Smitty had stuck the lens onto his finger before he left the bench, so he could hold it up and say 'Here it is!'"

Vannelli recalled how Brooks always came up with practice tricks that were not only completely unique, but were also designed to clear his players' minds of conventional ideas about the game. Brooks would move the two goals and bring a third goal onto the rink, positioning all three about equal distance apart, and none of them where a net ordinarily would be. Then the players would play three-on-three-on-three—three groups of three at a time. Anybody from one group could score in either of the other two goals, but they had to defend the third one, and the same went for the other groups. While playing wildly spontaneous rink-rat-style games with great enthusiasm, they were really also getting overload training because they were always playing three-on-six.

Steve Ulseth remembered the clever—and sometimes cutting—little one-liners Herbie would throw at his players and at referees. "One time, when I was a freshman, he asked me some question," said Ulseth. "It caught me off-guard, and I said, 'I don't know.' He said, 'Young man, you'd better get an opinion. You'll never go anywhere in this life if you don't have an opinion.'

"Another time, when I was a freshman, we had lost at Grand Forks, and Herbie was diagramming how we were going to change things around a little for the next game. I don't know if he thought Phil Verchota wasn't paying close enough attention, but after he diagrammed it on the board, he said, 'Phil, what do you think about that?'"

"I don't know," answered the startled Verchota.

"What do you mean, you don't know?" pursued Brooks.

"You've never asked me anything for three years, so I don't know," said Verchota.

The players all tuned in, however.

"That night, we're getting ready for the game, and Herbie comes in and says, 'Phil, I'm starting you tonight. What do you think about that?'"

Ulseth didn't disagree with my suggestion that the 1978–79 season was the greatest ever for skill level and competition in the WCHA. "Especially the way it worked out for us," he joked. He didn't necessarily think the players then were much better than they are now, but he thought defense has become more of a focus.

"It's always much easier to try to stop a team from scoring than to score against a team that's playing defensively," Ulseth said. "Look at goaltending equipment and how much bigger it got, which also makes it tougher to score."

But from the standpoint of sheer talent, when you look at the evolution of Gopher teams in the first decade of the twenty-first century—with coach Don Lucia recruiting players who mostly had accelerated their experience by playing a year or two in the USHL junior programs or at the U.S. National Development Team Program—the players, who are on average two years older as freshmen, certainly don't have the amazing statistics of the 1978–79 Gophers.

"I think that time also was the golden age of high school hockey in Minnesota, where there was so much talent coming out and suddenly was being noticed by the pros," said Ulseth. "If you look at my senior year [1980–81], Neal Broten won All-America and the first Hobey Baker. I was All-America too, and I was voted most valuable player of the WCHA, but Aaron Broten was voted the most valuable player of our team.

"The defensive systems became more prevalent and the goaltending might have improved in later years, but you have to wonder how Timmy Harrer would have shot the puck with a composite stick. We were using Christian Brothers and Northland wood sticks that were like logs compared to the players today. I'd like to see modern players try to shoot with the sticks we used."

Both Neal and Aaron Broten went on to glowing pro careers in the NHL, and both ultimately achieved the U.S. Hockey Hall of Fame—in the pure days, before USA Hockey took over that wonderful Eveleth icon and made inductions far more political. After a fling in pro hockey with the New York Rangers when Brooks was coaching there, Ulseth went into selling hockey equipment, so he knows all about the advances and how much tougher the WCHA was in those higher-skill days.

"We'd play North Dakota, and you'd come away with gashes on your ribcage from being hooked," Ulseth said. "We used to think they must have sharpened their stick blades to make their hooks do so much damage. And, of course, the gashes would never heal, because about the time they did, you were playing somebody else and getting hooked some more."

Ulseth was the embodiment of "Gopherhockey," the run-together term emblazoned on buttons to define the Herb Brooks coaching era.

"Bob Johnson and Herbie came to my house recruiting me," Ulseth recalled. "Bob Johnson said, 'I want you to come to Wisconsin to play left wing with my All-America center, Mike Eaves.' That was pretty impressive. Herbie came in and said, 'The only thing I can promise you is that if you make the team, I'll buy you a pair of skates.' That was it. So I walked on, with no scholarship help, because I wanted to go to Minnesota that bad.

"Sure enough, when I made the team, Herbie said, 'Go down to Steichen's and pick out a pair of skates.' He gave me a quarter of a scholarship at the end of my freshman year, and then I got a half as a sophomore. Brad Buetow moved me up to a full when I was captain."

Ulseth played 148 games over four years, compiling 84 goals and 118 assists, a total that was second only to the legendary Johnny Mayasich's 298 career points, and one point ahead of teammate Tim Harrer, who had climbed to second as a senior one year earlier. Ulseth's 93-point senior year was second only to teammate Aaron Broten's all-time Gopher single-season mark of 106 points set that same 1980–81 season. Ulseth also set the school record for the longest point-scoring streak at twenty-four games that season, which topped the twenty-three-game streak by Mayasich that spanned two seasons thirty years earlier.

Subsequent Gopher stars, such as Pat Micheletti, Corey Millen, Butsy Erickson, Larry Olimb, and Brian Bonin later compiled more career points than Ulseth, but those totals in no way detract from the walk-on-to-superstar status of Ulseth, a 5-foot-9 hustler who had only forty-eight penalty minutes despite never avoiding traffic. Consider that Neal Broten had seventy-four minutes and only played two seasons.

Brooks, of course, had moved on by the 1980–81 season, but Ulseth carried on the embodiment of everything Brooks loved about hockey, from his favorite saying that "the name on the front of the jersey is more important than the name on the back," to his fierce, swift, smart, but clean style of play.

If Ulseth was the perfect Herbie-type player, he hardly was free of Brooks' meaningful darts, however.

"When I was a freshman, somebody like Timmy Harrer was having some trouble on the power play," Ulseth recalled. "Herbie says, 'Ulseth, get out there for Harrer.' It was a big surprise to me, and as it turned out, I made a good play to Micheletti and we scored. I felt really good, and I came back to the bench, thinking Herbie might give me a big compliment. Instead, he says, 'See, Harrer? Even *he* can do it.'

"He threw a few of his usual shots at me. He tried me at center once and said I looked like a chicken with my head cut off, or his favorite, like 'a monkey bleeping a football.'"

That was another one he had borrowed from Glen Sonmor, and it became a standard Brooksism. "I think his genius was that he leveraged with each player what to say and how far to go," said Ulseth.

The rugged Mike Greeder, for example, could skate hard and had some skill with the puck, but without question, he was a Gopher for his unyielding ruggedness, a fact Brooks was sure to reinforce. That was another thing Herbie learned from Sonmor, who a decade earlier used to regale assistant coach Brooks and other listeners with his story about tough guys who typically lose their taste for playing tough and regress from being "a crusher, to a rusher, to an usher." Brooks had no need for ushers.

"We were playing at Colorado College when I was a freshman," said Ulseth. "Marc Pettygrove, who was from Minneapolis Roosevelt, played for CC, and he crosschecked Greeder right across the head. Dewey Markus was reffing, and Pettygrove hit Greeder on the head so hard, he broke his stick, but there was no penalty. Herbie yelled, 'Dewey, what the hell? He crosschecked him in the head!'"

Markus was skating past the bench and said, "I heard wood-on-wood."

And Herbie said, "Of course you did—it was Greeder."

Nobody was free from Herbie's torpedoes. "I remember when Herb coached the Rangers, and Patti went out there, but her credit card got stolen," Ulseth said. "Herbie said he didn't report the lost credit card for two weeks because whoever stole it was spending less than Patti."

"If you ever played for him, you carry Herbie with you every day," Ulseth said thirty years later. "The complete respect all his players had for him was amazing. If

I was sitting in a restaurant tomorrow and he walked in, I'd still feel like he was my coach. I'd still feel on edge, like I couldn't relax around him. Everyone stood up a little straighter, as though you were hoping he wouldn't ask you something. I think we all thought that someday we'd get to the point where we could just sit down with him and have that personal conversation with him. Then he died. The only time I ever had a talk with him like that was once when he called me on Christmas Eve. . . . I was home with my wife, and we talked for about forty-five minutes about life in general. On Christmas Eve."

Trainer Gary Smith, also an integral part of Brooks' earlier Gopher teams, was squeezed out by some political maneuvers at the U, and he left to start the Institute for Athletic Medicine. Herbie always appreciated Smith's loyalty and treated him as an assistant coach and confidante in an era when trainers weren't considered as important as they later were.

"There were times when Herbie would tell me how much he'd love to go out and have a beer with some of his players—one of them was Les Auge, an old [St. Paul] Johnson player," said Smith. "But he'd never let himself do it because he thought it might cut into his image of discipline. It was a different world then. To Herbie, having a beer with someone was the ultimate way to socialize. He knew I didn't drink, so our relationship was different."

The beer thing was always interesting. I never saw Herbie when he seemed even the least bit inebriated, even though I saw him drink a few beers now and then. He expressed admiration, and a little curiosity, of the fact that I had never taken a drink—beer, wine, anything. Herbie used to always say, "I don't drink either." I'd say, but what about beer? He'd say, "Oh, I like to drink a beer now and then, but I don't drink."

In Herbie's world, hard alcohol or wine was "drinking," but having a beer, especially with a couple of friends, was not drinking but socializing. In later years, some complaints and alcohol-abuse issues arose on campus, so the University of Minnesota ruled that alcohol could not be served on campus, and that no sports teams could be given beer or allowed to drink while on a trip representing the school. When Brooks coached the Gophers, though, it was a looser and more innocent time, and if the team had a long bus trip, he might direct Gary Smith to buy a case or two of beer, along with the usual soft drinks. Sometimes, Smith recalled, it would be one case of beer, or two if they'd won.

"That was always Herbie," said Patti, his wife. "Herbie loved to drink his beer, but he always called himself a nondrinker. It drove me nuts."

In 1989, members of the 1979 Gopher national championship team gathered at Herb (front row, third from left) and Patti Brooks' home. *Author photo*

Herb and Patti's kids, Kelly and Danny, grew up during that seven-year reign of Gopher coaching, but Herbie was consumed with coaching, and all the organizational and operational elements he created, which pretty much prevented him from watching them grow up.

"Through the years, I was referred to as 'the Widow Brooks' because I'd always go to Danny's games alone," said Patti. "Even if he was around, he felt that hockey parents were so pushy that he went to the other extreme."

Patti, meanwhile, went to every home Gopher game. She unashamedly acknowledges that no matter how many games she attended, she still had no interest in, or idea about, the tactics and strategy of hockey, because to her it was a social function. Throughout the Gopher years, various players often called the Brooks residence, happy when Herb wasn't there and they could talk to Patti instead. She enjoyed talking to them and said she felt mostly like a surrogate mom. She was surprised when I told her that to the players, she was more of a fantasy. Whenever they could talk to the coach's cute, young, vivacious blonde wife, who was always friendly and chatty, it was part of a Mrs. Robinson–type fantasy.

"I thought I was like their sounding board," Patti said. "But, I had my fantasies, too, like Les Auge in shorts, or Warren Miller. . . . Paul Holmgren and I would talk for hours, and Mike Polich and I would talk a lot. Pat Phippen, all these years, kept saying he was going to tell Herbie off, but he never could do it. Then there was Joe Micheletti . . . Reed Larson . . . Mark Lambert . . . Bill Butters . . . Ken Yackel Jr. . . . Dick Spannbauer was in charge of things when we renovated our kitchen, and we'd stand there and talk all the time, while his guys were doing the work, when I thought he should have been working too."

Meanwhile, Herbie was completely immersed in coaching his way: totally, thoroughly evaluating prospects, inventing tactics, plotting, and planning. He didn't have time to get away, although he grew to love golf as an escape. Even then, though, he'd either be asking for advice on how to improve his game, or be giving advice to those in his foursome if he thought he could help.

Being normally casual was outside of his scope. While I continued to kid him about having button-down collars on his team's jerseys, Herbie always looked as though he was stepping off the pages of *Gentleman's Quarterly*, while I have always been most comfortable wearing jeans. It was hard to visualize Herbie getting casual in a T-shirt and a pair of Levi's—not that he didn't try. Herbie loyally bought his clothes from Al Johnson's, a little men's store in Dinkytown—that tiny crammed-in area adjacent to the university. Al Johnson's persevered in that location for years, despite being too high-end in fashion and price for the common college student. Once, Herbie bought a pair of denim slacks there. I always gave him grief, pointing out that having a pair of denim slacks that you had dry-cleaned and pressed was not quite the same as throwing on a comfortable pair of Levi's. But that was Herbie.

Not that he ever positioned himself to seem pompous, but he always tried to help anyone he perceived as needing it.

"On any road trip, we'd have these huge team meals," Gary Smith said. "Usually they were buffets, and there was always a lot left over. So Herbie always gave me meal money, as if I had to go eat on my own. He knew I needed money, so he wanted me to pocket the meal money, then come in after the players were through and eat from all that was left.

"Back then we also got two tickets to every game, and I'd put on a trench coat and go outside and sell my tickets. I never sold them for more than face value, but that was Herbie's suggestion, just his way of trying to help me out."

Gary Smith's expanded role with the Gophers was a major reason why Brooks hired him to serve as trainer for the 1980 Olympic team, even though AHAUS had a different trainer picked out. Smith readily recalls some of his favorite incidents, besides the BU fight, while with the Gophers.

"We were playing in Michigan, and they purposely set it up so that some of their most obnoxious fans were seated right behind our bench," Smitty said. "A lot of them were drunk, and they got so abusive it got to some of our guys. Dan Bonk lost it and swung his stick at them. I was right in his line of fire, so I threw my arms up and he hit me right on the arms when he swung. I went down. Herb saw me down and yelled at the refs, 'Hey, those fans just jumped our trainer!'

"One of my favorites was at Michigan State, when we had to go three overtimes to beat them in the playoffs in 1976. After the first overtime, Herb says, 'What do you think?' and I said, 'I think you'd better get the fire going again.' As he walked into the room, I was walking behind him, and he all of a sudden grabs the garbage can and throws it, and I got hit with it. He read them the riot act. . . . Then when we went back outside he calmly asked me if I thought that was good enough.

"So after the second overtime, he says, 'What do you think now?' I told him to let me try something. So I went in and told them all to lie down on the floor. I didn't know what I was doing, but I said to them they should just picture all that blood and tiredness draining out of their legs and how energized they were going to feel. It was dark in there, but just about then Herbie comes in and says, 'What the hell are you doing?' I told him to get the hell out of there, and he did. Sure enough, we went out and won it right away in the third overtime."

A fellow I became good friends with was Art Kaminsky, a freelance journalist who enjoyed writing about college hockey for the *New York Times*. We met at an NCAA tournament in the early 1970s and stayed in casual contact through the next few years. He did a big feature story on Alex Pirus of Notre Dame in the *New York Times*, and later he got the Minnesota North Stars to sign Pirus before he completed his eligibility. Because I was covering the North Stars (as well as college, high school, and Fighting Saints hockey), general manager Jack Gordon and I had a long conversation about it. Gordon was one of the best people I ever met in the sport—a quiet, thoughtful, intelligent manager—and we had an excellent rapport behind the scenes. He explained the whole situation to me and asked what I thought about the ethics of a fellow who used a press pass to get into a dressing room, supposedly just to interview a player, then wrote a big story about the player in the *New York Times*, and then went to the pro team that had drafted that player and tried to get him signed. I had to admit, it sounded totally unethical. There were some loose rules about contact with an "agent" in those days, and it seemed that Kaminsky was broadening his scope to align more and more clients for the future, maybe the near future.

"I remember when Art Kaminsky came to Williams Arena and was in the dressing room interviewing our players," said Gary Smith. "Herbie was really mad, and he ordered me to go throw Kaminsky out. Then we go off to the Olympics, and Herbie hires Kaminsky as his agent."

I recalled that incident, but what I heard was Herbie ordering Warren Strelow to go "throw Kaminsky's ass out of here." When I brought it up later, Brooks, Strelow, and Kaminsky all insisted it never happened. Now I know what happened: Strelow balked at the order, so Gary Smith carried it out.

Phil Verchota looks back and recalls tactical cleverness as part of the thoroughness Brooks brought to his coaching realm.

"First of all, there was no question we were going to be in shape and never get beat on conditioning," said Verchota. "We also were never going to get beat on tactics. In the defensive zone, it was rigid, and disciplined. The center always stayed back to help the defense, and the centers had to be among the best skaters, because they were required to be offensive threats, too. The wings were also rigidly structured in our defensive zone. One wing would be on the boards for a breakout pass, but the off-wing would go to the slot to help the defense."

Once in place, it was quite simple to execute the plan effectively and, clearly, everybody bought into the plan or they wouldn't play. It was as simple as that. It also was an easy adjustment for Brooks to help his players break out from an inspired forecheck that might be bottling them up, as he did in the second period of the 1979 NCAA final against North Dakota. It was a simple adjustment from the system everybody was executing: the center and weak-side wing were holding in the slot as defensive support and were aware either of them would have to break back to the weak-side boards, because the defensemen were going to reverse the puck and ring it to the weak side to avert the pressure.

"But once we had the puck and got out of our defensive zone, I don't ever remember ever hearing about staying in a lane," said Verchota. "Offensively, I can't tell you that Herbie ever adjusted during a game."

That seems impossible, but that's how well-conceived Brooks' offensive plan was. First, he wanted players who could think independently and creatively and make plays on rushes. Instead of demands to stay in lanes, they could interact in any way that fit their fancy, improvising if necessary. His players thrived on the freedom to create, and I often thought in later years what a tragedy it was that he couldn't have coached Aaron Broten, Larry Olimb, or Dave Spehar, to name just three examples of highly skilled players who would have embodied the spontaneity of the fertile Brooks imagination.

Brooks hated dumping the puck into the offensive zone. "Why would you work so hard to get it, then want to throw it to the other team?" he'd ask. But he also was pragmatic, and added: "Throwing the puck in is an awful style, but it can be a good tactic." So while he much preferred passing the puck into the zone, or circling back to regroup for another attempt at entering the zone while controlling the puck, sometimes throwing the puck in deep was a springboard for gaining immediate possession deep in the offensive zone.

"We had one forechecking plan, but there were a series of keys that forced you to decide what to do," said Verchota. "For example, the first guy in would forecheck hard, going after the puck at full speed. The second guy in had to read what the first guy did—whether he chased the puck carrier, hit the guy, or whatever. So if the first guy went in hard and bodychecked the puck carrier, the second guy would go in hard to support the first guy. If the first forechecker chased the puck carrier behind the net, the second forechecker might head off the puck carrier on the other side of the net, or he might stay back if it didn't look like there was a good chance of getting to the puck carrier. The third guy stayed high, ready to help out defensively, unless we turned the puck over.

"Once you learned how to read and react to the keys, you never adjusted—because you were adjusting all the time, to whatever was happening."

Brilliant. A lot of astute, advanced, and creative coaches use different systems to deploy their forecheck, such as a 2-1-2, a 1-2-2, a 1-1-3, or some other fashion. In a 2-1-2, the first two forecheckers go hard, much as in the Swedish system. In the 1-2-2, one forechecker goes hard, with the other two staying back to patrol the area horizontally, at about the top of the circles. In a 1-1-3, which is very cautious, one forechecker goes hard, the second holds halfway, and the third lines up at center point, almost like three defensemen strung across the blue line. Those same diagrammed systems might be deployed in the neutral zone.

Many very well-coached teams go with an aggressive 2-1-2 to get ahead, or when a rally is needed, but once ahead, teams might fall back in a 1-1-3, or even a 1-4, to keep a foe from generating a strong offensive thrust.

In the Brooks plan, his players could deploy all of these structured systems, and more, simply because they were improvising the best way to attack on each particular rush. A team trying to figure out how a Brooks team was forechecking might see a particular line forecheck three different ways on a single shift. Not only did that system demand thought and anticipation from each player, but the versatility that resulted also meant that no opponent could adjust to escape it the same, consistent way it might against a more conventional, disciplined system.

Certainly there were times when one forward might botch the assignment, or cheat by failing to push himself to maximum commitment. When it got bad enough, Brooks blew.

"We were playing somewhere, and we had won the Friday night game," recalled Ulseth. "In the first period of the Saturday game, we played poorly and got behind. When we got to the dressing room, Herb said we were playing like a bunch of whores. We didn't know what that was supposed to mean. So he explained it. He said a whore takes any easy mark that comes by, and whatever she makes, she spends it all right away, while a high-class call girl might invest her money and move up in the world."

It was classic Herb Brooks, the amateur sociologist, stretching reality a bit to create an analogy to convince his players that they shouldn't take shortcuts in their responsibility, because while the easy route might lead to immediate gratification, it will bring no real lasting success. I think.

Brooks' reliance on Gary Smith expanded during those middle years. "He always knew I was in the same rowboat and I had his backside, rowing as hard as ever," said Smith. "He was just as loyal, and he did a lot of things to take care of me.

"Sometimes he'd unload on the team and you'd think he was really hot, then he'd walk out and calmly ask me how the players were taking it. He was a master manipulator, and he'd pick kids to recruit who he thought could handle the verbal abuse he'd give them.

"Sometimes he'd go recruiting and leave me to take the team on a trip. He did that when we flew to Michigan Tech, in 1975 I think it was. We changed planes in Green Bay, and when the security people were going through his stuff, Jeff Tscherne said, 'Do you think I'd put a bomb in there?' They pulled him aside, and it was my job to call Herbie and say, 'We're OK, but we lost Tscherne. He's in jail in Green Bay.'"

That was just after the Gophers had clinched the WCHA title and were playing Tech in the final series of the regular season. They wound up losing to Tech in the NCAA final in St. Louis that year, but on the final regular weekend, with the title already clinched, Brooks was mad that the Gophers were swept by Tech.

"After the game, they're all headed for the dressing room, and out on the bench, I noticed all the fans were still there," said Smith. "They had a ceremony all arranged to present us with the MacNaughton Cup for winning the title."

That made sense, because at the time the trophy was a Michigan Tech possession, given to the WCHA regular-season champion. Later, Tech gave it to the league to award each year.

"I went back to the dressing room and told Herbie we had to get back out there," said Smith. "He said 'Why?' and I told him they're waiting to present us with the MacNaughton Cup. Herbie said, 'You go get it.' So I had to go out there all alone and try to carry that thing back to the dressing room. Herbie was so mad, he canceled our return flight the next morning and called up and hired a bus, and he made the team get on the bus for the ten-hour drive back to Minnesota."

It was back at Williams Arena where Herbie gave the MacNaughton Cup its men's room dousing to show the players how meaningless a trophy is if a team doesn't play like champions.

Another "secret weapon" Brooks pulled out during the 1978–79 season was Jack Blatherwick—the same guy who had coached at Breck School when Brooks asked him if varying from the all-Minnesota scheme would be favorably accepted by high school coaches. Blatherwick was in grad school at Minnesota by then, and his knowledge of physiology and how it might be applied to hockey coaching was breakthrough stuff.

At that time, Brooks ran all of his Gopher teams through a notorious routine. Mondays would be killers, when the players would do the much-publicized Herbies until they were ready to drop from exhaustion.

"He would time us," said Reed Larson. "We'd do blue and back, then red and back, and that had to be done in fifteen seconds. Then the rest of it had to be done in thirty seconds. If you didn't make the first part in fifteen seconds, you had to do it again. We'd also do three laps around the whole rink. The first lap would be timed, and if you did it in fifteen seconds, then you had to do the second and third laps in the same time."

Bill Baker, whose term at the U went a couple of years past Reed Larson's, said he had heard about the killer drills while in high school—and then he was living them. By then, Herbie had found a way to make them worse yet. He used the drills to develop endurance, but also to establish discipline.

"The worst part is that he would choose two players, and it would always be somebody like Rob McClanahan or John Meredith, our fastest guys," said Baker. "They'd go out and light it up, going to the blue and back and red and back, and Herbie would time them at thirteen or fourteen seconds. Then he would insist that all of us had to do it in twelve seconds. If you didn't make it, you had to keep doing it. He knew we wouldn't make it, which was fine, because he had planned to keep us going. Sometimes we'd go a whole hour without pucks, then we'd take a break while they resurfaced, and then we'd go back out for another hour.

"We'd do at least forty-five solid minutes of 'Herbies,' then we'd do the three times around the rink in a pack, and you had to make it back to the spot where he started timing your lap in the same amount of time on all three laps. The third lap was the killer. He'd just stand there, hardly even turning his head."

Brooks always figured that superb conditioning could allow the less-experienced Minnesota players to offset the experience edge of the older Canadian junior players on opposing teams. As demanding and unyielding as Brooks was, though, his true brilliance as a student of the game was that logic could on occasion make him change his approach. That's where Blatherwick came in.

"I started talking to Herbie during that '78–'79 season about using better intervals in training," Blatherwick recalled. "I watched him run the team through endless 'Herbies' on Mondays, and I asked him what his objective was—to get the team in shape, or to exhaust them? Doing 'Herbies' meant going fast, then they slowed down from being tired, so they were anaerobic in the short term, but after the first time down and back, they were just aerobic—like jogging.

"He said no, they were also being executed to develop mental toughness. And I said, 'I don't believe you have to do something dumb to achieve mental toughness.'"

That was typical of the man Herbie took to calling Cardiac Jack. He always was forthright, and he would say what he knew to be true, just like Brooks himself. His assessment to Brooks was offered with such startling candor that it changed Brooks' practice strategy forevermore, although not instantly.

Blatherwick later refined his own quick-interval training scheme to short, under-five-second bursts of flat-out speed, followed by a slowdown period that was two or three times longer, so that it would resemble the intervals of games. Hockey players almost never go flat-out for more than five seconds, and they generally play a one-minute shift, followed by two minutes of bench time waiting for their next turn, so the same interval made sense for practice.

"I suggested he should run his practices at a super-fast pace, even the flow and complicated drills, and as soon as the players slowed down, practice would be over," said Blatherwick. "He didn't do that, but he understood. All coaches want their players to have the same speed at the end of a drill as at the start, or at the end of a shift as at the start."

The problem is, as soon as an athlete's muscles are spent, they don't work as well. The athlete may try as hard and put out as much effort, but the muscles cut corners for survival. Blatherwick's quick-interval drills were based on short-burst quickness, followed by recovery without the muscles becoming fully taxed. Players could do them for a full hour and not feel exhausted, if executed properly. Blatherwick proved that working on endurance could improve endurance, but at the expense of quickness, while working on quickness could improve quickness, and endurance would be improved as an exponent. This was unheard of in hockey—particularly tradition-bound North American hockey.

"Herbie did it better than any other coach I know of," said Blatherwick. "He didn't stop doing his drills during the '78–'79 season, but he went to Roy Griak to check on it and asked him about my drills. Griak said, 'He's right!'"

Griak was the legendary track coach at the University of Minnesota who won numerous championships and always was on the forefront of positive training for both quick-interval sprinters and long-distance endurance. Naturally, he trained such diverse athletes differently, and they succeeded at both extremes. Brooks always had great rapport with the so-called minor-sports coaches at Minnesota, because he knew how much harder they had to work to succeed in their sport, such as track, wrestling, and gymnastics, without the media spotlight or fan support. Those coaches appreciated Herbie for his genuine support.

Griak's endorsement of everything Blatherwick had recommended not only affirmed Brooks' impression of his new "eccentric scientist," but it also led Brooks to become the most progressive practice and training hockey coach in North America, and possibly in the world.

After that, Brooks' rigorous training and conditioning disciplines rivaled those of the Soviets. They were far beyond what any NHL team or Canadian or American program was doing at the time, while his inventive drills were incorporated to encourage the best traits of the inventive European game with his own ideas.

Actually, the only other North American team of that era that was incorporating anything resembling the European style was the Austin Mavericks of the Midwest Junior Hockey League, forerunner of the USHL, with which Lou Vairo was putting another new coaching concept to work. Vairo and I had many discussions, shared a mutual respect, and enjoyed discussing our mutual love for the game. We also argued quite vehemently when Lou tried to convince me that he preceded Brooks in dabbling with the Soviet hockey concepts of Anatoli Tarasov.

The still-blossoming junior league was just emerging back then, and the Mavericks were closer to playground hockey when compared to the large stage the WCHA had achieved. I told Lou that this made it far easier—and maybe less significant—to experiment with a "different" Soviet system there. Vairo was such a strong admirer of Tarasov, while Brooks was not a Soviet devotee. He was, in fact, like a latter-day Tarasov, in that he used only certain elements of the creative "other" systems—in this case, Soviet and European—that suited him, and integrated them into his own style and system.

It was significant and appropriate when Vairo was brought into the USA Hockey tent for his favorable influence, and he became more impressed with Brooks in later years, particularly when Brooks used him as a consultant with the 1980 Olympic team, and as an assistant coach with the 2002 Olympic team.

CHAPTER 19

OLYMPIC BLUEPRINT

To a man, the players who played for Herb Brooks at the University of Minnesota wouldn't trade the experience for anything. There was no time for Brooks to celebrate the 1979 national title, however, and no real transition from leading the Gophers to creating the 1980 U.S. Olympic team. He had known he'd be coaching it—third choice or not—throughout the 1978–79 season, and his job started immediately after the college season ended, when he coached the U.S. team in the 1979 World Championships in Moscow.

It was the perfect testing ground, maybe more so for Brooks than for his team. Some players made lasting impressions on him there.

Former Gopher Mike Polich was playing in the NHL by then, but he described it perfectly and eloquently: "Herbie knew who he could talk to and get a response, and who wouldn't respond. When it came to the Olympic team, he was going to select guys who could take it and respond. If you throw gasoline on a flower, it might wilt. Herbie didn't want that. He wanted to know that when he threw gasoline, there'd be an explosion."

Brooks had devised a plan to turn his coach-induced explosions from occasionally misfiring and needing a tune-up, to a program that might be more analogous to a finely tuned Formula 1 racecar engine. What would become the incredible story of the 1980 United States Olympic hockey team unfolded through an assortment of factors that included players, skills, styles, coordination—and an almost cosmic confluence of good luck and perfect breaks. All of it was pulled together, of course, by Herb Brooks.

The actual organizational structure began with the experience he gained during his seven years at the University of Minnesota, where his teams rang up a 167-99-2 record. Later coaches would put up better winning percentages, but all of them rode the wave of success Brooks had established in seven short years, leading the Gophers from the bottom of the WCHA to their first three NCAA titles. He fully intended to return to the U after the Olympics, during which Brad Buetow, his assistant, ran the program on an interim basis.

It may have seemed as though Brooks was gazing at the stars when he started his idealistic plot for the 1980 Olympic team. In fact, it took all of the stars aligning in a perfect pattern. It's possible, for example, that Mike Eruzione was considered for the team because four years earlier he had fallen asleep and missed a great opportunity. Eruzione, who helped Boston University reach four consecutive NCAA tournaments, was a young player on the U.S. National Team, run by John Mariucci's informal hand, for the 1976 World Championships in Katowice, Poland. Gary Gambucci, a former Gopher All-American who went on to play in the NHL, joined the U.S. National Team and was Eruzione's teammate at the time.

"On the plane flying across the Atlantic, John gave us a legal pad and a pen to be passed around among the players," said Gambucci. "We were all supposed to put down our names, and what position we wanted to play. Eruzione was sleeping, and nobody wanted to wake him up, so the pad got passed on and nobody thought anything of it. In the tournament, we had a couple extra guys, but I couldn't understand why Eruzione never played. He was great on the bench, always patting guys on the back and always positive—he was our best cheerleader. It turned out, he had never signed up for a position, and John went by that list, so he never put him in.

"Later on, I was having lunch with Herbie when he was just starting to organize his 1980 team. I told Herbie that story and I mentioned that Eruzione was such a great team guy, he might be perfect to consider as captain for his team."

Funny how things work out. Brooks, of course, was painstakingly thorough, and he focused on each player he invited to attend the midsummer 1979 National Sports Festival in Colorado Springs. He also stored away such nuggets of information from sources he trusted.

Brooks was patient when he took the U.S. team to the 1979 World Championships in Moscow. I kidded him that by going to the Soviet Union, he might find a city he liked less than Duluth.

"That was pretty much a team of misfits," joked Phil Verchota, who joined Gopher teammates Bill Baker, Steve Christoff, Eric Strobel, and Rob McClanahan, plus Jim Craig and Jack O'Callahan from Boston University, Mark Johnson from Wisconsin, and an assortment of others that included Bob Collyard from Colorado College, sharpshooter Joey Mullen, and a just-retired pro and former Denver University winger named Craig Patrick.

"I was a late add-on," said Verchota. "Herbie gave me a call, and as I recall, he didn't really ask me if I was interested in playing, he just told me I was coming on the team. I think he called me because he knew I had a passport. We finished something like seventh, but Jimmy Craig played pretty well in goal."

That tournament was where Brooks—always seeking a cure for his anxiety about goaltenders—decided that Craig would be someone he could trust in battle. The tournament was equally significant for Patrick and O'Callahan.

"I realized Herbie was a special guy from the first I met him," said Patrick, who was to become a thoroughly devoted and respectful ally of Brooks for the rest of his life. "We were teammates back in 1970, on a U.S. team that played in the World Championships in Romania. He played defense."

True, Brooks had been a free-skating forward throughout high school at St. Paul Johnson, college at Minnesota, and on U.S. National and Olympic teams beginning in 1961, but he moved back to defense and was there as captain of his final U.S. team in 1970. Maybe his personal experience was another reason why he always was eager to move a smart, good-skating and good puck-handling forward to the blue line.

Patrick, a winger on Denver's NCAA championship teams in 1968 and 1969, went on to play pro hockey with the California Golden Seals, St. Louis Blues, Minnesota Fighting Saints, and Washington Capitals. After the 1978–79 pro season ended, Patrick joined the Brooks-coached U.S. Nationals, where he was named captain for the trip to Moscow.

"On that team in Moscow, Herbie was trying to encourage us to do all those things he liked, opening up on offense," said Patrick. "I thought it was refreshing to be able to move your legs and do some weaving. It was a lot of fun . . . it was great!"

The World Championships went from late April into May 1979. The U.S. finished with a 5-2 loss to West Germany and placed seventh overall.

"Halfway through the World Championships, Herbie pulled me aside and said, 'I'm going to coach the 1980 Olympic team, and I'd like you to think about being my assistant coach,'" Patrick recalled. "He said he had asked someone else, but he suspected that person might turn it down. When we got back, he called and said the guy—and I never knew who it was—had turned it down, and he'd like me to be his assistant.

"I said, 'When do you want me there?' I took my family to St. Louis and went up to Minnesota."

Patrick came from one of the most prominent families in NHL history. His grandfather was Lester Patrick, a legendary NHL icon, and his father was Lynn Patrick, who branched off to run the St. Louis Blues during the NHL expansion in 1967. Craig was not only a good player on his own, he later become an outstanding NHL executive. He also is one of the genuine, good people in the sport, and his always-thoughtful, whisper-quiet, good-guy demeanor was one of the things that Brooks sought.

"Herbie was the master planner," said Patrick. "When I first got there, he said, 'This is what you're going to do: I'm going to be a real prick, and you will have to keep the guys together. The guys from the East and West hate each other, and the only way to keep them from hating each other is to make them all hate me.'"

O'Callahan, a tough, ornery defenseman, was immortalized in the movie *Miracle*, although he was not entirely a willing hero. When the movie about the 1980 team was being made, it had to be cut down from about four hours to two hours. O'Callahan said they couldn't cut a lot of his role out, because the kid playing him in the movie was from Boston, was playing at the University of Maine, and was so good he seemed to wind up in nearly every scene. "So we're going to make you a star," the filmmakers told O'Callahan.

O'Callahan's respect for, and rapport with, Brooks was formed on that 1979 U.S. team—a major shift from the hostilities that lingered from 1976, when Minnesota had brawled and beaten the Terriers in the NCAA semifinals. In the movie, O'Callahan has a fight with former Gopher Rob McClanahan at the first U.S. practice, and O'Callahan's character says it was because McClanahan was on that 1976 team. Actually, McClanahan was a senior at Mounds View High School in 1976.

"That BU–Minnesota thing was just a fight, and it was over with," O'Callahan recalled. "The East–West guys wanted to kill each other, but most of the animosity for me was from the '78 Sports Festival, when we had a bench-clearing brawl, and Steve Christoff and I got into it."

When O'Callahan played for Brooks in Moscow, he said, "I didn't think I played all that well, but after we got back, my agent called and said Herb Brooks didn't want me to sign a pro contract, because he wanted me to come out for the Olympic team. I said, 'He really said that?' because I didn't think I had played very well. My agent said he liked my character, my effort, my attitude, and who I was as a person. His assessment of me didn't have anything to do with how I played.

"He saw all that in me in three weeks? I came away with a whole higher level of respect for him—before the 1979 Sports Festival."

The Sports Festival was an annual summer gathering of top prospects who were invited to the Olympic facilities in Colorado Springs for high-level training and head-to-head competition with other elite players. Brooks was the busiest in the months before the festival, making an endless succession of telephone calls to points in Minnesota, Wisconsin, Michigan, and New England.

"A year before the Olympics, I remember we were over at Herbie's house for some big get-together," said his brother Dave. "Everybody was there, but Herbie wasn't around. I asked Patti where he was, and she said he was down in his office. So I went down there and walked in. He was on the phone. He was calling coaches and teachers and family members of all kinds of players, just trying to find out what kind of people those players really were and if they were good citizens. He wanted to know everything about them down to their traffic tickets."

His thoroughness left Dave shaking his head, but Herbie was covering all the bases. At the National Sports Festival, there would be seventy players divided among four teams. Certainly, Herbie had a pretty good idea about the nucleus of players he already liked, from his Gopher teams, to teams he had coached against, and the U.S. team he coached, but it might be difficult to make some selections. So he guaranteed himself a no-lose situation: If everybody invited was a high-character person, then he wouldn't have to worry about winding up with a whiner or a prima donna. That's as close to a guarantee that a coach could ask for, but no other coach would go through the hours of research Brooks spent investigating every candidate.

Because the movie *Miracle* met with such acclaim, and remains an inspirational source for many teams, hockey and otherwise, it is commonly considered factual, even though many parts of the true story were exaggerated or eliminated for convenience or cinematic effect. One major example is when the Brooks character casually tosses a sheet of paper at the Craig Patrick character and tersely says that's his team—already selected before the Sports Festival tournament. That not only made Brooks appear arrogant, even if the intention was to make him look sure of himself, but it also insults the unbelievably painstaking process he put all the players through for the sake of fairness.

Brooks ingeniously arranged and welcomed input all through the week—from general managers and coaches of pro teams, to college coaches and amateur officials, everybody was invited to participate. Many did, and many sidled up to Brooks and suggested he watch so-and-so closely. Brooks thanked them, with a "consider yourself considered" air of appreciation, when really, he kept his own charts and lists. It was masterful. I'd never seen him work so diplomatically and come so close to playing politics. Normally, he was so direct and blunt that he wasn't always tactful, and he despised the political games he frequently accused AHAUS of playing. (AHAUS, the Amateur Hockey Association of the United States, was the formal name of the governing body of U.S. amateur hockey until it changed to USA Hockey years later.)

Along with team officials, there were countless hockey dignitaries around. John Ziegler, commissioner of the NHL, was there, as was Tommy Ivan, the boss of the Chicago Blackhawks and chairman of the National Sports Festival Ice Hockey Committee. Brooks listened to everything anyone said, but he had his reasons for every move, and he explained it all before the festival got going.

"I was the last guy cut in 1960," Brooks told me, "and it was the day before we went to Squaw Valley. I was fortunate to last that long with guys like Tommy Williams and Billy Christian, because they had a lot of better players.

"I've worked hard to be honest with this. On day one, our advisory staff got together. We had written comments from every Division I and Division II coach in the country, and from [NHL] Central Scouting for their unbiased analysis. A couple of personal friends will also help with the analysis."

The friends were undoubtedly Jack Blatherwick and Warren Strelow.

"We had open tryouts and came up with a composite list, which we gave to the National Sports Festival," Brooks told me. "Here in Colorado Springs, we've had daily meetings with the staff, and each advisor gives a different assessment each day. We'll get recommendations about players on and off the ice. We've also given them all psychological tests, plus we have dry-land training with Jack Blatherwick and electronic tests of speed.

"We gave everyone a weight program to be done from April 1 to now, with stretching, flexibility, aerobic training for endurance, and anaerobic sprints for quickness, because we want to build strength and speed of reaction. We've got to zero in on what the players *can* do. All of the players have liabilities, but we want to be positive. We can't have all the same styles. We've got to build a house out of all different kinds of bricks. We can't go for all speed. The Europeans have strength in close quarters, and Lou Vairo suggests we don't overlook body strength.

"I'm trying to look at this through the eyes of a player. We want to recognize their ability, and their sacrifices, and try to complement it with management doing the same thing. By removing the politicking, any mistakes that will be made will be honest ones."

The players were divided up, with the New England team comprising the East's top players, while the Great Lakes team was mostly Michigan area prospects. Some Minnesota prospects and all of the Wisconsin and North Dakota prospects were on the Central team, and the Midwest team was all Minnesotans.

The coaches and general managers of each of the four teams were volunteers, and Brooks was determined to be straight and honest with players who might have alternatives if not chosen for the Olympic team. "We've got a player like Les Auge, who's got a possible pro contract," said Brooks. "Tom Ross has a possible teaching contract. We want to let them know their possibilities and not lead them on if it might cost them the chance to do something elsewhere.

"If I was a player, I'd like a moment to be by myself. So I've explained to all seventy players what we're doing. We've going to be tough on college underclassmen in the selections, because we can't move you up and down to college, the way we can with the IHL [International Hockey League], although we can bring them up if we need to.

"And no matter what anybody thinks about the selections, we cannot discount previous performance."

Perfect. And fair. If a great player was hampered by injury, Brooks left himself some wiggle room to select a player on known ability and performance, even if someone outplayed that player at the festival.

It was a totally comprehensive organizational plan, from the lowest-ranked player to the officials and executives. Brooks made everyone feel a part of the process and the decision. To this day, many of the team officials in attendance at the National Sports Festival in July 1979 might claim to have had some connection with choosing or administering the 1980 U.S. Olympic team.

But really, it was all put together, executed, and selected by one man: Herb Brooks.

CHAPTER 20

SPORTS FESTIVAL DRAMA

The National Sports Festival in Colorado Springs was a far more elaborate event than I had imagined. I was among those who shared a skepticism when AHAUS located itself in that city. It fit in so well with the stereotype of the organization—a group of hockey guys who became bigshots through their adept manipulation of amateur hockey throughout the United States.

Every American kid playing youth hockey winds up sending money to the group (now USA Hockey), which had to be located somewhere. To a Minnesotan, it seemed logical that the governing body might be in Minnesota, where more kids play amateur hockey than anywhere else. Once you've been to Colorado Springs, however, and gazed up at Pikes Peak while sucking in that crisp mountain air, you can understand why that location was selected. When the directors had to get out of the office to discuss important issues, what's better than doing business during a round of golf at the Broadmoor Country Club?

The Broadmoor is a palatial old resort that had a strange, old ice arena, and still has a fabulous golf course. But across town in Colorado Springs, there is an entire village set up with barracks-type housing, as well as extensive and complete training and testing facilities.

WCHA teams used to stay at the Broadmoor, albeit in rooms more like servant's quarters than in the upper-crust lodgings where patrons—and the occasional wandering journalist—enjoyed the good life. A walk around the courtyard pool brought you to the arena, which had a unique layout. The rink was almost square, a bit shorter than regulation, and maybe a bit wider, with seats at both ends, only a few rows for fans on the press-box side, and a large, barely sloping grandstand opposite. Clearly, the place was perfect for national and international figure skating events back in the days before large and glamorous arenas were built in every city, and it passed for a hockey rink with very deep, square corners.

The press box was something else. To get there, journalists from skinny to chubby walked up the few rows of seats to a wooden-rung ladder fastened to the wall, then, getting a firm grip on typewriters (in that era) and maybe a briefcase, climbed up and through a square trapdoor that measured less than 3×3 feet. I've seen some of my chunkier colleagues struggle to work themselves up through that opening. After that, covering the game was easy, although coming back down was no treat, either. The other special feature of the press box was that you had to crouch down like a poster boy for bad posture in order to walk along the actual press row, otherwise you would conk your head on the large boards presumably holding the ceiling up. Any exuberant reporter, or on-deadline hustler who leaped out of his chair to scramble after a quick postgame quote, would often jump up, then sit back down until the stars cleared from his sight.

It was there where the seventy players on the four Sports Festival hockey teams would do battle from July 27 through the first week of August.

Inside the arena, the results of the games didn't matter so much as how certain players played. Covering the selection process for the paper gave me the chance to watch carefully, looking for the attributes I knew Brooks liked, and weighing them with the skill level and dedication I knew that the Gophers and other WCHA players brought with them.

The Great Lakes team, led by center Mark Wells and defenseman Ken Morrow, beat New England 5-3; then the Midwest team, consisting wholly of Minnesota players, bombarded New England (Jim Craig notwithstanding) 10-5, and Great Lakes beat the Central team 6-1. Mark Johnson, from Wisconsin, was injured in one of the early games, as was Eric Strobel, leaving the Central team short.

But one of the interesting showdowns came when the Central team came back to beat the Midwest 6-4, outscoring their opponents 4-1 in the third period. There was a lot of rough stuff and chippy play in the second period. Central's Bob Suter, from Wisconsin, nailed Neal Broten in front, triggering a skirmish that saw Verchota fight Suter and Steve Christoff engage in another battle.

Steve Janaszak played brilliantly, blanking Central after Dave Christian's early goal and leaving with a 3-1 lead at the halfway point. His partner, Blane Comstock, was a solid goalie who had national team experience and had played at Bemidji State, but he struggled that night. Tim Harrer's goal restored a 4-3 lead for Midwest, but Central came back with two goals in fifty-eight seconds, and Christian hit an empty net for a hat trick.

Craig didn't play any more for New England, which outlasted Central 10-8. It was ragged and sloppy, and nobody did themselves much good in Brooks' view.

John Harrington, who had starred for three years at Virginia (Minnesota) High School and then four years at Minnesota-Duluth, had prepared himself superbly, first by taking Brooks' workout plan beyond its limits. He worked out with weights on Mondays, Wednesdays, and Fridays, and worked with a U.S. Air Force Academy physical-education instructor, running stairs and doing other cardiovascular training Tuesdays, Thursdays, and Saturdays. In addition, he worked on techniques and endurance with a figure skating instructor Monday through Thursday. He continued that regimen from the end of his college term right through to the Friday before the Sports Festival started. "I weigh 183 now, and I weighed 180 during last season," he said. "I gained the weight from lifting weights. I know it's been a lot of work, but all the guys from Minnesota are winners—all of 'em. And they go all-out, all the time."

Harrington knew that Brooks could have pretty much taken his entire Gopher team and made a representative showing at the Olympics, which also indicated to him what was required to make the team. Harrington and Mark Pavelich, his UMD linemate, both played amid most of the Gophers on the Midwest team. Mark Wells was similarly prepared for the Central team and trained with his Bowling Green teammate, Ken Morrow, at the latter's place in Flint, Michigan. "Brooks gave us all a training program, and we did a lot of running," Wells said. "It's a good thing we did. There are a lot of good players here, and they're all scoring."

Meanwhile, off in a corner of the dressing room, Janaszak was talking to Comstock. "We know what you can do, Commer, so just relax and do it." Interesting, the twenty-one-year-old kid just out of college trying to counsel the veteran. Comstock did come back with a strong game as Midwest beat Great Lakes 6-5. Scoring twice for Great Lakes was Mike Eruzione, a transplanted Boston guy who had played two years at Toledo in the International League, which wasn't considered a pro league at the time.

These were high-test, emotional games, and the "advisors," as well as Brooks and his staff, watched intently. As planned, all four teams played each other once each, and the bronze-medal game Saturday afternoon was between the Central and New England teams, while the tournament concluded Saturday night with the gold-medal game between Great Lakes and Midwest.

I had watched just as intently and kept my own chart of players. Brooks announced that he would tell the players at the end of the tournament who would be selected for the twenty-five-player roster. He also said he would release the team to the media after the gold-medal game. That, of course, would be after 10 p.m., and closer to 11.

I challenged Brooks on this because at 10 p.m. in Colorado Springs, it would already be 11 p.m. in Minnesota, Wisconsin, and Chicago, and midnight in Boston and New York. No major media in the biggest hockey-playing areas would get a sniff of the team when it was announced. But there was no way Brooks was going to change his mind.

So I came up with a plan. I pulled out my big wirebound pad and made some notes, putting together my own choices, but tempering some of them with what I suspected Brooks would want. It was time to read his mind for real. On Saturday morning I went to Brooks' room and rapped on the door. He let me in and invited me to sit down. I joked around with him about how I had watched all these hockey bigshots at the Sports Festival act like they were major influences on Brooks' decisions. I said I knew he was going to consider all the input, but I also knew he was picking *his* team.

Then I said that since there was no way the *Minneapolis Tribune* could get his official announcement into any editions of the Sunday paper, I was going to write a feature story speculating on who I thought would make the team. I would temper it with conditional terms, such as "it is believed these will be the goaltenders," and "it is expected that Brooks will take these defensemen." Plus, I told him, I had an advantage because I could read his mind. He laughed.

"I've made up my list of players, and I want to show it to you," I said. "I don't care if I embarrass myself, and you certainly don't have to tip me off to anything, but if I'm way off on somebody, you could avoid some embarrassment for a player I pick if he has no chance. So I'd like you to look over my list."

Herbie took the list, and I sat back in the chair. At the top, I had written goalies, and had Jim Craig from BU, Steve Janaszak from Minnesota, and Bruce Horsch from Michigan Tech by way of Halifax of the American League. "Well, you got the three goalkeepers," he said.

Below them, I had listed the defensemen: Bill Baker, Mike Ramsey, and Les Auge from Minnesota, Ken Morrow from Bowling Green, Jack O'Callahan from BU, Bob Suter from Wisconsin, Jack Hughes from Harvard, and Gary Ross from Bemidji State. "Hmmm," said Brooks, "you got all eight defensemen, too."

Then he started checking off my list of forwards: Phil Verchota, Steve Christoff, Rob McClanahan, Buzz Schneider, Eric Strobel, and Neal Broten, all from Minnesota; Dave Christian from North Dakota; Mark Pavelich and John Harrington from UMD; Mark Johnson from Wisconsin; Craig Homola from Vermont; Dave Silk and Mike Eruzione from BU; Dave Delich from Colorado College; and Ralph Cox from New Hampshire. Brooks got about halfway through, then reached down beside his chair and opened his attache case, pulling out a legal pad. "This is my own private list, which nobody else has seen," said Brooks. "I'm only pulling it out to show you that you got every player except one."

"Really?" I said. "And I'll bet I know which one."

Brooks asked me which one I thought was wrong, and I said, "You see where

Craig Homola's name is? Next to that, see the little star? That's an asterisk. Look down at the bottom of the page."

There I had written: "Played well enough to make the team, but you're going to send him back to Vermont and try to bring him up just before the Olympics."

"You son of a bitch," Herbie said. "That's exactly what I plan to do."

Mind-reading? No, just good hunches.

Only one thing, I told Herbie. In the bronze and gold games, somebody could score three goals, or a goalie could sieve out, and he might change his mind on more than one or two players. "You're right," he said. So I made one request. "I'm writing the story for our early edition, with all these conditional words to indicate that all twenty-five names are speculation," I told him. "So when the gold game ends, look at me in the press box. If you decide to make any changes, give me a thumbs-down, and I'll leave the conditional words in every paragraph; if you're not going to make any changes, give me a thumbs-up, and I'll pull all the conditional words to turn my conjecture into fact."

I hustled to write my story and sent it back to Minneapolis, explaining carefully to the desk guys what was going on. They weren't hockey types, but they understood a novel idea and went for it.

Central beat New England 7-4 in the third-place game, as Mark Johnson returned to the lineup to score a goal, although Strobel was still out. Both of them were cinches to make the team anyway, by anyone's judgment.

In the gold-medal game—a rematch of the game in which Midwest had beaten Great Lakes 6-5—Midwest jumped to a 2-0 lead in the first period. The second period remained scoreless until 19:30, when Homola, a slick centerman from Eveleth, beat Janaszak on a breakaway. Later, Homola scored again to cap a stunning 4-2 turnaround. The Midwest line of Pavelich centering Harrington and McClanahan buzzed the net, but Bruce Horsch was brilliant, stopping all fifteen shots he faced in the second half of the game. "I knew they were looking closely at maybe four or five goaltenders," said Horsch. "I was just trying to eliminate the bad goals."

After the final buzzer sounded, Herbie looked over at me in the press box and gave me a thumbs-up. I grabbed the phone, gave the word, and the sports desk pulled the conditional terms out of the story, which stood as a scoop for the whole world on the roster for the 1980 U.S. Olympic hockey team.

Brooks immediately realized that naming so many University of Minnesota players to his roster would have consequences, and he set about to eliminate the provincialism that he had described to Craig Patrick as a potential problem.

The problem at Minnesota was more imposing. Brad Buetow took over the Gophers without five key underclassmen: Christoff, McClanahan, Strobel, Broten, and Ramsey. The other Gophers Brooks named to the Olympic team—Janaszak, Baker, Auge, Verchota, and Schneider—had all completed their eligibility. Auge was playing at Oklahoma City in the Central League, and Schneider at Milwaukee in the IHL, while the others had just finished their senior seasons.

The National Hockey League amateur draft followed, and the benefit of having so many NHL executives and scouts at the Sports Festival became apparent when Mike Ramsey went to Buffalo with the eleventh pick of the first round, and Christian and Broten were drafted by Winnipeg and Minnesota, respectively, in the second round.

"I talked to [Buffalo general manager] Scotty Bowman, and he said he was very impressed with Ramsey and Broten," Brooks told me. "This is the fifth straight year we've produced the top American in the draft, with Ramsey, Christoff, Gorence, Reed Larson, and Russ Anderson."

CHAPTER 21

LONG SEASON TO PREPARE

As part of the exhaustive preparations Herb Brooks put together for the 1980 team, he created the most taxing schedule of exhibition games ever compiled for an Olympic squad. Obviously, while picking the roster and sending a few notable players back to their colleges for possible future consideration, Brooks was aware that there was much more work still to do.

The best way to test the players was to travel the world in search of the toughest competition, part of the typical Brooks overload training. Important as the competition was, Brooks also needed time to instill the intricacies of his philosophies in the team.

He had seven years to set up a Gopher culture in which freshmen joined up and fit right in with the already established systems. He had just seven months to try to get Team USA to become a true team—and, in fact, the first team to be called Team USA. A schedule of ten exhibitions in Holland, Finland, and Norway got things going in what would become legendary fashion. If Brooks wanted to assert his discipline on the team, the first of two games against Norway at the tail end of the European tour provided the opportunity, when the United States played to a tie against a clearly inferior team. Afterward, Brooks fumed the way he always fumed—by taking action. He kept the players on the ice, just as the movie *Miracle* portrayed it, and made them skate the hated Herbies.

The non-Gophers on the team thought the incident proved Brooks was capable of going psycho. Late-departing Norwegian fans were amazed, and the arena staff just wanted to go home. To the ex-Gophers, however, it was no big deal.

"Billy Baker and I were talking," recalled Verchota, twenty-seven years after the fact. "We were saying, 'Did Norway really happen?' It did, all right.

"The minute Herb said, 'Over here,' we all knew exactly what we were in for. We went for something over a half hour, literally until they turned the lights off. Actually, we had done those Herbies so many times with the Gophers that even the thing in Norway was light."

Buzz Schneider hadn't dressed for the game. Sitting in the stands with Craig Patrick, he felt guilty and asked Patrick if he should go put his equipment on and join the punishment skate.

"In the movie, they made a big thing of that skate after the game in Norway," Mike Ramsey said. "It wasn't that big a deal. A couple of us had been thrown out of the game for fighting. They called it really tight, and they weren't really fights, but we had showered and gotten dressed. When he started skating the guys, we all felt guilty and asked Craig if we should go back out there. He said not to, because they were almost done, but they kept on going—and they did turn the lights off."

Gary Smith, Herbie's trusted trainer and confidante, got a call from Brooks in the summer of 1979, after Brooks had picked the team, and agreed to go along as trainer. Smith had left the university when he got a disagreeable reassignment, and started a company called the Institute for Athletic Medicine in the Twin Cities after the 1976–77 season. He was happy to rejoin Brooks, and he recalled the Norway incident, too. "The people running the Zamboni came and asked us to leave, but Herbie kept skating them," Smith said. "A guy went to turn off the lights, and Herbie skated them in the dark. Nobody could believe it. Mark Johnson crashed into the boards, but he sent them again."

In the Gopher days, however, those drills might consume all of a Monday practice, continuing after resurfacing and with timed requirements, so the former Gophers got a chuckle out of it when their new teammates expressed disbelief, to say nothing of queasy stomachs.

The following night, Team USA beat Norway 9-0.

After ten games in Europe, the North American portion of the team's preparation called for 52 games in 134 days, from September 29, 1979, through February 9, 1980, when it would conclude the pre-Olympic tour against the Soviet Union's full team at Madison Square Garden, before both teams made their way upstate to Lake Placid. Those fifty-two games would be against teams from the National Hockey League, the American Hockey League, the Western Hockey League, the Central Hockey League, and the International Hockey League (including one with the IHL All-Stars). These would be interspersed with games against top U.S. college teams and other international teams, including eight against Canada, six against the Soviet Union, a single game against Sweden and Czechoslovakia—and one game against the Warroad Lakers, a senior men's team. U.S. teams had always played Warroad, a tradition that paid respect to Cal Marvin, who operated the team from the little border town that repeatedly won Canadian Allen Cups against senior teams from north of the border. Brooks was honored to maintain the tradition.

One of my pleasures as the hockey beat writer for the *Minneapolis Tribune* was covering the U.S. team as it practiced and played at Met Center in Bloomington,

Minnesota, and at Williams Arena and the Duluth Arena. All the while I continued to cover the North Stars, Minnesota colleges, and the high schools, as time permitted. Scotty Bowman was coach and general manager of the Buffalo Sabres, and he kept close tabs on Mike Ramsey after drafting him in the first round of the August 1979 draft, as well as on Rob McClanahan, a third-round pick in 1978, and Eric Strobel, an eighth-round pick, also in 1978.

"Ramsey is a great skater, McClanahan plays the way I like him to play, and Strobel has a great skating stride," Bowman told me before an October North Stars game in Buffalo. "And Brooks is a top coach, really strong on fundamentals, so Ramsey and those other players will be better prepared to step in at the NHL level. They're skilled, and with Brooks, they'll know what they have to do. Brooks gives them better training than the junior players we've drafted and will send back to junior."

Bowman monitored his prospects with the U.S. team by taping their telecasts off cable. Trying to break free of the NHL's stifling traditions, he also sent his assistant, Roger Neilson, to the press box and hooked him up to the bench by headphones, just as football teams do. "There has been no innovation in the NHL for many years," Bowman explained. "Nobody comes up with something different, and all the teams play the same way. Look at Europe!"

It's interesting that the top coach in the NHL was so impressed with Brooks, and was also impatient with the NHL's inability to keep up with the Europeans in innovative hockey. At the moment, Bowman was watching videotape of Team USA playing Canada. Craig shut out Canada 6-0, as Neal Broten scored three in the second period, and Steve Christoff, Schneider, and Baker each got one.

The U.S. squad returned to the Twin Cities for a game against the University of Minnesota at the St. Paul Civic Center. "When I was at the U, we beat the U.S. Olympic team 5-2 in Eveleth four years ago," Brooks recalled. "So we've spent a lot of time with the psychology of being ready."

With Brooks, of course, the psychology wasn't always gentle. John Harrington, from UMD, recalled getting what Herbie might have intended to be constructive criticism—with an edge.

Harrington had played for Dave Hendrickson at Virginia, Minnesota, and for his younger brother, Gus Hendrickson, at UMD. Both Hendricksons were astute, progressive hockey minds and good friends of Herbie's, so it was easy to see why Harrington had a progressive sense of the game before he got to Brooks. "When I was a senior at Duluth, we were playing Minnesota, and I saw Herb, and he said hello, and I thought, 'Whoa!'" said Harrington. "Then I scored a shorthanded goal at Minnesota, and I hoped maybe I'd had a good enough game to get a chance to be invited for a tryout."

He was, along with his centerman, Mark Pavelich. Things seemed to be going well, and when Team USA went over to the St. Paul Civic Center for a practice, it wound up on the ice in the adjacent old auditorium. "It was pretty dark over there, and I was sitting on a bench, bent over tying my skates," Harrington added. "I was aware somebody came and sat next to me, but I didn't look up while I tied my skates. Then this guy sitting next to me says, 'You might be the worst defensive player I've ever seen. Didn't those Hendricksons teach you anything?' It was Herb, of course, and apparently he didn't think much of my backchecking. I never looked up, and he got up and walked away.

"He was great for getting his message across that way. One time he went up to Dave Silk and said, 'I don't know if you can't skate, or if you won't skate, but I'm going to find out.' Then he walked out. Silk said, sarcastically, 'He must not like my skating.'"

The Gophers, especially players like Tim Harrer, Steve Ulseth, and freshman Aaron Broten, were sky-high to face the Olympic team, but it didn't matter. Brooks had the U.S. team psyched. McClanahan scored twice and Mark Johnson once for a 3-1 first period, then Christoff scored twice in the second period, and Johnson added two in the third for a hat trick. Silk scored on a breakaway pass from Ramsey, and it ended 8-2, before 13,765 fans.

"We can't get too sophisticated, too uppity, or we'll cut our own throats," Brooks reasoned, after the Gophers had outshot the U.S. team 39-37. "Mark Johnson is a helluva player. He's got all the skills. If he wants to play in the National Hockey League, he will. I'm a lot happier for those players from other teams to score now; you despise someone like Johnson when he's on the other team because he kills you."

Now the Gopher-dominated Olympians were the "other team" for the Gophers, and vice versa. "It was strange playing against them," McClanahan said. "It was a big game for us because we wanted to play well. It was weird when they played the rouser and to be on the other side. The Gophs have the championship and tradition, and they're gonna be good."

Brooks took the team to Flint to play that city's IHL club on October 30. "It was Ken Morrow day," Brooks explained. "They're doing a fundraiser and having clinics. So I left Jim Craig, Baker, Broten, and Christian home. I'm playing Pavelich with Schneider and Harrington; Johnson between Strobel and Eruzione; Christoff with Silk and McClanahan; and Mark Wells centering Ralph Cox and Verchota. Strobel hasn't scored since Finland. That's eleven games without a goal, and Verchota was in a slump of twelve games without a goal, and Silk has had one goal in his last eleven games.

"I want to split Janaszak and Horsch in goal, because it's tough on them to sit. Neither has had any work for the last nine games. I played Craig all through that stretch, because he was hurt at the Sports Festival, so he didn't get any work early, and we wanted to go with him. That's the American way: number one gets the job. I'm going to Craig in big games, because he's the one who can turn it around for us.

"Craig has a lot of poise and stands on his feet. He has good concentration, controls his rebounds, and knows his angles. And he doesn't come unglued. He's solid, and he knows his way around the net. He was MVP of our team in Moscow [in 1979]. I had followed him. I saw him at the Great Lakes Tournament at Christmas, and he wasn't that hot, but he became number one when he got the chance. . . . In Colorado, he hurt his hand, but his goals-against average is 1.50, and he hasn't given up any cheap goals, the kind that can demoralize a team."

Craig Patrick immersed himself in the assistant-coaching duties Brooks set out for him, and had an easier time of it because of general manager Ken Johannson's schedule. "Ken had a full-time job at the Mayo Clinic, so he asked if I could be assistant general manager as well as assistant coach," Patrick said. "That helped me, because I got to know the players better, and their families, and I could be something like their big brother."

Johannson was an exemplary manager—except for one detail. Brooks had everything so thoroughly arranged and managed that Team USA didn't really need anything more than a traveling secretary. From the start, it seemed Brooks was more often annoyed than aided when Johannson's well-intentioned organizational moves actually caused Brooks to have to change his plans. When I asked him if those clashes might not become a problem, Brooks said no, he could adjust and everything would be all right. That proved to be untrue, however, and Johannson turned the managerial duties over to Ralph Jasinski on November 1.

"I don't really know all the details of Ken leaving, but Ralph was fine, and he at least could see what Brooks had put in place and didn't try to do too much," Patrick recalled.

Brooks worked primarily through Art Kaminsky, who served as agent to many of the Olympians, to try to prevent key Olympians from leaving for the pros until after the Olympics were over. Interesting that when Brooks tried to do some things for the sake of some players, they misunderstood. He was going to send Gary Ross to Dayton of the IHL, but Ross said he might quit playing rather than go. Ralph Cox, whose rights were owned by the Boston Bruins, had a great shot, but his lack of outright speed was a concern to Brooks. Les Auge, another ex-Gopher and one of Brooks' favorites,

1980 USA Olympic Ice Hockey Team (as of August 3, 1979)

Front row   Steve Janaszak, Mark Johnson, Dr. Nagobads, Buddy Kessel, Ken Johannson, Jim Craig, Herb Brooks, Craig Patrick, Bruce Horsch
Middle row   Bob Webster, Jack O'Callahan, Steve Christoff, Mike Ramsey, Phil Verchota, Ken Morrow, Jack Hughes, Bill Baker, Dave Delich, Les Auge, Gary Ross, Warren Strelow
Back row   John Harrington, David Silk, Eric Strobel, Neal Broten, Rob McClanahan, David Christian, Bob Suter, Mike Eruzione, Buzz Schneider, Mark Pavelich, Mark Wells

Schedule

SEPTEMBER	29	Saturday	Minnesota North Stars - Met Sports Center
OCTOBER	14	Sunday	Canadian Olympic Team - Met Sports Center
	23	Tuesday	University of Minnesota - **St. Paul Civic Center**
NOVEMBER	4	Sunday	Birmingham (CHL) - Met Sports Center
	20	Tuesday	Salt Lake City (CHL) - Met Sports Center
	27	Tuesday	Canadian Olympic Team - Met Sports Center
DECEMBER	2	Sunday	Cincinnati (CHL) - Met Sports Center
	6	Thursday	Oklahoma City (CHL) - Met Sports Center
	30	Sunday	Russian Olympics - Met Sports Center
JANUARY	15	Wednesday	University of Wisconsin - Met Sports Center
	25	Friday	Ft. Worth (CHL) - Met Sports Center
	31	Thursday	Dallas (CHL) - Met Sports Center

ALL GAMES START AT 7:30 P.M.

A promotional poster advertising a portion of the 1980 Olympic team's barnstorming tour (as well as Schmidt beer). This team photo includes most of the roster's last cuts: Bruce Horsch, Jack Hughes, Dave Delich, Les Auge, and Gary Ross. Missing is another final cut, Ralph Cox.

was also on the bubble and unlikely to survive the cut from eight to six defensemen for the Olympic Games. Brooks told him that if he had the chance to sign a pro contract, maybe he should sign. "I had my mind set on trying to make it for a couple of years," Auge said of Team USA, "but I don't want anyone to do me any favors."

In November, the Birmingham Bulls of the Central Hockey League came to Minnesota to face the U.S. squad. George Brophy, a wild man of a coach, had a rugged team, and it was another lesson for the U.S. skaters. Brooks had just made Eruzione captain, and Eruzione celebrated with a goal at 19:59 of the second period to make it 3-1. In the third period, Mike Perovich tackled Ramsey, Serge Beaudoin dropped Strobel, and Christoff and Dave Hanson—the ex–St. Paul Humboldt tough guy who had played one of the Hanson Brothers in the movie *Slap Shot*—also tangled. Bob Suter dropped a Birmingham player in retaliation, so Ray Adduono kicked Silk's skates out from under him.

A Birmingham goal closed it to 3-2, then Hanson suckered Ramsey. "Just one of those things that happen," Hanson shrugged. It was doubtful the young Olympians would see anything close to that assault in Lake Placid, but they stood in there. When Bill Baker scored on the ensuing power play, and Suter shot one in off McClanahan's skate, they had a 5-2 victory.

McClanahan, always a target for Brooks because he came from the wealthy North Oaks suburb of the Twin Cities, said that "instead of taking the summer off, I worked my butt off with weights, and shot 200 pucks every day. I went to Colorado confident. We're doing some different things, and it's working with a more mature team."

On Thanksgiving weekend, Canada came to Met Center after the two teams had played three times in Calgary. McClanahan's first-period goal staked the U.S. team to a 1-0 lead after a period, but Canada—which, like the United States, was using amateur players against the best European elite-leaguers—tied the game in the second period, and Glenn Anderson, a future Edmonton Oiler, scored the winner in the third.

"That's the fourth straight game we've taken an early lead and lost after giving up goals early in periods," Brooks pointed out. "There's a lot of hesitancy in our game right now. We're in a slump and we're not forcing our way through it. We won ten in a row, and maybe we could lose ten in a row."

Brooks couldn't help but note that while the U.S. players struggled against the tedium of the long schedule—and their coach—the University of Minnesota lost twice at home to North Dakota. In the 7-6 overtime second game, Tim Harrer—one of those college guys Brooks sent back to school with an eye toward a possible recall before the Olympics—had scored a first-period goal, then three more in the second period to bring the Gophers close. Harrer's rocketry prompted North Dakota coach Gino Gasparini to say, "If Harrer can't play for the U.S. Olympic team, I'll get out of coaching. He's one of the best forwards in college hockey, and he's the best shooter."

Without a doubt, the U.S. forwards caught the comment, too. On December 2, the CHL's Cincinnati Stingers came to the Twin Cities, and Team USA went on a 6-1 romp. Oklahoma City, a CHL squad, came in next for a reunion of sorts, which the Olympians won 5-3. Afterward, Dave Delich, a forward from Eveleth, Minnesota, who Brooks had cut from the twenty-six-man roster, commented, "I haven't heard from Herb. Last time I talked to him, he said keep working. I'm trying to keep some of his ideas in mind in the pro system."

At the end of December, Gorky Torpedo from the Soviet Union came to play the Gophers and won 8-6, after the Gophers scored four straight goals in the third period to close it to 7-6. Tim Harrer had two of the goals in the rally, giving him goals in eight straight games.

Gorky Torpedo then faced Team USA, and the U.S. players unloaded in a 10-3 blowout. The United States was 33-12-1. "They underestimated us, damn right," said Brooks of the Soviet team. "We're throwing their stuff right back at 'em. I changed all the lines tonight, and I might make a couple changes. I'm not saying. Several players on this team don't have guarantees, while twelve or thirteen do."

Was it a veiled threat?

Late in the preparatory schedule, Brooks made a couple of critical moves. Dave Christian had played well at center, but Brooks had Mark Johnson, Mark Pavelich, Neal Broten, and Mark Wells at center, while Steve Christoff, Eric Strobel, and Rob McClanahan were strong centermen already playing wing. Brooks would never have cut Christian; in fact, he wanted to get him into more action. So he made a dramatic move and shifted Christian back to defense, a position he had never played at Warroad High School or at the University of North Dakota, nor would he ever play it after the Olympics, during a long and outstanding NHL career. But Christian became yet another player—like Joe Micheletti and even Brooks himself—who successfully used his speed, intelligence, and excellent puck-handling skills to become an outstanding defenseman.

Moving Christian to the blue line facilitated another couple of moves toward the mandatory cut-down to twenty players for the Olympic Games. Goaltender Bruce Horsch was a solid and capable performer, but he was third, behind Craig and Janaszak, and only two goaltenders could be kept. On defense, Gary Ross and Les Auge had already been let go, but the team was still two players over. It was difficult, but forward Ralph Cox and defenseman Jack Hughes became the final cuts.

CHAPTER 22

FINAL ROSTER FOR LAKE PLACID

By the time the long, exhausting exhibition season reached its legendary final game before the Olympics, Herb Brooks had carried off one of the most amazing tactical, strategic, physical, and mental team-preparation operations in the history of ice hockey, if not sports in general. To some of the players, it was complicated; to others—especially the former Gophers—it was just a step up from what they already had gone through. Some of the Olympians may not even have been fully aware of how cleverly Brooks had raised their level of individual and team play, while also altering and adjusting their view of how to play the game.

Athletes in all sports benefit from an ability to anticipate. In some cases it is purely guesswork, such as when a batter correctly guesses that a fastball is coming on the outside corner, or a linebacker predicts that the next play will be an end sweep his way, or a basketball player anticipates a no-look pass to the big guy in the paint. The best players hone their instincts to come up with the best guesses. In hockey, that all comes under the general heading of "hockey sense." Successful hockey players lift the sport to the highest level of spontaneity and excitement by constantly gauging their opponents, at a high speed and on both offense and defense, and trying to fool them. This aids coverage on defense and can create offense by playing to openings. The best hockey players not only anticipate openings, but also create openings that only they can foresee.

That's what made Wayne Gretzky, as well as Valery Kharlamov and countless other Europeans, seem so superior to their peers. Other players were bigger, stronger, faster, or more aggressive, but the best players had better hockey sense.

While many astute coaches assume that great hockey sense is a gift that allows certain players to "see the ice" better than their peers, Brooks believed all players could heighten and improve hockey sense with drills and training that enhanced skills and quick thinking. As demanding as his conditioning drills were, his systems were aimed at leveraging a disciplined sense of defensive play with unfettered creativity.

With the 1980 Olympic team, he had only those seven months, during which his players advanced from anticipating in a somewhat mechanical manner, to instinctively putting themselves in a better position to succeed.

Brooks called it "sophisticated pond hockey," because he knew that the freedom to experiment and develop skills, dekes, and passing is a staple of unstructured pickup games on outdoor ice. That lack of structure is what makes pond hockey so exhilarating, as players constantly seek to win one-on-one duels and to find—or create—two-on-one advantages. Brooks selected players for their perceived hockey sense in addition to their skill, and then tried to "unstructure" them into a pond-hockey mentality, where they might function well in the face of extreme pressure, or make a move they had never attempted before.

Brooks was astonished at the talent Neal Broten had brought from Roseau, Minnesota, to the University of Minnesota the previous year, when he scored seventy-one points and earned Brooks' praise as the greatest freshman player ever at Minnesota. Similarly, Brooks was most impressed by the skill level of three players who had given his Gophers so many problems over the years: Mark Johnson of Wisconsin, Mark Pavelich of the University of Minnesota-Duluth, and Dave Christian of the University of North Dakota.

That is not to demean any of the other players; all were capable of making plays that could lift fans out of their seats. But Johnson, Pavelich, and Christian did those things consistently enough that they became routine, and routinely expected.

Of the three, Johnson was the most refined, and was so smooth that when he beat you, it was almost painless. Christian was smooth, too, but played with a combination of pickup-game glee filtered through the grittiness of forceful determination. Pavelich was the least refined of the three because he was the truest rink-rat on the team, but he also was arguably the most skilled. He made spectacular plays with computer-perfect precision, yet on virtually every shift, he also created numerous "could've" or "should've" scoring chances by doing subtle things. You never wanted to take your eyes off Pav, because of the feeling that he hadn't yet made his greatest play, and that it might come on the next shift.

Johnson and Pavelich were three-year WCHA stars, Christian was at North Dakota for two seasons, and Broten had only one year of college experience. With each passing day, all drew closer to attaining a level of consistent creativity.

Arguably no other player could have done what Christian did. The son of Billy Christian, a star of the 1960 U.S. team's upset of the Soviet Union at Squaw Valley, California, Dave was a standout from youth hockey, through Warroad High School, and then at North Dakota, where, despite his brilliance in the title-clinching game against the Gophers, he was used more as a worker bee amid the Canadian-dominated talent recruited by coach Gino Gasparini.

Dave Christian's rink-rat days were spent on the Warroad River, and because his dad and uncles, Roger and Gordon, were all elite players and still competed with the senior amateur Warroad Lakers, there was always a key to the Warroad Arena around. "I can remember getting inside, and edging along the wall, feeling my way along in the pitch black to find the lights so I could skate," Dave said.

Always an adept scorer, Christian hadn't always been put in position to score. After recording eight goals and sixteen assists as a freshman with the Fighting Sioux, he had twenty-two goals and twenty-four assists as a sophomore. That looks impressive by today's standards, but in 1978–79 he was only tied for forty-eighth in WCHA scoring and ranked sixth on the team in league points.

"In high school, I visited two places: Minnesota and North Dakota," Christian recalled. "One of the reasons I decided on North Dakota was that Brad Buetow, who was Herbie's assistant, called me and said they were going to ask me to take less for my scholarship because they were trying to get enough together for a partial to another defenseman. I thought I deserved a full, so I went where they offered me a full.

"I was very frustrated my first year at North Dakota, and I talked to my dad about how if it was going to be that way, maybe I had made a mistake in where I was going. In my sophomore year, it wasn't much better until I went with the U.S. Junior team to the World Junior tournament over the holidays. When I came back, I played a lot more the second half of the season. But I killed penalties more than playing in offensive situations, because we had guys like Mark Taylor, Dougie Smail, and Kevin Maxwell, who played on the power play."

Billy Christian had scored the winning goal when the United States beat the Soviet Union 3-2 in the 1960 Olympics, but Dave wouldn't get that opportunity, because about midseason with the 1980 Olympic squad, his role changed. Brooks started to ask him if he'd ever played defense, then asked it more and more. "We were playing in a tournament at about Christmastime and he said, 'You're going to play defense tonight.' He put me with Billy Baker, and I wouldn't say I felt comfortable, but I didn't feel out of place, either," Christian recalled. "Honestly, as long as I played, I didn't care where I played, and the fact that Herbie trusted me to go back to D, I didn't think much about it."

Brooks had watched the great Johnny Mayasich switch back to defense in his later years with U.S. National and Olympic teams. Brooks had done the same thing with players like Joe Micheletti at Minnesota, and he himself moved back to defense to finish his years with U.S. National Team in the late 1960s. With Brooks, such a move was never intended to restrain a player, but to broaden the flexibility of the defensive corps by adding a dynamic rusher and playmaker.

"The interesting thing is that, at forward, we had a lot of forechecking things to key on, and at D, there really wasn't anything to think about," Christian continued. "You covered your position on defense, but when you got the puck, you could take off and go—the length of the ice if it was open. At forward, you had to be aware of what their second defenseman was doing, and read off keys about how much time you had to get to a guy before he could make a play. At defense, you just played."

So Dave Christian, who always tended to his defensive responsibilities as a forward, made a seamless transition to defense, where he paired up with Baker and played the rest of that season. Even with all the other outstanding forwards on the U.S. team, it is impossible to imagine any of the others switching back to play defense so efficiently. Maybe Pavelich, because of his rink-rat savvy, but Christian was perfect.

"The rest of my career, I never played defense again, in the NHL or anywhere," Christian recalled. "But every time I'd see Herbie, or run into him at any event, he'd always say that everybody else had me playing out of position, and if he ever coached me in the NHL, he'd put me at defense again."

Christian went on to play 1,111 games over fifteen years in the NHL with Winnipeg, Washington, Boston, St. Louis, and Chicago, and he scored 372 goals and 458 assists in a career that lasted through 1994—and all of it "out of position." Without question, though, his play on defense, particularly in view of injuries to Bob Suter and Jack O'Callahan, was a pivotal element of U.S. success.

As the team prepared for Lake Placid, the players had different perspectives on their treatment. Christian remembered the September trip to Holland, Finland, and Norway. "We took a bus from Tampere to some other city in Finland, and I remember looking across a lake and seeing the barbed wire on the border to the Soviet Union," Christian said. "And everybody remembers when we finished up the trip in Norway. We were looking at the girls up in the stands, and we tied 3-3. That's when he skated us after the game until they turned the lights out, and Mark Johnson crashed into the end boards."

Rob McClanahan was another unique case. He had been a star at Mounds View High School, a swift, high-scoring center sought by various colleges. That year, Brooks considered McClanahan, Steve Christoff from Richfield, and Eric Strobel from Rochester Mayo to be the bluest of blue-chippers, and he got them all. Brooks loved Strobel's magnificent skating stride and Christoff's aggressive temperament and quick shot. But I always felt he had a reservation or two about McClanahan. Because he was from North Oaks, a wealthy area just north of St. Paul, I thought Brooks tended to question whether he'd be willing to pay a price when the chips were down.

McClanahan disagrees. "I never felt that way," he said. "Herb didn't bust my chops at the U. Maybe he didn't use me in scoring situations, but I never felt that he picked on me."

Without a doubt, Christoff was the best goal-scorer of the three. McClanahan was assigned to frequent penalty-killing and defensive duties, which he approached with no less enthusiasm.

Team USA included eight of the top eleven scorers from the Gophers' 1978–79 NCAA championship team, plus goaltender Steve Janaszak, who played forty-one of the Gophers' forty-four games that season. Obviously, big and burly Don Micheletti didn't fit the mold of a lean and elusive Olympian in Brooks' mind, but he certainly could have gone to the net and scored goals. Tim Harrer was close to being picked up for the team, and Steve Ulseth was compact and quick like a prototype Olympian, but those two probably were not selected because Brooks feared unwarranted criticism if he had any more Gophers. Plus, he had former Gopher Buzz Schneider on the team as well.

If the 1980 Olympic team wasn't Team Gopher, it was pretty much Team WCHA. Of the top seven scorers in the WCHA in 1978–79, five made the team. Dave Delich of Colorado College made the original team but not the final roster.

"Herbie made a big effort to prove he wasn't our friend," McClanahan said. "When we were freshmen at the U, the World Junior tournament was just getting to be known. They wanted Strobel, Christoff, and me, but Herbie said they could only take one, and he wasn't going to let one go without the others.

"He was always able to get all the players to play at their highest level. When we won the 1979 NCAA title, we had a slump where we lost six of eight during that season. We played at Denver, and he ordered everybody back to the hotel. We thought we were in for it, but what we didn't know is he had beer and pizza waiting for us."

The uplifting ploys that had instilled camaraderie with his earlier Gopher team worked again. He still believed that buddies having a beer was normal team-building stuff. Later, McClanahan also played for Brooks with the New York Rangers, giving him a unique look at the progression of change in Brooks.

"He refined himself at the different levels," said McClanahan. "At the U, he implemented a lot of stuff with us, without using it in games—things he used with the Olympic team. But he refined himself and found a different way to motivate the pros. With the pros, he did more circling drills instead of stops and starts. At the U, he kicked our ass.

"At the U, we might do Herbies for three-plus hours, three days in a row. With the Olympic team, at our first practice out in Colorado Springs after he picked the team, he said, 'You will improve more this year than you ever have in your lives.' Offensively, he wasn't going to yell unless we were lazy. For those of us who had played for him at the U, it was a much easier year. When he did get on us and skate the heck out of us, like after the game against Norway, we'd just grit our teeth and say to each other, 'Don't let this bastard beat us.'"

Of course Team USA in 1980 didn't only consist of University of Minnesota players. Christian, Pavelich, and Harrington weren't Gophers, but they were from Minnesota. Even Mark Johnson, son of Herbie's favorite adversary, Bob Johnson, and from Madison, was born in Minneapolis, as his dad began his coaching career at Minneapolis Roosevelt High School. Because Brooks was so concerned with the abundance of Minnesotans on the team, he did everything he could to focus praise elsewhere.

Johnson and Pavelich were clearly the offensive catalysts—the stars of the team—at Lake Placid, but the books, stories, and movies created throughout the first twenty-five years after that Olympics have focused on Jim Craig for his goaltending heroics, Mike Eruzione for his huge goal against the Soviet Union, and Jack O'Callahan for a remarkable comeback from a knee injury during the Games. Part of this is because the major media focused more readily on New England than Minnesota, but Brooks also encouraged the media to point the spotlight away from the team's heavy Minnesota flavor. The four Boston University players made for colorful stories.

The puzzle of Eruzione is one for the ages. Eruzione and Schneider were the elder statesmen of the team, at age twenty-five. After moving on from his high school days at Winthrop, Massachusetts, and college at Boston University, where he helped the Terriers reach four straight NCAA tournaments, Eruzione went on to play for two years at Toledo in the International League. But in Brooks' constant reevaluation of his players, Eruzione's potential may have lagged behind that of his speedier teammates, partly because he had to overcome a broken hand he suffered in a practice at Aldrich Arena in suburban St. Paul. He had healed by the end of the exhibition season, but the recovery slowed his return to form, and he was vulnerable. Ralph Cox was available in New Hampshire, and Craig Homola was starring at Vermont. Brooks first made peripheral contact with Homola, who decided that being captain of a strong Vermont team precluded him from leaving at that time.

Harrer, a proven sniper who was in the midst of what would be a fifty-three-goal season for the Gophers, might well have bolstered the Team USA's offense. As word spread through the U.S. team of a possible change, the feeling was unanimous that the U.S. team had gone through a whole season of unification behind Eruzione, and that a late change would be ill-advised. Several players approached Brooks outside the team bus after a game against the International League All-Stars in Milwaukee to state their case.

"In the movie, *Miracle*, they had four players, with my character among them, talking to Brooks outside the bus," said Rob McClanahan, who then stated that he wasn't among those players. "But I can assure you that a meeting was held by some players and Herbie outside the bus in Milwaukee," he added.

Brooks yielded. That may have seemed out of character for someone who was always trying to improve the team, but Brooks, who himself had history as a late cut, had also been looking for a sign that the team had truly come together. Finding that players both East and West were unified behind Eruzione satisfied him that the elusive team chemistry might be in place after all.

Both Michigan players on the squad, center Mark Wells and defenseman Ken Morrow, arrived by way of Bowling Green. Morrow got plenty of publicity after the Olympics when he went directly from Lake Placid to the New York Islanders, which were on their way to winning the Stanley Cup. Morrow was outstanding, and also huge at 6 feet 4 inches. He was a powerful part of the team, but it was almost comical to read NHL writers gush that he had been the best player on the Olympic team because he won a gold medal and the Stanley Cup in the same year.

Wells remained comparatively anonymous, as did tough defenseman Bob Suter from Wisconsin, but both played solid contributing roles. Wells centered the fourth line, which was effective throughout. Suter broke his leg about three months before the Olympics, but overcame much skepticism to rejoin the team and play his usual hard-nosed style.

Dave Silk, a talented winger from Boston University, was the only one among the BU quartet who was overlooked in the media afterglow. He was a talented scorer and a good guy, and I had a good rapport with him, as well as with the other BU guys.

One day I was going out to Metropolitan Sports Center to watch a U.S. practice and catch up on the team's latest road trip. Brooks was running the players through some heavy-duty stuff, and a couple players came to the bench. I was behind the bench, but I stood up on the row of seats so I could lean over the Plexiglas and talk to the wheezing players. When I asked about how hard they were going, one of them quoted the popular hit song's famous refrain: "Well, you know, 'we are fam-i-ly.'" As I wrote it down, Silk gave me a quick glance and added, "But some of us are adopted."

I wrote that down, too, and I used the quotes in my story for the *Minneapolis Tribune* the next day. In the story, I identified Silk only as "another player." I knew that if Brooks was in the wrong mood, he might take the sarcasm for, well, sarcasm, and bench Silk for a game or two.

Twenty-three years later, at Brooks' funeral, I was able to renew acquaintances with those Olympians I hadn't seen in recent years, including Silk.

"I remember quoting your comment about 'some of us are adopted,' without using your name, because I knew Herbie might bench you for it," I told him.

"When you did that, I knew you could be trusted," said Silk.

That was true, because no matter how close Herbie and I were, anything said to me in confidence by any player remained confidential. An interesting side effect of Silk's unattributed quote was that, shortly after the Olympics, when agent Art Kaminsky decided to collaborate with Boston writer John Powers on a book entitled *One Goal: A Chronicle of the 1980 U.S. Olympic Hockey Team*, they came to Minnesota to research what had happened during the season. Even though I knew Art well—possibly too well—he didn't call me about the team, but he and his co-author did look through old issues of the *Minneapolis Tribune* and read the articles I had written. They lifted that particular quote, crediting me as the writer, and said that the quote probably came from John Harrington because I was close to him. If they had asked me, I might well have told them who really said it. Attributing that gem of a quote to a Minnesotan rather than one of the eastern players completely robbed it of its significance.

While the outside world went on plotting, scheming, Cold Warring, kidnapping, hostage-holding, and generally maintaining the status quo, Herb Brooks had built a figurative cocoon for Team USA. The focus and intensity, and the industrial-strength conditioning work, all came together at the right time.

"Herbie was a very good coach," said Christian. "To me, one of the best things he did was to rule out any excuse any of us could have. Nobody could say we got outworked, or we should have been better conditioned; nobody could say we needed more guys who could skate; nobody could say we had disruptive guys or we didn't all get along. Maybe some of our unity was because he tried to make us all hate him, but I always thought he was easy to play for.

"Sure, he had some rules—if you want to call it a system—but all you really had to do was play hard and be smart. When you play in a pickup game, you always try to create a two-on-one, and it works if you do it anywhere on the ice."

There was still one game left to play before going to Lake Placid, and that was a final exhibition against none other than the Soviet Union. At the time, it may have seemed like terrible planning. But in retrospect, it was a huge piece of the magic puzzle.

"Herbie felt we had to have that game," said Christian, "to see what they were really like, and so we wouldn't have to spend a period adjusting if we ended up playing them in the Olympics. We'd know what to expect."

CHAPTER 23

SUPPORT FOR HERBIE'S WORLD

As the world according to Herb Brooks turned, Craig Patrick became his most beneficial devotee at two National Hockey League stops. Patrick learned what Brooks could do from witnessing it as his assistant during that seven-month sprint from team selection to the world's stage at Lake Placid, and he believed Brooks was capable of more than maybe even Brooks himself imagined.

During the 1979–80 campaign, the quiet, analytical assistant went from peeking inside Herb's world, to being pulled willingly through the keyhole. At times, that world looked like it might be spinning off its axis. Brooks could be maddeningly stubborn, though always calculating and plotting. That can get wearisome, and sometimes it appeared that Brooks had climbed too far out on the limb, to where he had isolated himself and needed the support of someone loyal and capable enough to offer a hand.

That was Craig Patrick.

"Herb did a great job," recalled Patrick, who had the best possible vantage point for such an assessment. "He literally taught the team about eight different forechecks, and we could switch from one to another just by his order on the bench. He had names for some of the different systems to make it easy to use them strategically at different points of different games.

"Sometimes he'd take the team out in a field, or into a gym, and walk through these things as he put them in. When we were in a game, he could read the other team's systems from the bench—not just what players were giving us problems and how they were doing it, but the system they were using. That was a pretty good quality, and I realized I never saw any coach who was able to do that before."

Herbie's catch names for different forechecks were devised to be easily remembered by his players. One of his favorites was "assholes and eyeballs." There wasn't much doubt that his players would forget that one. The idea was that if the puck was in the offensive zone, and the other team's defensemen were chasing back after it, Brooks' players had to read and react, rather than just charge in. If the puck was on the end boards, for example, and a defenseman was going back for it, the attacking forwards would think "assholes or eyeballs." If they saw the defenseman's rear end, they should go all-out, because it meant the defenseman was still pursuing the puck, and by hustling they could cause an immediate turnover. If they saw his eyeballs, however, it meant the defenseman already had the puck and was coming out toward them, so they should approach more cautiously, in order to contain or turn him back.

As much as Brooks had done with the Gophers, he schooled the Olympians to be alert for those keys, and it heightened their ability to react. In Herbie's concept, he might call it "read and react," but he had trained them to more accurately "anticipate and act."

One of his favorite Brooksisms was: "If we're going to make mistakes, let's make mistakes of commission, not omission." He always urged his teams to act, not sit back.

"Before each game, Herb and I would talk over what was planned," Patrick said. "I should say *he* talked. I listened. The only thing I could offer was anything I might have picked up from the players. I couldn't offer anything about systems, because he was advanced and had them all planned. I've never seen systems like that before—or since."

The National Hockey League, which was so tradition-bound before 1980, was later subjected to some of the Brooks influence. But by 2010, seven years after Herb's death and thirty years after Lake Placid, the NHL has still resisted the European or Brooks influence.

"The NHL went the opposite way, really," said Patrick.

True, the only utilization of those European concepts was the increasing presence of players from Russia, Sweden, Finland, the Czech Republic, and Slovakia, who had to simplify their play to fit in among the best and most-skilled North American players.

As Brooks brought everything together with Team USA, he found a new and dedicated backer in Craig Patrick, who joined Brooks' trusted trainer Gary Smith, team doctor Doc Nagobads, equipment man Buddy Kessel, and old friend Warren Strelow, his official unofficial goaltender coach. That was Herbie's support group, although he willingly accepted more support when he found it.

The final and more obscure piece of the Team USA puzzle was Lou Vairo, a devoted hockey expert who didn't come by his expertise easily, but worked ceaselessly at it, even while being at odds with Brooks for a time. Vairo grew up in Flushing Meadows in the New York City borough of Queens, was fascinated by hockey, and started coaching, probably because of his personality, which was both gregarious and pushy. While training to become a chef, Vairo coached mites, peewees, other youth teams, and even City College of New York. His hunger for learning the techniques of the game was insatiable, and if he had grown up in Minnesota, he would have fit right in. Then again, he might not have pursued his passion to the ends of the earth.

"I was basically a roller-hockey player," Vairo explained. "We had a little rink in Flushing Meadows that was about as wide as it was long. But we had so little ice time we played a lot on rollers."

Then came his transformation: "Back in 1968 or '69, the Russians were playing Sweden, and it was on TV. I was at my grandmother's house in Brooklyn, and I remember watching the game on an old black-and-white TV, with aluminum foil on the antenna. It was the Russians, coached by Anatoli Tarasov, against the Swedes. I was fascinated. I had never seen hockey played the way they were playing.

"So I wrote a letter, and mailed it to: 'Anatoli Tarasov, Moscow, USSR.' To my surprise, about a month later, I got a reply! He wrote me back and offered me an invitation to come over there and watch up close. So I borrowed $500, and I took off for the Soviet Union."

Tarasov, the Father of Russian Hockey, took in this bold, brazen, but bluntly forthright American. Tarasov always insisted the Soviet Union players should never try to copy Canada, because it would doom them to always be second-best. Then he proceeded to make them the best in the world—by far—in their skill development and their totally unselfish teamwork, as well as their breathtaking circling, swirling, puck-control style of play. He was flattered, and perhaps a bit bemused, that a North American would want to come and observe his techniques.

"Everything he did, from dryland training, to practices, to their games was sensible to me," Vairo said. "But it was tough. When I got back and wanted to talk about it, I'd say the Russians could win the Stanley Cup, and I got laughed at, even by my closest friends. That was in 1970 or '71, and I'd always say, 'Just wait.'"

One of the better young players in New York was Bobby Crawford, who had played for Vairo. His dad was sending him out to Minnesota to play junior hockey and was impressed enough with Vairo to try to get him hired as coach.

"Bobby Crawford's dad asked if I'd want to go coach in Austin," Vairo recalled, "and I said, 'Texas is too hot for me.' I'd never heard of Austin, Minnesota. When I got out there, they said they had a bit of a financial bind, so instead of $12,000, they could only pay me $4,000, and I might have to give $2,000 of it back. I still agreed. They didn't know I was planning to open a pizzeria in Brooklyn, and I would have paid them to try these things out with a real hockey team."

Vairo knew nothing about Minnesota's great high school and college hockey history or its homegrown players, and he had never heard of Herb Brooks. He was busy overcoming all sorts of hassles with boosters, parents, and other Minnesotans when he tried to put in some Russian techniques in tryouts and training camp. "Some players quit," Vairo recalled. "Being dedicated, or committed, is important. It's like ham and eggs—the chicken is dedicated, but the pig is committed. Fred Shero told me that one."

So Vairo set out to turn the Austin Mavericks into a U.S. spinoff of the Soviet Union's Red Army. He got a job as a dishwasher in an Austin restaurant, where he worked every day before and after practice. He also painted houses. But the team played better and better. He coached from 1975 to 1978, winning a national junior championship in 1975–76. Junior hockey was still in its formative state in Minnesota. Few fans showed up, being more interested with North Stars, Fighting Saints, college, and high school hockey. A scrimmage between top high school teams drew five times as many onlookers as a junior game in Minnesota. The juniors were a bigger attraction, however, in Austin, where high school was the highest level of competitive hockey, and in Iowa and Nebraska, where there was no high school hockey.

I met Vairo during his run in Austin. I was impressed by him, but he always complained that I gave so much publicity to Herb Brooks and the Gophers, and seemed to be unaware that he—Vairo—had been installing Russian techniques before Brooks ever deployed such ideas at the University. I tried to reason with him by explaining that if an NHL coach in Montreal tried Russian tactics on one hand, and a squirt coach in northern Quebec tried it too, it wouldn't matter if the squirts did it first. The Gophers commanded the attention of the whole state, and indeed the whole college hockey nation, while almost nobody knew the Austin Mavericks even existed.

I'm convinced Vairo would have had the guts to do the same innovative Soviet stuff at a WCHA college, but the bigger point was that Vairo was copying what Tarasov had shown him, while Brooks wasn't copying anybody, but rather creating his own style. Lou was by far the first coach in the U.S. to install and implement the Russian style, but Brooks never claimed to have done that. He had his own inventive idea for how a team should play, and it involved complementing the altered Canadian/North American style with which he started with elements from the Russians, Czechs, Swedes, Finns, and anyone else who might have impressed him back in his playing days. Lou got an "A" for being "Anatoli West," but Brooks was completely unmatched for creating his own hybrid style and systems. Since Tarasov was such an unquestioned innovator, Herb Brooks was clearly the Tarasov of North American Hockey. "I agree with that," Vairo told me in 2008.

Tarasov's brilliance was in studying the rigidly disciplined way Canadians played while dominating hockey for decades, then deciding to create an entirely new style, so as to avoid being doomed to second-best. Installing a unique style in a nation like the Soviet Union, where hockey was in its infancy and didn't have a specific style, was impressive yet, at the same time, far easier than swimming upstream against the rushing flow of traditional Canadian—and by exponent—American style.

"No question, Tarasov couldn't have done what he did in our country," Vairo acknowledged.

Vairo and Tarasov stayed in close contact and admired each other tremendously. One time, while talking tactics, Vairo questioned a maneuver in the defensive zone, asking who supported the defenseman when he had the puck near his own end boards? Tarasov looked at him intensely, Vairo recalled, and said, "Do you think my defensemen are shit?"

"Tarasov had some amazing drills, and he always said that he made his practices so difficult that the games always seemed easier than the practices. He said the reason for that is he didn't want his players to be like Canadians, who think a good-conditioned team wins games in the last ten minutes. That's wrong, he said. They win in the first four minutes—by destroying their opponents' will.

"I asked Tarasov to give me five transition drills," Vairo recalled. "He said, 'You want five secrets of Soviet hockey? OK, but will you work for them? You will get five drills, after you present me with one hundred drills, in detail, and they must be here by 6 a.m. tomorrow. And that's not a request, that's an order.' I didn't sleep. I stayed up all night drawing up one hundred drills, with explanations. The next morning I brought them to him, and he read every one. Usually he would say, 'Nyet,' then go on to the next one. He liked about two out of the one hundred. But he kept his word and he gave me five transition drills. So I did the same thing, and looked at each one, then said, 'Nyet.' He got a big kick out of that."

Right about the same time as Tarasov was showing Vairo his secret drills, Herb Brooks was borrowing my notebook and drawing a rink outline, drawing X's and O's here and there, and then drawing a line to describe where a player should go. Then he drew a line to show alternative moves and routes, and soon the entire diagram was so covered with crisscrossing lines and circles that it was impossible to figure out what he had first intended. I have dozens of notepad pages with those diagrams.

It's interesting that Vairo was consumed with admiration for Tarasov and didn't even know who Herb Brooks was. The first contact between Vairo and Brooks was a classic. Brooks, like other college coaches, kept an eye on developing junior players and saw the Mavericks when they played the St. Paul Vulcans. During Vairo's first year, the phone rang.

"Herb called, and said 'This is Herb Brooks.' I didn't know who he was," said Vairo. "He said, 'I coach at the U,' and I said, 'The what?' I had never heard of 'the U,'

One of the many drill diagrams Brooks drew for the author over the years. First, Brooks would draw a line to describe where a player should go. Then he would draw a line to show an alternative route, and then another, and so on until it was impossible to discern what he had first intended. *Author collection*

so I still didn't know who he was. He went on to say, 'I want you to know, there will be two tickets for you to all our games.'

"I went up and watched the Gophers a few times in 1975, and they didn't do anything special. Things worked out for me in Austin, and I left there knowing that nobody played the way we played, and I always felt we never got credit for it."

It was true that in the early 1970s, Brooks was installing bits and pieces of his imaginative style, but he still kept his team playing conventional North American hockey. Without a doubt, Vairo would have been more impressed had he watched Brooks run a practice or two, but the time would come when Vairo would have ample opportunity to be impressed by Herbie.

And vice versa.

While becoming very close to Tarasov, Vairo remained a student of the game at the highest level. When the heavily favored Soviet Union was upset by Czechoslovakia at the 1977 World Championships, it was a classic example of how an imaginative tactic, when executed by a team totally committed to it, can upset a vastly superior opponent. That was the year, Vairo noted, when the Czechs switched from a normal two-man forecheck (where the second attacker supported the first), to the two attackers each going after a defenseman instead. Once the Czech forecheckers each got to a defenseman, it took away the Russians' favorite D-to-D pass to start their breakout. In addition, the strong-side Czech defenseman would crash in from the point when the puck was passed up the boards.

"The Russians couldn't get out of their own end," Vairo said. "It took until the next year for the Russians to beat it. The Czechs tried the same thing, and the Russian defenseman would fake one way, then reverse and dump the puck to the weak-side corner. Their center would come back and get the puck, and there would be nobody to pick him up."

Vairo had explained all that to me in the lobby of the Waldorf-Astoria, just before the third and deciding game of a series between the NHL All-Stars and the Soviet Union in 1979 in Madison Square Garden. After losing the first game, the Russians switched to the same style the Czechs had used to beat them, and it worked. Vairo had the keys to the kingdom when he was summoned to NHL coach Scotty Bowman's room at the Waldorf. He not only explained to Bowman what the Soviets were doing, but also described the antidote the Russians had come up with to beat that system.

"Scotty told me he didn't think he could get the NHL players to understand a new system in such a short time," Vairo added. So the NHL All-Stars played NHL hockey against the Soviets, and the Soviets blitzed them, 6-0.

A few months later, Herb Brooks was coaching the U.S. National Team, preparing to go to Moscow for the World Championships. Vairo went to Lake Placid to watch an exhibition tournament in which the U.S. played Sweden.

"The Swedes were flying one forward out of the defensive zone for a long pass," Vairo recalled. "Both U.S. defensemen vacated the blue line to cover him. I was sitting with Bob Fleming from AHAUS, and I said they shouldn't do that, because it made it easy for the Swedes to get out. Bob asked me to write it down, and he took it down to Herb. Herb called me to come down after the game, and he thanked me for calling it to his attention.

"Then he asked me if I would come along and be on the walkie-talkie to the bench."

Brooks and Vairo may have had differences, but they had a unique bond in their fascination for the game. Brooks knew when he had a valuable asset at his disposal, and Vairo happily accepted the opportunity and accompanied the U.S. team to Moscow.

"We played pretty well, but those other teams live for that tournament," said Vairo. "Jim Craig played good in goal, and when Herb asked me what I thought of him, I said I thought he had done well. I had a chance to get to know Herb a little on that trip."

And vice versa.

"We got a chance to go to the Bolshoi Ballet together," Vairo recalled. "There was a group of us, and I was sitting next to Herb. I had never seen anything like that, and I don't think he had, either. It was beautiful, but it wasn't really the sort of thing I was interested in. I fell asleep, at one point, and Herb elbowed me to keep me awake. Herb said, 'You enjoying it?' And I said, 'The dancing doesn't do much for me, but the band's pretty good.' He howled about that later. He couldn't believe I would call one of the best orchestras in the world a band."

Vairo might have been critical of Brooks at first, but when Brooks realized Vairo had some tactical knowledge that could help his team, he invited him to join up, even if it was unofficial, and he would be in the press box on the walkie-talkie with Craig Patrick at Lake Placid, too.

CHAPTER 24

NOT READY FOR PRIME TIME

On Saturday, February 9, 1980, everything was in place for Team USA to test its abilities against the most powerful hockey team in the world. The Americans met the Soviet Union's Olympic team at Madison Square Garden, just three days before they would face Sweden in Lake Placid in the first game of the Winter Olympics. It was time to show off all they had learned during seven months of preparation.

A crowd of 11,243 showed up for the game, but nobody had arranged for officials, so two fans with some refereeing experience were recruited from the stands. The Soviet Union's players skated out wearing new Jofa helmets. Their warm-up drills were more impressive to watch than some games, as they skated through a sequence of high-tempo one-on-ones, then two-on-ones, two-on-twos, and three-on-twos featuring quick, precise passes.

The USSR introductions were met with polite applause. When Team USA was introduced, the crowd cheered, and the applause swelled until it grew into a standing ovation. Ron Raines sang an emotional National Anthem, and when he got to "land of the free" he thrust his fist in the air, and the crowd roared loudly enough to drown out "and the home of the brave."

The puck was dropped by a fifty-two-year-old salesman who did games in a New Jersey junior league, and who just happened to be in the stands and willing to fill in. Helmut Balderis, a star from Latvia, drew a penalty, but the uptight and tentative U.S. team fizzled on the power play. When Balderis came out of the box, he immediately set up Alexander Maltsev for a quick shot from the slot and it was 1-0. Vladimir Krutov, a nineteen-year-old who broke into the Soviet lineup, scored the next two goals, the second by sneaking out to the center red line for a long pass from Zinetula Bilyaletdinov.

A minute later, Valery Kharlamov was faced with what amounted to a one-on-three, so he shot from wide on the right side and it was 4-0 at the first intermission.

Jim Craig steadied his play in the second period, and at the 10:43 mark, he skated off for the preplanned split with Steve Janaszak. There was no way to know that this would be Janaszak's final appearance for the U.S., but the Soviets didn't let up.

Finally, the U.S. team broke through when Steve Christoff set up Mike Eruzione, who drilled a quick shot home, cutting the deficit to 5-1. Another power play led to a goal by Boris Mikhailov nine seconds before the end of the period, and it was 6-1. The best, however, was yet to come.

With both sides short a man, Phil Verchota, who hadn't gotten into the action in the first period because the U.S. team was reduced to three lines, broke in from center ice, alone against four Soviet defenders. He veered toward the net and fired a shot, then cut around a defender and put his own rebound high into the left corner. But just as the U.S. team showed signs of life, the speedy Maltsev scored his second goal of the game on the play of the game.

Shorthanded, Maltsev rushed up the right side on the retreating Dave Christian. He made a slight deke, executed an electrifying counterclockwise spin, regained possession, and fired a backhander all in one motion. Janaszak had no chance. It was 7-2.

Vladimir Golikov put the Soviets into frolic mode by zipping a pass through Ken Morrow's legs to Sergei Makarov, who scored; Krutov came back twenty seconds later to complete his hat trick.

Christoff scored on a power play, then Balderis showed his stuff. Working from the right corner, he passed to Valery Vasiliev at the left point, then moved swiftly into position to deflect Vasiliev's return pass into the net.

After the game, Brooks was masterful with the gathered New York media. "I knew we were in trouble," Brooks began, "when they introduced the Russian players and my team applauded; then Maltsev scored that goal, and I applauded."

"I'll take full responsibility for this one," Brooks said. "I gave 'em a bad plan. I knew we'd be nervous, but we went stride-for-stride with them for a thirty-minute stretch, and we should have been more aggressive, but I gave them too cautious a checking plan . . . too conservative."

There was Herbie, taking the hit for a 10-3 loss, after an exhibition of sleight-of-puck passing and playmaking brilliance that pretty much negated whatever game plan Brooks might have concocted.

Viktor Tikhonov, the Soviet coach, was suspicious. "The U.S. team has a very good future," he said. "We showed what we can do in this particular game, and they didn't. The U.S. was holding something in reserve."

After the posturing was over, Brooks suddenly had some serious concerns. Jack O'Callahan, the tough BU defenseman, had left the game and his injury was diagnosed as stretched or torn knee ligaments. Rob McClanahan had taken a shot in the ankle, and Mark Wells had a serious sore throat.

"I wanted to go with four lines, but Wells couldn't play, so we had to cut back," said Brooks. "Now I don't know if Wells will recover, and we'll have to see how O'Callahan is. We have forty-eight hours to name our twenty-man player list for the Olympics."

Trainer Gary Smith remembers O'Callahan's injury: "The doctors said he tore his medial collateral ligament in his knee, so I talked it over with Herb right away. I told him it would be a tough decision, because that injury is something that usually takes three full weeks to recover, so there would be only a slim chance of him being ready."

O'Callahan was in the middle of the team's first real drama.

"Doctors looked at my left knee and said there was no way I could play," O'Callahan said. "Herb had come in and said, 'If you can't play, we'll still get you credentials, but you can't be in the Olympic Village. But let's wait because I don't have to make the decision for another day.' My parents were coming in, and I told them to come anyway, because this was the Olympics, and it was my team, and it was not all about me.

Brooks instructs members of the 1980 U.S. Olympic team, including former Minnesota Gophers Phil Verchota and Bill Baker (facing camera) and Bowling Green standout Mark Wells (back to camera).
AP Images/Douglas Ball

"But I had all the attention. All these doctors were there looking at me on Sunday, and said I had torn ligaments and I was done for a while. Then another guy walks in, and says, 'Is it OK if I take a look at him?' They said go ahead. It was Dr. Dick Steadman from Vail, Colorado. He's an orthopedic surgeon and had worked on a lot of big-name skiers and other athletes. He started poking around in my knee, checking, and he made me do all this movement stuff, where he'd hold my ankle in one hand and my knee in the other, and put resistance on it, then ask me to kick forward or pull back.

"We were working back and forth. He was sweating, so he took off his jacket. I'm sweating. And the other doctors were all watching, like they were in school. Then Dr. Steadman said he wanted to talk to the other doctors alone, so could I leave? I went out of the room, and then they called me back in. . . . They talked some more, and then he said, 'The rosters have to go in, and I'm going to encourage the coach not to take you off the team. The other doctors think you can't play, but I think you can. You have until 6 p.m. tomorrow night, then I want to reexamine you. If you'll do this rehab, I think there's a 25 percent chance you can play.'

"I said I'd do it, so I spent the next forty hours with one trainer, working together. I'd do really hard exercises on my knee and my quad, then electrical stimulation, and that would go on for an hour and a half, then I'd have an hour and a half rest. We kept doing that, over and over. Dr. Steadman thought by doing all this, it would make my recovery quicker, so we went to test it again, and Herbie was there, and so were the other doctors. They all concurred and said that it healed so incredibly that, in another day or two of working like that, I'd be ready to get back on the ice.

"Then Herb went off and talked to the doctors, and came back to me and said, 'I'm going to keep you on the team. I don't know how much you're going to play, but I need you on the team. If you're not playing, I still need you to support the team.' I missed the first two games, although I was on the bench, and then I played the next five."

In the movie *Miracle*, O'Callahan didn't play until he made a truly miraculous comeback against the Soviet Union in the crucial medal-round game. In reality, he played a fair amount from game three on, although he played much less in the Soviet game. The fact that he played at all was something of a medical miracle, because if it had been a normal college or NHL season, he undoubtedly would have been out for a month.

The heavy pre-Olympic schedule may have gotten the team ready and flying by the time the Olympics started, but the 10-3 loss to the Soviets made it all seem futile, and physically, the Americans were limping. In addition to O'Callahan, Bob Suter was still not 100 percent coming back from the broken leg he suffered three months earlier.

Brooks was undismayed, even by the drubbing at the Soviets' hands.

"That was a good lesson, and the players learned a lot of things," Brooks said. "We've done a lot of things, but not against teams of this caliber. We're not demoralized. Sometimes a good kicking is good for quality athletes."

Going to Lake Placid, Brooks knew he would probably go with four defensemen most of the time—Dave Christian, Bill Baker, Mike Ramsey, and Ken Morrow—and he had his four lines all set after months of constant juggling and experimenting. The only line that had been together consistently since Christmas was the "Conehead line": Mark Pavelich centering Buzz Schneider and John Harrington.

"I remember all the times right before games," John Harrington said. "Herbie would say, 'McClanahan, you play with Johnson tonight . . . Strobel, you're with Verchota.' Then he'd say, 'Pav, you guys stay the same.' I think he sensed we all played the same and knew we could work together, with Pav making the plays."

Mark Johnson centered Rob McClanahan and Dave Silk; Neal Broten centered Mike Eruzione and Steve Christoff; Mark Wells centered Phil Verchota and Eric Strobel. Then there were the Coneheads.

"Herb used to say we were the Coneheads and we were uncoachable," said Pavelich, who grew up outside of Eveleth on Ely Lake, where his dad helped shovel off a hockey rink.

"You learn the most when you grow up on an outdoor rink," said Pav. "We'd play on ponds, and then when the ice got deep enough on Ely Lake, we'd play there every day. After it got too snowy, we'd move to the outdoor rink that was a couple blocks away. But the regulars, who were more dedicated, would be out on the lake, too.

"Everybody in the neighborhood would be on the rink for big scrimmages on Saturdays and Sundays. There'd be players there from ages five to eighty, with thirty players on the rink. When you were little, you'd play against the older guys. You learned to improvise."

Bill Kangas, who played youth and high school hockey with Pavelich, was also out there on Ely Lake with him. "He was amazing," Kangas said. "Once in a while he'd be down there and say he forgot his skates, and ask if any of us had any skates he could borrow. Then he'd borrow a stick. It might be left-handed, and he shot right; it didn't matter. Pav could go out there with somebody else's skates on that were the wrong size, and using a left-handed stick, and he'd still be the best out there."

While he was quiet and rarely said anything, Pavelich was as clever away from the game as he was on the ice. People assumed Brooks came up with the Conehead tag for the all–Iron Range line. But it didn't happen that way. Brooks, in fact, had never watched *Saturday Night Live* and was unaware of the comical, alien Coneheads who were portrayed by Dan Aykroyd and Jane Curtin.

"We named ourselves," said Pavelich. "In practice, Herb would have the power play working at one end and the penalty killers at the other, so there'd be nothing left for us to do but be out in the middle of the ice, putting out the cones or rearranging them. I watched *Saturday Night Live*, and I enjoyed the Coneheads, so we named ourselves."

Coneheads fit perfectly once Pavelich suggested it. Brooks thought it worked, too, although he liked to joke about how they were from up in the sticks on the Iron Range, as though Coneheads was more to indicate the dunce hats that the slower kids in school used to wear.

The hockey sense—rink smarts—that came naturally to the Iron Range kids who played on outdoor rinks growing up couldn't really be taught. Brooks came closer than any coach to installing a rink-rat style on his teams, and he admired the free-flowing skills of the Northern Minnesota guys, even while he heckled them about it. At times it appeared the Conehead line was fourth in the pecking order, other times third, but often they'd be the second line off the bench or even start, because Brooks wanted to establish a high-tempo attack or change the pace of a game.

Schneider said, "Herbie left us together from Christmas on. We were playing in a tournament at Christmas at Met Center, and as we were about to go out, Herbie grabbed the back of Pav's shirt and said, 'Go out and get one.' He set me up and I scored. So later on, he did it again, and said, 'Go out and get another one.' And we scored again.

"It was interesting, because it seemed like Herbie would send us out almost like a checking line against the other team's top guys, and we'd score. Pav would just say, 'Go to the net, and I'll put it on your stick.' So I'd go to the net, and he'd put it right there. Pav was like an artist, going down the ice."

There wasn't much artistry from anyone on the U.S. squad, though, in Madison Square Garden on February 9. Perhaps on that night, Herbie and the U.S. team should have brought their own puck so they could play, too.

Team USA headed to Lake Placid, ready to take on the world, whether it looked like it or not. The *Minneapolis Tribune* had three of us in Lake Placid. Jon Roe would cover all the events except hockey, while columnist Joe Soucheray would write his "light and breezy" columns about any and every topic that popped into his head. I would cover just the hockey.

Our sports editor, Gary Libman, had planned everything, but he had made one enormous blunder; he hadn't secured us a place to stay. Overcome with pity for our plight of possibly staying one hundred miles away, a local realtor said that she had a two-bedroom apartment in the lower level of her home that she would rent out to the *Tribune* for the two weeks. It was directly across the street from the high school that had been transformed into the press center for the Olympic Games. The high school was across a driveway from the main arena.

Roe and Soucheray had to get up in the morning and head out for whatever venue they were going to—the ski slopes by shuttle bus, perhaps. Meanwhile, I could get up at 9:45 a.m., shower, eat breakfast, and stroll across the street with plenty of time for a 10:30 a.m. hockey game. The boss' oversight turned out to be a masterstroke of good luck for me, because I was able to see many games beyond just the U.S. games I wrote about. I could have written six stories a day for the whole two weeks and gotten by on four hours of sleep a night. I was wired. The pressure of writing good stories on deadline was no pressure at all. It was exciting, much like each hockey game, where Team USA went in without any pressure, because nobody expected much success from these college kids.

And anyone who did have high hopes had them pretty well adjusted by that 10-3 game in Madison Square Garden.

CHAPTER 25

MINI-MIRACLE AGAINST SWEDEN

The Winter Olympics, of course, consist of all sorts of events, some individual, some team-oriented. A speed skater, for example, can compete in a half-dozen events and conceivably win six gold medals. In hockey, teams and players compete in a full tournament, and only the final tournament team champion gets a gold medal.

Because the United States had done so poorly in international tournaments leading up to 1980, winning only two medals since the 1960 gold medal—bronze at the 1962 World Championships and the silver at the 1972 Olympics, when Canada chose not to participate—no consideration was given to the Americans for success at Lake Placid. Herb Brooks, who liked to fashion his teams as underdogs, had willing accomplices throughout the hockey world.

The Soviet Union, on the other hand, won no medal in the 1953 World Championships, then won the gold in 1954, and since then had filled their trophy case. The Soviets cruised into Lake Placid with a live string of fourteen golds, two silvers, and one bronze in the previous seventeen years of Winter Olympics and World Championships.

At Lake Placid, the teams were paired according to how they finished in the 1979 World Championships. In the Red Pool, No. 1 Soviet Union was joined by No. 4 Canada, No. 5 Finland, No. 8 Netherlands, No. 9 Poland, and No. 12 Japan. The Blue Pool featured No. 2 Czechoslovakia, No. 3 Sweden, No. 6 West Germany, No. 7 United States, No. 10 Romania, and No. 11 Norway. The ratings were pretty solid, with most people figuring Czechoslovakia as the Blue Pool favorite, but much-improved Sweden stood ready to bypass the Czechs if they were indeed showing signs of age on the national team. The United States was a true long shot, the youngest team facing a challenge even to move ahead of West Germany in pool play. In the Red Pool, the Soviet Union was the clear favorite, with most observers predicting Canada would be the second team to reach the medal round.

The U.S. team could hardly celebrate being out of the Soviets' pool because its first two games would be against Sweden and Czechoslovakia, the Blue Pool co-favorites. In those days, any slip in the preliminary round could cost a team the chance to make the medal round, where only the top two from each pool would advance to complete the round-robin format. The two from each pool that advanced carried forward only their result against each other in pool play, then added their results against the other pool's two teams in the medal round, resulting in a three-game standing to determine the gold, silver, and bronze medals.

The United States certainly was not looking past its opening game against Sweden when it hit the Olympic Fieldhouse ice on Tuesday, February 12. The day started with Norway meeting the Czechs, also at the Fieldhouse, while the adjacent Olympic Arena was the location of Canada–Holland, West Germany–Romania, and Poland–Finland. The USSR was slated to meet Japan in the nightcap at the Fieldhouse.

The Fieldhouse wasn't even half full for the start of the U.S.–Sweden game, and the press box wasn't nearly full either, even though hockey was the only event being held that day, which was actually the day before the official opening ceremonies. The crowd was, however, enthusiastic and loudly behind the U.S. skaters, and the team responded with a strong first period. Brooks was greatly concerned about his goaltending situation, saying, "Jimmy Craig has been fighting the puck and hasn't been on top of his game for about a month." He told Craig, "Jimmy, your curveball is hanging" and that he was considering starting Janaszak. Craig responded with considerable fire. "Don't worry, I'll be ready," he told Brooks.

It was time to find out. The strong, polished, and experienced Swedish team had a goaltender named Per-Eric "Pelle" Lindbergh, who would go on to star for the Philadelphia Flyers before his tragic death in 1985, when he lost control of his speeding Porsche Turbo. Mats Naslund, another future NHL star, led a group of highly skilled forwards. Several of the Swedish players were in their thirties, so even though they preferred a skating-passing game, they didn't take it lightly when the U.S. players checked them, and the hitting was brisk on both sides. "We don't pick our players to be physical," said Swedish coach Bengt Ohlsson, "but this is the first time we have a tougher physical team than the Americans."

Craig and Lindbergh dueled until 11:04, when defenseman Sture Andersson snapped a shot from the slot into the upper left corner of the net, giving Sweden a 1-0 lead. Late in the period, Rob McClanahan missed a shift and Gary Smith advised Brooks that it might be wise to send the forward to the dressing room for treatment from the AHAUS's trainer.

By the first intermission, McClanahan had been through a whirlpool treatment and was on the training table. "I was flat on my back, with a monster ice pack," McClanahan recalled. When the team came into the dressing room, Brooks spotted McClanahan on the training table. McClanahan still thinks the episode that followed was a psych job by Brooks to fire up the team. I'm less certain, knowing that deep down, Brooks always wondered about the inner toughness of the kid from North Oaks.

Brooks, a bit uptight from the pressure, asked what was wrong and was told it was a thigh bruise. "Well, that's a long way from your heart," Brooks muttered, and made a couple other comments indicating that he didn't think such a trivial thing should prevent McClanahan from playing.

"I don't even remember exactly what all he said, but I know I was about a second from throwing a punch," McClanahan said. "I jumped up and threw off the ice pack, yelling at him. He went out of the room and I chased him out into the hallway. The Swedish team was right next door, and their dressing-room door was open. They had to be wondering what the heck was going on, because there's the U.S. coach and one of his players yelling at each other."

McClanahan went back into the dressing room and started getting his gear on. A thigh bruise, even a deep thigh bruise, doesn't necessarily lead to further injury; it's more a matter of how much pain a player can endure. McClanahan was determined to show Brooks that he could play. In the movie *Miracle*, the Brooks character follows up the confrontation by walking past the Patrick character and saying, "That ought to fire them up." No such comment was ever made; Brooks wouldn't be that obvious. Even though McClanahan thinks it was a typical ploy Brooks often tried to get players to perform out of anger toward him, I think it was more Brooks venting a bit at McClanahan. My guess is that if Johnson, Christian, Christoff, or O'Callahan had been on that table, Brooks wouldn't have made those comments. Typically, though, during that two-week stretch at Lake Placid, whatever Herbie did, no matter the reason, worked out positively.

Sure enough, McClanahan rejoined the team three and a half minutes into the second period, with the United States still trailing 1-0. Late in the period, four consecutive strong shifts established a pattern of momentum, and when Mark Johnson's line took its next turn, Johnson deflected a Mike Ramsey pass to Dave Silk, who scored at 19:32.

"I came over the blue, and Johnson and Silk were together," said Mike Ramsey. "I threw it to Johnson. He knocked down the pass and it went right to Silk. We were so high-strung, we were ready to snap, and I think if we had ever gotten on top, we'd have buried 'em."

When the third period started, the aroused Americans had proven they could play Sweden even. The U.S. came out hot again. Sweden was not about to lose its poise, though, and regained the lead at 2-1. As the game ticked into its final minute, Brooks pulled Jim Craig for a sixth attacker with 0:41 remaining. Interestingly, in the first moment of true crisis, Brooks sent out the Coneheads—Pavelich, Schneider, and Harrington—with Ramsey and Bill Baker on the points, and Mark Johnson as the sixth attacker. Ramsey got possession at the left point and shot, and when his shot was blocked, Ramsey pounced on the puck and fed across to Baker on the right point.

"I just wanted to keep the puck in," said Baker, knowing that if it came out across the blue line, they might not get another chance. "Then I saw Buzzy in the right corner, so I fired it up the boards toward him. He deflected it, but the puck kept going around behind the net."

Pavelich, on the end boards toward the left corner, did what he did best: come up with the puck in traffic and create something where nothing appeared evident.

"Pav came up with it, and he made an unbelievable play," said Baker. "There was a guy right on Pav, but he's so quick that he gave him a little move and just sort of froze the guy. Mark broke up the slot, but he was covered, so Pav fed the puck right past Johnson to me."

Baker had already pinched in a bit from the right point, and he glided toward the slot to meet the pass. With twenty-seven seconds remaining, his low, forty-foot missile somehow found its way cleanly through the tangle of bodies and into the net behind Lindbergh. "It came to me and it was like in slow motion. I shot, but I still couldn't see where the puck went."

In an instant, he couldn't see anything because he was buried by a mob of blue-clad teammates, who poured off the bench. Referee Victor Dmbrovski from the Soviet Union had to dig through the bodies to identify the goal-scorer.

"We had some great goaltending out there. That's the best Jimmy Craig has played in . . . three weeks," Brooks said afterward. "He said not to worry, he'd be ready, and he was. I knew we'd be facing an excellent goalie in Pelle Lindbergh. I wish the Flyers had signed him when they drafted him. Overall, I wasn't satisfied with the play of our forwards, but when you take into account pulling the goalie, jockeying guys around, then we tie the game—I guess I'd have to say we were lucky."

Craig made thirty-four saves and was his usual self afterward. "My record speaks for itself," said Craig. "I only lost seven games all year, and six by one goal."

If Jim Craig sounded cocky, it was because he had a way of not being very tactful and of barking commands that rarely endeared him to his teammates. Most dismissed it with the usual shrug, saying, "He's a goalie."

"Jimmy had an uncanny ability to say the wrong thing at the wrong time," laughed Dave Christian, recalling all the times Craig's yapping annoyed teammates.

Nobody wearing a blue USA jersey probably had a care about Craig's cocksuredness at the time, and certainly not about the other results from the day. The United States didn't win, but the 2-2 tie with Sweden was a bigger upset than Romania beating West Germany or Poland beating Finland. It was a huge achievement for the youthful Americans.

The following day featured the Winter Games' official opening ceremonies, with athletes from all the nations marching in formation at an outdoor stadium in bone-chilling cold. One of the incredible spectacles at the ceremonies was the release of dozens of white doves, an obvious symbol of peace. As the doves flapped furiously into the cold, gray sky, most of them fluttered up, up, and away, but at least one didn't. As I watched, and as the athletes stood frozen at attention, one struggling bird headed toward the athletes. Just as it was about to clear them, it hurtled toward the ground in a final, fitful fall. It floundered there for just a moment before apparently expiring. The symbolism was inescapable: A white dove of peace crashed to earth and died amid the jackboots of the Soviet contingent.

CHAPTER 26

CANCELED CZECHS

The day after the opening ceremonies, the U.S.–Czechoslovakia game would conclude another six-game afternoon. Sweden opened the day with an 8-0 rout of Romania, as the Swedish scores suddenly took on added importance: If the U.S. and Sweden both were fortunate enough to reach the medal round, goal differential would determine their seeding. West Germany regained its touch with a 10-3 romp over Norway in the other Blue Pool game.

With the tie against Sweden, the United States had thrust itself atop the pool with the Swedes and Czechs as a contender to reach the medal round. Certainly, any loss could hinder that possibility, but it put extra emphasis on the game with Czechoslovakia. "The Czechs are better than the Swedes," Brooks said. "They're like counter-punchers. They lay back, making sure of their defensive play and waiting for an opening. Then they blitz you."

When the clichés and Brooksisms had all been fired off, I got the feeling that Herbie had more confidence in his team's chances than respect for the Czechoslovakian team. Maybe it was because his U.S. National Team had tied the vaunted Czechs a year earlier in Moscow. Maybe it was because the Czechs were more predictable in style, with their left-wing-lock system. Or maybe it was just that after the tie with Sweden, Brooks seemed loose and confident, and it rubbed off on his players.

There were 7,125 fans in the 8,100-seat Olympic Fieldhouse, which was far better than the Sweden game, where estimates ranged as low as 3,000. The Czechs had several future NHL stars on their roster, including Peter, Marian, and Anton Stastny, the famous brothers who played on the same spectacular line. But the Americans proved that a little confidence and optimism can go a long way. All agreed that the game was the catalyst for tying the U.S. skaters together in unity.

After Jaroslav Pouzar got Czechoslovakia off to a 1-0 start, Brooks came back a few minutes later with a faceoff trick that worked better than he could have hoped. Neal Broten was at center, but with a wing and a defenseman flanking him, and only one defenseman back. Mike Eruzione, the absent wing, had made as if skating to the bench, but then lined up there, near the boards. Amazingly, the Czechs didn't seem to notice him. Broten won the faceoff, stepped ahead, and passed to Eruzione, who was breaking off left wing in the clear. Eruzione drilled his shot from the left circle past goaltender Jiri Kralik, making it 1-1.

A minute after that, John Harrington missed a Buzz Schneider rebound, but Mark Pavelich converted it, and the U.S. led 2-1—the first lead for the Americans in two games. The goal aroused the crowd—the same crowd that created the now-famous chant of "USA . . . USA. . . ."

The Americans rallied, but Kralik came up with big saves. At the twelve-minute mark, Craig stopped Peter Stastny, but Marian lifted the rebound over the fallen netminder for a 2-2 tie. As he did throughout the tournament, Craig got better as the game went on, but there was little indication of the outburst that was to come.

Craig stopped another Peter Stastny chance to open the second period, and then the Coneheads struck again. Pavelich was in the right corner, apparently well covered, but he made a sudden move, instantly eluded the checker, and passed to the goal mouth, where Schneider scored. A 3-2 lead further inspired the U.S. players. With five minutes left in the middle period, Steve Christoff's forecheck got the puck loose, and Mark Johnson beat a defender coming out of the left corner, veering to the slot where he scored with a backhander for a 4-2 lead.

In the third period, Dave Christian bolted in with a great move and nearly scored, and Phil Verchota batted in the rebound at 2:59. "I didn't get it, Wells got it," protested Verchota, but the official scorer remains Verchota. Exactly a minute later, Harrington picked a breakout pass out of the air, raced in on the left side, circled behind the net, and waited until he spotted Schneider arriving in front. Pass, goal, and a stunning 6-2 U.S. lead.

The Czechs got one back, but at 10:54 of the final period Rob McClanahan raced in on the left side. A Czech defenseman tripped him, but McClanahan still got a good shot away. When the puck went in, the U.S. bench cleared to congratulate the winger who had missed the previous day's opening ceremonies to get treatment for his thigh bruise.

The last nine minutes of the game were close to warfare. Jan Neliba blasted Johnson from behind with a crosscheck, leaving him in a heap on the ice. Brooks was enraged. He was caught on videotape shouting, "I'll shove that Koho right down your throat," although other reports suggested Brooks may have suggested an alternate orifice. When the Swedish referee didn't issue a penalty, Brooks leveled a verbal outburst at him, too, language barrier notwithstanding.

"The ref gave me a hand wave across the front of his face. I don't know what that meant in Swedish, but I gave him a few hand gestures of my own that I think he understood," Brooks said after the game. "It was a cheap shot, interference, and a crosscheck, and Johnson could be out a while."

After the game, like after every game, the media hustled across the alleyway to the large high school auditorium to get a seat and await the appearance of the competing coaches, most of whom brought two chosen players. Brooks didn't want to single out players, and when he learned the Soviet Union wasn't going to bring players, he was happy because it meant the organizers couldn't make him do it. The reporters mostly grumbled about it, but none seemed to realize the players would be exiting the adjacent arena after showering and dressing. I simply stood outside in the snow and caught any player I wanted as they came out the side door.

"The U.S. skiers are falling down, Beth Heiden lost, and everybody is talking about them and all the problems the U.S. athletes are having," Harrington said. "We go along, and maybe nobody hears about us, but we just played our two toughest games right off the bat, and we're undefeated. We're too young, maybe, but we spend our emotions on the ice.

"Herbie pushes you, and sometimes you hate it, but it's good, because we know how hard we can go now; we know the threshold and we know what we can do."

Pavelich, always an economist with words, shrugged. "A little luck and a little hard work," he said, offering only a bit of a grin and that terse account to explain the three goals the Coneheads had just scored. Then he pushed past the fans and was gone.

"Nothing flashy, we just go with what we've got on our line," said Schneider, who had scored two goals. "We know where each other is. Harrington gave me a late pass on one, and Pav set me up on the other. I was all alone, but I wasn't complaining. We weren't nervous. After you've played in the Hipp, nothing can make you nervous."

The Hipp is the Eveleth Hippodrome, the legendary old brick arena with inflexible dasher boards, where Pavelich grew up and where Harrington and Schneider had to play every year. Brooks gave full credit to his all–Iron Range line for my *Minneapolis Tribune* account of the game. "I kept going to the Pavelich line tonight because they were hot," Brooks said. "They set the tempo for us tonight, so they became our first line. They're from the Range, and they have a tradition. This kind of performance is expected of them, by their fathers and their uncles. They're the product of a hungry environment, and what they did for us tonight didn't surprise me."

Brooks, who loved having adversaries to conquer, found another one with the media in the official postgame press conference. That morning Mike Lupica, a columnist for the *New York Daily News*, wrote a column ripping Brooks for being on a runaway ego trip, saying the coach was so anxious to get all the glory for himself that he wouldn't allow any of the players attend the postgame interviews. I found that humorous, because Brooks had expressed to me for several days that he didn't know how he could prevent players from being singled out. If that happened, it would undermine his attempts to unify the players. When the Russians refused to bring players to the press conference, Brooks saw his chance to do the same.

At one point during his post-Czechoslovakia victory press conference, Brooks asked, "Is there a Mike Lupica in here? Never mind, you don't need to raise your hand or stand up. I've never seen you or talked to you, but that didn't stop you from writing what you wrote in the paper. If you wanted to know why I'm not bringing players in here after games, you could have asked me. Instead you wrote what you did. But if you think I'm coming in here for my ego's sake, from now on you can ask your questions to Craig Patrick, my assistant, because I'm not coming."

The journalists recoiled, but Brooks wanted more: "Not only that, the press is welcome to talk to players on practice days, but not game days."

As he stalked out of the auditorium, I fell into step with Herb and asked, "What are you doing?"

He said, "Don't worry. You know, downstairs at the arena, the media can't go past the barrier to the dressing room, but just short of the barrier there's an arena manager's office, and I've worked it out with the manager so I can go in there and hide out. I'll just meet you in there after every game."

Brooks told the same thing to Gregg Wong, who was at the Olympics alone for the *St. Paul Pioneer Press*. Wong had to cover all the big events in every sport, so either he wasn't at the hockey game, or he had to hustle to get somewhere else afterward. Basically, after every game, I had an exclusive interview with Brooks. Then I'd run outside and catch the U.S. players as they exited into the snow, while the flowers of American sports journalism sat inside the auditorium complaining that nobody was bringing them their interviews. Herbie had no intention of enforcing a ban on the media talking to his players, and he didn't need to because only a couple of other even tried to talk to the players.

In *Miracle*, that whole impasse is kissed off in a brief scene where a postgame press conference is set in a classroom-size room. A reporter raises his hand and Herb cordially asks, "Yes, Mike?" The reporter, also quite cordially, asks if it's true that Brooks isn't bringing players so he can get all the attention for himself. Brooks answers, "No, Mike," and continues his pleasant discourse with the journalist. An otherwise well-done and inspirational movie could have benefited from accurately portraying the open hostility that prompted Brooks to end his attendance at the press conferences.

After Brooks began his boycott, I would hustle down to meet him in the arena manager's office after the games, then get back outside just as the players were leaving. If there was any extra time, I would run in the auditorium and try to catch the opposing coach's press conference. Rather than risk missing any nuggets from the press conferences, I made a deal with Bob Verdi, a columnist from the *Chicago Tribune*. If Verdi would cover me on any auditorium stuff, I would give him one Brooks quote after every game.

Throughout his life, Herbie tended to look for windmills he could out-tilt. His searches for worthy adversaries were often attempts to develop "us against them" scenarios to get his players' adrenaline pumping. Sometimes the University of Minnesota administration would be "them," or maybe it would be the general manager or even owner of a pro team against whom he could unify and rally the "us."

In 1980, Herbie and his Team USA took on the whole world, and after two games, a tie and a victory against the two best teams in the United States' pool suddenly thrust the team from overlooked to contender. If unappreciative media types wanted to line up on the "them" side, Brooks was more than willing to accommodate them.

CHAPTER 27

NORWEGIAN BREEZE

There were various reasons to anticipate a rout when the U.S. faced Norway in a Saturday matinee, switching from the Fieldhouse to the Olympic Arena for the first game of six that would fill the two buildings. In its favor, the U.S. had the youthful exuberance that overran Czechoslovakia, the Blue Pool's top seed, in a 7-3 romp that still had the whole hockey tournament buzzing. Meanwhile Norway, the tournament's lowest seed, had lost 10-4 to West Germany and 11-0 to the same Czech team handled by the United States.

On top of that, it was Norway that had almost ruined the U.S. team's ten-game European trip by forcing the U.S. to come from behind for a 3-3 tie, leading to Brooks' famous postgame skate-a-thon. The U.S. came back and hammered Norway the next day to complete the trip, but Brooks wasn't about to let his players forget the humiliating tie: "Norway tied us 3-3 back in Oslo in September, and not only that, they didn't tie us, we tied them. . . . If we're looking past Norway, we're in trouble. If we think it'll be easy, and we can just go out and finesse them, we're crazy."

Brooks wasn't even calculating the possibilities of reaching the medal round. The U.S. and Sweden were both 1-0-1, but Sweden still had to play Czechoslovakia, the 1-1 team the U.S. whipped. If the Czechs beat the Swedes, the Americans had a shot at not only reaching the medal round, but also being the No. 1 seed out of the Blue Pool, so long as they didn't stumble big-time against Norway, Romania, or West Germany—a team that always had been tough for them. West Germany had beaten Brooks' U.S. team twice in the 1979 World Championships. If Sweden got by Czechoslovakia and carried that tie with the U.S. into the medal round, goal differential would determine the seeds. While running up the score on an overmatched foe was not enticing to Brooks, Norway was susceptible to giving up a lot of goals, having been outscored 21-4 in their previous two losses.

Jack O'Callahan was still out with his fast-recovering stretched knee ligaments, but the training staff did an excellent job on Mark Johnson's shoulder. Johnson, who had been crosschecked from behind, away from the puck, by a Czech defenseman late in the game, had his shoulder and arm taped up like a mummy, restricting his movement but not preventing him from playing.

So the Norway game should have been a breeze, right? That's not the way it works in the Olympics, and certainly not the way things worked for the U.S. in its insistence on doing things the hard way. Early penalties left both teams skating a man short, and barely four minutes in, Geir Myhre deflected a shot from the blue line by Oeivind Loesaamoen past Jim Craig, and Norway led 1-0.

Norwegian goaltender Jim Martinsen stood firm in the opening period, and Norway took that 1-0 lead to the dressing room. The second period was different, mainly because Mike Eruzione capitalized on another power play in the opening seconds for a 1-1 tie. Johnson, with one arm taped down tight, got free in the slot, took a feed from McClanahan, and scored on a quick twenty-five-foot shot, and Dave Silk converted a feed from Mark Pavelich to make it 3-1.

The U.S. may have had trouble comprehending Norway's strategy, because the Norwegians were very defensive, even when they fell behind. "They sent in one guy and dropped the other four back on their blue line to defend," Johnson said, as quoted in my *Minneapolis Tribune* account. Erik Pettersen, Norway's coach, explained the strategy: "We are the lowest-seeded team in the tournament, and there is a large difference between the best and worst teams in the tournament. . . . So we try to defend in our games and keep the score down."

True, when Norway lost 11-0 to Czechoslovakia, it held the Czechs scoreless through the first period and six minutes of the second. Holding the U.S. scoreless through the first was another achievement in Norway's scheme. Nevertheless, the U.S. pulled away for a 5-1 victory.

In our private postgame meeting, Brooks praised the Bowling Green duo of Mark Wells and Ken Morrow: "Morrow is playing with a separated shoulder from the Czech game, and Wells is a battler who was the last player named to the team, and he stuck it out and now is rewarded."

Harrington pointed out that "We played OK, but we were still cruising a little from the last game. We never worried, we knew we were better, and we'll be much better in our next game."

Brooks had suggested as much. "The only way to beat that style of containment," he told me, "is to fall back, set up, and draw them out, or throw the puck in." After his yearlong effort to get his players to abandon the North American dump-and-chase mentality, Brooks still believed that while dumping the puck in was a bad style, it still was a good tactic when necessary.

"We were coming off a big, emotional victory, and I was extremely concerned about this game," he added. "We were brutal. . . . we stopped thinking. We broke down and didn't use all five out there; we were expressing ourselves with one or two at a time. I didn't do any screaming or yelling. I just wanted us to get back in rhythm. We'll be a better hockey club now, against Romania and West Germany."

Brooks didn't mind the final score, even though a chance to bolster the goal differential got away. In Red Pool play, the Soviet Union opened with a 16-0 romp over Japan, then beat the Netherlands 17-4. "I don't think it's in the best interest of sportsmanship for the Russians to score seventeen goals," Brooks told me, adding, "I'm not sure we could score seventeen goals in five games.

"I told our players we do not have enough talent to win on talent alone," he added. Then he caught himself, realizing how often he used that phrase through his Gopher days. "The guys from the Gophers must be sick of me. But young American players are selfish—if things are going good, they want more. That's the American way."

That day featured some other very interesting games, giving me a bearing on the rapidly unfolding tournament. Sweden beat West Germany 5-2 to join the U.S. at 2-0-1 atop the Blue Pool, but the Red Pool had the day's big surprise: Finland upset Canada 4-3. The Soviet Union, meanwhile, pounded Poland 8-1—the Russians had outscored three victims 41-5.

CHAPTER 28

ROMANIAN ANTI-ROMP

E ven though the U.S. team was 2-0-1 and holding its own destiny in its suddenly capable hands, Brooks knew his players weren't hitting on all cylinders, at least not to his satisfaction. Having scoring balance is great, he mentioned, but he needed to see some scoring from his top guns.

Brooks also outdid himself in his pregame motivation. Herbie told me that he had warned his players about losing to Romania after all they had accomplished, telling them that "playing in these games is a great opportunity. And being in the position of controlling your own destiny, as we are, is a miracle opportunity. Don't blow it. If you do, you'll carry it to your graves." Then he walked toward the door, turned back, and added, "To your [bleeping] graves."

That speech became one of the more moving parts of the movie *Miracle*, although it was shuffled in the film to become a pivotal part of Team USA's final medal round game against Finland. That adjustment wasn't necessarily just dramatic license. Brooks and his players were not in possession of daily notes, as I was, and their recall when the movie was made, twenty-three years after the fact, was understandably varied. Some remembered it as being before the third period of the Finland game; others thought it was in Brooks' pregame speech. Eric Strobel said he thought it came on the practice day before the Finland game. But there it is, in the old, yellowing pages of the *Minneapolis Tribune*, where I quoted Brooks making that statement before the game against Romania. The movie also had Jack O'Callahan returning from his stretched knee ligaments in the Soviet game, but actually he made his return against Romania and got an assist.

Brooks had reason to prod some of his top gunners into action. Steve Christoff, the team's pre-Olympic scoring leader, had yet to score after three Olympic games, nor had Neal Broten, the team's fourth-leading pre-Olympic scorer, or Strobel. Late in the Norway game, Brooks moved Christoff up to join center Mark Johnson and left wing Rob McClanahan, and shifted Strobel to the right side with Broten at center and Mike Eruzione on the left.

Brooks stuck with those changes for the Monday game against Romania, which was the day's finale. The spark Brooks was looking for flared to life: Christoff, Strobel, and Broten all scored their first goals of the Games, and the United States cruised to a 7-2 victory.

Brooks was so anxious to get his big guns firing that he seemed to overlook the Conehead line, which had been so instrumental in the team's success to that point. The Coneheads got the call to start and set a high tempo, and for the first twelve minutes, all four lines flew, creating dozens of scoring chances but doing little except making Romanian netminder Valerian Netedu look like a Hall of Famer.

Finally, the U.S. broke through, and when it did, it was the Coneheads, with Schneider scoring on a classic tic-tac-toe passing play. The U.S. led 4-1 after two periods. The Coneheads had figured in three of the four goals, but barely saw the ice in the third period.

"Don't be afraid to give us a few shifts," said Harrington, sarcastically, after the game. "He said we weren't moving the puck, so we got out three times in the third period. And we got the last twelve seconds of a power play as one shift."

Pavelich? He was typically against anything that sounded even remotely critical. "He's right. I wasn't moving," said Pav.

Impressive as 7-2 sounded, Romania had been socked 8-0 by Sweden. The goal differential, like it or not, was widening in Sweden's favor.

Brooks had said he was thinking of starting Steve Janaszak in goal against Romania, but changed his mind, giving Jim Craig his fifth start in ten days. It would have been the perfect opportunity to give Janaszak a game in which he was certain to shine, and bring back a refreshed Craig for the last game and the medal round.

Years later, McClanahan said, "The only mistake I think Herb made in the whole Olympics was in not playing Janny."

There could have been two reasons for his decision to leave Janaszak as the only player who didn't see ice throughout the Olympics, but they didn't seem pertinent at the time. Craig, of course, had matters well in hand, and it seems most likely that Brooks' well-documented lack of confidence in his goaltenders could have made him stay with the status quo. Bolstering that theory was the presence of Warren Strelow, Brooks' goaltending assistant who always was an advocate of staying with the hot hand in goal.

A more bothersome possibility is pure speculation. Janaszak was a loyal, four-year trouper for Brooks at the University of Minnesota, never yapping, never spouting off. But there is a wonderful story of the time he felt he had taken enough. Brooks pulled him from a game in which the Gophers were playing poorly. When the backup goalie was less lucky, Brooks, on the bench, said, "Janny, get ready," to which Janaszak snapped back, "[Bleep] you, I'm always ready."

It's a great story, but not the sort of thing that I wrote for the *Minneapolis Tribune*. Dan Stoneking, covering for the *Minneapolis Star*, asked if I thought Janaszak would be up to the task, and if so, why he hadn't played already. I told him Janaszak was a strong competitor and could easily be the regular goaltender on the team. To underscore my theory, I told him about Janaszak's colorful retort on the Gopher bench from the previous year.

When Craig got the start against Romania, it occurred to me that Stoneking was prone to "talking inside" with some sources, whether he knew any inside stuff or not. After the Olympics were over, I wondered if Stoneking had sidled up to Brooks and, in an attempt to get him to talk about Janaszak, told him that anecdote without revealing the source. I have no doubt that if he did, Brooks would have wondered why Janaszak was telling that story at such a crucial time. It would have been sufficient grounds for Brooks to not play him. If true, it would go down as my only regret from the Games.

For his part, Craig offered perspective on how the team was winning, but also on the pressures it was coming under. "The situation is getting to be a little itchy," Craig said. "It's getting to the point where we don't do the things we've been doing all season, like teasing someone who misses a shot . . . because we all realize a mistake could cost us a medal."

Playing the last game of the day against Romania, the U.S. knew that Sweden had beaten Norway 7-1. Meanwhile, a couple of intriguing happenings in the Red Pool caught notice. It was a mild upset when Holland beat Poland 5-3, but it was huge news when Finland almost upset the Soviet Union before falling 4-2. I watched that game, and Finland clearly had the Soviets in trouble. At 2:38 of the third period, the Finns went ahead 2-1. Seventeen-plus minutes are too long to sit on a lead by icing the puck, but the Finns tried to do exactly that. It almost worked, too, but late in the third, Russia scored three goals in a span of one minute and nineteen seconds to escape with a 4-2 victory.

It proved once again that even if the Soviet Union was not on top of its game, it could turn it up and score in a decisive burst. It also showed that Finland was far better than anyone realized.

CHAPTER 29

ESCAPE FROM WEST GERMANY

Maybe because the preparations had been so long and exhausting, or maybe because of the sudden elevated expectations for the U.S. hockey team, it seemed as though the preliminary round went by in a flash. Six hours before the seventh-seeded U.S. team's late start against West Germany at the Olympic Fieldhouse primary rink, the top seeds in the Blue Pool collided and Sweden, seeded third overall, defeated pool favorite and overall No. 2 seed Czechoslovakia 4-2. Nobody made a point of it, but that outcome also meant that the U.S. was guaranteed the other Blue Pool medal round slot before it took the ice for warm-ups. The Czechs were 3-2, and even a loss to West Germany couldn't sink the U.S. lower than 3-1-1.

In the Red Pool, Canada still had a shot at the medal round, having stayed only one game behind the USSR until the surprising loss to Finland. The teams entered the final preliminary games with the Soviets 4-0, Canada 3-1, and Finland 2-2. Only one problem: the top seeds were paired for the final day, so No. 2 Canada had to face the top-seeded Soviet Union, while Finland faced Holland.

Playing immediately before the U.S., Canada made a run at the Soviets, leading 3-1 in the second period. The Soviets scored thirteen seconds before the period ended to cut the deficit to 3-2, and then did what they did so often: rally to fight off another upset. The Russians scored twelve seconds apart to open the third period and vault ahead 4-3. The Canadians tied it a minute later, but the Soviets scored the final two goals to win 6-4 and keep their perfect record intact at 5-0.

When Finland beat Holland 10-3, the Finns moved into a tie with Canada at 3-2 for the second Red Pool place in the medal round. Canada had a clear edge in goal differential over Finland, but it didn't matter, because the first tie-breaker was their head-to-head result, and Finland had beaten Canada, thus claiming the second Red Pool spot in the medal round.

Brooks, of course, wasn't into doing the math or worrying about the other games. The U.S. had to stay focused and keep improving to go into the medal round at full tilt. A big victory could still secure the No. 1 seed from the pool, delaying its now inevitable meeting with the Soviet Union until the Sunday finale. Some of the players had done the math and realized the team trailed Sweden by six in goal differential. The U.S. would have to beat West Germany by at least seven to claim the top spot.

The warm-up was where the night's drama got more interesting. Some players had indicated that they were often annoyed when goaltender Jim Craig shouted orders and criticism at them during games, and that they might occasionally shoot a puck or two about head-high in practices. Craig's old BU teammate, Dave Silk, was never close to Craig and could be accused of whizzing a few head-high shots in warm-ups. But this time it was Mike Eruzione, another BU teammate, who sent a wrist shot at Craig while Brooks was still downstairs in the dressing room. I watched, startled, as Craig went down. He lay there motionless for a few minutes, and then was helped to the bench. "I was just trying to warm him up, and I hit him in the throat," said Eruzione.

"I almost blacked out," Craig said after the game. "It stunned me."

Yet when the game started, Craig was between the pipes.

Herbie and the players who had been with him on the 1979 U.S. National Team needed no warning about West Germany, which had beaten them 6-3 and 5-2 in the 1979 World Championships. That memory, plus the fact the Germans always seemed to play the U.S. tough, made winning by seven an unenviable task. Before the first period was over, that task was replaced by merely trying to win.

Before the game was two minutes old, West German defenseman Horst-Peter Kretschmer came across the neutral zone and dumped the puck into the U.S. zone—on goal. Craig looked mesmerized as the puck flew past him—clang!—and it was 1-0 for Germany. Up in the press box, I wondered why Brooks, whom I had not yet talked to, had started Craig if he was a bit woozy from being hit in warm-ups.

The U.S. came storming back, but Sigmund Suttner held firm in the West German goal. This was not good. The U.S. had started considerably better than it had in several earlier games, but things weren't clicking, and the deficit stayed 1-0 until fifteen seconds remained in the opening period—then it got worse. After a skirmish, Mark Johnson and Dave Christian both went to the penalty box with one German, giving West Germany a power play at 19:41. Udo Kiessling flung a shot on goal from the point, no screen, and Craig missed it—2-0.

The teams traded rushes and scoring chances in the second period, and Craig seemed to find himself, and the U.S. fought back to a 2-2 tie.

Rainer Philipp opened the third period by firing a shot off the right pipe. The U.S. team immediately broke back the other way, and Rob McClanahan drilled one home for the first U.S. lead of the game. Exactly three minutes later, Phil Verchota deflected a shot past Suttner, and Craig was by then sharp enough to hold on for a 4-2 victory.

It was with relief, more than momentum, that the U.S. completed the preliminary action at 4-0-1 to remain even with Sweden.

"The Germans always play well against the U.S.," Brooks told me afterward. "They get us to the point of not thinking, then we lose our poise and composure and play ragged.

"Seven goals. It was a bad plan to mention that we had to win by seven. If we played our game, we might have gotten seven goals. After one period, we needed the game; don't worry about scoring seven. We were not mentally sharp . . . and obviously we haven't played as well in our last three games as we did in our first two. And the last three is how we were playing coming in here."

Brooks was alluding to the flat spot the U.S. team had hit in the weeks prior to the Olympics. "Craig was fighting the puck all night," Brooks added. "They blew that first one by him, and I talked to him after the first period. I thought of replacing him after the first, but he said he was OK.

"Obviously, we haven't been as sharp as we can be, but we've gone five games undefeated. My worry is that we're not mentally sharp. I stayed away from the Sweden–Czech game and spent the time answering some hate mail. I thought knowing that we were automatically in might affect our performance. But the main thing is I didn't want us to go into the medal round with a loss."

I asked Herbie if he'd considered starting Steve Janaszak. "Why would I?" was his quick retort.

"Because Jim Craig was knocked out cold in warm-ups," I said.

"What? He *what*?!" he asked.

Brooks admitted that he had no idea Craig had been hit, but it explained the near-disastrous start.

CHAPTER 30

MEDAL-ROUND INTRICACY

A s the Olympic hockey tournament rounded the final turn and sailed into the medal round, compelling angles were everywhere. Sweden, the No. 1 seed from the Blue Pool, was fast, precise, and smooth, but totally intimidated by the very presence of the Soviet Union's overwhelming team. Finland, a true sleeper, was as technically skilled as any team at the tournament. Such future NHL stars as Jari Kurri and Reijo Ruotsalainen, both nineteen at the time, were on the squad, plus the explosive veteran Reijo Leppanen. But Finland was also so intimidated by the Soviet Union team as to abandon any chance of winning its preliminary-round game against the Soviets.

The Soviet Union's team was very similar to the Red Army–dominated outfit that had humbled the NHL All-Stars 6-0 in Madison Square Garden one year before, with the now-familiar names bolstered by Helmut Balderis from Latvia and the final player selected, Vladimir Krutov—the amazing nineteen-year-old who had emerged as a standout performer every bit as impressive as Valery Kharlamov or Slava Fetisov. On paper, probably not a single player on the U.S. team could have made the Soviet team.

Then there was the USA outfit, Herb Brooks and his disparate gang of college guys, welded together by their coach's progressive view of hockey and his ability to push all the motivational hot buttons in each player's psyche. True, the U.S. team was undefeated, but its players were still feeling their way. They weren't getting sufficient goal output for their effort, and Jim Craig, told by Brooks in that classic challenge that his "curveball was hanging," had yet to find his fastball.

There was a magical quality heading into the medal round. After the Russians had beaten the Canadians, coach Viktor Tikhonov grabbed each player as he came off the ice and kissed him on the cheek, just as he had done after the team escaped Finland 4-2. It was reported that he repeated this act in the dressing room. This was not a show of affection so much as a smooch from a coach who seemed totally relieved at surviving another game. How relieved would Herb Brooks have had to be before he would kiss Phil Verchota?

Tikhonov's display belied a curious vulnerability in the Soviet domination. That sounded absurd then—the Soviets had scored fifty-one goals in their five victories, more than twice as many as the U.S—but had the big red machine rolled on for so long that it was more than just overconfident? Hah. The Soviets had just humiliated the United States 10-3 in that final exhibition at Madison Square Garden. Even if Tikhonov was concerned, his players had to be thinking they could breeze through one more game against the Americans, then put it all together to snuff Sweden in the final game.

Tikhonov didn't attend the press gathering after the Russians had come from behind to defeat Team Canada, but assistant coach and spokesman Vladimir Yursinov said that Tikhonov "chewed out the players on the bench. What he said is very hard to translate."

When Clare Drake, Canada's coach, was asked how it felt to come so close to beating a supposedly unbeatable team, he said evenly, "I think it's possible to beat them. I thought we were going to do it today. And if I were a betting man, I would bet the Americans will do it, right here."

Meanwhile, when Sweden beat Czechoslovakia on that final preliminary day, thirty-six-year-old Swedish coach Bengt Ohlsson was asked about his team's chances for the gold. "We are heading for a silver," he replied. "The gold is out of the question. The Russians are the best. . . ."

Similarly, when I asked Frank Moberg, one of Finland's coaches, why the Finns had tried to sit on a 2-1 lead for most of the third period against the USSR rather than forcing play, he said, "We couldn't have beaten them. Just holding the score down and keeping the game close is good for our hockey program."

I couldn't believe that Sweden's program, which was based on such an intellectual style, was so pragmatic that it couldn't adjust its sights and shoot for the sky. Nor could I believe, based on all the so-called stubborn "Finlanders" I knew in Northern Minnesota, that Finland would take such a submissive outlook. Perhaps the impressive play of so many Swedes and Finns in the NHL since then has helped change their competitive mindset, but in 1980, the best they hoped for was to finish second.

Brooks was irritated that his team was undefeated but still seeded second behind Sweden going into the medal round. He didn't fully understand the round-robin format that made the medal round so intricate, nor did the U.S. players.

The U.S., for example, was 4-0-1, but the medal round was a new round-robin, with only the preliminary game between each pool's representatives carried forward. Team USA and Sweden both entered 0-0-1, because of their tie in the Blue Pool, while the USSR was 1-0 and Finland 0-1, based on their game in the Red Pool. If both Sweden and the U.S. could beat both Finland and the Soviets, goal differential would determine the gold between the Swedes and Americans. Finland, in fact, could only win the gold if it beat both Sweden and the U.S., and if the Soviets lost to both.

"Russia isn't playing that well, and Finland will be just another game," said Mark Johnson.

Johnson wasn't being overconfident, just expressing relief that the U.S. team not only had made the medal round, but also had a legitimate chance at a medal of some sort. Any medal would be a huge bonus for such a year of hard work.

Brooks tried to put blinders on and keep his focus on getting his team back to playing at its best.

When I told Herb that Canadian coach Clare Drake had predicted the U.S. would beat the Soviets, he was astounded. "He said that?" Brooks asked incredulously. He was genuinely moved that anyone from Canada would pick the U.S. to beat the USSR, especially when always-proud Canada had just lost such an excruciating game to the Soviets.

Privately, Brooks had realized after the first two games, against Sweden and the Czechs, that his players had an excellent chance of making the medal round, which meant they would face the Russians again. So he started dropping little remarks here and there to privately heckle the Soviet players. He mentioned several times how Boris Mikhailov looked a lot like Stan Laurel of Laurel and Hardy fame. He made repeated remarks to his players that "something is wrong with the Russians," and followed up by saying they were not their usual invincible selves.

All of Herbie's background machinations, plus what I had observed in watching Tikhonov and his players move through the preliminaries on cruise control, made for an interesting scenario. I wanted to flat predict that the U.S. would upset the Soviet Union. But how could I write anything so crazy sounding for the *Minneapolis Tribune*?

Turns out I couldn't, but I had a great idea for how to house it. On a free shuttle bus, I had overheard a young husband tell his wife that he wished he had brought along their piano. When his wife asked why in the world would he want to have brought the piano, he replied, "Because I left our tickets on it."

You can't make up stuff like that. I decided to write an off-the-wall feature as a letter home to my family. I wrote about how cold and crowded it was at Lake Placid and about the story of the guy without his piano. I asked how things were going back home and mentioned how I regretted that by the time I got home, the outdoor ice would probably be melting, which would end our neighborhood pickup games.

Then I got to the next-to-last paragraph where I would house my prediction—the real purpose of the story. I wrote about how well the U.S. was playing under Herbie.

The Russians were still the big favorite, although they were not playing anywhere near their peak. Then I wrote that even though we were far apart, maybe if we all focused our concentration on pulling for the U.S., all of that cosmic energy would come together and help the U.S. team pull off the greatest upset in hockey history.

Then, in the final paragraph, I wrote that I had to get going so I could get the letter in the mail and file a story. I added that I had been so busy that I hoped I didn't mix up the two documents. I thought the idea worked.

Late that night, I was talking to a sports slot-man at the *Tribune*, the guy who laid out the pages. He said that there was quite a disagreement among the newspaper executives and editors. A fair number said they didn't think that my "letter home" should run in the paper. In 1980, such pieces weren't considered worthy. Also, my piece said we all should be pulling for the U.S, which was out-of-bounds. However, it seemed quite natural that since the entire country would be pulling for the U.S. against the Russians, flat-out saying it might be acceptable.

The slot-man said that he was in the minority in the disagreement and had to fight hard for it. In the end, the decision was made to run the piece. It wasn't until a week later, after getting home and wading through all the old newspapers, when I came to that one. To my complete frustration, the whole "letter" ran—except for those last two paragraphs. The compromise to run it meant cutting the paragraph that predicted the U.S. could beat the Russians.

In view of how journalism has shifted toward feature reporting, such background features are now commonplace.

It must also be pointed out that Lake Placid during the 1980 Winter Olympics became a world unto itself. The Cold War was still raging and there were still hostages in Iran, but in Lake Placid there was precious little sense of the real world. For the players, their world was the arenas and the Olympic Village, which I visited one day to check out the almost-prison-like compound where the world's athletes resided. The place was, we were told, to be turned into a prison after the Olympics.

One real-world item that did circulate was that President Jimmy Carter was considering withholding U.S. athletes from participating in that year's Summer Olympics in Moscow. Herb and I had a major disagreement over that. He thought it made sense to support the boycott, and I asked how he might have felt if a boycott had kept the U.S. hockey team from playing at Lake Placid. Never mind where the venue was; my concern was for athletes who had trained intensely for a year, the way the U.S. hockey team had, before being told they couldn't play because of political gamesmanship.

On the day before the medal round, a Canadian television broadcaster told me "Canada is throwing its whole support behind the American team." That was made evident by the relative shortsightedness of the ABC network and Olympic organizers. While Canadian television altered its schedule to carry the U.S.–Soviet game live and in its entirety across that country in both English and French, ABC seemed worried about cutting into its afternoon soap opera schedule. The bigger mistake, though, was that tournament organizers chose to put the game on at 5 p.m. (4 p.m. in the Midwest and 2 p.m. on the West Coast) rather than in the Friday night primetime slot, which went to the Sweden–Finland matchup. ABC battled with organizers to change the game time, and when it didn't happen, the network decided to show the 5 p.m. game on videotape delay at 8:30 p.m. eastern standard time, which was already reserved for Olympic coverage.

Whatever was going on behind network and Olympic doors, Herb Brooks was loose and ready, and his mind was whirring at maximum efficiency.

"We could play our best game and still get blown out," Herbie said, in comments I used in the *Minneapolis Tribune* which *did* get into the paper. "But the 10-3 loss in New York does us good now. I made the team play a cautious forechecking style in that 10-3 game. Now we're going to try what we did against the Czechs. We'll forecheck aggressively from the top of the circles in, but once they get out past the top of the circles, we'll fall back to set up almost a 1-4 zone between the top of the circles in their end and our blue line.

"I don't know what's wrong with the Russians. They haven't had their usual intensity in their last two games. Maybe they consider this a comedown after having beaten the NHL's best pros. But if Russia takes us lightly, if they play like they did against Finland and Canada, they could be in trouble. When the smoke clears, I want our players to know that their maximum ability has been spent on the ice."

Then Herbie cracked a sly grin. "If Tikhonov loses, he goes to Siberia," he said. "If we lose, I go back to East St. Paul—that's not bad, because that's where I'm going anyway."

The tournament had been all-consuming, but Jack O'Callahan provided a dose of reality. Looking ahead, he said, "The saddest part of this whole thing is that Monday morning, we bus to the Albany airport and we scatter. And we'll never be a team again."

The sun was shining brightly, and the cold snap was over, but the reality was that this team wouldn't have a "next" season. This weekend, Friday and Sunday, would be it. Then it would be over.

CHAPTER 31

RUSSIAN MASTERPIECE

B y the time Friday, February 22 rolled around, the scene at the Olympic Fieldhouse was decidedly different from the casual circumstances of the U.S. team's first game against Sweden. The tickets were gone, scalpers were on hand, and the colorful arena was filled to capacity. Same with the press box. Many of the big-time columnists and reporters who couldn't be bothered by "ice hockey" at the start of the tournament were now elbowing their way into every available vantage point, and some unavailable ones.

The place was buzzing, and I took my usual seat, where I had a good view and could shoot photos. Media types got either a press box pass or a photo pass. I had the press box slot, but I also had my camera, so I was able to shoot from a unique vantage point.

Next to me was a very interesting fellow from Switzerland named Andreas Wyden. He was a media representative, but he also was the manager of the Lugano team from the professional Swiss Elite League. Wyden was a true student of the game, seeing it from the European perspective with knowledge of the North American style, which was the perfect balance for me, who conversely saw the game from the North American perspective but with an understanding and appreciation for the European style. We had interesting conversations every game and he was intrigued by this American team.

If every corner of the Fieldhouse was electrically charged, it was nothing like the inside of the Team USA dressing room, where Herb Brooks had been prodding his players into readiness.

"We were nervous as hell," recalled Eric Strobel, twenty-eight years after the fact.

The intricate masterpiece that was a year in the making was nearing completion. Nobody at that moment could have appreciated that in Herbie's mind, this masterpiece was really paint-by-numbers.

Ever since putting together his list of tryout candidates for the Sports Festival, Brooks had been running his own private experiment, believing he could organize and prepare a like-minded group to the fine edge of capability. There was no thought among the Americans of upsetting the Russians, only the thought of getting to the point of being prepared to compete with *anybody* in a crucial game by "playing our game." After the U.S. tied Sweden and beat Czechoslovakia, Brooks realized that the medal round was not only within reach, but a virtual certainty, barring a complete collapse against a lesser team. That, of course, would mean another shot at the Soviet Union, so he began planting the seed in his players' minds that the Russians perhaps were not invincible after all, that something was wrong.

No matter the teams' history against one another, it was time for more magic from Herbie, who walked into a dressing room filled with very quiet players and palpable tension that had each of them on a private emotional roller-coaster.

If the collective mood of the U.S. team could be likened to a hand grenade, Herbie was about to pull the pin with possibly the greatest pregame speech ever delivered:

"You were born to be a player. You were meant to be here. This moment is yours."

Mark Johnson, who went on to success as an NHL player and later as coach of the University of Wisconsin women's NCAA team, said, "Herb's pregame speech captured the moment. That's why he was so successful. He had vision, he was the ultimate salesman, he sold us on what he was teaching, and we believed it."

Herbie could overstate, belabor, repeat, and drive the players to distraction with his constant attempts at motivation, but this was brilliant. He showed confidence in what brought the players to this point and demonstrated his certainty that they had reached the highest plateau. If it was the Kentucky Derby, they had rounded the final turn and needed no whip, but merely to be turned loose to sprint for the finish.

"It was a really powerful speech," Strobel said. "Everybody was so nervous, and we were still scared shitless. But he was a really, really good coach. In practice, he'd have us doing something, but if there was any reason you didn't understand or disagreed with what he was doing, you could always tell him, and he'd listen patiently, and then explain it in a different way so it made sense. As great as he was with X's and O's, his mental approach was amazing.

"He knew you can't coach spontaneity, and that emotion has to come from within. Herbie was unique; he motivated everybody differently, and he made it hard not to be buddy-buddy with everybody on the team. As a player, maybe you were looking for more guidance, because players are always looking for guidance and wanting reassurance that they're doing what they're supposed to be doing. But once in a while, you have to find your own way. That's what Herbie wanted. He wanted to get us to the point where we could find our own way, and he knew that sometimes he had to be a hard-ass to get things done."

The 1980 team celebrates its stunning victory over the Soviets. *Author photo*

To say Team USA was ready was an understatement, but the Soviet players were unimpressed, emotionless, as they lined up in their red uniforms. The puck dropped, and immediately there was warfare in front of the net. Boris Mikhailov was penalized for hooking just 3:25 into the game, but the U.S. power play was uptight and futile, despite the chanting of the full-house crowd and its newly coined "USA! . . . USA! . . . USA! . . ."

The U.S. was playing through the nerves and tension. The Russians kept getting shots, but it was scoreless until 9:12 of the first period, when defenseman Alexei Kasatonov fired a shot from the right point. There was no screen, and Jim Craig looked set, but Vladimir Krutov got his stick on the puck and deflected it ever so slightly into the lower right corner—1-0 for the Soviets.

Five minutes passed. Steve Christoff came out for a turn with Mark Wells on the fourth line, and Dave Silk skated with Mark Johnson and Rob McClanahan in a switch of roles by Brooks. The Soviets pinned Team USA into its own end. Brooks didn't wait.

"At about the eight-minute mark of the first period," Herbie told me afterward, "they were coming at us so hard, with their strong-side defenseman pinching in, and we couldn't get out of our zone. So we started flying the strong-side winger, with the center cutting across behind him, and we had the weak-side wing drop back deep into the corner. That meant their defense couldn't pinch in on the strong side, and if we reversed the puck to the other corner, our weak-side winger was back deep enough that their weak-side defenseman couldn't get to him if he pinched."

Technical stuff, maybe, but it worked. In the normal setting, one defenseman might be behind the net with the puck or passing to his partner in one corner, making it the strong side, while the wing on that side would be posted on the side boards awaiting a pass. The Soviets had obviously scouted the Americans and figured they could forecheck hard with two forwards going at the two U.S. defensemen. This would force a hasty pass to the posted winger, who could be immediately stopped by the pinching Soviet defenseman. The third Soviet forward would shadow the U.S. center, who would curl and skate up the middle, while the U.S.'s weak-side winger would sag toward the slot as a defensive sentry. It was the same Czech tactic Lou Vairo had described to Scotty Bowman when the Soviets beat the NHL All-Stars.

With all that action on the strong side (or puck side), the weak-side defenseman would generally fall back in defensive mode. But Herbie's change did two things: by having the strong-side winger simply take off, flying up the boards and out of the zone, the Soviet defenseman had to fall back with him out of caution against a long, breakaway pass, instead of pinching down the boards. Meanwhile the center, cutting straight across, might also escape his check and get open. As a safeguard, it also meant the U.S. could reverse the puck to the weak side, where the winger was waiting deep in the corner with nobody on him.

Another gem of Herbie's coaching. By suddenly having to concentrate on a change in system, the Americans had something to focus on besides how uptight they were. In his usual manner of involving everybody, Brooks advised Craig Patrick to call upstairs with notification of the change, and to ask for Vairo's approval. Suddenly, the U.S. players seemed able to break out of their end much more easily.

"When we started flying the winger in the first period, it worked," Brooks said. "It jolted them, and they fell back. . . . We had practiced it, and we tried it against Canada in an exhibition.

"In a way, we were giving the Russians a little dose of their own medicine, and they didn't expect it."

Getting out of the zone was one thing, but there still was that 1-0 deficit. Leave it to the Coneheads. Mark Pavelich broke from his own blue line, up the right side. Buzz Schneider sped up the left. As anticipated, both Soviet defensemen fell back in good position, and it looked like no serious threat. Pav made a subtle little deke, as if to dart to the outside. The defenseman tensed up, and Pavelich instead zipped a perfect pass precisely on the tape of Schneider's stick. Buzz cranked and fired his shot past Vladislav Tretiak and into the net at 14:03 for a 1-1 tie.

The crowd erupted in a flag-waving, chanting uproar. The Coneheads stayed intact, while Brooks kept juggling the other lines, trying to unrack his other guns. Neal Broten centering Mike Eruzione and Steve Christoff put on a big shift. Then Mark Wells came out with Phil Verchota and Strobel, and the aroused U.S. forced more of the play.

With 2:26 left in the first, Alexander Golikov got loose deep on the right side and sent a pinpoint pass to the slot, where Sergei Makarov gunned it into the upper right corner of the net, and the Soviets regained the lead at 2-1.

With only a few seconds remaining in the period, the puck came out of the Soviet zone and just a bit across the U.S. blue line. Everyone in the building knew that the period would end that way. The Americans were doing pretty well, and they weren't out of the game at 2-1. But then came the play of the game—maybe of the entire tournament. Dave Christian hustled the puck out to center ice and, with 0:03 showing, fired a ninety-foot slapshot at Tretiak.

"Tretiak let it bounce off his pad, but he left the puck," Christian recalled.

Johnson, breaking past two relaxing defensemen, got the rebound first.

"When Tretiak blocked the shot, I happened to be right where the puck went. I made a little move and shot, and caught him by surprise," Johnson said afterward. "When the puck went in, I looked up at the clock and it said 0:00."

The officials signaled that the puck had gone in before time expired. Tikhonov quickly hustled his players off to the dressing room, as if their departure might assure that the period was over. It took awhile, but the officials ordered them to come back out and take a faceoff for the last second to be official. Tikhonov sent out only three skaters and his goalie—but it was Vladimir Myshkin, not Tretiak. The puck was dropped and the period ended.

The USSR had outshot Team USA 18-8 in that first period, and while the Soviet players had to be frustrated and certainly aroused at the sudden turn of events, the game still seemed like so many others in which holding their emotionless poise would allow the Russians to prevail.

When the teams returned to the ice for the second period, Brooks was astonished to see Myshkin in the Soviet goal. Brooks seized the moment to fire up his troops some more, saying, "They've just decided to keep the best goalkeeper in the world on the bench." Afterward, there were outrageous rumors that Tretiak had pulled himself, although years later I asked the legendary Russian goalie and he said only that Tikhonov was a fool.

It didn't make an immediate difference. On the power play, Alexander Maltsev put on a burst of speed to get past the defense, then cut for the net and fired a shot past Craig for a 3-2 Russian lead. The Soviets attacked with renewed force, and while the U.S. skaters battled back, they mostly failed to get any shots on net. Midway through the period, Craig was penalized and Johnson put Schneider in shorthanded, but his shot missed the net. The Soviet Union outshot the U.S. 12-2 in the middle period. Trailing by just one didn't seem that bad.

"I told our guys we had . . . as many thrusts as they did," Brooks said. "We just were not getting shots. When we didn't get shots, it eliminated one of the most effective parts of our game—forechecking—because they'd get control and we were falling back in backchecking patterns.

"I told the guys, 'Stick to the system, stick to the system.' You get your heart right in your throat while saying it, but I kept saying it, and we stuck with it."

Craig was playing his best, holding the U.S. firmly in the game despite being outshot 30-10. While it was true that the U.S. players had missed a fair number of good chances, it was an impressive selling job to convince them they weren't being outplayed.

In the third period, the fiery Vladimir Krutov was called for high-sticking at 6:47. The Russians pressed to keep the Americans from setting up on the power play, but Bill Baker moved in from the left point and passed to the right of the slot, where Johnson slammed the puck from between a defenseman's feet to beat Myshkin and tie the game.

Again, the arena was rocking, and the chanting and cheering reached a fever pitch. Baker didn't make the official score sheet with his pass, but nobody cared.

At precisely 10:00—the halfway point in the period—the Conehead line got rolling again. Buzz Schneider, always disciplined, carried out of the U.S. zone, blasted the puck into the offensive zone from the center red line, and then veered to the bench for a change as Harrington and Pavelich sped in deep, in hot pursuit of the puck. Myshkin turned the shot aside and into the left corner as Mike Eruzione came on for Schneider. Bill Baker, the left defenseman, thought Eruzione would be too late to help the attack, so he jumped at the chance to join the rush. Harrington's hustle got him to the puck first and he knocked it up the left boards. Pavelich never really took possession of the puck, but as it came up the boards out of the corner, he knew he would get to it first. He also knew a Russian player would be right on him, so he made a deft one-touch backhand pass to send the puck back toward the slot. Chances were Baker might be there, and if not, the puck would go through to Dave Christian on the right point.

Baker was too far in to catch the pass, and as Christian moved toward the slot for it, Eruzione, who probably should have stopped at the point to cover for Baker, cruised diagonally toward the slot, reached back to gather in the puck, and fired through the traffic. The puck puffed the netting behind Myshkin, and the crowd erupted.

"Buzzy came off early—my pal, he owed me one," said Eruzione, who was just late enough to be right on time. "Harrington worked the corner to Pav, who fought a guy and got it to me some way. I kept walking in, and a defenseman screened the goalie, so I shot."

Christian, the centerman playing brilliantly as a defenseman throughout the tournament, laughed about the goal years later. "That might've been the only time Billy ever beat me to the crease," Christian told me. "Eruzione always said that if he hadn't scored that goal, he'd have gone back to painting bridges. He got that goal by coming straight from the bench. The puck was coming right to me, and he poached it. Too bad. I might have scored that goal instead, and Mike would have looked good painting bridges. Instead, he's never worked a day in his life because he's turned that one goal into a career."

With the U.S. holding a 4-3 lead, the crowd screamed every time the Americans cleared the puck across their own blue line. Then the fans cheered every time a U.S. player touched the puck. Steve Christoff flattened Sergei Starikov along the boards. Mike Ramsey flattened somebody almost every shift. The youthful Americans weren't sitting on the lead—they were spending their exuberance to flawlessly cover every possibility, making the smart moves to stop Soviet attacks, chipping the puck back out of the zone, advancing to the next zone, and overwhelming the Russians by hustling for every loose puck.

The Russian players held their storied, emotionless poise, but seemed baffled by how smart and tenacious their opponents were. Not only was Team USA's conditioning (all those Herbies) paying rich dividends, but its players also seemed to have even greater quickness after Eruzione's goal. The crowd kept cheering, chanting, and waving giant flags. Otherwise hardened journalists cheered in the press box. I scarcely remembered to exhale, and if I muttered anything, it was to Andreas Wyden, my Swiss friend sitting next to me. But I didn't cheer, surprising myself with my own discipline.

Wyden was eloquent in his analysis: "When the U.S. was behind, they had to invent something to get ahead, and they did. . . . Now that the Russians are in trouble, they are poised. But they don't need poise, they need emotion."

The clock was not yet an ally; there was still too much time left. A full five minutes remained; with exactly that time remaining, the Soviet Union had trailed Finland 2-1, then pumped in three goals to win 4-2. Could the American skaters keep it up? The U.S. defensemen were brilliant, even though Brooks played just four blueliners almost all the way: Christian and Baker on one unit, and Ramsey and Morrow on the other. Jack O'Callahan had come back and played against Romania and West Germany, but he obviously wasn't near 100 percent on his injured knee. Bob Suter was hotly competitive as usual, but he had never quite regained the quickness he had before breaking his leg and missing much of the latter part of the team's exhibition slate. On top of that, Morrow, the 6-foot-4 giant, was hindered with a separated shoulder from the Czech game.

O'Callahan, a bundle of energy, was very active on the bench. "OC was so involved in the club that he was practically coaching the team through the last five minutes," Brooks said. "All I was doing was changing lines."

"Against the Russians, we learned some things from the 10-3 game that definitely helped us when we played them in the medal round," said Christian, the converted defenseman. "They'd have the puck coming at you, and then they'd turn back and throw it all the way back, maybe to their goalie, and about the time you changed directions to move back up, they'd go end-to-end in about two seconds. Just as Herb thought, by playing them before the Olympics, we knew what to expect. And I don't think the Russians counted on the condition we were in."

Mark Johnson still had his arm taped up extensively from his shoulder injury against the Czechs, but it didn't seem to bother him. "There were no broken bones, and it wasn't really separated," said Johnson, "so it was more like a bad bruise. I'd get treatment for it, then get taped up enough so it restricted things, but when you get playing and sweating, it becomes a moot point. You can be sore after the games end."

With three minutes remaining, the Russians remained cool and poised. Brooks read Tikhonov like a book and matched him page for page. "They didn't have a good scoring chance through the last ten minutes," said Christian.

"We went right at 'em with what was almost a Russian system," said Harrington, right after the game. "Herbie cut down the shifts. We weren't trying to match lines, but when they changed halfway through a shift, we did too."

Down below, the building shook: "U-S-A! . . . U-S-A! . . . U-S-A! . . ." The chant rained down from the rafters, as the clock hit 2:00, then 1:59, and the crowd rose in a standing ovation. The aggressive Americans were clogging passing lanes, and the always-precise Russian passing game was suddenly not precise at all. Attempted passes went for icings, and each drew an even louder ovation.

There was 1:29 left and the Soviets rushed again. Boris Mikhauilov, looking like a very concerned Stan Laurel, forced a shot and missed the net with forty-five seconds remaining. Vladimir Petrov fired. Wide again. Remarkably, the Russians didn't pull

Myshkin for a sixth attacker. Perhaps the Soviet Union had been behind so rarely that it had never practiced pulling its goalie.

With twenty-five seconds to go, Ken Morrow was checked off the puck behind the net, but Mark Johnson flipped the loose puck clear. The crowd was standing and yelling itself hoarse, the giant flags were waving. As the clock went to ten seconds, Johnson sent the puck up the side boards. McClanahan was there to take possession, but instead he skated along with it, like a hired escort, protecting it as the clock went from 0:03 to 0:02 to 0:01. When it hit 0:00, he leaped into the air like a high jumper, thrusting his arms to the rafters, as his teammates poured onto the ice in a massive celebration.

Who could ever forget ABC's Al Michaels' now-legendary call as Rob McClanahan escorted the puck up the side boards to safety and the final seconds ticked away?

Michaels, in what has become the signature phrase of a long and illustrious career, marked those final seconds by asking, "Do you believe in miracles?"

Fabulous line. Michaels later said he knew it would require a special final tag line from the announcer's booth, and his famous phrase just popped into his mind.

Among those who question that are Keith "Huffer" Christiansen, a splendid but pint-sized centerman, and Mike "Lefty" Curran, a quick, left-handed goaltender. Both played high school hockey at International Falls, Minnesota, where nicknames are prevalent, if not mandatory. Both were fantastic players, Huffer at Minnesota-Duluth and then with the Minnesota Fighting Saints, and Lefty at the University of North Dakota, before rejoining Huffer with the Saints.

Both were also teammates on the 1972 U.S. Olympic team, which created its own history by winning the silver at Sapporo, Japan. They said that each member of that 1972 team had received a video record of their silver-medal games. The tape shows that in the closing seconds of their silver medal–clinching game, play-by-play announcer Curt Gowdy asked, "Do you believe in miracles?"

Gowdy's color commentator on the telecast was a bright young broadcaster named . . . Al Michaels.

Regardless, the U.S. college kids had just beaten the mighty Soviets 4-3. The exuberance of youth, driven to what they thought was excess by their coach—and incredible conditioning from those dreaded Herbies—dominated the Russians through the third. The U.S. practically toyed with the most powerful hockey team in the world through the final minutes with a display of defensive cohesion that left Brooks repeating, "Play your game."

Immediately after the final buzzer, the movie *Miracle* shows Herbie leaving the bench and going downstairs to stand against the wall of the darkened and silent corridor to put his head in his hands and sink to the floor in a puddle of spent emotion. Great theater. In reality, he went downstairs to the dressing room, where trainer Gary Smith found him in the bathroom.

"I was one of the first to the dressing room, because I didn't go on the ice, either," said Smith. "I found Herbie standing alone in a stall in the bathroom, looking at the wall, as if to say, 'What have we done?' I looked at him, and he didn't say anything."

And then he went to the little arena manager's office. I walked in and Herbie was behind the desk, grinning like a Cheshire cat. Emotional meltdown? Far from it. Herbie's memorable words were: "This is going to cost Giel a ton," referring to Minnesota athletic director Paul Giel.

We both laughed. Lou Nanne came busting through the door, his jacket tied around his waist and hanging down past his rear end. He had torn the crotch of his pants when he jumped out of his seat at the finish.

"President Carter called," Brooks said. "He said we made the U.S. proud, and he invited us to the White House. My banker called, too. I don't know what he wanted, but I'm afraid to call him back."

Herbie was loose and laughing. I wanted to stay, but I had to run upstairs to catch the players as they left the arena. As I was about to leave, Herbie stood up, and then he grimaced, and rubbed his hand on his chest, right about at his solar plexus. "What's wrong?" I asked, thinking that maybe he was having a mild heart attack.

"When the game ended, O'Callahan was so excited, he hit me," Brooks told me. "At least, I *think* it was because he was so excited."

O'Callahan was a competitive character from the tough Charlestown neighborhood in Boston. He might not have been healthy enough to play regularly against the Russians, but that didn't mean he might not have been doubly emotional—frustrated at not playing more shifts, and ecstatic at the upset unfolding in front of him. For twenty-eight years, I wondered about that, and then, five years after Herbie's death, I got the opportunity to reprise that incident in a phone call with O'Callahan.

"I can't believe he told you that," said O'Callahan. "I did punch him. It wasn't really a punch, but I was pissed at having spent the whole year on the team and that he kept me after I got injured, and then we pulled off the win against the Russians. He came at me to give me a hug, and I threw a forearm and caught him right in the chest. I caught him really hard, too. But I didn't think anybody knew about it."

Outside, in the snow, a throng of people jammed the area where I had always had the players to myself. A few other journalists were out there, too, for the first time in the whole tournament.

"It's just crazy," Bill Baker said. "I still can't believe it. They weren't as physical this time, but Jimmy Craig proved he's a big-time goalie. We were singing 'God Bless America' in the dressing room after the game—although we had to teach a few of the guys the words."

I spotted a side door to the arena opening, and Mark Wells came out, wearing a jacket that was different than the team jackets all his teammates were wearing. I caught up to him, and he said, "Shhh, don't tell anyone. I'm trying to sneak out," then adding, "The Russians were actually sitting on a one-goal lead from the middle of the second period. We had good flow, and we knew we could do it."

Back in front of the door, the crowd pushed so close that I could barely take notes, as I caught John Harrington. "It will take me a while for this to soak in," he said. "We never gave up, even though we were reeling a little for two periods. . . . We went to school on their last two games. We knew going into the third period that we're younger than they are, so we're gonna bust our butts and take it to 'em."

I thanked John, and as he pulled away, I heard whoever it was behind me call, "Mark! Hey, Mark, wait a minute." As I edged through the crowd the other direction, I glanced back and saw that it was Dave Anderson, the well-known *New York Times* sports columnist. He had been standing right behind me, taking notes as I interviewed Harrington. I didn't realize until later that he thought I had been interviewing Mark Johnson.

I still had time to run into the auditorium, where I caught Vladimir Yursinov, Soviet assistant coach and press conference spokesman. "Merit must go to the other team. They played a fantastic game. The best of the tournament."

The Soviet team and its officials could seem cocky, almost arrogant, when they won, but through Yursinov, they proved classy and gracious after an excruciating loss that rocked the entire hockey world. Maybe that's the Russian way.

Back outside, the crowd was still clustered around the Olympic Fieldhouse exit. As the players trickled out, one and two at a time, the nightly medal celebration down on the nearby lake was beginning, with a hail of fireworks lighting the Lake Placid sky. People stood around, bathed in the combined glow of the fireworks over the lake and the U.S. victory. Suddenly, a guy thrust his fist in the air and shouted, "Got two for the Sweden–Finland game. Fifty bucks!"

That's the American way.

CHAPTER 32

FINNISH FINISH

The day off on Saturday flashed by, and the United States sailed into its Sunday, February 24, final medal-round game on an incredible high from beating the Soviet Union and putting Olympic gold directly in its sights. The U.S. players certainly didn't share my concern on their behalf for what they could be in for against Finland. Nor did the U.S. fans, who flocked eagerly into the Olympic Fieldhouse, passing scalpers who were asking—and getting—$125 a ticket. Finland tied Sweden 3-3 and stood 0-1-1 to the 1-0-1 of the U.S., 1-1 of Russia, and 0-0-2 of Sweden.

What kind of a story would it be to have Team USA practically romp through the preliminary round and shock the Soviet Union, only to lose to Finland and have to get up on the low stand to accept the bronze medal behind the USSR and Finland?

Hard to imagine, yet I had watched Finland closely throughout the tournament and was very impressed with its players' talent, speed, playmaking, and scoring abilities. They had beaten Canada, which had pinned three exhibition season losses on the United States, and they had the Soviets down 2-1 with five minutes to play. As I had discussed with various observers, there were a number of brilliant forwards in the tournament, especially Soviets Valery Kharlamov and Vladimir Krutov, Mats Naslund of Sweden, and the three Stastny brothers of Czechoslovakia. But my favorite player, the one who had impressed me the most out of all the teams other than the United States, was Reijo Leppanen, who had five goals and four assists through the first five games for Finland.

When I discussed with others how good Leppanen was, I continued to hear about Finland's best defenseman, Tapio Levo. Leppanen was a smooth and polished thirty, and Levo was twenty-four, so their experience made them vital parts of the dangerously explosive Finnish team, which also starred Jari Kurri and defenseman Reijo Ruotsalainen, a pair of future long-term NHLers.

In addition, while both the Swedish and Finnish teams were mentally intimidated to the point of believing they had no chance to beat the Soviet Union, they held no such respect for the U.S. I explained my concerns to Herbie, but he was already well aware of how good Finland was—even if his players weren't convinced.

My optimism was pretty subdued in the press box as the crowd filed in, bearing flags and starting their rhythmic clapping and chanting before the game even started. Then the press box address system announced the lineup: "From Finland, scratch No. 22, Reijo Leppanen, and No. 8, Tapio Levo."

I had to shake my head. Herbie's magic had worked again. Here was the U.S. team with the gold medal on the line, and their opponent would be playing without its best forward and most impressive defenseman.

Referee Vladimir Subrt from Czechoslovakia dropped the puck in the packed Fieldhouse, and the U.S. team played a full rotation of strong shifts. The U.S. team got a power play at the five-minute mark, but couldn't beat Jorma Valtonen in the Finnish goal.

At 9:20, Mikko Leinonen, who scored two of the goals to tie Sweden 3-3 in the Finland's first medal round game, broke on the left and passed across to Jukka Porvari, who blasted a fifty-foot slapshot. The Finns liked to use off-hand shooters for a better angle, and I thought Porvari's shot surprised Jim Craig. Porvari got all of it, but it was unscreened, about a foot inside the right post, and found the net about glove-high.

Again, I smiled at the thought that this might be part of the puzzle—Craig gave up a shaky goal to start almost every game, then came on as each game progressed. This time, the U.S. outshot Finland 14-7 in the first period, but trailed 1-0, even though Finland mostly played only two lines because of the loss of Leppanen.

The U.S. had some chances, but also had some trouble making plays against the skilled and well-drilled Finns, who roamed freely and interacted with each other to defuse the U.S. passing. Pavelich set up John Harrington to start the second period, but Harrington misfired. Then Mike Ramsey went off for roughing. Neal Broten and Steve Christoff went out to kill the last part of the penalty, and when Broten pestered a Finnish player, Christoff swiped the puck and broke in, scoring with a backhander from the slot, two seconds after the penalty had expired.

The 1-1 tie was short-lived, however. Buzz Schneider was called for slashing at 6:00 and this time the Finnish power play clicked. Leinonen rushed in on the left and dropped a pass back to the left point. As Hannu Haapalainen cranked up to shoot, Leinonen swung behind the net and came out on the right side, perfectly positioned to bank in Haapalainen's hard pass at 6:30. The U.S. players tried to rebound, but fizzled on a power play.

The score remained 2-1 at the second intermission, and the Americans were twenty minutes away from having Finland pull the rug out from under their miracle. Snapping things back into focus would take one last, wonderful period in which

Team USA did it all—all the rushes, all the plays, all the shots, all the goals, all the saves, and even all the penalties in a final, twenty-minute celebration of what the whole season meant to the team.

Two minutes into the final period, Dave Christian took off with the puck and broke straight up the middle for the net. Just as Christian got in position to score, he snapped a pass to his left, and Phil Verchota, breaking hard, drilled his shot home to tie the game.

Mark Johnson came on for a line change at the six-minute mark and went deep behind the net to gain possession, quickly feeding out front where Rob McClanahan had just arrived at the right edge, unnoticed by Finland's defense. McClanahan slipped the puck under Valtonen to give the U.S. its first lead of the game.

The U.S. and Finnish teams shake hands after the Americans secured the gold medal at Lake Placid. *Author photo*

The teams traded rushes through the middle part of the period, but then Verchota went off at a critical time. With only 4:15 remaining, the Finnish power play could tie the game, recapture the momentum, and still ruin the whole show for Team USA. The U.S. players knew that Jim Craig liked to get a clear view of the shots, but they stayed busy by throwing themselves in front of repeated Finnish shots.

Short-handed, Christoff barged in against the tiring Finnish defense, and when he got the puck and found himself alone against two Finns, he knew somebody had to be coming. He passed out toward the blue line where, sure enough, Mark Johnson was coming from the bench. Johnson caught the pass just inside the blue line and carried it in for a shot. Valtonen made the initial save, but couldn't stop Johnson from jamming in his own rebound. The short-handed goal made it 4-2 and put Team USA into a comparatively comfortable position. Craig held firm, and the U.S. finished the gold medal–clinching 4-2 victory.

The U.S. team poured onto the ice. Craig, whose mom had recently died, skated over near the glass, and a fan tossed him a large American flag. He unfurled it and draped it around his shoulders like a cape in what became an iconic image of the U.S. team, as his eyes searched the throng for his father.

Vice President Walter Mondale had come to Lake Placid to pay personal tribute to the hockey team. When he was escorted to the dressing room, Mondale, a Minnesotan, asked, "How many of you are from Minnesota?"

Before anyone could answer, Brooks said, "Nobody is from Minnesota, Mr. Vice President. We're all from the U.S.A."

Herbie's reappearance at the postgame press conference in the huge auditorium was well-timed, and he brought his entire team to the stage.

"Much has been said about the players and the press conferences," Brooks said. "You people have been watching a group of people who startled the athletic world, not just the hockey world. If you're a father, you kick your sons in the ass a few times, and as a coach, I do, too. You love your sons, as I love this hockey club."

The still-celebratory media were throwing a few questions out, but mostly, we were all entertained by the group, which included players throwing Brooks' "Brooksisms" back at him and heckling their coach.

Somebody asked if the players, having accomplished so much, would like to stay together and keep playing.

"I would like to take two weeks off, first," said Eruzione. "We jelled into a team in six months. No coach or anyone could have experienced the kind of season we've had.

Members of the U.S. team celebrate after defeating Finland 4-2 on February 24, 1980, to clinch
the gold medal. Pictured from left are Rob McClanahan, Bill Baker, Buzz Schneider, Mike Ramsey,
Bob Suter, Neal Broten, Phil Verchota, Eric Strobel, and Steve Christoff (partially out of frame).
AP Images

Who knows if I'll ever see John Harrington or David Christian again? That's a shame
. . . and maybe a relief, too."

Everyone laughed. Then Jack O'Callahan, who returned to play in the preliminary
round, but barely touched the ice in the medal round, jumped onto the table with a
beer in one hand.

"My question is to coach Brooks," he shouted, even though the players booed on
cue. "Do you expect to be coach again?" Then he added, "Gong that question."

Brooks said, "In a short period of time, I'll be known as 'Herb Who?' to these guys."

Brooks also seized the chance to send a well-aimed zinger at AHAUS. In recent
years, the Colorado Springs–based governing body of U.S. amateur hockey had lost
touch with grassroots hockey. Instead it had turned to politics by getting to the right
congressmen to hustle through the citizenship papers of, for example, Lou Nanne,
and later Bryan Trottier. The act of naturalizing Canadian NHL stars for the sake of
improving the lot of American hockey rankled Brooks. In fact, his brother, Dave Brooks,
had attempted legal action when Nanne took the place of a U.S.-born player.

"This team's success proves that AHAUS should look at the grassroots youth
programs, and maybe look at college hockey programs in a little more depth, as the

sound basis of American hockey," said Brooks. Most in the audience probably didn't have a clue as to what Brooks was alluding.

One reporter mentioned he had heard about somebody chronicling the various Brooksisms uttered by the coach during the season, and John Harrington was called on for a brief summary:

"Well, 'we were damned if we did and damned if we didn't.' 'Fool me once, shame on you, fool me twice, shame on me.' 'We went to the well and the water was cold and the water was deep. We went to the well again, and the water was colder and the water was deeper.' 'We looked like a monkey screwing a football out there.' For lack of a better phrase, that just about wraps it up."

Everybody laughed, including Brooks.

With that, the U.S. team got up and stormed out of the auditorium, coach and all. The gathered media trooped after them, understandably perhaps, but also quite rudely, vacating the press conference auditorium, even though the Finnish delegation was just coming in. Too bad. A couple of reporters from Finland and I were the only ones who stayed in the large, vacant auditorium to hear coach Frank Moberg deliver some of the most moving comments of the entire tournament.

"Everyone knew the Soviets were the best team. But now, the USA has the gold medal, and the Soviet team has something else, depending on their last game. So the U.S. team is better," he began.

"We knew before the tournament that the U.S. had a good team, and as the tournament progressed, it was proving to be a *really* good team. And now, obviously, they are the best. They work hard and skate hard, and they have some European elements when they play, with more diverse style than NHL teams show."

Moberg was asked again about the U.S. performance.

"It was a small surprise," he said. "I say small, because we had Russia wondering for a while, and Canada had Russia wondering for a while. But the U.S. worked real hard, hustled all the time. And," he added, as he reached out his right hand and slowly turned it from a grasping hand to a clenched fist, "they have this . . . this *spirit*! You can almost touch it!"

The most eloquent and thoughtful description of the Herb Brooks magic that had been channeled into the Team USA miracle had been offered by a coach of an excellent but just-vanquished team, in the deserted auditorium of an abandoned press conference.

Next door, in the final game of the tournament, between the two top seeds, the Soviets blasted the Swedes 9-2.

CHAPTER 33

AFTERMATH

After the emotional post-Olympic celebrations, it was time to start writing, but I couldn't yet, because next up was the official medal ceremony back out on the ice at the Olympic Fieldhouse, which in 2005 was renamed Herb Brooks Arena.

The Swedish players, called up one at a time to get their bronze medals, each took a turn stepping onto the lowest of the three medal stands. The U.S. players stood in something of a ragged line, still wearing their blue warm-ups they had worn to the press conference and unable to conceal their glee. Next, the Soviet players stepped onto the middle pedestal one at a time to accept their silver medals.

When it came time for the U.S. players to be summoned, also one at a time, each went up onto the tallest of the three stands and had his gold medal draped around his neck. Each, in turn, raised his arms in triumph and set off a new round of applause and chants of "U-S-A! . . . U-S-A! . . ." among the spectators.

Captain Mike Eruzione was the last player called to the stand. Always a bit of a ham, he had a great idea. Instead of standing there all alone while his teammates cheered him on from fifty feet away, he waved them to come forward and join him. The team ran across the ice and clamored up on the stand.

At the ceremony, the Olympic Committee distributed twenty gold medals, one to each player. There wasn't one for Brooks, and he later said sarcastically that he had missed a gold medal in 1960, and now he missed one again, in 1980.

Afterward, the team had a large, official get-together—great food, celebratory drinks, and, overall, a jovial atmosphere. The players let loose, and so did the peripheral guys, including Lou Vairo, whose counsel from up in the rafters via walkie-talkie was an interesting element. It was valuable to Herbie's peace of mind, most notably when Brooks changed systems to escape the defensive zone against the Russians.

"The happiest moment of my life," Vairo told me years later, "was to be at Lake Placid and see that wonderful victory."

Herbie remained true to his personality, far more adept at creating fantastic scenarios than he was at accepting accolades or celebrating. And his mind kept racing to the future. In this case, the future was the next morning, when the players would

The mighty Soviets congratulate the 1980 U.S. Olympic hockey team prior to receiving their silver medals. *Author photo*

have to rise early, clean up, and get dressed to be whisked by jet to the White House for a meeting with President Carter. Herbie was concerned that too much partying might leave a few of the lads too off form to make the proper impression during such a formal occasion, so he gave the call to the troops: "Come on, guys, let's get going. The party's over."

His announcement received a mixed reaction, and Ralph Jasinski, the amiable fellow who had taken over the team's general manager role midway through the exhibition season, told Herbie to lighten up, that the games were over.

Later, Brooks told me, incredulously, "AHAUS fired me." I asked him what he meant, and he told me about that party and his attempt to get his players to break it up and go back to the Olympic Village. Herb said that Jasinski, a loyal AHAUS representative, had told him his job was over, that he was no longer in control. In reality, Jasinski had tried to get Herbie to quit being the taskmaster—the general—and to relax a little, but Brooks took it as a dagger.

Vairo supported my theory.

"Ralph Jasinski wanted the party to continue," Vairo told me. "Herb announced to his players, 'Come on, we got to get ready to leave,' and Ralph said, 'Herb, you're

President Jimmy Carter welcomes Olympic medalists to the White House. He is surrounded by members of the hockey team, as well as speed skater Eric Heiden (right). *Photo by Keystone/CNP/Getty Images*

not coaching anymore.' Herb said later, 'He fired me.' But it didn't really happen the way he thought."

Brooks' tenure as the 1980 Olympic coach may have come to an end, but his players had come to admire their mentor. John Harrington, who had played under such great coaches as Dave Hendrickson at Virginia High School and Gus Hendrickson at Minnesota-Duluth, and now Herb Brooks, tried to put it in perspective, twenty-eight years later. "The biggest difference is that Herb pushed and pushed until he got the absolute best out of every player," Harrington said.

Gary Smith, Herb's loyal trainer, remained amazed at Brooks' motivational tactics even after Brooks' death. "Back in the first game against Sweden, I told Herbie on the bench that I didn't think Robby McClanahan could go and we should send him to the dressing room for treatment," Smith recalled. "I walked into the room behind Herbie, and he made some crack to McClanahan about his thigh being a long way from his heart, and Robby, who was on his back with a giant ice bag on his leg, straightened his leg and the ice bag went flying, and he chased Herbie into the hallway.

I thought to myself, 'My god, we're in the first game, and he's lost it!' But you know, the whole team played much better from then on.

"And in the Russian game, we made a change on a penalty kill, and Neal Broten went on the ice. I counted the players and reached out and grabbed Broten by the back of the jersey and pulled him back, or we would have had a too-many-men penalty. Herbie walked down the bench and gave me a little tap, and said, 'Way to stay in the game.' Bob Suter, sitting on that end of the bench, looked up at me and gave me a big grin."

Mark Pavelich, who always said that whenever he wasn't sure what Brooks wanted, he just went harder, turned out to be the perfect example of what Herbie wanted.

"The things other coaches did drove Herb crazy," Pav recalled. "He never let it rest. It was a lot more than a daily job. He was totally consumed with it. We always had good workouts with Herb. A lot of other coaches weren't as smart. He would space it out, with drills, skating, and game situations interspersed. We always practiced with a lot of energy and got real-life conditioning. He always expected a lot of you, and you always had to do your job.

"We had to do so much with Herb. He pushed everybody, and he always seemed to know how much he could push. That was the best learning part of my career, because I gained so much. But winning always makes it a lot more fun."

In 2008, McClanahan looked back and reflected on playing for Brooks in college and on the U.S. team. "At the U, he implemented a lot more than he used in games," McClanahan said. "He kicked our ass everywhere we went. But you know, whether he understood it or not, he never knew how to run a power play.

"With the Olympic team, he told us at our first practice that we would learn more this year than we ever learned in our lives, and he said that, offensively, he was not going to yell—unless we were being lazy. I remember after a lot of our exhibition games with the Olympic team, we'd be sitting there saying to ourselves, 'Don't let this bastard beat us!' He was conservative about some things, but he really wasn't."

Dave Christian said, "By the time we got to the Russian game, we had twenty guys who all had confidence in everybody else on the team. I probably thought it was a possibility we could beat the Russians—why can't it happen? For me, it was the game we were playing that day, and I approached it the way I would whether it was a pickup game back on the Warroad River, or the biggest game I'd ever play in.

"I told my kids, years later, to imagine that they can do anything, and to shoot high. Do you know how many times I dreamt it, and saw myself winning the gold medal? When we got to that game, it was a great opportunity for competition at the highest level, and I was young enough and naïve enough to look at it as just another game."

A Golden Gopher cheerleader escorts Brooks during a post-Olympic victory parade down Washington Avenue on the University of Minnesota campus. *Author photo*

Buzz Schneider recalled going from playing for Brooks at Minnesota to his vagabond stretch in the lower minor leagues to maintain his amateur status. "When I left the U in 1975, I went with the 1976 Olympic team," Schneider told me. "I played for Badger Bob, and he was awfully positive, while Herbie often coached from the negative. But I was more comfortable with Herbie because when you did something wrong, you knew about it, right away. He gave grief to everybody, just trying to help motivate us. We always did a lot of weaving and changing. By the time I got back with him on the Olympic team, he had it figured out. He had studied what the Europeans did, and he did things, like each line had a different power play."

Schneider's course was meandering before he came back to Brooks in 1979. "I went with the U.S. to the 1975 World Championships, and I got a hat trick against Tretiak. After the 1976 Olympics, I was supposed to go to Pittsburgh in 1976–77, but Wren Blair went there and he wanted me to come to camp without a contract. I went to the Pittsburgh camp, and they wanted me to go to [minor league affiliate] Hershey, and then to Saginaw. I came home and worked out with Herbie's team at the U, then I went to Oklahoma City, and Birmingham of the WHA wanted me to go to Hampton, Virginia . . . in the Southern League. Then I went up to Springfield, and then went with John Mariucci to the World Championship. In 1977–78,

I went to Toronto's camp, and they were sending me somewhere, but I went to Milwaukee instead, and wound up playing there, when Mike Eruzione was in Toledo [in the same league].

"I had a chance to go to Europe, but Herbie said to stay stateside. At the end of the 1978–79 season, I had a cast on my hand and couldn't play in the playoffs. Then I got the chance to play for Herbie on the Olympic team."

Pavelich appreciated playing with Schneider and John Harrington, his Conehead line mates. "I think our line stayed together because Herb knew how hard it was to get three guys who always did the same thing," said Pav. "Buzzy was such a good skater and had a big shot, and John became quite a student of the game as a coach. I was surprised that they didn't pick John [as head coach] at Minnesota-Duluth when they named Scott Sandelin. He would have been a great head coach in the WCHA."

I arranged to introduce Pavelich and Harrington to my new friend, Andreas Wyden, who signed them to play the next season for Lugano.

Mark Johnson, the 1980 team's consensus offensive catalyst, had the most reason to be concerned about joining the Brooks entourage, simply because Brooks and Johnson's dad, Badger Bob, were such intense rivals as college coaches, with feelings that ranged from dislike to hatred. Jack O'Callahan later recalled how everybody wondered how secure they were on the team right to the end, but Johnson actually might have been the most secure.

"Obviously, I had some concerns at first, about how the year would unfold and what our relationship might be," Johnson remembered. "When he had our first training camp and then went to Norway, he pulled me aside for a one-on-one in his hotel room. He put it all aside in that meeting, by telling me how he saw me, what he saw as the role I was going to play, and what I'd be able to do. I knew then that I'd have the chance to play a big role and do what I was capable of doing.

"That put me at ease, and our relationship grew as the season went on. All of the players respected what he did, and his respect for me grew, and mine for him as a coach grew. A lot of guys on the team thought he was crazy, because of his daily approach. But we were a bunch of eighteen- to twenty-three-year-olds, and we thought we knew everything, and then you get someone like him, pushing you outside of your comfort zone. There was some resistance, and some animosity. But as we had some success, I think everybody realized his stuff was working.

"At some point, everybody got to trust him and what he was doing. The main thing was to respect what he was doing, and everybody was different, so there was a chunk of players who never got comfortable until the final roster was decided. Then we had Tim Harrer and Les Auge coming in, and a lot of guys were wondering who's next? We didn't have a lot of options. We could go to the minor leagues or go back to class. But I felt pretty comfortable in the guy running the ship."

Since he went on to such successful NHL and coaching careers, perhaps Johnson understood, in retrospect, the remarkable nature of the U.S. gold medal better than some of his teammates, who might understandably go through the rest of their lives feeling as if they couldn't possibly have lost at Lake Placid. After all, as Brooks himself had told them, they were "meant" to be there.

Johnson went to Halifax, Nova Scotia, in May 2008 to accept, on behalf of his 1980 teammates, the International Ice Hockey Federation honor for directing the biggest story in the IIHF's one-hundred-year history. While there, he noted that the IIHF presented its one-hundred-year all-star international team, which consisted of forward Wayne Gretzky, defenseman Borje Salming from Sweden, and defenseman Slava Fetisov, goaltender Vladislav Tretiak, and forwards Valery Kharlamov and Sergei Makarov, all from the Soviet Union—and all from the team that the 1980 U.S. team conquered.

"If we played the Russians one hundred times, they'd have beaten us ninety-nine," Johnson said in his acceptance speech. "Unfortunately for the Russians, they got us on the one hundredth game—on February 22, 1980."

In 1980, Jack O'Callahan might have seemed to resent Brooks' heavy-handed coaching style. Twenty-eight years later, working in Chicago, O'Callahan said his respect for Brooks couldn't be more enormous

"I give speeches to kids or groups, and whenever I'm talking, I talk about Herb," O'Callahan told me. "He did so much work and was so driven, that he didn't have to do much. He had done such a tremendous job that we had become such an extension of him, all he needed to do was open the door.

"After all he'd done, at Lake Placid we finally could quit listening to him. But he had the last laugh—because he already resided in our heads and our hearts."

CHAPTER 34

THE SOUND OF DAVOS

Despite his comment that his success with Team USA was going to "cost Giel a ton," Herb Brooks had pretty well decided he would seek a pro hockey coaching job after the Games rather than return to the University of Minnesota, where he had already accomplished everything possible. At some point during the Olympics, Herbie somehow had the time and the foresight to do a little back-guard planning on his own behalf. He sent a message to Craig Sarner, a former Gopher player who came to the U when Herb was freshman coach, and who played on the 1972 silver medal U.S. team.

"I was playing pro hockey for the team in Davos, Switzerland," Sarner recalled. "Herb sent me a postcard either just before the Olympics, or just after they started, saying, 'I think we're ready, but whatever happens, I'll be looking for a job.' We had a playing coach who wanted to just play, so at the end of the Olympics, when the U.S. had won the gold medal, I said to our general manager, 'Let me call Herb. It probably won't happen, but if it does, it'll be great publicity.' He thought it was a great idea."

Brooks was still in Lake Placid when the wheels were turning in Davos. Meanwhile, Brooks had Art Kaminsky trolling for every possible NHL team that might have an opening or be thinking of a coaching change. Everybody seemed interested, but most of the teams were reluctant to take a chance on a proven rebel—a progressive-minded coach who would thumb his nose at tradition and convention and insist on doing it his own way. The offers were lukewarm, at best.

"New York contacted me," Herb confided, "and said, 'Don't move without talking to us.' They made an offer. I turned it down."

Then he went back to breaking down the Olympic triumph, bouncing from topic to topic almost as if by stream of consciousness. "We're tired physically and tired mentally," he began. "The players sang 'God Bless America' in the dressing room, over and over. I don't think I'll ever witness anything like it . . . I was going to get a haircut this morning, but I just didn't have time. . . .

"Screw New York."

It was just that abrupt. He was figuring he might get a big offer to step right in and coach in the NHL, but it didn't appear forthcoming. Then Herbie was back to the game aftermath.

"I was good 'til my wife started crying—then I started crying," Brooks said. "Bob Fleming of AHAUS said, 'You might be human, after all.'"

I asked him if the players saw him crying. "No," Herbie said. "I turned the other way. Each team got twenty medals, helluva deal. I missed one in 1960, and I miss another in 1980. Bob Fleming said, 'I'll buy you one.' It's pretty ironic that twenty years later, I'm here, in a different role. Jack McCartan said, 'Herb, it's meant to be. It'll happen.' Jack was the last guy I talked to in 1960 at the Denver Arena, when the team went one way and I went the other. . . . Unbelievable. A college team wins the Olympic gold . . .unbelievable . . . unbelievable.

"I feel a little let down, really. Nine or ten months preparing before the Sports Festival, now everybody will be gone. Everybody splits. But as years go by, this'll mean more. As a first-time coach, I had a hard time eating. Just forced two six-packs down and went to work."

Herbie laughed. I asked him if or when he coached in the NHL, would he do the same things he did with the Olympic team—the same systems he practiced and experimented with at the University of Minnesota and executed with Team USA?

"I would insist on a system like this," Brooks said. "I would do it, even if it cost me. I'd do it, and let them fire me."

What did he think he might do in the 1980–81 season?

"Maybe I might be coaching bantams in Mounds View," he said.

Little did Brooks know that an offer was coming from Davos. He and the Gophers on the U.S. team returned to Minneapolis for a motorcade to Williams Arena at the University. Washington and University Avenues were lined with cheering fans as Brooks and the ex-Gophers—plus Neal Broten, who would return to the U, and Dave Christian, the former Fighting Sioux—sat on the back of convertibles and drove through gray February weather. A brief ceremony was held for them inside the arena, and then Herbie was off to numerous speaking engagements.

"I got hold of him," said Sarner. "He was speaking all over, but I got him and said to at least come over to visit Davos. He agreed to do it, and when he flew to Zurich, I think there were about ten newspapers that had reporters there to meet him. It was really a huge deal over there."

What few people know is something that Herbie once confided in me—that his favorite movie of all time was *The Sound of Music*. Maybe Lou Vairo wouldn't have liked Julie Andrews dancing through the flowers in the Alps, but Herbie loved it. When he was driven from Zurich to Davos, a beautiful little picture postcard town in the Alps, Herbie must have felt like he was realizing that dream scenario.

"He agonized over it," Sarner recalled, "but he was smart enough to realize he was not getting viable offers from the NHL."

Elite league teams in Europe could have two "imports" each. Usually, these were players from Canada, or maybe Sweden. Davos had two Americans: Sarner, from North St. Paul, and Wally Olds, a former Gopher All-American from Baudette, Minnesota.

"When Herbie showed up, it was still snowing," Sarner said. "I took him up skiing, got him completely outfitted, and went up there with an instructor giving him twenty minutes of training. The instructor kept insisting that he was doing it wrong, and Herbie was getting pissed, until I said, 'This guy is you. That's the way you are when you're coaching.' He laughed. I told him to wait and keep talking to him, while I made a run. I went down one time and came back up, and Herbie was gone. I couldn't believe it. He just took off. He had no idea what he was doing or where he was going, and if you go down the wrong side of one of those mountains, they might never find you. But he came up the tow, looking like a Yeti, covered with snow. I said, 'If you're going to kill yourself, at least let me watch.'"

The Davos team was a whole 'nother thing for Brooks. He spoke no German, and the players spoke little English, so everything he said had to be translated by Sarner. "We had a quasi-amateur attitude," Sarner said. "These guys were probably working for $40,000 at a job, and getting $30,000 to play hockey. Everybody was going thirty miles per hour, and Herbie wanted them to go faster. I said, 'Enjoy the ride for a year. You'll be in the NHL, but for now, sit back and enjoy the ride.' But he was so impatient.

"It was an incredibly tough transition for him. He's so good at verbal communication, and everything he did on our team had to go through a third party. He was going stir crazy, but the players enjoyed him; they were enthralled by him."

Herb brought his family over with him. Patti seemed to enjoy the experience, and daughter Kelly flourished in school. But her big brother had some problems. Danny was a quiet, almost surly kid. Hard to believe that he grew up to be a great guy, an engaging, intelligent, successful businessman, because at that time he simply didn't communicate. He hated it over in Switzerland, and he complained a lot.

I got a letter from Herb, dated November 14, 1980, and he wrote:

Greetings—the Alps are full of snow. Looks like an early ski season. Time is going by fast, hard to believe. Our team is coming back from a slump. We lost five out of six, primarily due to Olds and Sarner being hurt. Both are starting to come around. We now have won four of our last five, and we're four points out of first place. It will be a close race between 5–6 teams.

Last Saturday we played in Bern, vs. Buzz Schneider's team, and won 4-1, before 16,700 people. Pavelich and Harrington are playing good, from reports, especially John. Their team [Lugano] is in third place, six points out. Both players should be in the "A" league, because "B" is too easy. But Dave Gardner and Jacques Lemaire are in a B league, also. The money is good whether it's A or B.

Brooks, ever the coach, added:

John, did you write your article on why St. Thomas, Bemidji State, etc., should go up to the WCHA? As I mentioned before, more opportunities must be provided for the up and coming players. The state of Minnesota should have more than two Division I teams. You could open a lot of eyes. Write it.

Everything is going well over here. Swiss hockey mentality is hard to figure out. Kelly is fitting in real good . . . but Dan wants to come home. We may send him home early, because his school is lagging behind because of the language, and at his age, this is not good. Say hello to your family, and tell Jack to hang in there at Breck. It will pay off. Hard work always does.

Regards, Herb

Danny moved back to Minnesota and lived with Warren Strelow's family and went to school in Mahtomedi.

After the Davos team had played in the Spengler Cup holiday tournament, Herb's attitude changed, Sarner noted. "He had never been in a situation where he couldn't evaluate and pick his players," Sarner said. "We weren't winning, and he wasn't happy.

"One day, he wanted to talk to the players, and he started ripping the management. I had to translate, and I wondered what the heck he was doing. He said, 'I don't trust your management. . . . Do you realize they offered me $25,000 under the table just to be here?' I didn't translate it, and he said, 'Tell them.' But I didn't. I asked if I could see him outside.

"We went out and I said it would sound foolish to repeat that, because all these guys were being paid under the table. He laughed. 'Oh really?' he said. 'I should have taken that money, then.' It turns out he was being righteous instead of mercenary, because he didn't realize that they had budgeted to pay him under the table.

"I realized, though, that he was ripping management because he didn't want to be there any longer," Sarner continued. "A lot of his best assets couldn't be put to use. I'd been in Europe playing for six years, and the innovative stuff that was new to North America wasn't all new over there. He was still great at pointing out things that players need to be aware of. A coach has to give you enough looks in practice so nothing could surprise you in a game, and if you were paying attention in practice with Herbie, you knew what to look for."

Shortly after the Spengler Cup, Herbie packed up his family and returned to his home in Shoreview.

It wasn't only that Brooks was impatient, however. While Brooks went off to Davos, Craig Patrick got a job at AHAUS, the forerunner of USA Hockey. For two months, Patrick was executive assistant to Hal Trumble in Colorado Springs, but soon had offers from the Colorado Rockies, New York Islanders, and New York Rangers. "I interviewed with the Rangers on July 15, 1980, and took over general manager duties there," Patrick said. "Fred Shero was GM and coach, but he didn't like the GM work, so my title was director of hockey operations, but really I handled the general manager duties. Shero had done a great job with the Flyers, but by the time he got to the Rangers, at least when I came, it seemed like he was afraid of being fired and he was reluctant to make any adjustments. We started out 4-13-4, and they let him go."

With the Rangers in those days, the triumvirate of Sonny Werblin, Jack Krumpe, and William Jennings made the decisions.

"They asked me what we should do, and I said, 'Hire Herb Brooks.' We tried, but he couldn't get out of his contract [with Davos] until the end of the season," Patrick recalled. "So rather than hire someone else, I was pretty sure we could get Herbie for the next season, so I took the team over.

"After the season . . . Sonny wanted me to coach and Lou Nanne to be brought in as GM. I said, 'No, you've got to bring in Herb Brooks.' All I knew about coaching was from Herbie's stuff that I had witnessed. I had tried to do more flow stuff, and I told the guys they were great athletes and 'You do what you want on offense, but play defense this way,' and I adjusted the defense to suit the players."

Way off in Switzerland, Brooks' impatience might well have been compounded when he realized his Olympic assistant, Patrick, was now the man managing the hockey operations for the Rangers, and that he wanted Brooks to coach there.

So long, *Sound of Music*. Hello Broadway.

CHAPTER 35

PLOW HORSES TO THOROUGHBREDS

What a difference a year makes. Herb Brooks returned to Minnesota a hero after the 1980 Olympics, but when he returned from Davos to his home in Shoreview in January 1981, he returned as someone who had been on an extended vacation, after what had to be considered a mediocre half-year in the Swiss Elite League.

"I came home, and I'm shaking," he told me, shortly after returning. "I'm afraid to answer the phone, and I feel sensitive about everything I say being misinterpreted."

Some of the reports were misleading, going back to the Olympic team. One of these regarded Craig Homola not being taken to Lake Placid. "Homola wanted a guarantee to be on the team, and I don't blame him," Brooks said. "He showed concern for the guys on the U.S. team and his Vermont teammates, so it was better for him to stay [at Vermont]."

Other reports linked Brooks to the Colorado Rockies, one alleging that he had told people he should have taken the Rockies coaching job, while other reports linked him to the Rangers. Still others speculated on his sudden departure from Davos in midseason.

"I got a call from Craig Patrick, offering me the Rangers job, and I knew I was under contract in Davos," Brooks said. "The bottom line is, whatever I'm going to do, my future is in the U.S. So if I'm back here, something might break in hockey. If not, the next year and a half is valuable startup time for me in the business world."

Herb was in monologue form, so I restrained myself and did not say that those same circumstances were in place when he decided to go to Davos in the first place. He left out the part about being impatient and feeling unfulfilled by not being able to build and drive a team at his preferred pace.

"The only thing good about the Ranger thing is it made me look at the bottom line, and where I want to be five, ten years from now," he said. "I made adjustments in Davos. Life is a series of adjustments. I adjusted my ideas of tactics and conditioning, but the process of dealing with quality athletes is the same. I believe in them and challenge them, so that their innate talent comes out. . . . You use those tactics because players are good, and the NHL is the pinnacle of players. To do less than that would not be doing a job for them.

"For somebody to say I can't do it in the NHL, do they mean I can't make NHL players think and be creative? Break down the stereotypes? Get them in shape? Our American players are just as good as the Swedes, Finns, or Russians, but you've got to give them the environment where they can come out.

"My whole thing is belief in the players. No NHL player I've talked to has said anything other than that they'd love to do it. I have a profound belief in the ability of the players, and it bothers me to see other people kicking our rear ends.

"They say I can't do those things in the NHL. That's not an indictment of me— it's an indictment of the establishment. I'm not talking about the Scotty Bowmans of the world. You've got to give players an environment of practice-work-rest ratio, so you can stimulate players with drills. It's tough to travel and play eighty games, but when you challenge quality players, you get better motivation and consistency. I've been fortunate to have been blessed with quality people."

There were also rumors that in the Olympics Brooks served the roles of coach and general manager, and he wouldn't be able to work under someone else. "If I worked in the NHL, I'd be very happy working under someone, as long as I could be involved in open communications," Brooks countered. "I have no interest in being a general manager. I've been talked to, talked about, and had words put in my mouth. Like I got a master's in business from dealing with high-level people.

"[Agent] Norm Caplan called and said somebody in the Whalers organization brought up my name. There's nothing now, and they might stick with Larry Pleau, but I could be considered at the end of the year. I don't want to be GM, I just want to coach and have communication with the GM.

"Bruce Bennett [sports editor of the *Duluth News Tribune*] called me and asked if I would coach UMD. I said, 'No way.' I'm not interested in a college coaching job. Replacing coaches is not the problem in college hockey: it's the expansion of Division I schools, to give all the good Minnesota players an opportunity to play. I remember applying for the UMD job eight years ago, and I couldn't even get an interview."

As for his non-hockey world? "I'm helping our neighbor build a new closet," Brooks said. "Or, actually, he's building it and I'm watching."

Brooks didn't have to wait long for something to develop. Craig Patrick had done a good job of guiding the New York Rangers to a respectable finish in 1981, after replacing Fred Shero, a legendary coach in his days with the Philadelphia Flyers whose almost mystical touch seemed lost in Manhattan, where he didn't have a Bobby Clarke. After finishing the season so well, Sonny Werblin, Jack Krumpe, and William

New York Rangers GM Craig Patrick welcomes Herb Brooks as new head coach of the team for the 1981–82 season. Brooks would stay on through the midpoint of the 1984–85 season. *Photo by Bruce Bennett Studios/Getty Images*

Jennings wanted Patrick to continue, but he insisted that Brooks was the proper route for the 1981–82 season and got him signed.

"At the Rangers training camp, when Brooks came in, he was feeling his way," Patrick recalled. "I'm sure he would have liked to come in and instantly install everything he'd done with the Olympic team, but he was smart enough to come in slow and see what would work. With the Olympic team, he had to hurry, because we only had seven months. He tried some ideas, and I heard it later.

"Guys like Ron Duguay liked what he was doing a lot. All the players seemed to adapt to it well."

Mark Pavelich came home from Switzerland and signed with the Rangers, mainly to be reunited with Brooks. In Manhattan, he joined the nucleus that included Ron Duguay and brothers Dave and Don Maloney.

"It would have been a tough decision if Herb wasn't there," Pavelich said, "but he was the reason I went. It was quite different for a guy from Ely Lake being in Manhattan in early September. But the first time I took a walk downtown, I ran into a guy who was from Duluth and was a big UMD hockey fan."

"Pavelich fit in so well, it was quite a surprise," Patrick recalls. "The players really were neat about accepting him."

Pavelich was the exact opposite of Duguay, who was a central character in the Big Apple's social whirl, with his flowing shoulder-length hair and fashionable suits. Pavelich had one sport jacket, which he got from the Olympic team, and a nylon windbreaker with "Tuna's Bar, Eveleth, Minn." emblazoned on the back. The two were at opposite ends of the sophistication scale, yet they clicked amazingly well.

Herb used to tell me about seeing the two of them walking along the sidewalk in Manhattan, on their way to Studio 54: Pav, wearing his sport jacket with the bottom hanging out under the nylon Tuna's Bar windbreaker, and Duguay, with his trademark hair blowing in the wind, his full-length mink coat draped around him, and his arm around Pav's shoulder, leading him inside.

"Doogs was a big shot," Pavelich recalled. "You never had to stand in line when you went anyplace with him. Duguay lived in a different world. He was actually a very good hockey player, which surprised me, but away from the game, he was going out with Cheryl Tiegs and Farrah Fawcett."

The two also clicked on the ice. Once again, Pavelich was a physical extension of Brooks' imagination, playing his own brand of sophisticated pond hockey and setting up Duguay, as well as everybody else, with his creative playmaking. Pavelich played with Duguay his first couple of years with the Rangers, facilitating a remarkable team transition. The Rangers went from a somewhat plodding traditional style to one that suddenly was circling and abandoning lanes. It was as if the most traditional up-and-down NHL team was transformed virtually overnight into the 1979 Red Army team.

When I first wrote about seeing the likes of Nick Fotiu, Don Maloney, and Ron Duguay circling back to maintain puck control and interchanging lanes to attack from all angles, I wrote that Brooks had, in two months, taken "plow horses and transformed them into Kentucky Derby thoroughbreds."

It helped that the Rangers acquired Reijo Ruotsalainen, the small but extremely gifted Finnish defenseman previously on the 1980 Finnish Olympic team, who was on the same creative wavelength as Pav.

In his first season with the Rangers, Brooks called me at home one time, shocked and angry at an interviewer. "We went into Toronto, and a guy from *Hockey Night in*

Canada came to interview me," Brooks said. "He says, 'Well, Herb, how does it feel to be coaching in the NHL when you know that everybody hopes you fail?' Then he shoved the microphone in my face.

"Why would anyone hope I failed? I don't get it. I don't begrudge another coach for doing what he's doing, and I'd never hope for anybody to fail. Why would people in the NHL hope I fail?"

It was an indication of how deeply the Canadian tradition of up-and-down-the-lane hockey was engrained. Teams played it and understood it, and so did their fans. Soviet players had yet to enter the NHL, so nobody challenged tradition. Swedish players who were coming in enjoyed the simpler NHL game and never complained. It was sort of like asking a trigonometry whiz to take money for doing single-digit addition. Brooks, however, was trying to revolutionize the game and was viewed with fear, concern, and even scorn for what he might do to those sacred traditions.

In spite of all that, with Brooks behind the bench, the Rangers won one hundred games in fewer tries than with any other coach before or since. Brooks coached the Rangers for three and a half years, and after attempting to move his family to the East with him, he sent them back to Minnesota for stability while his children were in high school.

The Rangers had on their roster Anders Hedberg and Ulf Nilsson, a brilliant pair of Swedish stars who had played with the WHA's Winnipeg Jets. In Brooks' first season with the Rangers, the team invited the Swedes' former Jets linemate, Bobby Hull, to training camp.

"We had training camp at the Rye rink in Westchester, as usual," Patrick explained. "But we decided to go to Finland for some exhibition games. Bobby Hull came along with us. But we decided not to sign him after he played in training camp."

Hull, speaking five years after Brooks died, said he gained tremendous respect for his coaching style and regretted never being able to play for him, because it would have suited his skating and shooting game.

Not everybody was unanimous in their acclaim for Brooks, however. Phil Esposito, the former Boston Bruins scoring star who finished his career with the Rangers, was doing color commentary on Rangers' telecasts and was often very critical of Brooks' coaching tactics. That shouldn't have been surprising, since everybody connected with the club figured that Esposito had designs on taking over the team. In addition, Esposito made his fame by going to the net, planting his immovable self, and steering pucks in. If he ever understood or appreciated what Brooks was attempting to do, it didn't come through on the broadcasts.

Interestingly, Esposito took over that commentary role from a guy who seemed like the perfect analyst for a Brooks-coached NHL team: Mike Eruzione. "The difference in the Rangers from before Herb took over until after was like night and day," Eruzione recalled.

During those years, the Rangers were one of the best half-dozen teams in the NHL, but they had one problem: the New York Islanders. The Isles had Billy Smith in goal, Denis Potvin on defense, and the likes of Bryan Trottier and Mike Bossy up front. They dominated the Stanley Cup playoffs until Wayne Gretzky and the Edmonton Oilers displaced them.

Each year, it seemed that Brooks had the Rangers perfectly poised to take on the Isles, but the Rangers would meet them in the first or second round and lose a long, six-game series, after which the Islanders would blow out everybody else in four or five games. Brooks employed a defensive-zone penalty-killing box system against the Islanders in those playoff series, containing Trottier's playmaking at center and thus stifling Bossy's goal-scoring.

"I remember that system," Pavelich told me, "because I'd cover Trottier. I had played with Duguay my first couple of years, but then I played center with [Mark]

Brooks watches the action during a game at Madison Square Garden during the 1981–82 season. Former 1980 Olympian Dave Silk is hopping the boards. *Photo by Focus on Sport/Getty Images*

Osborne and Anders Hedberg. Hedberg was fun to play with, and the first time we were together, he set me up for a hat trick."

"Can you imagine how that Ranger team would play with the rules the way they've been changed, with great skaters like Nilsson, Hedberg, Pavelich, and Ruotsalainen?" Eruzione asked in 2008, referring to the NHL's recent crackdown on obstruction infractions. "They were great even then, when everybody really worked them over. Nilsson and Hedberg had welts on their chests after every game.

"And Pav was spectacular. They always wanted me to interview Pav, but he'd say, 'Rizzo, you know that's not important,' and he'd go back in the dressing room. Finally, we worked out a deal . . . I told him if he did [the interview], he'd get this gift certificate to a sporting goods store and he could buy all kinds of fishing rods. So he said OK and came on."

Like Pavelich, an inveterate outdoorsman, Brooks still loved Minnesota, although Herb admired idyllic lakes and woods, fresh air, and clear, million-star nights more from an idealistic perspective than a practical one. Herbie took his friend Billy Christian up on an invitation for a family trip before he went back to New York for his third season.

"We were out there fishing off an island in Lake of the Woods," Patti told me at the time. "We fished for a week, and Herbie never had a nibble. I always thought Danny was back home sticking pins in a walleye. I'd noticed Herb was sleeping in the back of the boat, so I said, 'How will you know if you get a bite?' Then I realized that his line wasn't even in the water."

Later on, when I asked Herb about the trip, he said, "We went to Warroad to get away. Two days in the boat, and all the beautiful scenery, but I'd rather be *doing* something. I've got to be more active."

Back in New York he still enjoyed the challenge, but not the political undercurrents that came with an NHL coaching position. Nor did he enjoy living away from his family in Minnesota. And pros or not, Brooks kept close tabs on the developmental structure of U.S. amateur hockey.

Later, Herb would finally come to have more respect for the organizational efforts of Art Berglund, who had worked his way up the AHAUS ladder to an executive position. Back then, however, Herb was anything but respectful. Berglund was from Fort Frances, Ontario, and Brooks thought he had ridden some political coattails to a position of authority in American hockey, which, in the mind of Herb—and his brother David—was constantly being overrun by Canadians. Lou Nanne, a good friend of Herbie's in college, had come from Sault Ste. Marie, Ontario, and earned

All-America status playing defense at Minnesota. AHAUS officials gloated about pulling all sorts of strings to rush Nanne's naturalization papers through the necessary channels, so that he could become a citizen in time to play on the U.S. National team in 1967–68.

"They were trying to naturalize some more Canadian players so they could play on the U.S. team," Dave explained. "There were several players, one of them was Bill Masterton, who had played at Denver. So I went to Congressman Joe Karth, and he stopped it. Louie called me up and gave me hell, and asked if I wanted the U.S. to be in the 'B' league forever, and I said, 'Who cares, if they're American kids? Someday we'll make it to the 'A' level.' Masterton was a great guy, and I saw him when he was playing for the [1966–67] U.S. team in an exhibition game. He came up to me and said, 'I don't think it's right, either.'"

Herb liked to call Berglund "Holiday Inn." When I asked him why, Herbie delighted in saying, "Because he's America's guest." Then he added, "Every time a Canadian gets a job like that in U.S. hockey, a lot of U.S. people who have contributed to the development of U.S. hockey by standing out in the snow banks get left out."

When Herb was hired by the Rangers, he also kept close tabs on his Olympic players. Most of them played pro hockey and reached the NHL level, with Mike Ramsey, Dave Christian, Neal Broten, Mark Johnson, and Ken Morrow probably gaining the greatest fame. Eruzione went back to BU and got a permanent job in its sports development department, ruining the myth that he never worked a day in his life, thanks to his game-winning goal against the Soviets.

When Eruzione was supplanted from his Rangers television job by Phil Esposito, the prospect of the New York Rangers leading the entire NHL into a new era were greatly diminished. But it was fantastic to watch while it lasted for those three and a half seasons, during which Rob McClanahan and Dave Silk played a short time with the Rangers, and Pavelich became a popular mainstay.

"Herbie had refined himself because he had to have a different way to motivate the pros," McClanahan recalled. "He couldn't threaten 'em, and he needed the support of his captains, which he had."

Pavelich, who maintains he learned more from Brooks than from any other coach, confirmed McClanahan's assessment. "He couldn't really yell at Barry Beck," Pav said. "At that time, he couldn't do what he had done with us on the Olympic team.

"Switzerland was a top place to play, but I had to be real choosey who I signed with when I came back. I had been told all the way along that I was too small to play, and I started to accept it. Herb had told me Art Kaminsky would be a good agent to sign with, but I don't know. After my first year with the Rangers, Jack Krumpe ripped up my contract, which was a two-way, minimum-wage deal with a bonus, and gave me a better contract. After my second year, he did the same thing again. So my first contract wasn't very good, but I went in and talked myself and got more."

Pavelich still looks back wistfully at his five years with the Rangers and thinks about what might have been, and how odd it is that some critics claimed that Brooks was a failure there.

"It was really unfair, because we were a good team under Herbie, up in the ninety-point range, and the only problem we had was that the Islanders were always there," Pavelich recalled. "Having the eighty-game NHL schedule was difficult in some ways for Herb. After so much time, how he pulled everybody together by making himself the enemy was hard to do. He tried to do the same thing, but it didn't work as well with the Rangers.

"But everybody respected him . . . I got the chance to get him a few times when we sat down and had conversations, but it was always with him doing the talking, and he'd usually give me some crap about the [UMD] Bulldogs."

When Brooks left the Rangers, it was pretty well a forced issue by Brooks, who much preferred that to quitting.

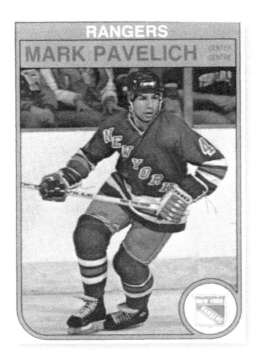

Crafty playmaker Mark Pavelich was a physical extension of Brooks' ideas about the game. As a star forward at Minnesota-Duluth, the Eveleth, Minnesota, native played against Brooks' Minnesota Gopher teams before being named to the 1980 Olympic squad and then signing with Brooks' Rangers.

"If there was a problem, it might be that some of the players stopped listening to him," said Patrick.

"The Rangers might have been his greatest coaching job," added Jack Blatherwick, who came to training camp as Brooks' prime consultant and soaked up a lot. "He knew he had to change what he had done. He got a board with little magnetic things instead of a chalkboard. Half the guys couldn't speak English, and the other half didn't give a shit. Then you had guys like Pavelich and Ruotsalainen who were perfect for Herbie. Pav always said, 'Don't worry about what he says, just go somewhere fast.'

"The first day in practice, I remember watching guys like Steve Vickers, Ron Duguay, and Carol Vadnais. Then the team went to Finland for two weeks, and when they came back, I was on the ice with them and Herbie blew the whistle. They sped right up to him and had rapt attention for every word he said. He turned a bunch of partiers and dissidents into true believers."

CHAPTER 36

LEAVING NEW YORK

Herb Brooks was ready to return for the challenge of his fourth season with the New York Rangers, having accomplished so much already, but he regretted leaving home. He had pretty much left the raising of Danny and Kelly to his wife, Patti, who seemed fine remaining in her parallel universe while Herbie was off chasing pucks. By the time Brooks was leaving for that training camp, Danny was just starting the eleventh grade at St. Thomas Academy, and Kelly was eleven years old.

Danny had grown up—and kept growing. He was playing defense on the hockey team and showing more and more talent for the game. He also had reached an age where he could be the subject of his dad's barbs. "Danny doesn't beat me at golf yet, but he will," Herb said. "He eats so much, that instead of feeding him salad these days, we just throw some vinegar and oil on the lawn and let him graze."

Herb was heading back out to New York for the last year of his Rangers contract, when we sat down for a long, freewheeling conversation. I could tell he was weary from fighting the establishment. "Just being away, and worrying about it, is a chore," Brooks said. "Patti never says anything about my job, that I spend too much time away or anything. But four months at home over the summer is precious time.

"This will be our toughest year ever. The main group should have been a magnet for the fragments. I've dealt with some personnel problems, but a couple major ones have been overlooked. We'll have two-hour practices, and the drills are important for us to make a positive push. There is some backstabbing and grumbling. But we've made the transition for players like Nick Fotiu. We got 40 percent of our wins with him in the lineup, and 15 percent without him. We've had some turmoil, and I've suggested we get rid of some."

Wayne Thomas, a former goaltender, and Carol Vadnais, formerly a smooth and polished defenseman, were his two assistants. Herb had always liked Thomas, and he saw great potential in Vadnais. "When I came here, Vad was an eighteen-year veteran," Brooks said. "He became a big fan of the conditioning plan after he saw the reasons behind it. Vad is intelligent, analytical, and gone along with the things we've done.

"We just came off the best year in eleven years for the Rangers, with forty-two wins and ninety-three points, but I'm so sick of the mentality, and of guys unwilling to sacrifice. I did it their way, and I'm tired of it. I'm not putting up with malcontents. I've handled them as delicately as possible, first as a family, then making suggestions to management, and I'm not going to prostitute myself for the job.

"We've moved from the middle of the pack to the top one-third, and once there . . . any of the top half-dozen teams could win the [Stanley] Cup. I've changed from living in a motel to an apartment near the practice rink. A lot of coaches do the same thing; I'm not trying to be a hero about it. Patti has been the ideal coach's wife. Kelly has been great, no problem. Danny has lived up to some of my expectations, and he's typical—if he'd been born out East, he'd have wanted to be back there, so he wants to be home in Minnesota. Kids that age need peers more than parents.

"But it's a dog's life."

Having vented his innermost thoughts, Brooks turned back to his inner drive. "All of that doesn't diminish my intensity," he said. "I'm chasing a dream—the Stanley Cup. How much time can you be granted to chase the dream? Some of the dreams, hopes, and aspirations must propel you beyond a contract. Coaches are very idealistic and sometimes forget the pragmatic application that is necessary. Sometimes you have to reduce the net profit to produce a winner."

As for his refined system, he said, "I struck out against the stereotype. I never read 'the book.' I went to the seminar and came up with a hybrid application. I started to recognize when you play against the Swedes, the Czechs, or the Russians, they're moving all the time and they have the puck captive. You can't hit what you can't catch.

"When I got the U job, we got the hell kicked out of us. You couldn't be so idealistic as to not survive. When Neal Broten came along, we could open it up more. . . . I held the system in reserve and was not willing to go with it. In 1977–78, we did a little—flying a player, deliberately coming back. When I got the Olympic team, I figured, 'Let's go with it.'

"I don't think there are too many secrets in this game. Execution is what counts. Hard work, companionship, a sense of destiny, change the 'I-me-myself' to 'we-us-ourselves.' It works in football and basketball, where the best teams might be very predictable, but they execute and play with high intensity."

Turning back to his present situation and the NHL, Brooks continued, "The players we've had in New York enjoy what we're doing. Everything I've done is out of respect for the players' talent. Their hearts and minds are very willing. Don Maloney is a better overall player. He's still a thirty-goal player, but he's been forced to improve specific skills. All the players in the league are capable of doing anything, to varying degrees. Our system gives them a lot of freedom.

"My first year in New York, I said no, I'm not backing down from what I believe in. We came back from 6-1 to 6-4 against Pittsburgh, and [Pittsburgh coach] Eddie Johnston said, 'Stay with it, and good luck.'"

Brooks went on to presage some rules changes that the NHL wouldn't implement until the new millennium. "I'm excited for the game of hockey in the '80s," he began. "Maybe we still need some rule changes. We should use the red line for icing only, and move the nets out. Going to overtime was a great move. We've got the fastest, most creative game in the world, so why restrict it? It's an international game. And personally, I would rather write a book than read a book."

I asked if there might come a time when Herbie would like to get out of the NHL whirlwind and maybe take a run at helping operate in amateur hockey.

"I love amateur hockey," he said. "I'd rather be involved in the structure, and it would be an easy transition. I've coached three years in the NHL, and I could see becoming a general manager at some point. But as far as amateur hockey goes, I sent them a letter and got no answer. I was not invited to the AHAUS meeting.

"I've got my own ideas, and it would be to combine everything. I'm receptive to all ideas. I'd like to see an American hockey program. We shouldn't copy anybody. Don't forget who we are, and incorporate some of the best ideas into our own style. There's nothing wrong with being a North American hockey player. We don't want to forget our past, our chemistry, but refine it, better it, and assimilate different things to improve it.

"I think our '80 team built a house; we've got one layer down. We can polish that while we added another layer. Our game was part of the past and part of the future. Dump the puck? There's nothing wrong with that, if you do it for tactical reason. You look at Edmonton, Quebec, and how they open it up. The North Stars at times wheel and deal. They're exciting hockey clubs. I can appreciate the Washington Caps because of their discipline, and the Islanders too. I respect them so much. But, you've got to stay with tactics suitable for the club. The players you have dictate what you can do tactically."

Brooks also confided that he had taken to watching a lot of New York Knicks basketball games, and he was impressed by how similar the two games are. The center and two forwards are much like a forward line in hockey, and the two guards are like the point men on defense. Watching the Knicks verified Brooks's concept of how a hockey team should interchange and play.

"One key word that is very important is 'transition.' We want to make a basketball-type transition from the freedom on offense to the checking game," Brooks explained. "Sometimes a player gets lazy when you give them freedom. At first, you make quick transitions to offense, but now we're at a plateau where we have a corresponding obligation to switch to a checking game."

As for the future?

"We can't duck making decisions," Brooks said. "A great game in New York is 'CYA'—cover your ass. So many people want credit, but nobody likes to be responsible when things go wrong. The fans in New York have been unbelievably loyal in support of the Rangers. One minute they boo, the next they cheer. You might question their tactics, but not their unwavering loyalty to the New York Rangers—and that's the ultimate compliment."

Brooks admitted that he had realized he had to change how he treated his players when he went to the NHL. "With amateurs, I treated them more as a group, in college and with the Olympic team," he explained. "I was fortunate to have some who would stand up to it, and sometimes thrive on it. The first year I flat out went with innovative offense was the Olympic year, and it helped to have players like Pav, Broten, Mark Johnson, and David Christian."

In his downtime? Brooks had been a high-level fast-pitch softball player after college. "I tried fishing, but I need active rest," he said. "I went back to softball and got three hits in eight games—but I didn't strike out. I played lots of golf. I'm so bad, but there's not a lot of time to let my mind wander because I need so many swings. Every day I think about something, whether it's being out of hockey school, or playing over that last game with the Islanders. . . ."

Then it was back to hockey. Herb grabbed my yellow legal pad and started drawing rink diagrams and checking schemes, with his little lines turning into a maze of lines, then circling, circling, until the whole diagram was a mishmash of converging lines. Then he'd draw another rink diagram and start anew.

"I've talked to some basketball coaches to see what might apply to hockey," Brooks said. "We use decoys and influences to reduce the clutter of ten in a zone to seven—as long as we have four of the seven.

"Against the Islanders, we played what amounted to a basketball man-to-man, full-court press. Our defensive forward shadowed their center from the offensive zone out as soon as the puck came loose. That made them have to have their wings carry the puck and try to pass rink-wide, which was much better for us to defend against. Then when we got the puck, we moved it back, one forward moved up and the other two crisscrossed and filled holes."

As for his three years at the helm, Brooks turned reflective.

"I felt the barriers of tradition three years ago," he said, "but not anymore. Glen Sather and Michel Bergeron do it more all the time, and it's exciting."

Sather, of course, was coaching Wayne Gretzky and the Edmonton Oilers, the new dynasty that was about to take over, and Bergeron had the Quebec Nordiques playing a wide-open offensive style.

"Edmonton wins 1-0 on the road, and they're playing a freewheeling game," said Brooks. "That's exciting."

The progression started, of course, back when Brooks was just getting going with his Herbies and his drill-sergeant coaching. If the Rangers moaned about hard practices, the ex-Olympic players on the team knew they had it tougher with the Olympic team; on the Olympic team, his ex-Gophers knew they had it much tougher with the Gophers. Over in Philadelphia, Paul Holmgren had risen to prominence after spending just that one 1974–75 season under Brooks with the Gophers. "I named my dog Herb," he said. "Now whenever I get mad, I can kick Herb."

Herb also was a source of good humor for some of the officials around the NHL. In one game, after referee Andy Van Hellemond had called his fourth straight penalty on the Rangers, there was a long delay before the Rangers came off the bench. Finally, Van Hellemond skated over to the Ranger bench, and Herbie said, "I like your new helmet and I think you look real cute in it, but your refereeing sucks!"

Van Hellemond could only laugh as he skated away.

When Brooks went back for his final season with the Rangers, he was of a different mindset. He drove from Minnesota to New York for the start of training camp, accompanied by Jack Blatherwick.

"Herbie said, 'I hate going out there. I talked to my dad, and I know it'll be the last time I'll see him,'" Blatherwick recalled. "When he left the Rangers, he forced them to fire him."

Blatherwick recounted a high-level meeting, before training camp, when some renovations were supposed to be done at the practice facility. Jack Krumpe was there, as was Craig Patrick and the team doctor, who argued that the Rangers' trainer was not doing a good job.

"Herbie said, 'Well, I don't have a Mercedes convertible and a blonde bombshell, but I do know that . . .' and the doctor left. He just got up and left the meeting.

Herbie then said, 'What's the status of the rink?' Jack Krumpe, who everyone called Mr. Krumpe, answered, and Herb said, 'Jack, if you can't get it done, I'll come out and get it done.' That was another step toward the end."

I knew Herbie was distracted when I talked to him on the phone. "A month ago, my dad died," he told me. "I'm not with anybody out here, so my mind wanders and I think about life's values that take on a different meaning. People might talk about 'em, but it's lip service. Then something like this happens.

"My dad was a catalyst, a rallying point. I was more his son than he was my father. He radiated leadership."

There were other distractions, too. Rob McClanahan retired. The Rangers were going to send him to their American League farm team, and he decided he wasn't going to the minors, Brooks explained.

"I told Robby, and Bill Baker, that we're all going to be extinct, but we can fear extinction without distinction. We have peace of mind knowing we distinguished ourselves."

Patrick said that he thought some of the players might have started tuning Herbie out, and his patience seemed more strained. "He didn't like Ron Duguay being out late every night," Patrick recalled. "But Duguay would practice, then go home and sleep for four hours, then stay out late."

Blatherwick said defenseman Dave Maloney had told him, "Herb Brooks is the greatest coach in the world, but I don't think I could play my whole career for him."

With Brooks seeming to force the Rangers to dismiss him, I asked Patrick whether Herb quit or was fired. "He definitely got fired," said Patrick, who actually did the firing, although in the Ranger hierarchy, Patrick was carrying out what the governing triumvirate of Sonny Werblin, Jack Krumpe, and William Jennings decided.

"They had a press conference downtown," Herbie told me in a phone call from New York. "Legally, all I can say is it's done. I kept the answers general and superficial. But I'm so totally drained."

Brooks may have wanted to come home and may have forced the issue with his behavior, but the Rangers were hit with a rash of injuries, including losing Pavelich for an extended period. And Brooks didn't want to leave his quest unquenched.

"We had the best record in eleven years and we were 6-6 against the Islanders, but I met Craig at the rink Monday morning and he said he decided he wanted to make the change," Herbie said. "Success is doing your best, really. Some people said our playoff series with the Islanders was the best in recent years. And we knocked out the Flyers two years in a row, once after they had won the division. But Patrick is not willing to accept injuries as a reason for our problems."

Still, knowing that Patrick remained a great admirer of Herb's, I asked him if Phil Esposito's influence on Sonny Werblin might have been a factor in the organization's decision. "I guess so," Patrick replied. "After Herb got fired, they got rid of me too, and hired Phil. I made a mistake and didn't pay any attention to Phil on TV. We had great draft picks. The year I got fired [1986], we had made it to the semifinals again, and I had just drafted Brian Leetch with the ninth pick, and a month later, I was gone."

Glen Sonmor, Herbie's old mentor with the Gophers, spoke at a Gopher Blue Line luncheon later that week as coach of the North Stars. Typically, Glen put things in his unique perspective. Brad Buetow was coaching the Gophers then.

"Herbie may become governor, president of the University, president of Jostens—whatever that is," Sonmor began. "He may become athletic director at the U, he may get my job, or maybe Louie [Nanne]'s job as GM [of the North Stars], although Brad, I don't think he's got time to get around to your job. But I make my living doing what I love to do, so to complain about it is senseless. To hear about a coach of Herbie's ability getting fired shouldn't be a surprise, because Pat Quinn, Red Berenson, and others have recently gotten fired, too.

"But to think Herbie can't coach anymore. . . . Barry Beck said on TV, 'Herb is not able to get through to us,' and get this: one reason is his office is on the second floor at the practice facility! The guy is an excellent coach, but when things don't go right, the coach goes.

"I learned early, from John Mariucci, a man I've always respected and admired. John said, 'Going to coach? Get a mobile home.'

"We survive by having a good sense of humor. I remember when my good friend Harry Neale fully expected to get fired. He was told the players don't particularly like his practices, and he said, 'Well, I'm not particularly fond of their games.'"

CHAPTER 37

TEAM MINNESOTA MIRACLE

W hen Herb Brooks returned home after coaching the New York Rangers, he had time to reflect on a whirlwind career, as well as spend time with his family. However, it didn't take him long to get busy—and then ultra-busy—traveling the country to give motivational speeches at major corporations. Reactions were always favorable, because everybody wanted to hear some uplifting words from the man who captivated the nation via a hockey tournament in Lake Placid.

At the time, the Minnesota North Stars still were struggling for some stability since undergoing a "merger" after the 1977–78 season that was actually a takeover by the Cleveland hockey club. Cleveland Barons owners, the brothers Gordon and George Gund, had brought some of their top players, including goaltender Gilles Meloche and centerman Dennis Maruk, to Minnesota and blended them with the best of the North Stars.

Quiet negotiations began between the Minnesota North Stars organization and Brooks to make Herb their new coach, but things broke down. Brooks was always very demanding in his attempts to assure himself of some security, and the Gunds backed away. Gordon, who was blind from having suffered a retinal ailment many years earlier, was the more shrewd businessman of the two, while George was a soft-spoken fellow more likely to enjoy the good life, but a friendly, affable man who was no less a strong partner for it.

When the talks broke off, Brooks made some ill-conceived comments, including one about "telling Gordon Gund where he can shove his white cane."

It was bold, it was brash, and it was absurd, because the Gunds had enormous amounts of what is commonly called "[bleep] you" money.

The following year, Brooks made a brief but rather astonishing plunge into amateur hockey. It was an interesting venture, proving once again the depth of Brooks' love for Minnesota high school hockey, its players, and its history. It also proved there were no boundaries to the magic that Herb Brooks could generate for a given situation. He selected a team of senior players from all over the state, but not before performing considerable political wrangling to put them together in the spring of 1986.

From the players' perspective, it was a no-brainer.

"None of us knew what we were doing, except we were getting the chance to play for Herb Brooks," said Tom Sagissor, a centerman from Hastings.

Minnesota's well-deserved pride in its hockey rose to an unmatched pinnacle with the success of the Brooks-coached University of Minnesota teams in the 1970s and was capped, of course, by the 1980 Olympic gold medal. It's easy to take success for granted, however, and Minnesota's unequaled high school hockey structure continued with the status quo. It was an assumption of superiority that was soon challenged. The Miracle on Ice had inspired the whole nation, and areas such as New England and Michigan had made enormous strides since. While they lacked the great numbers produced by Minnesota high schools, they excelled in developing high-end players by stressing "AAA" bantam and midget select teams, or by sending players via the junior route. In both instances, players played many more games than Minnesota high school kids, including best-against-best tournaments for elite players.

Minnesota had always done well against outside competition, but suddenly Minnesota teams were starting to lose, and then by lopsided margins. The rising level of outside competition was overlooked amid the controversy of Minnesota State High School League rules restricting competition outside its control. In the case of post-season hockey tournaments, athletes who participated were ruled ineligible for spring varsity sports. Therefore, many top hockey players had to decide whether to play and forfeit participation in baseball, golf, or track, or pass up the hockey and remain eligible for those sports.

Larry Johnson came up with the right plan at the right time. As an amateur hockey official who was always respected by Brooks, Johnson was a rare find, and he calculated that since Herbie had been off for a year after three and a half years coaching the Rangers, he might be enticed to take on a new quest: Team Minnesota. Part of the reason Brooks agreed might have been because his son, Danny, had grown to be a 6-foot-3 defenseman at St. Thomas Academy who was bypassed by the Gophers and instead accepted a scholarship offer from the University of Denver. He would be a valid candidate for the team, making it the first time Brooks had ever coached his son.

Typically, Brooks organized everything flawlessly. The tournament, held in Lowell, Massachusetts, and in New Hampshire, still ran afoul of the restrictive Minnesota State High School League rules, until Brooks convinced its executive director Orv Bies that the event was actually part of the Olympic development structure, which was not only true due to AHAUS's governance of the tourney, but also earned it an exemption from Minnesota State High School League rules. Brooks enlisted Dave

Knoblauch, a loyal behind-the-scenes supporter of the University of Minnesota, to help as general manager, while Larry Johnson was the AHAUS administrator to the team. Jack Blatherwick and Craig Sarner, the latter now back home from Europe, agreed to assist. Herb got scouting reports from Chuck Grillo, Jack Barzee, and Blatherwick. Gene Vacanti donated uniform equipment.

Then Herb set off to hastily check out some of the top high school players. After a year away from coaching, working with this eager crop of high school seniors reawakened the flame. I was writing about high school, college, and pro hockey all at the same time, so it was fascinating to see some of the high school standouts I'd been watching converge at Augsburg College for practice.

Some of the players Herb picked went on to college or even pro stardom, but at the time, they were just another batch of good high school players. In goal, Herb took Robb Stauber of Duluth Denfeld and Scott Nelson of Grand Rapids; on defense, Danny Brooks and Randy Skarda, both of St. Thomas Academy, Dennis Vaske of Robbinsdale Armstrong, Lance Pitlick of Robbinsdale Cooper, Jeff Pauletti of Hastings, and Bob Broten of White Bear Lake. Up front, Tom Sagissor centered Hastings teammate Brad Stepan and big George Pelawa of Bemidji; Steve Rohlik of Hill-Murray centered Scott Bloom of Burnsville and Tom Quinlan of Hill-Murray; Tod Hartje of Anoka centered Ross Johnson of Rochester Mayo and Sandy Smith of Brainerd; and a fourth line had Jeff Mehl centering Fergus Falls teammate Blaine Rude and Jim Rokala of Armstrong.

Almost all of the players were giants, led by Quinlan and Rude, both 6-foot-4, and Pelawa, who was 6-foot-3 and 240 pounds. Vaske was 6-foot-2, and only a couple of the quicker forwards were shorter than 6 feet.

"I've really enjoyed working with this group," Brooks told me during the training camp for a story I was writing in the *Minneapolis Tribune*. "All twenty of these players have been leaders of their respective teams. All of our players have their own personal qualities and they lead by their own examples. It reminds me of what Mike Eruzione said at Lake Placid: 'I'm just a captain among captains.'

"This team has rekindled the flame. It's made me realize that I've got to be involved in hockey somehow. I'm not talking about anything like an NHL job; if I can help out the Minnesota Amateur Hockey Association, the high school coaches, and some young men, that's fine. I've found out something about myself from this—that I've got to do something with hockey, on the ice."

The players were mostly multi-sport stars who might well have passed up the opportunity if their spring eligibility hadn't been cleared. Hartje, who went on to star at Harvard, was perhaps the state's best quarterback; Smith and Mehl were breakaway running backs; Pelawa, Bloom, Vaske, and Pitlick all were powerful, line-smashing fullbacks. Smith, in fact, couldn't straighten his leg fully and needed a brace since surgery for a football injury.

"Smith is tough and has great hands, and he might be a surprise because a lot of people haven't seen him," Brooks said. "He might be as good a forward as we've got. But I guess I can't say there are any surprises, because everybody has something to contribute."

Hartje and Stauber—a future Hobey Baker Award winner at Minnesota—were on their schools' golf teams in the spring, while Bloom was on the tennis team and the Hill-Murray tandem of Steve Rohlik and Tom Quinlan were baseball standouts. Rohlik went on to play hockey at Wisconsin and coach at Hill-Murray before becoming an assistant at the University of Nebraska-Omaha and later Minnesota-Duluth. Quinlan went on to baseball stardom and played for Toronto in a World Series. Hartje, a five-handicap golfer, joined the Anoka baseball team after it lost some players to a disciplinary ruling. In his first game, he was two for four, and he tripled in his second game.

As high school seniors, the players were only prospects, and the pro scouts had only Pelawa ranked as a potential first-round selection in the NHL amateur draft. Brooks put them together and ran them through six weeks of semi-regular practices, distilling what chemistry he could find and going low-key on exotic systems.

Brooks also contributed off the ice. Dave Knoblauch, known to everyone in Gopher hockey circles as "Knobby," told me that Brooks continued doing some motivational speaking, but during the weeks he coached Team Minnesota, he instructed anyone who hired him for a speaking engagement to make out the check to the team to help defray its expenses.

The challenge on the ice was imposing. One year earlier, New England won the tournament with a 3-0 record, Massachusetts and Michigan tied at 1-1-1, and Minnesota was 0-3. For 1986, the tournament expanded to six teams, with Minnesota in a three-team pool, meeting Massachusetts on a Friday in Lowell, and facing the West At-Large team (which included eight Minnesotans) on Saturday in Manchester, New Hampshire. In the other pool were Michigan, New England, and the East At-Large team. The top team in each of the two pools would play in a championship game on Sunday afternoon.

"A lot of scouts have written us off," said Brooks. "The eastern clubs are very good. I think Massachusetts is the favorite in our bracket, and Michigan has something like seven kids off the St. Clair Shores team that just about won the national junior tournament. I just hope we can make our guys better players for college and represent Minnesota as best we can."

As the team was preparing to go to the tournament, Knoblauch told me, "I don't know if I've ever seen Herb as calm and mellow. He's taught what he can, and he's so efficient. He's altered his knowledge to what will work at this level. There's been a lot of improvement universally in six weeks. We didn't know how much difference could be made. We have a very interesting mix of kids, a lot of nice kids. All of them had burgers together. They're becoming a team."

Lance Pitlick, a tough heart-and-soul defenseman who went on to star at the University of Minnesota and play eight years in the NHL, said, "To be chosen for that team was pretty special. I just remember Herb as someone I was in awe of. It was the first time in all of our cases where we were picked to play for a team like this. My biggest thing with Herbie is he brought out the best in everybody in a positive way. Most of us didn't know each other, but we all got to be friends. I got to know Danny Brooks pretty well and spent some time at their house, where I could see Herb as just a regular guy."

The players got an enormous kick out of Danny Brooks' impersonations of his dad, which would crack up the whole dressing room. He also would talk back to him in a manner no other player—college, Olympic, or NHL—would dare. There was no way Herbie would tolerate that, so he maneuvered around it. Besides, he wasn't going to be the drill sergeant taskmaster with this group. In fact, during warm-ups before practice, Herbie got in his licks with Danny when they played keep-away, and Herbie held onto the puck as long as he wanted with deft stickhandling. Danny presumably made up for it by eating everything at the house.

Years later, Danny called Tom Sagissor "probably our best player." Sagissor, who led Wisconsin to an NCAA championship four years down the road (on a team that also included Rohlik), perhaps has the best memory about the tournament.

"We wanted to do what every other player who ever played for Herb Brooks wanted to do, and that was to win," Sagissor said. "None of us knew what we were doing at first. Very few of us knew each other, because at that time, there weren't the countless 'select' teams at every age level that came about later on. We might have been the first one from Minnesota.

"Herb threw us into a game with the St. Paul Vulcans junior team, and we were scared shitless about playing them; after all, we had heard about the clutch and grab style of the USHL. Herb said even if they play that way, we aren't. So we played 'em, and it was pretty chippy, but we ended up 3-3 with them. We're trying to avoid all the garbage, but at the end of the second period, Herb had had enough. George Pelawa had been bothered by Shaun Sabol of the Vulcans all through the game, so Herbie told George to 'go out and get him.' He went out, and they went at it. Big George was throwing 'em right and left, and right then—that's when we became a team."

Officially, the Vulcans matchup was a "scrimmage," and officially, Brooks had seen all he wanted to and called it off after that second period ended.

"Then we went down to Chicago to play Team Illinois, a triple-A team," said Sagissor. "We beat them twice. I was centering George Pelawa and Brad Stepan. In the first game, we're losing 2-0 or 3-0, and Herb was upset. On the bench, you could feel his intensity pick up. George looked at me and said, 'We gotta get 'er going here,' and I said OK. We went out there and George hit a guy with an unbelievable bodycheck. The guy was four feet from the boards, but he flew up into the glass and shattered it. The guy fell right through the glass and out of the rink. Glass was shattered all over, and my eyes were bigger than eight-balls.

"Back on the bench, Herbie just had this little smirk. The ref skated over and said to George, 'You, get in the penalty box for charging.' Herb yelled, 'What? Charging? You can't call that charging, it was a clean hit. The ref said, 'Coach, your guy just put a guy into the first row of the seats. That's charging.' And Herb said, 'It wasn't charging. If you're going to call anything it should be two minutes for vandalism.'

"George was a great guy, and while he was 240 pounds, he had about 8 percent body fat. When he'd come down from Bemidji for practice, he'd stay with us at our house in Hastings. My dad would make pancakes for us in the morning, and George would just keep eating until the whole box was gone."

Pelawa, a magnificent specimen, had a full scholarship to North Dakota and a pro career ahead of him, but it was all cut short when he was killed in a tragic auto accident later that summer.

Minnesota opened the tournament with an impressive 6-4 victory over Massachusetts. Then it faced the West At-Large team, which had eight Minnesotans. Brooks had allowed most of them to join Team Minnesota's practice sessions, an amazingly generous gesture. In a seesaw battle, Rohlik set up Scott Bloom for a 4-3 Minnesota lead, and Stepan's goal clinched a 6-4 victory.

In the other bracket, all three teams were 1-1, and it took goal differential to declare Michigan the entry for Sunday's final game against Minnesota.

The final had a pretty bizarre start. With Stauber in goal, the Minnesota team was bedeviled by the quick, darting Michigan team, led by Chris Tancill, a future

Badger teammate of Sagissor and Rohlik, and Kip Miller, a future Michigan State star. Michigan was overrunning Minnesota, so Brooks pulled Stauber and sent in Scott Nelson, the Grand Rapids goaltender who had made thirty-seven saves in the victory over the West At-Large team. When Stauber got to the bench, Brooks told him he was just getting a rest, and he'd be going back in. No matter, the Michigan team roared away to a 7-1 lead in the first period.

"When it's 7-1, you look at each other and wonder how soon you can get it over and get out of there," said Sagissor.

Brooks walked into the locker room at the first intermission and said, "Look, guys. I'm not nervous. We didn't beat ourselves. They made some great plays, and we should shake their hands. But they can't do that all night. People spend their whole lives looking for chances to prove themselves, and competition is a way to prove yourselves. So we should be laughing, because we've got the chance in the next forty minutes to prove ourselves."

Then he said Stauber was going back in goal, and the team would go with an aggressive 2-1-2, with the strong-side defenseman gambling from the point.

"The other thing Herb said before the second period," Sagissor recalled, "was, 'Guys, don't learn to lose. You're all going to scatter to different teams for college, and you can learn to win or learn to lose. You can start right now. Learn to win, right now.'"

Minnesota shut down Michigan in the second, and, with four seconds remaining, Dennis Vaske scored, cutting it to 7-2. In the third period, the momentum swing continued in a rush. Up in the seats, Glen Sonmor asked the rest of the pro scouts assembled, "If Herbie brings this Minnesota team back, will you guys then realize I'm right when I tell you he's a superior coach?"

The third period began, and Pelawa scored at 1:25. Sagissor recalled, "When we came off, Herb said, 'You guys get ready, you're going right back on, next shift, to get another one.' Sure enough, Scott Bloom scored [at 1:45], and we went right back out and George scored again [at 2:20]."

Minnesota scored three goals in fifty-five seconds, and the 7-2 deficit was suddenly 7-5. Then Stepan scored to make it 7-6, and the teams traded goals, with Randy Skarda scoring twice to sandwich a Michigan goal.

"Herb's magic," said Sagissor. "He knows the chemistry set. All of a sudden, we were tied 8-8."

But that wasn't all. Michigan came back and scored not one, but two goals, regaining a 10-8 lead, surely breaking Minnesota's spirit—or, maybe not.

Later, Brooks told me, "I said, 'Hey, guys, no sweat. Pat them on the back, because it was a good goal, but we've been doing this all game.'" Minnesota got one goal to get the momentum back, then Tod Hartje scored shorthanded to tie it 10-10.

The third period ended that way, and Michigan's coaches insisted on calling it a tie and leaving right then so that both teams could catch flights home. Brooks stood at center ice, arguing his case with officials and the Michigan coach. In position for a faceoff was the Minnesota team, with Stauber in goal, while the Michigan players were on their bench.

Brooks won. Michigan came out on the ice, and Hartje scored again—the game-winner—and Minnesota won 11-10 in overtime.

"This game would have blown the socks off every hockey fan in Minnesota," Brooks said. "In our first two games, we didn't play that well, but we succeeded because of our heart. I told the players we're out of the cocoon of high school now, but we wouldn't be going to Lowell, Massachusetts, for a bleeping holiday.

"They gave us a big trophy. Knoblauch was crying, there were about two hundred fans and one hundred scouts in the audience, and they said they'd never seen a game like that. . . . and I'll guarantee you no matter how much hockey they go on to play, these kids will never forget that moment."

CHAPTER 38

A LITTLE COACHING,
A LOT OF INFLUENCE

After leaving the New York Rangers, Herb Brooks spent the most time he'd ever spent at home, landscaping, building and rebuilding the deck on his Turtle Lake home in Shoreview, and pretty much driving his wife Patti to distraction. Often, when I'd call to talk to Herb, she'd ask, "Will you find him a job?"

Herb went to work for Jostens, a Minnesota company that specialized in making commemorative items such as class rings. He did well and seemed to enjoy it, although coaching was never far from his mind. And he used his prohibitive influence wisely, whenever necessary.

I had some great and lengthy interviews with him during those years in the mid-1980s.

"It's a culture shock, in a lot of ways, to not be coaching," Brooks told me during one of those interviews for a *Minneapolis Tribune* feature. "I'm learning a new language, with not as many 'bleep-bleeps,' and it's a different life, a slower pace. It's nice. Not bad." Brooks was one of those rare individuals who actually said "bleep" instead of the usual coarse words of the dressing room and the referee-baiting life he had left—temporarily at least.

"I went off for my first day of work—put on a shirt and tie, took my briefcase and my turkey sandwich, got in my little Honda, and drove off to work. The first thing I thought about was, 'Where do all these people come from?'" Welcome to the rush-hour gridlock of the real world.

"I read somewhere that I was another college coach who was a failure in the NHL," he said. "Whoever said it, it was an indictment of the writer. I'll stand on my record with the Rangers. The dream of winning the Stanley Cup is all-consuming, all-encompassing, but I think winning the division is an accomplishment, and moving up into the top one-third of all NHL teams is another one. Personally, I know I can coach in the NHL, and there are a lot of college coaches, junior coaches, and minor league coaches who also can coach in the NHL. But they may not get the opportunity because of the good ol' boy network.

"I had my experience in the NHL, and it was a thrill to be there, even though there's always room for improvement. I know that NHL teams had never done some of the tactical things we tried, but most of the players picked it right up. The first month, we were running into each other out on the ice, but most of them ended up enjoying it. People don't give the players enough credit; you've got to give them challenges that meet their ability level. And everything I've done has been out of respect for the players' talent.

"In football, there are a lot of different tactics, but in hockey, if you deviate, you're almost considered an outcast. In the NHL, it's tough, because you don't have a very good practice-to-game ratio. With amateurs, it's easier to be experimental, but in pros, a coach has to stay alive in the organization. My first year in New York, we were up by one against the Rockies, and I decided to run the clock, like they do in basketball. Our guys were out playing catch with the puck in the neutral zone. I was having a heart attack on the bench, and I wanted to yell to dump it in, but we proved we could make it work."

Brooks reflected often on his dad, Herb Sr., who continued to influence him more than anyone could realize. "My dad taught me that there are certain things in life you should react to and lash out against even if you have to be combative, but there are also certain things you've got to accept—things you can't do anything about," he explained. "The key is knowing which to accept and which to rebel against. When my dad died, it was the first time anything like that had happened in my life, and it made me reflect a lot and put things in a different perspective. It made me think of my responsibility to my family more, because you can get caught up and become oblivious to the things around you.

"For some things, you need a hammer . . ." he paused, cracking a slight grin, "and for other things, you need a sledgehammer."

Vintage Herbie.

It remained important to him to convince himself that he didn't really get fired by the Rangers, even though Craig Patrick knew he had carried out that official duty.

"Going into my fourth year, I knew it would be my last year in New York, unless my family situation changed," said Brooks, meaning bringing his family with him. "It was still open-ended, and I talked to management about it. They had discussed me not coming back. What bothered me was something like, in my second year, when [longtime UPI sportswriter] Milt Richman wrote a story about me going to the North Stars before they hired Bill Mahoney. From then on, everybody looked at me like a short-term guy. That was tough, because an otherwise knowledgeable and gifted writer made a mistake.

"But I thought the media was good in New York, fair and objective. There are some good, some not so good, and I tried to be honest and above-board with them. They get a bad rap, and they weren't as bad as I had been told they were. All I ever asked was to just get the facts straight. I realize they had to sell papers. Some people wrote that Craig Patrick and I were feuding. That was totally ridiculous. We had been through a lot. At times we didn't see eye to eye, but if you don't have different ideas, then one guy could do both jobs as coach and general manager. If I had the chance to be both, and combine the two, fine. But I would not want to be GM and not coach. For me, coaching is the dynamic of the game. That's the fun; that's the challenge.

"I never had a problem with players like Ron Duguay. I pushed him because I thought Ron had the ability to get to another plateau. I wanted to show him and others that there were new plateaus to reach. It was never anything personal.

"I thought we could win it all. I think [Rangers coach] Ted Sator will find it a lot easier to do some things now, and I think the Rangers are primed to make another move up. The Islanders were at the peak of their game, and it was a thrill to compete against them. We played them twelve times in my years with the Rangers, and we won six of them. There are different kinds of thrills in sports, and winning championships is a thrill. It's not necessarily better in the pros, and there are a lot of similarities. Achieving the ultimate is a variable, but both match the same height."

When he left New York, Brooks maintained it was a decision of convenience. "I wanted to proceed one way with our personnel, going for the present and the future, and they wanted to go a different way, so we got into a bind—a philosophical bind," he said. "It was locked in. I had offered to resign, but they didn't want me to. I didn't get fired, and I didn't resign. It was a mutually agreed upon parting. There's a difference between disappointment and discouragement, and animosity. I was disappointed, but I didn't have any animosity.

"Even more important than the Stanley Cup is having peace of mind. I'm sure the Cup will come to New York, and when it does, I will know I had some hand with my input, just as the scouts and everybody else did."

Brooks also said he had decided his next coaching job in the NHL would be with the North Stars or nobody, so that he could live at home. When negotiations broke off between his old friend Lou Nanne, general manager of the Gund brothers' North Stars, Brooks may have been a little bitter, but he overcame it.

"Louie did what he had to do on the basis of how he perceived the job," Brooks said. "There were three different things I wanted, and I didn't get any of them. I accepted that. I agreed to everything, with the exception of one small thing: a reasonable signing bonus. We started out at $75,000, and I came down to $50,000, and Louie came back with $10,000. I wanted some control of players, but I agreed I would be consulted, but that Louie was general manager and he would have final say."

At the time, Nanne said, "It's dead, completely. From my side, it's dead. We made three offers, and that's enough. It's over, it's done. We just felt if he was enthusiastic about taking it, he would have taken it. Two weeks ago, I thought we had it done. I wanted him. I offered it to him three times. It's not even worth another phone call."

Brooks maintained that the only point of contention was the signing bonus. "What difference does it make whether there's one point or more than one?" Nanne retorted. "One is enough to prevent it from happening."

Both men were stubborn and unyielding. Nanne had power and Brooks wanted some assurances. "I never was told directly that negotiations were over," said Brooks, who had Art Kaminsky negotiate. "Louie told Art at the draft and I read it in the paper. It's ridiculous. It's not worth going to battle for. I love the area and I was very interested in coaching the North Stars. Unfortunately, it didn't work out. It got down to the financial package, and it didn't come together. If Louie didn't get that from my agent, then it wasn't communicated very well. Some people said Louie and I couldn't work together, but we know each other very well, and it might have worked out very well."

Brooks, again turning philosophical, said Kaminsky had heard that the North Stars were going to hire Lorne Henning, who had been assisting with the Islanders since playing for them. "The last thing in the world I want to do is take anything away from Lorne Henning," said Brooks. "He's a good guy, and he'll do a good job."

He added, "I just don't want to be involved in a controversy as my last thing in hockey. Who knows if it's my last thing in hockey? I can stand on my credibility. Let Louie stand on his record, and I'll stand on mine. My mind is clear. Let the people make up their own minds."

Finally, Brooks needled himself a little. "I've been giving so many motivational speeches," he said. "Lately, I'm starting to believe my own bullshit."

Feeling that he might be leaving pro hockey behind, Brooks looked forward to returning to a level he loved. "Now I hope to switch things and get involved with amateur hockey, and maybe fill a little vacuum there," said Brooks. "I'd like to help some things in the state of Minnesota, with amateur hockey and the high schools, and I've talked to Walter Bush about AHAUS. The Minnesota area has to show some improvement. We've got to develop our hockey players better and pursue improving high school and college, with the Olympics as the ultimate, and not necessarily worry about preparing players for the pros."

Brooks ruled out returning to the University of Minnesota. "I had accomplished what I wanted there," he said. "Had I known the North Stars thing wouldn't work out, that might have been more of a temptation. But now I'm working for Jostens. Maybe I won't wear a ring, but maybe I can sell one."

Meanwhile, at the U, Paul Giel had dismissed Brad Buetow as coach after the 1984–85 season and named Doug Woog as his replacement. Brooks helped make that decision far more than Woog ever realized. Woog was an interesting case. I always enjoyed talking hockey concepts and tactics with Woog, and we agreed on a lot of things, particularly the insistence that the Gophers should all be from Minnesota, both because of tradition and because it was such a unique concept for any major college sport.

Once in a while, we would disagree. Sometimes Doug would say to me that if I talked to players who played for both Brooks and him, I'd find that players thought he was the better coach. It didn't matter if we were in a crowded hospitality room at the WCHA playoffs or in private. Of course, Brooks had three NCAA titles, an Olympic gold medal, and was voted by his fellow NHL coaches as the league's outstanding coach after his first year with the Rangers. Doug, on the other hand, had coached South St. Paul High School to several state tournaments, but never won any.

When Giel followed protocol and named a committee to search for a new coach, Mike Sertich, who had led UMD to back-to-back WCHA titles and two Final Four trips in 1984 and 1985, was offered the job but chose to stay in Duluth after much soul-searching. The committee worked through a huge list of candidates, filtering it down to finalists that included Dave Peterson, Chuck Grillo, Mike Bertsch, Terry Abram, and Woog. I knew Herbie knew all of them, and some, like Grillo, were close friends of his, but he was convinced Woog should get the job because he had played for the Gophers.

I wrote features about all five finalists. Most were pretty straightforward, but my favorite was my piece on Abram, a former South St. Paul star and All-American defenseman at North Dakota. He gave me a great comment, about how his only regret was not being recruited by Minnesota, because whenever he heard the rouser his blood ran maroon and gold. The day after the story ran, I got a call at home from John Mariucci. He said it was a great quote, but it wasn't true. Maroosh loved how Abram played and had tried his best to recruit him, but he couldn't get him academically qualified for a scholarship. So Abram went to North Dakota, which didn't have the loftier Big Ten requirements.

Mariucci's call bothered me a lot, because I didn't like being a conveyer of misinformation, regardless of how good a quote was. But it bothered me more a week later, when I got a tip from a committee member late one night. Woog, it turned out, had a very poor final interview and was ranked the lowest on the list. The announcement was due the next day, the source told me, and Giel would name Terry Abram. I was gripped with the idea that the committee might have been as impressed with that quote as I was.

It was after 11 p.m. when I called Herbie at home. I asked if he still felt Woog should get the job, and he said yes, and he was sure Woog would be named the next morning. I told Brooks what my source had told me. When I told him of Mariucci's call, he recalled that Maroosh was right, he had gone after Abram out of high school. I said, "Well, there is only one person on the planet who could still influence Giel at this point and that's you, Herbie. If you feel that strongly, even though it's 11:30 p.m., you've got to call Paul."

He did. And the next day, Giel announced at the press conference that Doug Woog would be the new Gopher coach.

A year later, after Woog had completed what would be the first of eleven seasons as Gopher coach, and Herbie had worked his mini-miracle with Team Minnesota, there was a new challenge at Brooks' feet. He agreed to take over as coach at Division II

Brooks directs practice at St. Cloud State University in October 1986. He took over the program for one season, helping to lay the groundwork for the school's move to Division I. *AP Images/ St. Cloud Times, File*

St. Cloud State University for the 1986–87 season. His plan was to help carry out John Mariucci's dream of realizing more Division I teams than just Minnesota and Minnesota-Duluth, the latter of which Mariucci had helped push to D1. Brooks began plotting to guide the Huskies to Division I and convince the state to support a new Olympic-development National Hockey Center at St. Cloud State.

Amazingly, he got Wayne Ferris of the Minnesota Amateur Sports Commission involved with lobbying for the new facility, and Brooks went and spoke to lawmakers whenever asked. His year at St. Cloud was impressive. The Huskies played harder and better than ever before, going 25-10-1 in the tiny St. Cloud Arena and, remarkably, reaching the small-college Final Four.

Construction of the magnificent new facility made accommodations for two Olympic-sized ice sheets, one for games and one for practices and smaller-scale games. Brooks' master plan, undoubtedly driven by Mariucci, who was dying of cancer, was to create another major opportunity for Minnesota high school players to play for a Division I program. Brooks brought in a loyal assistant in Craig Dahl. Their relationship went back to 1980, when Brooks was about to move his family to Davos. They weren't sure what to do with the house on Turtle Lake, when Patti came up with the idea of posting a notice on the bulletin board at Bethel College in nearby Arden Hills. It was a religious-oriented college, so Patti reasoned there was a good likelihood that someone responding to the notice would be of good character and trustworthy. Craig Dahl, who was coaching Bethel's hockey team, had been best known as a football player while growing up in Albert Lea, Minnesota, and he and a friend responded to the notice. After it was apparent to Herb and Patti that he fit their requisites, they agreed to let Dahl housesit for the year.

Dahl accepted the coaching job at nearby University of Wisconsin-River Falls and did a flawless job maintaining the house. When Brooks agreed to take the St. Cloud State job, he asked Dahl to come along as his assistant. It was a crash-course in coaching, but it was taught by a master. St. Cloud's team was typical of a good small-college operation, with a number of former high school stars who had not gotten big-school offers. Most were from north suburban high schools, within sixty miles of St. Cloud.

Brooks noted one way the college game had changed since 1979. "Damn face-masks," he told me. "All you can see is the players' eyes. I walk by guys off the ice, and I'm not sure who they are."

When relating his expectations for his new role, he said, "I've got to devise a system to fit the talent. But they work hard. I don't know what to expect in the league, but it doesn't matter."

It would be the Huskies' final year in the Northern Collegiate Hockey Association. "We'll have thirty-eight games next year, and we're committed to play thirty games against Division I teams, with Minnesota and UMD committed for two years from now," Brooks explained. "It's like starting a business and getting big orders from the biggest companies."

Regionally, other small colleges, such as Bemidji State, under coach Bob Peters, and some of the Wisconsin state colleges had strong traditions. "I know Mark Mazzoleni always has a good team at Stevens Point," said Brooks. "And Mike Eaves will do a good job at Eau Claire. Peters has done a fantastic job at Bemidji. We might get a thousand fans in a rink that seats about two thousand, but the students will be big winners if we can get the facility built, because it will be a hockey arena and a phy-ed place for intramurals and training."

When St. Cloud State played at River Falls, it found that the Wisconsin school's new coach had come from a successful Canadian junior program and had instilled smash-mouth, junior-style hockey there. "I've been in enough junior and pro and college games, so I know the difference between tough, aggressive hockey and cheap, dirty hockey," Brooks fumed, afterward. "There were forty-some-odd penalties, and I told our athletic director to tell their AD he'd better clean it up before they come to our place.

"I was in the locker room when we went out for warm-ups at River Falls. One of their guys speared our goalkeeper, and others were knocking our guys' sticks out of their hands. Now we go out for the game, and it went from there to a ridiculous, running-around game. At one point, I was telling our guys to accept the hits and skate through the sticks. We had a bad game, and River Falls has got a good team. Our guys took a lot and tried to stay out of the rough stuff, and they beat us."

Brooks said he figured the rematch up in St. Cloud would be a lot more controlled. But when the teams went out to warm up, it was more of the same. "Vic Brodt got slashed on the back of the legs and went down. And Mike Brodzinski got crosschecked under the chin," Brooks said. "When it was time to go out for the game, I went into the men's room and somehow I got locked in there. I finally got out and I was laughing about it, when I heard some noise. I ran out to the bench to see what was going on, and it was half over. There was a huge hassle, and they threw one of our fans out."

Sure enough, Jack Brodt, the feisty father of Vic Brodt, went onto the ice to try to lend a hand. But locked in the men's room? Was it a ploy, like former Gopher trainer Gary Smith concealing a contact lens while Herbie stalled the refs? At any rate, it assured Herbie's "innocence" and outrage.

"One of our guys got speared and skated away, and got speared again," Brooks recounted. "A River Falls guy two-handed one of our guys. Mike Vannelli got knocked onto their bench and one of their assistant coaches kicked him and challenged him. It had Canadian Junior A marks all over it. A lot of teams might run and hide from it, but we didn't. It turned into a bad scene, and now there'll be an inquiry.

"Maybe they think they're tougher because they played junior up there, so they think they can kick the heck out of these American college kids. One time, big Tony Schmalzbauer came to our bench for a change, and I said, 'Get back out there and don't let anybody get into a two-on-one with any of our guys.'"

The Huskies didn't win the division title, but beating Bemidji to reach the Final Four in Springfield, Massachusetts, was a big achievement. Bemidji had thirteen players with national tournament experience, while it was St. Cloud State's second time ever to the finals.

With things happening fast and St. Cloud State's campus quickly becoming turned on to hockey, Brooks could well have stayed and enjoyed the run to the independent Division I schedule. But his old buddy Lou Nanne came calling. Louie was always crafty, but more of a seat-of-the-pants decision-maker compared to Herbie, the meticulous planner. Perhaps the Gund brothers, who had good reason to not want Brooks as coach, had grown impatient. Nanne sold the Gunds on the fact that the public wanted Herb Brooks, and they acquiesced. So finally, Nanne hired Brooks to a two-year contract with the North Stars with a minimum of difficulty. One key element of Brooks' decision was Glen Sonmor's advice to take the job and run with it. Brooks didn't need the security he had previously sought, because this time around Louie obviously was his champion and Glen offered further insulation as Louie's assistant.

Minnesota fans were thrilled that their hero was finally taking over their NHL team, and it seemed like a match made in heaven for the 1987–88 season. This was the perfect opportunity to confirm a coaching legacy that needed no confirmation to a state full of hockey fans who already worshipped what he had done. In fact, among the state's grassroots hockey fans, Herb Brooks had more credibility than the North Stars organization.

Brooks got the North Stars to circulate and adopt his puck-control style. It was fascinating to watch Neal Broten plug right in during training camp. Optimism ran high, as fans anticipated Dino Ciccarelli becoming even more effective once acclimated to roaming, Brian Bellows coming into his own and thriving, and a young gun like Scott Bjugstad, a great skater and a deadly shooter, flourishing under his boyhood idol.

In one exhibition game, I was covering the North Stars as they circled and swirled. Brooks let J. P. Parise, his assistant, coach the team while he sat at the right end of the press box to get a perspective on who was doing what. Ciccarelli sat out this game, and as he walked through the press box, he paused at my station to discuss how training camp had been going and how enthused he was to play in an offensively creative system. Doug Woog, an interested observer, approached us from the left end of the press box. Doug and I exchanged pleasantries, and as he started to walk on, he asked Ciccarelli if he could talk to him. The two stepped away from me, although not far enough, and I couldn't help but overhear their conversation. Woog asked Dino various questions, all aimed at what practice drills the team did to get the players to circle and weave the way they were. It struck me as curious, because with twenty more paces, Woog could have asked the maestro himself. Brooks, still a staunch Woog backer, would have gladly drawn up a dozen of his circling diagrams while divulging any information Woog might have wanted.

The season started off slowly for the Stars, which shouldn't have surprised anyone, considering the players were learning a new system. Overlooked amid the optimism was the fact that the franchise was woefully thin beyond players such as Broten, Ciccarelli, Bellows, and Bjugstad. The only hope was that staunch, proven veterans like Dennis Maruk and Steve Payne could come through for them.

Then came a succession of injuries. Broten, the key to Herbie's hopes as the offensive catalyst, missed much of the season and was hampered when he did play. Bjugstad, a hard-shooting former Gopher, was healthy for only thirty-three games. Deprived of Broten's setup artistry, he managed just ten goals.

Every time we talked, Herbie said that key injuries forced him to back off his free-flowing system in favor of a more conservative, pragmatic approach. His hope was that just getting by would lead to new personnel who could stabilize things. He also said how much he appreciated the players' attitude, because they remained upbeat and positive no matter how things were going.

But nothing stabilized. The once high-scoring veterans faded, as Maruk managed just seven goals in twenty-two games, and Steve Payne had physical problems and played only nine games before retiring. Even the team's leading scorers were subpar. Ciccarelli led the team with forty-one goals, but had scored fifty-two goals just a year earlier.

Nanne made a couple of trades and called up everybody he could think of, but the best evidence of how bare the cupboard was came when the final season tally showed the worst record in the league at 19-48-13, even though Brooks used forty-six players as the season went along!

Brooks' ill-fated 19-48-13 season with the injury-plagued 1987–88 Minnesota North Stars. The gesture says it all. Former 1980 Olympian Neal Broten is second from left. *Photo by Bruce Bennett Studios/ Getty Images*

Nanne wasn't around for the finish, having stunned the state's fans and the organization by abruptly announcing his resignation in midseason. The entire team was thrown into even more turmoil. Nanne's presence was Brooks' only security, and with Nanne gone, Brooks' future with the Gund brothers was as vulnerable as wherever Gordon Gund chose "to shove his white cane."

At the end of the miserable season, it was all Brooks could do to muster determination for improvement the following year, but the new general manager would be a pivotal selection. After much deliberation, the Gunds introduced Jack Ferreira as the new general manager. Ferreira seemed like a decent fit, and he even contacted Brooks. But then, a press conference was held to announce that Brooks was done. Ferreira brought in Pierre Page as the new coach.

Brooks was angry. "Ferreira comes in and either retains or rehires whoever he wants," said Brooks. "A couple of weeks ago, Ferreira called me and asked me to stay on as coach, and our meetings have all been cordial. Now I get feedback that he went to the Gunds, and they put it down.

"It's confusing that they are having a press conference to announce I am not being rehired for a job I never applied for, even last year. How many times can they shoot me full of holes? Their management technique is to wipe the slate clean. I did not feel comfortable with the team ownership, and now they're conspiring on how to save some public relations. Jack's a good fellow, but I felt that the well had been poisoned somehow.

"To be frank, I have no desire to work for the Minnesota North Stars. That is no way a reflection on the players, who were a great group to be associated with. All season, we were decimated by injuries and had little to show for our effort, other than a good attitude. The players didn't quit or blame others. They stepped on the scale of adversity and measured up very well. With everybody returning next year, and with a new GM, I believe the team can challenge Detroit in the Norris Division."

It's intriguing how close the arrangement between Brooks and the North Stars actually came to working out, big time. Craig Patrick—Herbie's loyal assistant on the Olympic team who rose to assistant general manager with the Rangers and hired Brooks for that job, and who was summarily dismissed after Brooks' three and a half years, while Phil Esposito emerged from behind the scenes—had stayed active. While Brooks took a year off, then coached Team Minnesota, raised St. Cloud State's fortunes, and finally suffered through the miserable season with the North Stars, Patrick had gone out to Denver to be the athletic director of his alma mater.

In 1989, Patrick went to Pittsburgh, where he did a fantastic job guiding the Penguins to a couple of Stanley Cups. But before he went to Pittsburgh, he checked on some other NHL openings. One of those was with the Minnesota North Stars.

"I interviewed with the North Stars when Jack Ferreira got the job," said Patrick.

If Patrick, not Ferreira, had been hired by the Gund brothers, he would have been adamant about retaining Herb Brooks, who was still under contract with the North Stars at the time. The two undoubtedly would have worked in concert to bring about the kind of the success craved by the Gunds, to say nothing of Minnesota hockey fans. As it turned out, a whirlwind two-year span in Minnesota had ended, but not without Brooks proving that his impact on the state was deeply appreciated. If his efforts didn't always result in a championship, maybe that just proved he was human after all.

CHAPTER 39

STUBBORN SUCCESS IN THE 1990s

Herb Brooks had enough varied experiences during the 1990s to constitute a fantastic career in hockey. When that decade is prefaced by his achievements and experiences throughout the 1980s, it's mind-boggling.

The 1990s got off to a great start for Herb Brooks when he was inducted into the International Ice Hockey Federation Hall of Fame and the U.S. Hockey Hall of Fame. The selection committee for the latter, on which I served, had honored the entire 1980 team earlier, but Herb's induction was a deserving tribute. Herb asked Mike Eruzione to present him, which thoroughly surprised Eruzione, who hadn't had much contact with Brooks since 1980.

"It's not easy to stand here and talk about a legend," Eruzione began in his presentation at the Eveleth, Minnesota, facility's official ceremony. "The first time I met him was in Denver in the [1976] NCAA semifinals, when Herb sent all his best players out to beat us up.

"He gave me the opportunity to play for him and be the best I could be. John Mariucci believed in Herb and gave him the opportunity, and John is probably proud of Herb being inducted here, and proud that an Italian is talking about him, but he might be upset that it's a Bostonian."

Eruzione added a few of Herbie's best lines, then said, "He had us so prepared at all times because he was totally focused. Anybody can coach great players, but Herb was committed as a coach, day in and day out, to be the best coach he could be. That's all he asked of us—to be the best we could be.

"In the six months we had, he made a great development into the European style of play that would allow us to win the gold medal. He had stubbornness, to a degree, but he always said, 'We have a talented team, so I'm going to give them a chance to show it.' He may not let many people get too close to him, but he made us depend on each other and develop chemistry, and to believe not only in ourselves but in each other. For those reasons, he might be the greatest coach."

Then Brooks stepped up to the podium and said, "You've just seen why Mike Eruzione hasn't worked for ten years."

Then he touched all the important bases. He thanked his wife Patti, who "could be described as the ideal coach's wife. She has to be something special to put up with me. I have to think of my father, who introduced me to this great game of hockey. . . . My father's words were profound when we won the state tournament at St. Paul Johnson, when he said, 'Don't go to Michigan; go to the University of Minnesota. If you're good enough, you'll play for Mariucci; if you're not, you won't.

"Mariucci had a profound effect on my life. I had to work hard to play on some good teams and some great teams. Of all the players I had a chance to play with, the best was John Mayasich."

Brooks also offered his philosophical views: "The game is in a state of flux, and there were things I thought we could do, including some things that other countries are doing. The U.S. is not genetically inferior, but needs an environment that allows our natural ability to come out. In my first year at Minnesota, we were getting twenty-five hundred fans and the situation had to be changed fast. I had great captains in Bill Butters and Jimmy Gambucci, and two years later, we were able to win the national championship. It answered a philosophical question, saying we could play. . . ."

Herb didn't want to pass up the chance to motivate—to coach—the AHAUS organization that governed U.S. amateur development.

"In 1980, we had to get better. Today, our country has to change. We're not done; we're just getting started. I was alienating the 1980 players by design, and Mike knew that. We couldn't have done what we did without a captain like Mike Eruzione. We now find ourselves at a crossroads of hockey. We've got to change our development plans because we're not doing justice to our youth. We've got to adopt the attitude of 'How can I make the game better? How can I make them, better?' The Bible says, 'Apply your hearts to instructions and your ears to words of knowledge. . . .'"

In 1990, the plan was underway to separate the Winter Olympics from the Summer Olympics by two years. With both Olympics already planned for 1992, the Winter Games would be held again two years later in 1994, while the Summer Olympics would follow as scheduled in 1996. Thereafter, both would proceed on traditional four-year plans.

Brooks believed that the ideal circumstance would be to name one coach with a four-year plan to prepare and maintain a team to represent the United States in 1992 in Albertville, France, *and* in 1994 in Lillehammer, Norway. It made good sense to me, and to some within AHAUS, but Herb went at AHAUS boldly with his beliefs, when subtlety might have been more effective.

"I've raised my hand and I've brought up issues," Brooks said, "and I've been ostracized for it. They haven't called me in ten years. We did something in 1980 they'd never done and haven't done since. They know where I'm at. I won't be hard to find."

Brooks had maintained that others should get the chance to coach the Olympics and that he wouldn't be interested in returning. The two-term scheme appealed to him, however, reflecting a theme that continued for the rest of his life: he didn't want to be perceived as chasing positions or applying for them—he wanted to be pursued.

Lou Cotroneo, the colorful long-time coach at St. Paul Johnson High School who had been an assistant coach back when Brooks played for Johnson in the 1950s, asked me if I saw Herbie often. When I said yes, he said, "Say hello to him for me, because he's my idol. He's the only hockey coach I've ever known who has gotten paid more to not coach than to coach." I told Herbie that line, but he didn't laugh. I thought it was fantastic, because people overlook that when he was dismissed or forced teams to fire him, it was always with remaining time on his contract, so he got paid after leaving.

As the time neared to name a 1992 Olympic coach, Walter Bush, the president of USA Hockey (formerly AHAUS), said, "Herbie is a candidate to coach. He contacted some of our people. He'd like to coach, but I haven't talked to him."

Larry Johnson, still a USA Hockey executive and still a strong proponent of Brooks, told me, "You know I want Herbie because he's head and shoulders above anybody else out there. He's the best available coach, so he's got to be a candidate."

Brooks was elusive about who was contacting whom: "A week ago or so, a guy said Larry Johnson asked if I'd be interested. . . . I've raised my hand. I'm not applying, but they've got my number. But it's got to be a four-year plan. I've said I'd like to see others get the chance to do it, but this two-year arrangement [with Olympics in 1992 and 1994] is a once-in-a-lifetime thing. I'm not going to apply, though. I'm interested if they would be willing to do a four-year deal, and if they come to me. . . ."

The impasse continued. I tried to suggest to Herb that he should be the coach, but that the job description was for the 1992 team, not for the 1992 *and* 1994 coaching jobs. He insisted that USA Hockey should pursue his idea, and while I didn't disagree, I urged Herb to at least try to get the job that was available.

The final interviews were conducted in Chicago. Herbie called me the night before flying there, and I urged him again to try to work with USA Hockey rather than challenge the organization. "Think about it in this way," I told him. "The best possible thing for USA Hockey would be to adopt your plan, because they could lock you into a four-year contract, and then whatever happens in 1992, they've still got you committed for 1994 at the same figure. The best possible thing for you would be to take their plan for 1992 only. Then, if your goalie doesn't play like Jim Craig and you lose, you could get out of 1994. At the same time, if you win the gold medal in 1992, you could hold them up for a king's ransom for 1994, and they'd have no choice but to hire you.

"In other words, you technically are arguing for a plan that would be best for USA Hockey, and they are arguing for a plan that would be best for you. But you're too stubborn to accept their plan."

He called me again, just before going inside for his interview. I urged him in the strongest possible terms: "At some point, the question will arise about whether you will accept the job that is open, or hold out for both 1992 and 1994. Herbie, take the job that's open."

An hour or so later, he called me again. He was mad and said USA Hockey already had its mind made up and wasted his time. After he calmed down, I asked, "One thing, Herbie: when that moment arose and they asked if you would take it for 1992 alone, what did you say?"

He hesitated before finally answering. "I told 'em no, that it had to be for both terms," he said. I told him that I wouldn't have hired him either, under those circumstances.

In 1992, Team USA finished a dismal 0-3-3, placing eighth and barely making the inflated field of quarterfinalists, where they promptly lost 6-1 to Finland.

Herb Brooks could go off with an "I told you so" air, knowing that USA Hockey needed him more than he needed USA Hockey. I told Herbie that the individuals working for USA Hockey are basically good people, hoping to do the best they can for youth hockey, even if they lacked his foresight and ideas. I agreed with him that USA Hockey should quit spending so much money developing players already selected as "elite," and instead should distribute that money to try to improve greater numbers of marginal players and thus broaden the talent base. I told him I thought he was the best person to take over and thoroughly renovate USA Hockey, but in order to do that, he had two choices: to get into USA Hockey and work toward evolutionary changes from within, or to stay outside and throw rocks at it with no chance of forcing any changes, even when he was right.

Brooks said, "I'm not anti anything, but some things bother me and have to be addressed. I'm against pro athletes in the Olympics. We've got something better if we have development rungs. But it's shortsighted, disjointed, and fragmentated. . . ."

"Fragmentated"? Herbie *could* invent words, or maybe slip a bit as the torrent poured out of him.

"USA Hockey wants one-week camps all over," he continued. "You might introduce a concept, but you don't teach anything in one week. They call it 'ROI'— return on investment. And it's not there. They're selecting by quota with no continuity. They pick it up, drop it, and go somewhere else. The broader the base of the pyramid, the higher the peak. Right now, the pyramid is too short.

"My suggestion is a satellite program, with a half-dozen centers around the country. You get sixty kids to each one for three or four days a week, for four or five weeks. After 1980, tons of money came into USA Hockey. When you receive that much, you have a fiduciary responsibility. The pros are a Band-Aid application [for the Olympics]. It's a no-brainer to use minor league pros or recycled pros. We can do better by developing our own amateurs better. The college coaches are upset. You throw these carrots out to select teams and play in the Sports Festival in hopes of getting Olympic jobs, but that's all meaningless if the pros take over. The democratic process works, and I'd like to see it done in USA Hockey. But it's not being done now."

In 1991, it had all become a moot point anyway, because Brooks was hired to coach within the New Jersey Devils organization. Lou Lamoriello, former head coach at Providence College, was running the team, and he hired Brooks on a two-year contract to coach and teach the younger players and prospects at the team's Utica, New York, farm club, while Tommy McVie would coach the Devils with Robbie Ftorek assisting him.

"I'm looking forward to going to work as coach and GM at Utica," said Brooks. "That's an American League club, and it's the perfect way for me to go back into the game and blend in. I've been painted one way, and I think it's unfair."

Herbie's sensitivity to criticism was consuming, and it was important to him to know he did what he thought was right, even if management and other factors prevented him from carrying off his plans. When Lamoriello dismissed McVie after the season, he brought up Brooks to coach the big club. It was the 1992–93 season, and Herbie was back in the NHL with a good club that had high aspirations.

"We came off the best year we've ever had, and I'm pleased with what Herb is doing," Lamoriello told me, when Herbie was first getting going with the Devils. "We still have some transition, but we have a plan, a direction. Herb has a way of doing things. Herb and I spend a lot of time together. His greatest asset, besides being such a progressive thinker, is that he's not afraid to experiment, and he has such great adaptability. Certain things don't change, such as the fundamentals of the game. Every system will work if all will pull together. The game is changing, and some other teams are trying to force a system like this, but it won't work for them. No question that was part of my interest in going after Herb.

"I never saw a guy enjoy coaching as much as Herb does," Lamoriello added. "Perfection is part of his vocabulary, but the greatest change he's made is that he's a little more patient. He has his thoughts on how the game should be played, and his love to teach a progressive style matches up well with the players we had going into the season.

"We're looking at the total season. In training camp, Herb attacked the neutral zone first, then worked from there to the offensive and defensive zones. Sometimes it took adjustments, but he got us to play with constant movement. Everybody flowed, and he'd say, 'Go to your legs.' He incorporates everything together. He had Jack Blatherwick out here for eight days, and we're in the greatest shape."

"I like Lamoriello's management style," Brooks commented. "As the game has changed, I've come to understand management's role better. Some things bothered me with the way I handled things with the North Stars. I was right, but I handled it wrong. It can make you paranoid."

Brooks added, "[Peter] Stastny is out here with us, and he's going to walk into the Hall of Fame someday. We're working on taking the traditional approach and stretching the zones. It doesn't happen overnight. We played Pittsburgh almost straight up, and they're probably the best team we've seen, because the new time-out rule means they can play two lines almost all night and keep Mario Lemieux out there. We lost to the Islanders, but the next night we went into their building and beat them.

"Most teams do some motion things now, and there's a lot more freedom with the puck, but you still have to play intelligent defense. I believe in a defensive game, but not defense only. In the '90s, we still need some rule changes," he said, going on to suggest several rule changes, just as he had done when I interviewed him before his final season with the Rangers. "We've got to get rid of the red line and use it for icing only," he said, referring to the two-line passing rule. "You want to get rid of the hooking, holding, and slowdowns, take the red line out. And we should move the nets out from the end boards and give the game to the athletes. I don't mind fighting, if the fighters can also play.

"The teams in our division are all tough and can beat you offensively or defensively. With Philly, Washington, Pittsburgh, and the Islanders, it's tough finding holes, finding lanes—I think it's great. When I started doing some of this stuff at the university, I was striving for the best of Canadian and European styles. With the '80 Olympic team, I let it all hang out. I did some things with them that I haven't done since. Now we've got Russians, Czechs, Finns, Swedes, Americans, and Canadians, and some of the players who fit this system best are Canadian pros."

Brooks was enthused about his players. "Bobby Holik can shoot. Tom Chorske may not score much, but he's such a great skater and he does some other things." Slava Fetisov, a likable fellow who starred on defense for the Soviet Union team that was the victim of Brooks' magic at Lake Placid, was a key player, as was a young prospect named Scott Niedermayer.

"I used the word 'transition' in New York and was subjected to some ridicule," Brooks said. "Now everybody uses it. Offense has more personality, but defense takes more character. I'm trying to get our defense more involved with the offense. They've always run into a red light before. I've sort of got it to yellow, although it's not green yet."

Brooks was living away from home again, but Patti came out for visits. "It would be OK if I could find Patti a penthouse on Fifth Avenue," Brooks said. But before that could happen, after just one season, an amazing development brought an end to Herb Brooks' term at New Jersey.

"He had some problems with just a couple of players," recalled Jack Blatherwick. "Herbie thought Claude Lemieux was a bad actor, and he had Stephane Richer, who had scored fifty-one goals at Montreal but was a lazy player."

Lemieux had a reputation for being a great playoff scorer, but it might have been because he underachieved all season long and then perked up at playoff time. Brooks told me of an ugly incident he heard about that so outraged him, he demanded Lemieux be dismissed from the team. At a gathering of players and wives at a restaurant, the story goes, Lemieux arrived escorting a somewhat questionable woman and paid her to commit a quite shocking act among the mixed company. Brooks made his demand.

Lamoriello might well have gone along with Brooks, but the club president, Dr. John McMullen, had taken a personal liking to Lemieux and refused to get rid of him. When Brooks insisted one of the two must go, it turned out to be Brooks. A couple of years later, Lemieux was quoted ridiculing McMullen and subsequently was gone. McMullen, a strong leader usually possessing a good feel for people, died in 2005.

As for Brooks, he was back home with a year to go on his contract and more reason to be Lou Cotroneo's idol.

But the 1990s were far from over, and Herb Brooks took it to the hilt when he was invited to coach the French national team in the 1997 World Championships and the 1998 Winter Olympics in Nagano.

Brooks became a coach in constant transit, commuting to and from France, but he kept in contact with me and spoke about his frustrations. The French hockey players, he said, were surprisingly skilled, but they played for fun and there was very little organization, instruction, or development. The players dispersed to various pro teams in Europe, and when it came time for an international tournament, including the world championships or Olympics, they simply got together and said "Let's play!"

Brooks reacts to a call at the 1998 Winter Games in Nagano, Japan, where he coached the French Olympic team. Some USA Hockey officials accused Brooks of throwing a game to bump the U.S. to the relegation round. *AP Images/Kevork Djansezian*

It was very difficult for Brooks to organize the French team, mainly because he spoke no French and therefore relied on translators, just as he had in Davos all those years ago. He told me repeatedly that the players were good, but they weren't accustomed to conditioning or drills. Still, he persevered and said they eventually seemed to respond. In the World Championships held in Finland, the team pulled off the unthinkable: France, coached by Herb Brooks, upset the United States 3-1. Score one for passion . . . and one for tactical wizardry.

Later in the tournament, controversy ensued. With France tied going into the final minute of a game, Brooks was aware that his team could only advance by winning and that a tie would be as bad as a loss, so he pulled his goaltender. Unfortunately, the other team scored into the open net. The team that beat France bumped the U.S. into the relegation round, from which it would have to win a qualifier to return to the top international division for the 1998 Olympics in Nagano. USA Hockey officials actually accused Brooks of pulling his goalie to throw the game, knowing it would knock the U.S. out of the top level. If nothing else, it proved that Brooks was not completely paranoid about the intensity of his impasse with some members of USA Hockey.

The Olympics in Nagano were noteworthy for the use of pros. NHL players dominated, although the U.S. team was tougher on its hotel than it was on its foes, causing an off-ice controversy and losing 4-1 to the Czechs in the quarterfinals. France, without any NHLers, played everybody tough, and even though the team finished eleventh, it made an impact and added another amazing chapter to Brooks' career.

When he returned home, he stopped by and we discussed the stint with France. I told him he should have brought some France game jerseys back with him. "You mean you would want something like that?" he asked.

I said, "Of course."

He left, only to return about twenty minutes later and give me a game-worn France jersey, complete with black streaks from hockey tape. It was worn during the world championships when France beat Team USA.

A victory against Team USA, an Olympiad, an NHL team, and three Hall of Fame awards—not a bad decade.

CHAPTER 40

GROW, NURTURE,
TRANSPLANT, REPEAT

When you drove to the Brooks home on the north end of Turtle Lake in Shoreview, Minnesota, you entered a gate and went up a slight rise. Immediately, you were taken by the flowers and shrubs, precisely poised to escort you along as the driveway curved gently and then descended toward the house. More flowers and plants and trees and shrubs—must have been a thousand of them. The place was like an arboretum, and a visitor would have had to assume that such a busy and impatient man as Herb Brooks must have hired a great gardener.

The gardener was Brooks himself. He was as patient with his plants and flowers and shrubs as he was impatient with players who took shortcuts. The kicker was that after Herbie spent hours, days, weeks, and months planting, pruning, and nurturing all those flowers and bushes to the peak of their lives, he would dig it all up again and start over. If everything pleased his unyielding eye and sense of perspective, Brooks might even declare it perfect, but it didn't matter. Building the perfect garden was more important than possessing the perfect garden.

When Herb was coaching the New York Rangers, his time at home was limited, so he enlisted Patti and his dad to get things prepared. "One time Herbie's dad and I drove out by truck to get seventy-five of these special plants," Patti told me back then. "Then Herbie came in from New York for one day and planted every one of them.

"The amazing thing is that everything he touches grows bigger than you can believe. He can make flowers grow in sand—nothing but sand. And he can get some sick-looking plant to grow bigger than it's supposed to get. I don't know what he does; I think he just touches them."

There is perhaps no better comparison to Herb Brooks the hockey coach than Herb Brooks the gardener. Think of Brooks selecting a variety of players—and not just the most skilled ones—and working them in with older players until he achieved just the right balance. About the time the players all pulled together in perfect harmony, the season and playoffs would be over, certain players would be gone the following season, and Brooks would go out and carefully select the right flowers to transplant here and there.

By the time the twenty-first century rolled around, Herb Brooks had compiled far more than a lifetime of hockey achievements, although a lot of things had changed for both of us. He and Patti had moved to a large and classy home on the southern edge of White Bear Lake, selling their Turtle Lake place, and both Danny and Kelly had married and presented their parents with a new crop of grandchildren. I had left the *Minneapolis Tribune*, which had been renamed the *Star Tribune* in 1982 to make the downfall of the afternoon *Star* seem less of an issue. So to speak.

I was embroiled in a controversy over a series of NCAA violations in the University of Minnesota hockey program that I reported to my supervisor but was never allowed to write. A plot by an official at the U, who later wound up in jail for other indiscretions, succeeded in discrediting me with newspaper officials, who chose not to give me a chance to respond to the accusations, despite thirty years of service. The paper reassigned me even as the exclusive story I had offered the paper became the state's biggest sports story of the year. I could see no future with that operation and accepted an offer with a new network of community newspapers based in my hometown, Duluth. It was at the same time the McClatchy Company newspaper empire bought the *Star Tribune*. In a compromise arrangement, twelve members of the guild, including me, were offered buyouts. I got about a year's salary and a full pension to leave, which prompted me to wisecrack to Herb that "the only thing better than saying '[Bleep] you' to your boss is saying '[Bleep] you and give me a bag of money.'"

Brooks, like some other insiders in Gopher hockey, was aware of most of the rumors and some of the facts. He hated the fact that someone he trusted to write the inside facts was basically forced to leave, and he knew the University's campaign of false accusations had been a factor. Every time we talked, Brooks tried to bolster my spirits, but he didn't just do it with words. The University came up with a public relations move in 1996 to celebrate seventy-five years of Gopher hockey. The plan was to bring back the most prominent people behind the program's long trail of success and introduce them on the ice between periods of a game at the new Mariucci Arena. Since Brooks was the only Gopher coach at the time to have won an NCAA title, he was clearly the most prominent figures. But he was also the only prominent figure who refused to attend the game. "After what they did to you, I want nothing to do with them," he told me. I argued that his ties with the program's history were far bigger than my hassle, but he was steadfast. I was reminded of Gary Smith recalling how Brooks always ranked loyalty to a friend above all.

Herbie's unwavering loyalty was best shown in his ties to St. Paul's East Side. He went back to his Payne Avenue neighborhood as often as he could, whether it was for a haircut (long before his hair got long enough to need one) or to stop in at Vogel's Bar to enjoy a beer with old friends, those people who never forgot the national hero who never forgot them.

Another former associate who never forgot Brooks was Craig Patrick, who had accepted the general manager position with the Pittsburgh Penguins in December 1989. The Penguins would win two Stanley Cups with Patrick as GM, the first in 1991 with Brooks' nemesis Badger Bob Johnson behind the bench. The fact that Johnson and Brooks had been at sword's point throughout their careers was well-known, even though Bob's son Mark was one of Brooks' favorite players ever. "Both were great guys," Patrick said. "They were both completely different in their approach to the game, but both great coaches."

A few years after Johnson's death in late 1991, and after Herb's stint with the New Jersey Devils, Patrick hired Brooks to scout for the Penguins, undoubtedly thinking that having him under contract could be a benefit if Brooks ever wanted to return to coaching. In 1999, things weren't working out with Penguins head coach Kevin Constantine. Patrick dismissed Constantine and coaxed Brooks, who was now director of player personnel, into coaching. Herb was able to adapt to the team's personnel and lifted them to a strong second half, claiming his two hundredth NHL coaching victory while guiding the team to a 29-23-5 finish and a playoff berth.

Herb expressed to me several frustrations with the Penguins, the greatest of which was the unfulfilled potential of Jaromir Jagr. Brooks said Jagr was probably the most talented player in the NHL but he had taken to coasting through practices. Brooks prodded the Czech star and told him that no matter how long he played in the NHL, he was cheating himself out of a few more productive years by not forcing himself to be his best. Maybe partly because of such frustration, Brooks insisted he wouldn't return as coach after that fill-in stretch.

"It was interim only," Patrick said. "He really only did it as a favor to me. He wanted me to bring in Ivan Hlinka, a Czech, who could take over after a year. We tried it, because we had three or four Czech players, including Jagr, but Hlinka wouldn't learn English and we had to let him go a couple years later."

Brief as Herbie's return to coaching was, it seemed that he should still be coaching when the 2000–2001 season rolled around. He was forever young, and, to paraphrase his old favorite line, every day he coached better than the day before, and today he was coaching like it was next year.

"Next year," it turned out, would be 2001, when Brooks agreed to return as coach of the U.S. Olympic team.

CHAPTER 41

OLYMPIC FLAME REKINDLED

I t was a major decision for Herb Brooks to coach Team USA in the 2002 Olympics. These players were not going to be Brooks' selections—the NHL had taken over the Olympic hockey tournament. In return, the Winter Olympics became something of an NHL promotional tool.

Brooks had spoken against pro involvement, going so far as to suggest turning the Olympics into an under-20 tournament for national junior teams. Nevertheless, he accepted the chance to put together a group of elite NHL players. "Instead of the Dream of 1980, we have the Dream Team of 2002," Brooks said.

The situation seemed like old news by the time the USA selection camp was held in Colorado Springs. My wife Joan and I stopped to observe the preliminary USA selection camp in Colorado Springs while on our way to scouting out the situation in Salt Lake City. Don Cameron, the former editor of *College Hockey* magazine, was chosen to assemble the reporting staffs for all thirteen venues. These staffs would write immediate result pieces, assemble post-event quotes, and cover press conferences. A reporter covering the entire Olympics could have slept through the day, clicked on the Olympic intranet in the evening, and gotten complete coverage of all events at every venue. Cameron asked me to direct a staff of six for all the games at the ECenter, the men's hockey venue.

In Colorado Springs, Brooks gave the players a couple of preliminary talks and then spent some time on the rink with a diagram board. His plan was to free them up to use some of the wide-rink techniques the Europeans would use. This team wouldn't be together again until the day before the Olympics, so Brooks had to work fast. During the first practice, he came off the ice and told me he had several steps he wanted to cover, but after the first drills he went right to the last one because the skill level was so high. Jeremy Roenick, for example, made an unbelievable move during a scrimmage to create a scoring play. Brooks skated up next to him and said, "Jeremy, that was the kind of play that makes you truly an elite player." Roenick looked at him and said, "Thanks, Herb."

"There's only one thing," Brooks replied. "Now I want to see something like that every shift."

You could argue the point, but Roenick has rarely played harder, better, and more consistently than in that tournament.

In Colorado Springs, media questions focused on the NHL rivalry pitting U.S. players against their Canadian counterparts. "I don't know what the Canadians are doing, and I don't think they care what we're doing," said Brooks. "The rules are the same for everyone, but not always. I respectfully disagree with the NHL saying it will be the same for everybody. Don't forget, it will be old-home week for the Europeans when they get on the big rink."

Turning to his roster, Brooks added, "I sense a real energy from this group. I hope everybody will understand the importance of cohesiveness and the importance of the synergy we'll have to develop. We're part of the USA Hockey movement, but we're going to do some different things. We're going to put in more movement and try to bring out all their personalities, extract them and find the right combinations."

Jack Blatherwick, Brooks' conditioning expert, went along as part of Herbie's staff. "We had preliminary tryouts, and Chris Chelios was dying," Blatherwick recalled.

Chelios, who would turn forty just before the 2002 Games, might have seemed questionable because he seemed to be out of shape. "Herbie called him, and asked if he really wanted to play on the team. Chelios assured him he did, so Herbie says, 'Let's meet,' and he flew out to Los Angeles to meet Chelios at the airport. I'm sure Chelios thought he might not make the team. But Herbie asked him if he wanted to be on the team enough to be a true leader and to pay the price by training harder than ever and do extra work on his legs for the Olympics. Chelios told him he'd do anything to make the team and Herbie said, 'All right, Chris, then you're the captain.'

"Since then, Chelios has been a model of what you have to do to be physically at your best," Blatherwick continued, noting that by 2008, when Chelios was forty-six, he was still a formidable player on the Stanley Cup champion Detroit Red Wings. "One of Herbie's greatest passions in life was to prod people to be the best they could be."

Of Chelios, Brooks said, "I was so moved by his sincerity, conviction, and desire, and he's an absolute warrior. I was personally moved by his commitment. I'd never bet against this guy, and his signature will be on this team."

Brooks also brought in John Cunniff, who was fighting cancer, and Lou Vairo as his assistant coaches, with Warren Strelow as goalie coach. None other than Craig Patrick was the team's general manager, and Larry Pleau was associate GM. The roster was solid, with Mike Dunham, Tom Barrasso, and Mike Richter in goal; Brian Leetch, Chelios, Phil Housley, Brian Rafalski, Gary Suter, Tom Poti, and Aaron Miller at defense; and Mike Modano, Brett Hull, Roenick, Keith Tkachuk, John LeClair, Tony

2002 U.S. Olympic coach Herb Brooks addresses the media. *Author photo*

Amonte, Brian Rolston, John LeClair, Chris Drury, Adam Deadmarsh, Doug Weight, Scott Young, and Mike York at forward.

Patrick cautioned that this might be a "Dream Team," but when the NHL talked of a Dream Team, they were referring to Team Canada. And Russia, the Czech Republic, Sweden, and Finland were full of NHL players, as well. "There are about five other Dream Teams," Patrick said. "If you go through each roster, there are some great players. But we're every bit as good as any of them. So it's all about team-building."

"I've known Herbie a long time, but this will be the first time he's coached me. He knows so much about the game, and he's been through it," said Housley, a South St. Paul native. "North American players go up and down lanes, Europeans have moving systems. They can adjust to the North American game, but it's easy for them to go back.

In the NHL, you don't see many players flying the zone, because they'd be flying right back to the bench. I'm looking forward to what Herbie might have in mind for us."

"We're one of six or seven with a shot at this," Brooks acknowledged. "Canada, with Mario there, has speed and creativity, and could give Canada their first gold medal in fifty years. Russia, on paper, might be the best skill-wise, and they have the hottest goalkeeper in the world. Slava Fetisov is the coach, and he played for me in New Jersey and was on their 1980 team. The Czechs are the champions until somebody beats them, with Hasek in goal. The Finns can play. They've got good talent, and Teemu Selanne. The Swedes are talking about trying the torpedo system, with one D staying back and the other moving up on attack. And watch out for an upset, by somebody like Belarus or Switzerland. The way it's set up now, a team could lose three games and still win the gold medal."

Brooks also was aware that NHL commissioner Gary Bettman was rumored to be considering some changes in NHL rules to open up the game. The 2002 Olympics could force him to do exactly that. "I read where Steve Yzerman said it was about time when the Canadian players can't just show up and outwork everybody, that you've got to think these things through," said Brooks. "It's like saying the emperor has no clothes. It's why some great NHL players may not be great international players on big rinks."

When the tournament began there were undertones that this could well come down to a U.S.–Canada gold medal finish. Because of pressure from U.S. television dollars, a preliminary round basically eliminated the weakest teams from the least-competitive nations, while the final round pitted the preliminary round survivors against the top powers in three-game round robin pools called the "final round." Eight teams then advanced to the medal round, which would be conducted in a bracket format.

Canada, with Wayne Gretzky as high-profile general manager and Pat Quinn as coach, had Mario Lemieux, Joe Sakic, and Paul Kariya on the top line, and Steve Yzerman, Jarome Iginla, Brendan Shanahan, Eric Lindros, and Joe Niewendyk adding depth to the offense. Chris Pronger, Scott Niedermayer, Al MacInnis, Rob Blake, Adam Foote, and Eric Brewer led the defense, and Martin Brodeur and Curtis Joseph tended goal.

In the final round, Russia beat Belarus 6-4 in a tough struggle while Canada lost to Sweden in a stunning 5-2 decision. The Swedes flew out of their zone, running deep buttonhook patterns into Canada's end and curling back to deflect long passes to fast-breaking teammates in a modified torpedo style. The great Mario Lemieux said, "It seemed like we were standing still."

The shock of that game was still reverberating around the ECenter when the U.S. came out against Finland and recorded a convincing 6-0 victory. Brooks said he thought his team adjusted well after one period.

The "USA" chant, which started in 1980 in Lake Placid, pretty much ran from start to finish against Finland. "I can hear the crowd, and it's good to have them," Brooks said. "Twenty-two years ago, I was so damn scared I couldn't hear the crowd."

Finland bounced back to beat Belarus 8-1 before the Russians and the Americans engaged in a spectacular game that ended in a 2-2 tie. "It was an excellent brand of hockey with end-to-end rushes," said Modano. "Everybody's been able to check their egos here, for the good of our team."

Brooks noted that he did some juggling, putting Hull with Modano as a jumpstart. "It was a tough match, and we were on our heels a long time," he said. "I don't want to say we adjusted faster [to the larger ice surface] than the Canadian team—but we did adjust."

Brooks continued, "I told our guys, how many games you play in the NHL—eighty? Then I said, no you don't play eighty games—you play one game eighty times. They all laughed like hell. I think we've had as tough a draw as possible; we played a good team like Finland, then a great team like Russia."

The tournament continued with Sweden struggling to a 2-1 victory against the Czech Republic. In the third and final pairing of the final round, the U.S. trailed Belarus 1-0 after a period, then cruised to an 8-1 blowout.

Brett Hull wisecracked that he was enjoying the hockey so much that in his next contract negotiations he might insist that Herb Brooks be hired as his coach.

Brooks said, "I wish Mr. Bettman was here so I could debate it with him publicly. We have such great athletes, and we're in the entertainment business. When you take out the red line and have the big ice, you have such a high-tempo game that who knows what will happen?"

Herbie was his old, sharp self when told that when the lower-seeded teams were asked about the medal round quarterfinals, Germany's coaches said they'd like to play the U.S. "They said that?" Brooks asked. "Maybe that's why they lost the Second World War. I'm kidding. . . . Historically, Germany always has played well against the United States."

Later that day, the Canadian team, which had been ridiculed from Nova Scotia to Vancouver Island for getting pounded by Sweden and narrowly escaping Germany 3-2, faced the Czech Republic, with Martin Brodeur going against Dominik Hasek in a goaltending duel. The most controversial goal of the tournament came with the Czechs up 2-1. Hasek blocked and appeared to smother a Mario Lemieux shot against his side

Opposite: Brooks takes a shot at the author. Never one to pass up ice time, Brooks takes advantage of a pre-tournament skate in Salt Lake City. Tom Poti is in the background. *Author photo*

with his arm before falling to the ice. Paul Kariya dashed to the net for a rebound that wasn't there. Two Czech defenders converged on Kariya and all three were pushing as Hasek wound up partly across the line and the net became dislodged. The goal light flashed, signifying only that the puck had crossed the line, without regard to how it got there or when the whistle had blown. The referee, NHL mainstay Bill McCreary, skated over to the scorer's booth for what turned out to be a long review. Eventually, McCreary skated out and signaled a goal. Officials in the replay booth ruled that the puck was in Hasek's glove, that momentum carried his glove over the line, and that he was not pushed, even though all three reasons were in error and the net had been dislodged.

After another pair of goals, the game ended 3-3. Gretzky, general manager of Team Canada, spewed emotion. "It was clearly a goal," he said. "They couldn't skate with us in the third period. They should have had four or five penalties, and two or three suspensions. Right now, it's comical to listen to what's being said, because I'm such a proud Canadian, such a fan of Canadian hockey. All the negative things being said about Canada is just American propaganda."

During a press conference before the quarterfinals, a veteran sportswriter tossed a soft one at the Great One and asked if his "American propaganda" comment wasn't an attempt to stir up a story and deflect criticism that was being leveled at his team. "You think I'm not being honest?" Gretzky snapped, angrily challenging the questioner. "What I meant about American propaganda was that every time I came in, there was a different rumor coming out of our locker room."

While the Canadian media may have been hanging on every missed goal and lackluster performance by Team Canada, the fact was the U.S. media was too busy hanging on Team USA's run to rip the Canadians.

Brooks was more concerned with his team's game against Germany than with any perceived media bias. "They play a conservative style and they execute it very well," Herbie said. "Their philosophy is more on the defensive side. We'll have to handle the offensive blue line right, and draw them out of their posture."

The first quarterfinal saw the biggest upset of the tournament, when Belarus—the bottom seed—knocked out Sweden 4-3. Belarus coach Vladimir Krikunov was a piece of work. Asked if he noticed the crowd cheering for a Belarus upset, he replied, "Try to love us more and we'll try to play better."

In the other quarterfinals, Team USA struggled early to find room against Germany, but a barrage of three goals in a 2:05 span during the second stanza spotted the Americans a 5-0 cushion that remained to the end. Canada, meanwhile, beat the Finns 2-1 and the Russians topped the Czechs.

That set up a semifinal cakewalk for Canada, which cruised past the emotionally spent Belarus 7-1, while the U.S. faced a rematch with the same Russian team it had tied 2-2 a week earlier.

Down 3-0 after two periods, the Russians came out determined in the third. On the opening faceoff, Alexei Kovalev beat everyone to a carom and snapped a quick shot past Richter at 0:11. Vladimir Malakhov followed suit and suddenly, the 3-0 lead was 3-2. With Hull off for hooking midway through the period, the Russians pelted Richter. At one point, he went down for a shot by Sergei Samsonov and the puck hit the right post, ricocheted across the crease and hit the left post, and was left spinning in midair right above Richter, who was sprawled flat on his back in the crease with Samsonov and Sergei Fedorov looming over him.

The Russians argued, but this time a review upstairs ruled no goal. The game ended 3-2, and as McCreary left the rink, Markov escorted him to the exit. It didn't appear to be a heated exchange, but afterward McCreary issued a gross misconduct for verbal abuse, which meant Markov would be suspended from playing in the bronze medal game.

Slava Fetisov—who earlier had answered a request from Herbie, his former coach at New Jersey, by sending him an autographed photo of himself in a CCCP uniform—was tactful about McCreary's officiating. "Every controversial play is reviewed up above," he said. "These are NHL referees, professional people, but they live here. They're American and Canadians, and it's just human reaction, they're not going to call penalties in some situations."

"We knew we were really going to be under siege," Brooks said. "We had to try to get back to the rhythm of the first forty minutes. Now we go from the frying pan into the fireplace."

You had to love Herbie. When he was cooking, sending out so many of his little Brooksisms, he could be excused for misfiring every once in a while.

The day off between the semifinals and the gold medal game was the perfect stage for more intrigue. Earlier in the tournament, NHL commissioner Gary Bettman had appeared in Salt Lake City and sounded ready to lead a charge to revise NHL rules to open up the game, which was exactly what Herb Brooks had been promoting. The idea of widening rinks from eighty-five to one hundred feet was even broached by Mike Modano and Brett Hull, but it seemed far-fetched to expect club owners to give up revenue by removing the first couple rows of seats on both sides of their rinks.

"It's been terrific," Bettman said of the Olympic matchups. "We decided this year not to make any rule changes . . . because we knew this would be a good laboratory for us to be looking at things. We're going to evaluate what we've seen here when we meet with the general managers."

Clearly, Sweden's resounding 5-2 victory over Canada was the call to order for that press conference. Even hardened NHL fans had to realize that the long-passing, quick-striking Swedish offense was hockey's most electrifying attraction since, well, the USA gold medal run in 1980. Team USA's success in going unbeaten through the tournament also caught the attention of the NHL executives. The fact that the NHL was addressing Olympic hockey as a catalyst for potential changes was a breakthrough on its own.

But with the tournament down to its final game, Wayne Gretzky and the Canadian players were saying that because the final was down to all North American NHLers this was the first gold medal game that could be called like an NHL contest. The suggestion became something of a groundswell, and only Herb Brooks stood up to it.

"I think our team is very adept to playing a hybrid style," Brooks said. "I think the refs can definitely be influenced by all the talk. We just want to play the same style we've played so far, but I told the players, never underestimate the ability to influence refs."

When someone asked why he was against the traditional dump-and-chase style, Brooks said, "That's Canada's style and philosophy. They like it."

But why doesn't the U.S. play that way? "I think the game is a little more profound than that," he said. "The ability of the players allows them to do so much more."

What is it, he was pressed, that he doesn't like about that traditional style? "To me it seems stupid to work so hard to get the puck and then say, 'I'm going to give it back to you, and then try to get it back again,'" Brooks replied.

I asked clarification questions to make sure Brooks' opinions about his coaching were completely separated from his opinions about Canada's style. But the Canadian media had been inflamed by Gretzky's passionate tirade against "American propaganda."

Sure enough, on the morning of the gold medal game, one Canadian newspaper had taken Brooks' explanation of why he preferred a hybrid style, and turned it into a blatant insult of Canadian tradition. "Brooks calls Canada style 'stupid,'" one headline blared. It was picked up across Canada, and Brooks' personal preferences for the game of hockey were presented as his thoughts about Canada.

The teams took the ECenter ice after Quinn, Gretzky, and Canadian players had repeatedly insisted the final could be called like a typical NHL game, while Brooks and a few U.S. players had said no, it can't. The referee was McCreary. He had done a very good job, overall, of adapting to the international protocol of calling a second penalty even if that team was already short-handed. Now it was his responsibility to decide whether it would be an international game or just a normal NHL game.

In the opening minutes, McCreary called Canada's Scott Niedermayer for interference. Canada responded with a more-than-spirited penalty kill. As Mike Modano moved up the right side, Canada defenseman Adam Foote grabbed him and hauled him down. McCreary's arm didn't move. The whistle never went to his lips.

Without question, a day earlier McCreary would have called the flagrant second penalty and the U.S. would have had a two-man advantage. Instead, Canada easily killed the single penalty. The U.S. went up 1-0 when Tony Amonte drilled a five-hole shot past Martin Brodeur, but a Paul Kariya one-timer beat Mike Richter for a 1-1 tie. Late in the first, Jarome Iginla slipped behind the U.S. defense and rammed the puck in for a 2-1 Canada lead.

The second period was another test of the U.S. skaters trying to free themselves, and Canada playing an inspired, physical game that occasionally went to excess. The U.S. went two men short for 1:08 when Aaron Miller was whistled with Hull already sitting out, but generated a huge roar by killing it. The U.S. got a power play with five minutes to go in the second and tied it when Brian Rafalski's shot glanced off Chris Pronger's stick and through Brodeur's pads.

Then McCreary penalized Jeremy Roenick, and Sakic came through again, scoring on a deflection for a 3-2 Canada lead after two.

The third period was fantastic, high-intensity hockey, with both teams trading chances. At 13:43, McCreary whistled Steve Yzerman for tripping. Yzerman blew his cool. As he glided toward the penalty box, he screamed at McCreary. It was a lip-reader's delight and a truly uncharacteristic outburst by Detroit's classy, longtime captain. This figured to be a huge advantage for the U.S. After all, McCreary had ejected and suspended a Russian player for a postgame discussion; surely he would have to give Yzerman a misconduct, a game disqualification, or at the very least a double minor. Instead, McCreary swallowed what must rank as the most abuse he ever allowed to go unpenalized in his long and impressive career.

Yzerman sat out his two minutes and a successful penalty kill lifted the Canadians. It also had an amazing effect on Yzerman, who hit the ice flying and fed Sakic for a blast that Iginla tipped off Richter's glove and into the net.

True, even under normal NHL officiating, Yzerman would have still been in the penalty box; instead, he returned to the ice and created the game-clinching goal. The U.S. gambled and tried to attack, but Canada controlled and Sakic added another for a misleading 5-2 final score.

The 2002 Games, which saw Brooks' return to the USA Hockey fold, were notable for the USA's emotional silver medal finish behind Team Canada. *Author photo*

U.S. players didn't whine or complain, but accepted the loss with class. "A big monkey is lifted off Canada's back," said Roenick, adding, "We hope we set a precedent for USA Hockey. . . . I think we've done a lot to encourage hockey in this country."

"I think I speak for all coaches, to see the immense talent out there was an inspiring thing," said Brooks. "Canada has an excellent hockey club, but I don't think we had the legs today. We came through a real tough match against Russia, and Canada did a real good job defensively, but it was 3-2 with four minutes left, and I think they had better legs than we did at the end. Sometimes that's how tournaments go.

"USA Hockey is a cause for me," he continued. "I've seen our country come a long way. We went from apprentices, to journeymen, to masters of the trade. I want to see us build our own hockey culture, and I hope to be involved with the American hockey movement if called on."

Brooks then lightened up and talked about his boss, Penguins player/owner Mario Lemieux. "Mario came over and shook hands," Brooks said. "I didn't ask him for a raise; maybe it was a good time to do it."

In the euphoric rush of praise for Canada's exceptional final game, Gretzky took the microphone, looking much more relaxed. "This was a great game for the NHL to have, and for North American hockey," he began. "The U.S. team had a great tournament. We just happened to come out on top today." Somebody then asked Gretzky what he thought about Brooks calling Canada's hockey style "stupid," still cross-wiring comments from the day before. "It was an emotional time, and maybe he got caught up in it," Gretzky replied. "He had not lost a game before in the Olympics, and you always hate to see a friend of yours lose."

Unfortunately, Canada's gold medal created a misperception that no rule changes were necessary in the NHL. It wasn't until another Olympics passed that the NHL finally eliminated the two-line pass. Some traditions die hard. That one had been put in place during World War II, when many young players had gone off to fight and the league decided that a rule assuring aging defensemen wouldn't have to skate as far would be better than shutting down the league. It stuck for sixty years.

Had the U.S., playing Brooks' hybrid style, or the high-flying Swedes won the gold medal, perhaps Gary Bettman would have hastened to make the changes that came years later.

USA Hockey has taken great pride in winning the silver medal at Salt Lake City. Herb Brooks never celebrated the second-place finish, although he never publicly complained about all that happened in Utah. After that final game on Sunday, February 24, it seemed as though everyone in the Western Hemisphere had descended on the Salt Lake City airport to leave town. My wife and I got in a line that snaked at least a block down the sidewalk from the terminal. A few hours later, we got close enough to at least see the security gates. There, believe it or not, we spotted Herbie, being searched by hand and with a wand. Herb Brooks went unrecognized and was singled out for extra scrutiny.

VISIONARY INTERRUPTED

The most endearing evidence that Herb Brooks mellowed with age was when his son Danny and daughter Kelly presented him and Patti with a posse of grandchildren. Their famous dad had spent a lot more time away from home than they would have preferred while they were growing up, but they grew up well under Patti's fine hand. It might not have been until Danny and Kelly both finished school and got married that Herbie realized the lost time that he could have spent with his son and daughter.

Danny and wife Marne had their first child, Grace, in 1997. After 2000, things got a bit more hectic. Kelly, who had married Marc Paradise, son of hall of fame defenseman Bob Paradise, gave birth to Olivia Patricia; a year later, Kelly had twins, Tom and Joe, who were followed by Danny and Marne's second child, Lucia.

The Brooks household took on a different demeanor. Patti was amused by how much Herbie loved it. "They mauled him," Patti recalled. "They bossed him around and rode him like a horse and did things he wouldn't even have let our kids do. Gracie, Danny's first, used to run him ragged. And he'd call Kelly and say, 'Why don't you drop the kids off?'"

Danny remembers that his dad was almost never around to watch him play hockey games through high school. Kelly, however, remembers the times she wrestled around with her dad as a little girl.

"He wasn't around much in the winter, but I was at school," Kelly recalled. "I thought all dads were probably gone a lot, and I didn't think it was anything out of the ordinary. He was around a lot every summer, when we were there, too. My fondest memories of him are from summer, and then he started that hockey camp in Brainerd—I hated it, although he'd let us come up there some of the time.

"It was really something to see my dad with my kids, though. It is amazing when I see there is so much of him in my twins. My dad sort of gravitated toward Tommy, and he has a lot of the same, quiet tendencies. But both of the twins almost immediately seemed to be really good at hockey and baseball."

There was speculation Brooks would return to the NHL to coach the Rangers under Glen Sather. Lou Nanne had arranged for Sather and Brooks to meet, and thought the two would be an ideal combination. Sather coached the Edmonton Oilers in the Wayne Gretzky era, when they played a style similar to that which Brooks ran with the Rangers in the early 1980s. When Brooks turned it down, many thought it was just Herbie being wishy-washy. But Kelly knows. Herbie missed too much time away from home when his kids were young, and he wasn't about to miss out on the second chance with his grandchildren. "He enjoyed being with his grandkids so much, that was why he turned down the Rangers," Kelly said.

While some coaches seemed apprehensive about approaching Brooks for his system secrets, Brooks was unwavering in trying to spread his ideas and tips for opening up the creativity he found so attractive in hockey. Once I told Herbie that Duluth East High School coach Mike Randolph was one of the most progressive coaches in the state, and that I knew he would love to talk to Brooks. So when East was in the Twin Cities for a holiday high school tournament, I arranged a meeting among Herbie, Randolph, and Mike's assistant, Larry Trachsel. Afterward, Randolph gushed about what a great experience it was, and all the little tricks Herbie shared to teach players how to read keys and react to them. "Larry didn't say a word, but he soaked up everything Herbie said," Randolph told me. After a quick instructional session with their players, the next night, Trachsel implemented a few of the Brooks tips and Randolph said they used many of his methods from then on.

Herb Brooks enjoyed watching that East team, knowing that Randolph had installed many of his ideas and turned all his players loose to play it wide-open. Late in the 1995–96 season, East played at Grand Rapids in a crucial battle between heated Section 7AA rivals striving for the No. 1 playoff seed. I was driving up to watch that game, and Herbie was eager to ride along. Inside the arena, we spotted Gus Hendrickson and John Bymark, a great friend of both Herbie and me. Hendrickson was an outstanding coach who had lifted Grand Rapids to its first state championships in the 1970s, then coached Minnesota-Duluth through its rebuilding years and the Mark Pavelich–John Harrington–Curt Giles era. He was unceremoniously fired, and worked with Randolph's program for one year. Gus and I stood at one end of the packed arena, while Herbie and Bymark stood at the opposite end. Noting Gus's body English, I realized how close he was to the Rapids team, and having moved back to Grand Rapids, he was helping coach Lyn Ellingson. That meant old college coaching rivals Brooks and Hendrickson were at opposite ends watching the teams they had adopted. With the score tied at 3-3, both teams raged back and forth for the last eight minutes. In the final minute, there was a faceoff in the East end. Gus breathed a sigh and said, "Well, looks like overtime." Mainly to heckle him, I said, "I don't know, there's still almost a minute to go, and here comes Spehar and Locker." Amazingly, Chris Locker won the faceoff and flipped the puck ahead. David Spehar broke between the point men like a sprinter, beat them to the loose puck, and scored on the breakaway for a 4-3 victory.

It was frustrating for Herbie to watch the University of Minnesota for the next four years, when first Doug Woog and then Don Lucia restrained Spehar more and more, snuffing his scoring touch to occasional flashes after a promising freshman year. The most prolific scorer in Minnesota high school history wasn't used in scoring situations or with a puck-moving center, but reduced to an ordinary two-way player.

Brooks shook his head as he watched a style so controlled that it was diametrically opposed to his philosophy of extracting the best out of every player. Herbie grew more and more distant from the Gopher program he loved, but he continued to advance his theories to anyone interested in evolving their philosophy of the game. He got Jack Blatherwick to work with him to develop a plan for USA Hockey that would expand the grassroots base of the game rather than focus on only the select elite players USA Hockey seemed interested in.

Perhaps another reason Herbie mellowed during this time was that the magnitude of some of his achievements caught up with him. One example was in the spring of 2000 when he and his 1980 Olympic players were summoned to New York for a huge event, where *Sports Illustrated* was naming its choices for the top one hundred sports stories of the twentieth century. Team USA of 1980 was number one.

"They pushed us out there on stage," Herbie said. "I was first, and I looked down and there was Michael Jordan smiling up at us. Carl Lewis congratulated us. Hank Aaron, too. And Tiger Woods. Wayne Gretzky was there and was excited for us, but he said to me, 'I'm happy for you, but this is the United States, and I didn't think they'd pick a hockey game.'

"All these great stars were there and *Sports Illustrated* recognized many of them—Rocket Richard, Evander Holyfield, Willie Mays, Jim Brown, Dick Butkus, Joe Montana, Kareem Abdul-Jabbar, Larry Bird, Magic Johnson, Jack Nicklaus, Muhammad Ali . . . and they picked us. Can you believe it?"

I could believe it. Without a doubt, the U.S. team at Lake Placid, and particularly that 4-3 victory over the Soviet Union, was the sports story of the century. Herbie was genuinely surprised that the team would even be considered among the accomplishments of all those other heroes, and it may have been the first time he realized how much the nation—and the world—appreciated what he and his college guys had done.

Other accolades were more subtle. When he first stepped in for that interim year with the Pittsburgh Penguins, Mario Lemieux was recovering from Hodgkin's disease and wasn't playing. No matter, he went to work and convinced the players that his hybrid style was in their best interest. "From the top of the circles in our end, forward, it's your game," he told them. "Find seams, regroup, whatever." It was good to hear Herbie energized as he told me about his chore. "I told them we wanted to play an upbeat, progressive style, and one player said, 'We handled the puck more in our first practice with you than in any of the eleven years I've played."

Pittsburgh general manager Craig Patrick said there was no question that he could see a huge difference in the Brooks who coached the 1980 Olympic team and the Brooks who coached the Penguins into the playoffs a decade later. "Herbie was definitely different at Pittsburgh," Patrick said. "He was more comfortable in his skin. During the 1980 Olympic year, I never got the feeling he was comfortable in his skin. Never."

Out in the real world, Herbie's interests were varied. He was approached to run for political office more than once. In fact, he holds the unique distinction of being recruited to run by both the Republican and Democratic parties. He didn't take either up on their offer.

Mellower, perhaps, but he still kept the façade in place. He disliked the politics at USA Hockey and he continued to criticize them and describe ideas that were much more logical for the development of younger players. Lou Vairo may have had a hand in coaxing him back to USA Hockey. "I saw Herbie at a camp in St. Cloud in 1999 or 2000, and I told him I had just come back from Moscow," Vairo told me. "I told him I had asked Anatoli Tarasov if he had even a single regret in his entire life in hockey, and he said, 'Yes. I disagreed with the Soviet Ice Hockey Federation, and I lost. I couldn't speak against the bureaucracy; they got stronger against me, and I lost. But so did they. They lost me. So the real loser is Soviet hockey.' I told Herb that I couldn't help but think of him in the same way, and I didn't want him to be outside USA Hockey, because in my mind, there was only one person who should coach our Olympic team in 2002, and it was him. I invited him and Jack Blatherwick to come out to Colorado Springs because he needed to know a lot of his criticisms are shared, but we're not running things. You don't always get your way, because the staff has to fulfill the policy of the people."

Vairo, an assistant coach at the 2002 Olympics, also recalled that there was no lack of intensity from Brooks in the first few games. "We were all sitting in the dressing room and Herbie asked our opinions on who should start in goal," Vairo said. "We were playing Belarus and I said I thought he should start Tom Barasso, then Mike Richter would be ready for the next game. He started Barasso. I was sitting in the upper deck, talking to [assistant coach] John Cunniff on the walkie-talkie, and Mitt Romney, the politician, was sitting right next to me. Belarus comes out and scores in the first twenty seconds and when the puck went in Herbie was glaring up at me from the bench. . . . Romney leans over and says, 'Boy, I can see why guys did what he said in 1980!'"

Vairo also recalls that after the 2002 Olympics, Doug Palazzari from USA Hockey congratulated Herb, and Herb thanked him. "Then Doug said something like, 'Now let's see if you can quit attacking us all the time in print.' That did it. Herb was steaming. That set him off again."

Palazzari might not have meant anything by it, but to Brooks it was like he was saying "If I congratulate you for doing a good job, then you have to stop criticizing us." Still, Brooks set out to work within the structure, to create a new development plan to broaden the base of youthful hockey players. He had previously devised the idea that led to Minnesota's spring and fall Elite League games. He thought that the USHL junior league was doing a great job of improving the caliber of its players, but he also knew the league was recruiting prime Minnesota high school players rather than developing eighteen-year-old high school graduates, and that taking high school players early could only hurt the caliber of Minnesota high school hockey. Brooks determined that offering another thirty games or so before and after high school hockey's season would induce players to stay in high school and give them the extra games they needed to develop. With the Elite League up and running, Brooks turned his attention to his idea for the whole country.

"We worked for hours to prepare a plan for USA Hockey," recalled Blatherwick. "No matter how popular he became, Herbie stayed close to the roots of hockey. Our idea was to get each of the USA districts to have a coach-in-chief to oversee tryouts, which would get down to forty players at each of four age groups in thirteen districts. Each coach would have a group of players to be responsible for, and it would be as much to teach the coaches as the players. Herbie went to many NHLers for support, and not one said he wouldn't help or contribute. But every one of them said they'd only contribute or be involved if it was Herbie's program and Herbie was in charge.

They wanted their contributions to go back to developing these kids and not to the USA Hockey general fund."

Herbie was close to pulling it off, to becoming the architect who broadened the base of development that he always had envisioned—a structure in which he could help coax the coaches into a more progressive approach and thus expand the number of players with a more creative outlook on the game.

But something went wrong. There were bureaucratic hang-ups and Blatherwick said that when they talked to Neil Sheehy, who was working with USA Hockey, he urged them to trust him to help even if the money had to go to the general fund.

"I know that within USA Hockey there was a general feeling that Herbie had a lot of good ideas, and a lot of things they did were patterned after his ideas. But often when he suggested something, they might have to go through a lot of steps to get it on the next budget, and he sometimes took that as a rejection," Sheehy said, although he didn't recall the exact details of the last discussions between Brooks and the organization.

But when USA Hockey decided to not go ahead with the Brooks plan, he was enraged. He called me and vented his frustration, insisting he would never again work with "those people" at USA Hockey (actually, he used a euphemism for "people").

"When I came to work in AHAUS, I had a chip on my shoulder because I had come from an area that never had rinks or money," Vairo said. "AHAUS had a coaching program in place, leading up to the junior national team. I wanted them to expand it, to form a national camp for development, and I brought it up at a meeting with a lot of big-time hockey people present, including Herb, Bob Johnson, Tim Taylor, Gus Hendrickson, Dave Peterson, Jeff Sauer, and others. When I brought up my idea, it got defeated by a vote. They said there were six hundred players in Minnesota better than all the players in California, so it didn't make much sense having separate camps for areas that don't have much hockey. They said maybe in fifteen years they would be able to get programs in the lesser areas. After it got defeated, I'll never forget this, Herb got up and said, 'I'll support you.' And then so did Gus and then a couple of others. It was not a democracy, and we got it through. It did my heart good, because only a few years later, Florida won a championship with all Florida players."

That was always Herbie's stance: make something available to the people who can benefit from it the most, and maybe to those who are not affiliated with the hierarchy of the sport's existing elitism.

When USA Hockey decided to start its National Development Team Program in Ann Arbor, Michigan, for example, I thought it was a good idea for some areas, but not for Minnesota, which already had the unequaled high school program for development.

The plan was to hold a tryout, and skim off the top twenty among seventeen-year-olds and the top twenty among eighteen-year-olds, and take them away from home to be housed, fed, schooled, and cloistered together in a hockey-intense environment. At the time, it was declared vital to creating better players for future Olympic teams, an idea that lost all credibility when the NHL took over the Olympic teams, eliminating the chance of any non-NHL player ever again making Team USA's roster. Years later, everyone trumpets how successful the program is because, except for a few players who might fall by the wayside from hockey burnout, Development Team players all go on to college and pro futures.

However, taking the best players from Minnesota high schools couldn't help but dilute high school hockey, where the best players raise the level of all their teammates; losing them seriously erodes the largest base that USA Hockey is supposedly trying to broaden. Also, the elite forty players placed on those two teams would be elite players whether they stayed in high school, went to the Development Teams, or spent a year rink-ratting on a backyard pond. True, having the best play the best can accelerate the development of a small group, but it also leads to self-fulfilling prophecy in which merely identifying elite players can be mistaken for developing them. If USA Hockey really wanted to improve the skill level of a broader base of players, it should reverse things—don't invite the top forty players in those two age groups but rather forty promising but not-yet-elite prospects and develop them. If USA Hockey developed forty new elite players, it would at least double the number of elite players at those age levels, fulfilling the theory that the broader the base of the pyramid, the higher the peak.

Herbie agreed with that assessment, but he was more blunt. "For the money they're spending on forty kids a year, they could be developing a thousand kids across the country," he said.

He was really fired up, however, about the chance to work within the USA Hockey system, and he was ready to compromise in order to install his grassroots development program. He was angrier than ever when it didn't work out. I listened to him, agreed with him, and I heard him say he'd never work with USA Hockey again, but I held out hope he might still work with USA Hockey. His concepts were simply too good.

Herbie told me he was going to Biwabik on the Iron Range that weekend, where he would represent the 1980 team at a U.S. Hockey Hall of Fame fundraising event that included some golf at Giant's Ridge. Herbie was willing to go even though he knew he would miss the second birthday party for Kelly's twins. He felt the responsibility and he knew he'd see old friends and countless former teammates and players he had once coached.

Herbie wasn't a bad driver, just an incredibly impatient one. He liked cars and he occasionally asked my opinion about buying a new car. I'd pick out something that was innovative but inexpensive, and knowing many Twin Cities dealers would love to have Herb Brooks driving a car from their lot, send him someplace where it was a snap to get a good deal. The dealer would give him an offer that was below cost, and Herbie would ask me if it was a good deal. I'd say, "Herb, unless they pay you to take the car, you can't do any better." Then he'd turn it down.

A month later, he'd want to start the process again. One Honda dealer told me that it got to the point when he saw Herbie walking in the front door he'd sneak out the back. The art of making a good deal and then turning it down became a lot, it seemed to me, like transplanting the flowers in the yard. Get every detail arranged to perfection and then walk away and try for something better.

It often crosses my mind how I wish I had been home to drive Herbie to that Hall of Fame function. I never saw him again. He drove the family Toyota minivan up to the Iron Range and played a dozen holes on Monday with his buddies, including Dick Meredith. "We're out there on the course and Herbie's showing guys some tips on how to hold their forearm when they hit their drivers," Meredith said. "No matter what he was doing, he couldn't help coaching if he thought he could help someone."

Herbie broke off from that game before finishing the round so he could make it home in time for a flight to a speaking engagement in Chicago. Someone else needed motivating and Herbie was the guy. He was tired, friends said, from a busy schedule and from staying up late and reminiscing the night before. "My mom was in Las Vegas, so Dad had called me about noon to see if I'd come over to the house and let the dog out, because he was running late," Kelly recalled.

It was Monday afternoon on August 11, 2003, just six days after Herbie had turned sixty-six. Driving south on Interstate 35, he had just passed Forest Lake. Inexplicably, Herbie was driving in the far right lane even though he had to be in one of the two left lanes to get to his Birchwood home. Witnesses behind him said the van's two right-side tires drifted off onto the shoulder then suddenly the van swerved back to the left. They said the van's brake lights never came on, never flashed, supporting speculation that he might have dozed off then abruptly awoke and overcorrected to the left. The van veered across all three of the southbound lanes before flying off into the wide central median, where it barrel-rolled several times. He wasn't wearing a seatbelt, and when the driver's door flew open, he was thrown from the vehicle, which rolled over him in the deep grass before coming to rest on all four wheels. An emergency medical technician who happened to be following in another car stopped and ran to the van. When she and others found it was empty it took a minute to find him in the grass. They tried a respirator, as emergency vehicles were summoned, but Herbie died at the scene.

Word spread rapidly, through the area, the state, the nation, and the world. I was in California when I got the news. *St. Paul Pioneer Press* reporter Bruce Brothers, who knew I was the closest media person to Brooks, asked me what I was doing before he told me the horrible news. I was devastated. My whole family was devastated. The entire hockey world was devastated.

The media jumped at the opportunity to do features on the importance of wearing seatbelts, implying Brooks would have lived if he'd been wearing one. Kelly said, "He always yelled at me about putting my seatbelt on." Patti said that when the law changed making it a violation to not wear a seatbelt, they would be driving along and Patti would say, "Herb, there comes a police car." Herb would reach up, grab the seatbelt buckle, and hold it against the receptacle until the policeman passed, then let the belt retract back into the pillar.

I told them that I used to con him into wearing a belt by saying that the new car we were in wouldn't start unless we were both buckled in. However, all the speculation notwithstanding, we had to accept that Herbie didn't want to wear a seatbelt, and that none of us ever knew another person in the world who was more adamant about not being restrained in any way.

Reaction around the world was moving and heartfelt. The Associated Press distributed an item that quoted former Olympic and Islander defenseman Ken Morrow as saying, "Coach may have been the greatest innovator the sport has ever had. When it came to hockey, he was ahead of his time. All of his teams overachieved because Herbie understood how to get the best out of each player and make him part of a team. And like everyone who played for him, I became a better person because I played for Herb Brooks."

"It's certainly a sad day for American hockey" said Mark Johnson. "We lost one of the finest coaches. On a very sad note, we lose not only a great coach and innovator of the game, but a real good friend."

Herbie, if he could be given the last word among such luminaries, might have quoted one of his favorite movies, *Willy Wonka & the Chocolate Factory*: "We are the makers of dreams, the dreamers of dreams. We should be dreaming. We grew up as kids having dreams, but now we're too sophisticated, as adults, as a nation. We stopped dreaming. We should always have dreams."

"People all over the country who were old enough to be cognizant in February of 1980 can still tell you exactly where they were and what they were doing when Team USA beat the Soviet Union in the Winter Olympic hockey tournament," I wrote. "Hockey fans all across Minnesota will also remember where they were on August 11, 2003, when they heard that Herbie had been killed. I was in California, looking at bottled water. Later, gazing at the magnificent moon, I realized life goes on, the world keeps turning, and we're all helpless to do anything about it. But we can focus on doing our best, and we can persevere. Herb Brooks changed things he could and was frustrated when he tried to change things he couldn't. For sixty-six years, he was impatient, his mind always working to stay one jump ahead of everybody. He did it his way, and he did it well. Now he's been cut short, and for all we know, his best accomplishments might still have been ahead of him. Because nothing was beyond his reach.

"Everybody, not just hockey zealots, can take inspiration every day and in any endeavor from Herb Brooks and his inner drive and desire to succeed. But from now on, it's going to be a lot tougher. Herbie is gone, incomprehensible as that may be, and there is no one who can ever take his place."

AFTERWORD AND ACKNOWLEDGMENTS

The Twin Cities can be stifling with heat and humidity in mid-August, and it was sweltering inside the St. Paul Cathedral for both the wake and the funeral of Herb Brooks. Estimates ran as high as 2,500 for those of us who stood in a line that curled around the pews of the huge cathedral before winding its way up front where the family stood to greet the throng. It was there that David Brooks told me, through his tears, "I just want to be Herbie's little brother again." Leave it to Patti Brooks to lighten the moment when it seemed destined to become overpoweringly ponderous. When Lou Nanne, Herbie's former semipro roommate, gave her a hug, Patti whispered to him, "OK, now you can tell me which one of you really had to sleep out in the hallway." Louie insisted, still, that it was Herbie who was "entertaining" in the room and locked Louie out. Of course, Louie also realized that he was the only remaining witness.

Bill Butters and Mike Eruzione gave stirring memorial tributes at the funeral, which was attended by more hockey dignitaries than had ever assembled in the state of Minnesota for any reason. The whole 1980 Olympic team was at the wake, and all but the elusive Mark Pavelich, who returned to his North Shore home, attended the funeral as well. National Hockey League dignitaries, including Mario Lemieux and countless others, also attended, mingling with the common folks—East Siders who had known Herbie all his life. The Reverend John Malone, in fact, was an East Sider himself, although he attended Harding High School while Brooks was a Johnson stalwart. Malone said we could all only imagine, after all of Herbie's achievements, what more he might have done had he gone to Harding. Outside, thirty-two of us lined the long staircase, holding hockey sticks in an archway as Herbie's mahogany casket, followed by those in the funeral procession, descended and left for Roselawn Cemetery in suburban Roseville. Vintage military airplanes flew overhead in the traditional "missing man" formation, and a lone bagpiper played "Amazing Grace." It was a funeral fit for a king or a president, and it was indeed a tribute to all the people Herbie had touched.

As emotionally draining as that scene was, my mind raced back over all our unique and memorable times together, and how disappointing it was that the book I always promised Herbie I would write about his coaching would now have to be done differently. The celebration of the boldest and most creative hockey mind in history would now have to be something of a memorial, as well. The book now had to be done with some urgency, starting with hauling out and perusing numerous storage bins filled with my old notebooks going back to teams and games in the 1960s. Those notes spoke volumes and have been amplified here so well by the voices of Glen Sonmor, Jack Blatherwick, Craig Patrick, Lou Vairo, and many of the players Herbie so indelibly touched.

Patti, Danny, and Kelly—Herbie's immediate family—also provided valuable input. A high school friend of Patti's from Yankton, South Dakota, was moved when he heard of Herb's death and contacted Patti to offer his condolences. They were later able to rekindle their friendship, and it ultimately led to Patti marrying another wonderful man.

I must thank my own family because we all knew Herbie so well; my wife, Joan, has had to put up with me and all my saved notes, and our sons, Jack and Jeff, have always been sources of inspiration. I must acknowledge all of the former players, friends, and Brooks family members as well. One in particular is Pauline Brooks, Herbie's mom, for the delightful conversation we had at her assisted-living facility. In her mid-nineties, she was razor-sharp with her thoughtful and witty recollections. She would only have a few months left in her long and rich life, and I regret that she won't get to read this, but in some ways it memorializes her incisive comments.

Contacting every single player coached by Brooks would have been ideal but impossible. I want to thank those I did reach and apologize to the rest because all would have had valuable input to offer. Also, there was the problem of space and time. For example, I bypassed details regarding Herbie's pre-1980 career, including the 1979 U.S. National team and his trip to the 1978 World Championships in Prague, Czechoslovakia, simply to observe. A St. Paul attorney named Keith Hanzel, who had become a player agent on a limited basis, was there trying to find playing outlets for some of his clients. All the NHL general managers and scouts were at the tournament, but in those days, they were only interested in watching Canada play. "They had seminars where the top hockey minds from every country spoke at a roundtable discussion," Hanzel recalled. "Herbie and I went to hear about ways to change the tempo of a game, and progressive practice ideas and training techniques.

None of the NHL people attended those things, but Herbie and I did, and we also went to all the teams' practices. Herbie took notes on everything—from how they did their stretching, their skating drills, and how they warmed up their goaltenders, to how well they caught passes on their backhands. Everything. We even watched a peewee team practice, to see how they operated."

Imagine the effect on the blossoming Brooks hockey mind. He selected and inserted elements into his own coaching methods—which he revised every season—every day. Then fast-forward through all that receptive intensity, and picture him relaxing at home, on the floor, enjoying all the abuse that could be administered by his flock of new little grandkids.

Herb Brooks will live on, with tangible things like the Herb Brooks Foundation and the Herb Brooks Training Center, a facility at the Blaine National Sports Center complex that allows developing athletes the opportunity to train through dry-land and other off-ice work, as well as on the many ice sheets available there.

Of all the acknowledgments, of course, the main one must go to Herb Brooks himself. Rest in peace, Herbie, and know that this book will have accomplished its objective if it helps keep you alive, and forever young, the way we all remember you best.

INDEX

CPSIA information can be obtained
at www.ICGtesting.com
Printed in the USA
LVHW101459191122
733598LV00005B/138

9 780760 339954